PITCHED BATTLE

Ensign Sprague barreled in, raking the nearest submarine with effective machine-gun fire. But the Germans were firm believers in the "fight back" tactic and quickly filled the air with lead. Sallenger's TBF was the unfortunate recipient of most of this fire.

As he raced in, his plane shuddered from several hits that started a fire in the bomb bay and knocked out the radios and the electrical system. Because of the damage, Sallenger was unable to release his bombs on this pass. Nevertheless, he doubled back to once more face the antiaircraft fire.

The enemy fire again ripped into the Avenger, this time starting a fire in the left wing root. Sallenger's plane was in bad shape, but Sallenger dropped his two depth bombs manually, and they exploded near one of the submarines. . . .

HUNTER-KILLER

U.S. Escort Carriers in the Battle of the Atlantic

WILLIAM T. Y'BLOOD

BANTAM BOOKS

NEW YORK · TORONTO · LONDON · SYDNEY · AUCKLAND

*This edition contains the complete text
of the original hardcover edition.*
NOT ONE WORD HAS BEEN OMITTED.

HUNTER-KILLER

*A Bantam Falcon Book / published by arrangement with
the Naval Institute Press*

PRINTING HISTORY
Naval Institute Press edition published 1983
Bantam edition / June 1992

CONTENTS

PREFACE

The longest continuing battle of World War II was the Battle of the Atlantic. Many books have been written about the battle, primarily about the U-boats and the convoy escorts. Unfortunately, there has been a sort of veil, a murkiness, covering the operations of the U.S. Navy's escort carriers in that arena. About the only thing most people know about the escort carriers in the Atlantic is that the *Guadalcanal* captured *U-505*. But the "jeeps" were much more involved in actions in the Atlantic than that one isolated incident would indicate.

A passage in the recently declassified Tenth Fleet/Op-20-G history of communications intelligence in the Battle of the Atlantic, while not specifically concerning escort carriers, places their role in this far-reaching battle in a clearer perspective.

"The peculiar nature of the U-boat war, or the Battle of the Atlantic," it states, "does not lend itself readily to the stirring descriptions which may mark the history of a series of major fleet engagements. It is not an impressive succession of majors but an attrition of minors. To the Allies this battle may have been inglorious, for it was a battle to deliver supplies. When seen as a whole, however, these minor engagements add up to a major battle upon whose outcome week by week the future prosecution of the war abroad depended. Whether striking or hiding, however the U-boat turned to or from attack it always threatened and exacted countless hours of ceaseless watch and patrol. An engagement, which goes on so long, is so devoid of spectators and correspondents, and is so vi

far to the rear of the battle lines is apt to recede in memory with the passage of time, for it lacks the classical unities of the drama, being neither one in place nor the time nor the action."

Thus it was with the escort carriers in the Atlantic—"an attrition of minors . . . being neither one in place nor the time nor the action." It is hoped that this book will lift the veil, help to blow away the "fog of war" that covered the actions of the "jeeps" in the Atlantic.

I would especially like to thank Dr. Dean C. Allard and his assistants at the Naval Historical Center's Operational Archives Branch for all their help. Without it this book couldn't have been written. I am also indebted to the many ex-CVE veterans who contributed material. Not all of their stories and comments could be used, but, once again, without them there could be no book. A special thanks to my editor, Constance MacDonald, for her very fine efforts. Finally, with deep appreciation, I must thank my wife, Carolyn, my daughter, Laura, and especially my son, Kent (who took on some of my burden by helping with the typing of the manuscript). They all gave me inspiration and encouragement when I needed it.

HUNTER-KILLER

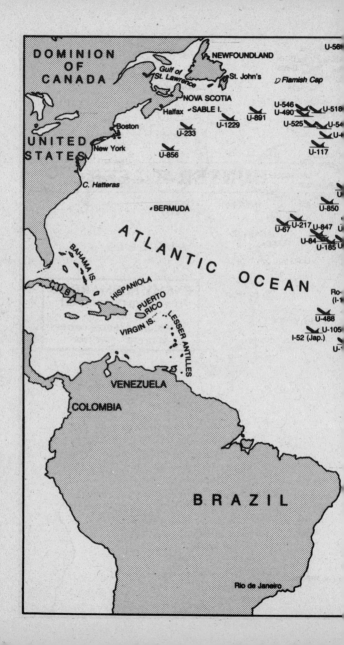

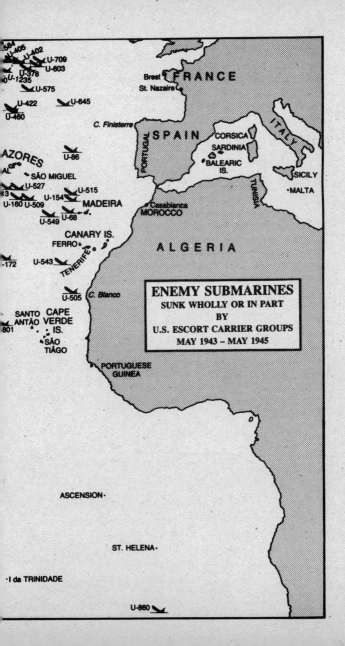

U-584
U-405 U-402
U-709
U-378 U-603
U-1235
U-575

U-422 U-645
U-460

C. Finisterre

FRANCE
Brest
St. Nazaire

SPAIN

PORTUGAL

CORSICA
SARDINIA
BALEARIC
IS.

ITALY

SICILY
MALTA

TUNISIA

AZORES

SÃO MIGUEL

U-86

U-527 U-515
U-154
U-160 U-509
U-549 U-68

MADEIRA

Casablanca
MOROCCO

ALGERIA

CANARY IS.
FERRO

-172 U-543
TENERIFE

ALGERIA

U-505 C. Blanco

SANTO CAPE
ANTÃO VERDE
801 IS.
SÃO
TIÃGO

PORTUGUESE
GUINEA

ENEMY SUBMARINES
SUNK WHOLLY OR IN PART
BY
U.S. ESCORT CARRIER GROUPS
MAY 1943 – MAY 1945

ASCENSION·

ST. HELENA·

·I da TRINIDADE

U-860

1

"THE LORD LOOKS OUT FOR DRUNKS, LITTLE CHILDREN, AND CVES"

On 3 September 1939, when German troops surged across the Polish border and World War II was ignited, the German Navy had only fifty-seven U-boats. Just twenty-two of these (the 626-ton Type VII and 1,032-ton Type IX) were really operational. The rest were smaller types useful only for training or coastal work. Kommodore Karl Doenitz (promoted to Rear Admiral and Flag Officer, U-boats, or *Befehlshaber der U-boote*, in October) had stated prior to the outbreak of war that at least 90 submarines would be needed in the Atlantic and 300 needed overall. Hitler (believing the war would be short) did not authorize a building program for some time, however, to the later good fortune of the Allies.[1]

On the same date on the other side of the Atlantic, a weapon that would later come into direct conflict with the U-boat was hardly a gleam in the eye of U.S. naval planners, let alone built. This weapon was the escort carrier. Still, the seeds that germinated into the escort carriers of World War II had been planted years before.

Just after World War I the Americans became interested in British activities in the field of aircraft carrier development. In 1916 the British had converted a merchant ship to a carrier and thus obtained the 15,775-ton HMS *Argus*, which could carry twenty aircraft and steam over 20 knots. (It is interesting to note that the *Argus* could steam a bit faster and was a bigger vessel than the World War II *Bogue*-class and *Casablanca*-class carriers.) Noting the success of the *Argus*, the Americans began planning their own aircraft carriers. The first fruit of these plans was the *Langley*, converted from a seven-year-old collier.

Conversion of the ship began in 1919, and the *Langley* was commissioned on 20 March 1922. The *Langley* displaced 11,050 tons, had a flight deck 534 feet long, and could steam at a leisurely 15 knots. The "Covered Wagon" was frankly considered an experiment, but the tests she was involved in regarding equipment, training, and operational techniques led directly to the successful U.S. carriers of World War II.

During World War I the British had also been experiment-

ing with conversions of light cruisers to carriers, though when the war ended these studies were discontinued. The idea of a cruiser-hulled carrier kept generating interest, however. When the Washington Fleet Conference of 1921–22 imposed limits on the total tonnage of aircraft carriers for the great naval powers, and the 1930 London Fleet Conference placed further limits on the building of battleships, cruisers, destroyers, and submarines, the idea of small carriers was rekindled. Several loopholes in the Washington agreement left the Americans with the chance to use up to 25 percent of the allotted cruiser tonnage for conversion to ships with flight decks. However, in the mid-1920s the Navy's General Board decided that it would not be a good idea to "sacrifice" a cruiser for

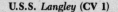

U.S.S. *Langley* (CV 1)

a carrier that would displace less than 10,000 tons. The
minimum displacement for a satisfactory carrier had to be
14,000 tons.[2]

But the idea of a small, or light, carrier would not go
away. In May of 1927, Lieutenant Commander Bruce G.
Leighton wrote an impressive paper on light carriers. His
forecast of possible use for these smaller vessels proved to be
remarkably prescient. In his paper Leighton foresaw the use
of these ships in *antisubmarine warfare*, fleet operations
support, reconnaissance, attacks on enemy warships, and the
reduction of enemy shore bases. Leighton was also concerned
that the loss of the *Lexington* or the *Saratoga*, both just
becoming operational, would seriously weaken fleet operations, whereas the small carriers could operate in groups, and
the destruction of one would not be a serious setback.[3]

About this time the Navy was quite taken with the idea
of a "flying deck cruiser." This hybrid vessel of approximately
10,000 tons would be a cross-pollination of light cruiser and
aircraft carrier. About 650 feet long, the forward half of this
vessel would be a 6-inch gunned, triple-turreted cruiser. The
after half would have a 350-foot *angled* flight deck (a design
years ahead of its time), with hangar space for twenty-four
aircraft. It was an imaginative concept. The only comparable
designs actually built were the two Japanese battleships *Ise*
and *Hyuga*, which were fitted with short flight decks in
World War II.

The flying deck cruiser would never be built. When
Franklin D. Roosevelt became president in 1933, the Navy
became the beneficiary of a new emphasis on shipbuilding.
With money now available for the construction of true carriers, the need for a hybrid carrier was gone. The idea of the
flying deck cruiser, though kept alive until 1940, finally
disappeared into the land of what-might-have-been.[4]

The concept of a small, or escort, carrier was not dead,
however. As early as 1935 the Navy's Bureau of Construction
and Repair had been considering the conversion of ten fast
passenger ships to carriers. Plans had been developed "for
quick action when the war emergency required the conversion of merchant type vessels to auxiliary aircraft carriers."[5]
These plans were allowed to lapse in 1940, though such
individuals as Captain John S. McCain, then commanding the
Ranger, were pleading in early 1939 for eight "pocket-sized"
carriers capable of cruiser speeds.

But the war in Europe was beginning to have an impact on American naval planners as they watched the British fighting the U-boats. Supplies, including aircraft, had to reach England. Small carriers could be used to deliver these aircraft as well as provide convoy escort. The instigator of what would become the escort carrier turned out to be President Roosevelt. In late October 1940 Roosevelt, through his naval aide, directed the chief of naval operations to obtain a merchant ship for conversion to an aircraft carrier. This ship was to displace 6,000 to 8,000 tons and have a speed of not less than 15 knots. She was to be capable of operating eight to twelve helicopters (though the Navy had none yet, nor would have any for some time) or aircraft. The purpose of this vessel was to carry aircraft for convoy escort, submarine detection, and the dropping of smoke bombs to mark the position of submarines located for surface craft to attack.[6]

In a series of conferences held in the office of the chief of naval operations between 31 December 1940 and 23 January 1941, it was decided to obtain two diesel-powered C-3 merchant ships from the Maritime Commission. Use of helicopters/autogiros was ruled out for these vessels. Because of the need for aircraft, these vessels would have a full-length flight deck.

Speed of construction was essential, as the president continually pointed out to the chief of naval operations. Nevertheless, the Navy believed that it would take a year and a half to convert the ships. Roosevelt was in no mood for this timetable and told the Navy that any plan that would take more than three months would be unacceptable.

Finally, by 17 January 1941 the Navy presented a proposal that was acceptable. On the 27th the Maritime Commission told the Navy that the C-3 diesel *Mormacmail* would be available for conversion about 1 March. A second ship, the *Mormacland*, was also to be available for conversion and assignment to the British. Further impetus for this conversion program was received in February of 1941 when then-Rear Admiral William F. Halsey (with strong endorsement from his superior officer, Admiral Husband E. Kimmel) urged the conversion of merchant vessels to carriers, and the sooner, the better.

On 4 March 1941, the Navy acquired the *Mormacmail*. At a cost of $1,500,000 she was converted at Newport News, Virginia. On 2 June, just a few days before the president's time limit of three months expired, she was commissioned as the *Long Island*. Initially she was designated APV-1, but this was changed to AVG-1 on 31 March 1941.

[The designation of escort carriers changed two more times during the war. From AVG (Aircraft Escort Vessel), the carriers were redesignated ACV (Auxiliary Aircraft Carrier) in August 1942, and finally CVE (Escort Carrier) in July 1943. These changes reflected the growing importance, or "respectability" as Henry Dater puts it, of these vessels in the U.S. Navy.]

The *Long Island* was 492 feet long overall, with a beam of 69 feet 6 inches. Initially she displaced 13,500 tons with a full load. She could make up to 16½ knots. To handle the proposed complement of SOC Seagull aircraft safely, a flight deck of 362 feet was built. She was fitted with one elevator aft and had one catapult forward on the port side. The carrier had no island; her bridge was just below the level of the flight deck at its forward end. When tests showed that a longer flight deck was needed, the *Long Island* went back into the yard in the summer of 1941 to have an additional 77 feet added. Because this additional length extended over the bridge, the ship now had to be conned from wings on either side of the flight deck. Certain other improvements were also made at this time. After she came out of the yards, she had a full-load displacement of 14,953 tons, but her speed had increased to over 17 knots.[7]

The *Mormacland* was acquired at the same time as the *Mormacmail* and was converted to a similar configuration. The main difference between the two ships was the small island on the *Mormacland*'s starboard side. She was transferred to the Royal Navy as HMS *Archer* in November 1941. Before receiving the *Archer*, the Royal Navy had been experimenting with several types of vessels that could be used for convoy escort. One stopgap measure was the CAM-ship (Catapult Aircraft Merchant ship). This cargo vessel could carry only one Hurricane fighter, which, when catapulted, could not be recovered. Nevertheless, a number of these ships provided very valuable service in 1941 and into 1942.

While the CAM-ships were being converted, the British were proceeding with a different type of conversion. In early 1941 they captured the German merchantman *Hannover*. Work was begun immediately to convert her into an "escort carrier." In June of 1941 she was placed in service as HMS

SOC-1 Seagull

Audacity. She was small—only 6,000 tons—and could carry just six aircraft. But she proved to be very successful in a brief career, being sunk by *U-751* on 21 December 1941. The experience the British gained with her and the *Archer* whetted their appetite for more escort carriers.[8]

To satisfy this appetite the Americans converted five other C-3 hulls for the British based on the improved *Long Island* plan. These had a flight deck 440 feet long, with a small island to starboard, but still only one elevator. One of these ships, the *Charger* (BAVG-4, then AVG-30, and finally CVE-30), was returned to the U.S. Navy on 2 March 1942. The *Charger* spent virtually her entire career on the East Coast in a training role.[9]

It would be some time before the British would receive more CVEs, because of higher priorities in both the United States and England. So they cast about for other possibilities. What the British came up with was the MAC-ship. Nineteen of these Merchant Aircraft Carrier ships were converted in 1942–43; they were former grain carriers or tankers that would still be used in a cargo capacity. A flight deck was added to their superstructures, and the ships carried four

Swordfish torpedo planes. By mid-1943, however, more true
escort carriers were becoming available, and the MAC-ships
operated in secondary roles for the remainder of the war.[10]

Meanwhile, like the *Langley*, the *Long Island* was being
used quite extensively for experimental purposes. Results of
the tests with this ship indicated the need for another aircraft
elevator, a longer flight deck, and an increase in antiaircraft
armament. The outcome of these tests would be the *Bogue*-
class escort carrier.

War came to the United States on 7 December 1941 at
Pearl Harbor, and four days later Germany declared war on
the United States. Doenitz wanted to take advantage of the
confusion that would surround America's entry into the war,
but commitments elsewhere left him with only about twelve
submarines that could operate at any one time off the United
States. Of these twelve boats only five or six actually initiated
Operation *Paukenschlag* off the U.S. East Coast on 13 January
1942.[11]

Nevertheless, these few U-boats created havoc off America,
encountering "the greenest pasture the war was ever to
offer."[12] United States defenses took an inordinately long time
to organize countermeasures to the U-boat threat, and merchant sinkings along the East Coast skyrocketed. In the first
six months over 400 ships totaling over 2,000,000 tons were
sunk in the area. But the Germans couldn't keep up the pace,
and, finally faced with more convoy operations and increased
antisubmarine forces, Doenitz moved many of his boats back
out into the North Atlantic in May. A number of submarines
remained in the Caribbean and Antilles areas, however, to
create trouble throughout the summer.[13]

In the meantime, the United States had been at war less
than three weeks when the secretary of the navy on 26
December 1941 approved the conversion of twenty-four C3-S-A1
hulls for the 1942 escort carrier program. Because the diesel-
powered *Long Island* and the first British carriers were
thought to be too slow, these ships employed steam turbines
and a single shaft to drive them at speeds up to 18 knots
(which was really not much faster than the earlier vessels).
Small smokestacks just aft of amidships vented the exhaust
gases overboard.

At 442 feet 3 inches long and 80 feet 10 inches wide, the
flight decks of the *Bogue*-class ships were slightly longer and

wider than the *Long Island*'s deck. Most of the vessels had a single catapult on the port side forward and inboard about 10 feet. Benefiting from the experience of the *Long Island*, these carriers had two elevators, nine arresting wires, and three barriers. The hangar deck was much larger than the *Long Island*'s, extending about 240 feet between the elevators. However, the shear of the main deck had been retained in the hangar, which created some plane-handling problems. A small island about 6 feet wide was an important improvement to these vessels. The island incorporated the captain's and navigator's cabins, an open bridge and lookout platforms, and a chart room.

Armament of the *Bogue*-class carriers was greatly improved. Main deck sponsons to hold two 5-inch 51s were built on the starboard and port quarters. These guns were eventually changed to 5-inch 38s. Eight to ten 40-mm twin mounts and approximately twenty-seven 20-mm mounts rounded out the defensive armament.

These new carriers could carry more than twice the fuel oil of the *Long Island*. They were better compartmented and much stronger with the addition of several more transverse bulkheads. Finally, owing to the lower flight deck (four feet lower than that of the *Long Island*), they had greater stability.[14]

The 1942 escort carrier program included twenty C-3 vessels and four *Cimarron*-class oilers. Ten of these first *Bogue*-class ships went to the British. A further twenty-four C-3 hulls were converted during the 1943 program, with the last delivery of these on 18 February 1944. Of these twenty-four ships, only the *Prince William* remained with the U.S. Navy, the rest being delivered to the British. In all, the British received thirty-eight escort carriers from the United States through lend-lease. The *Prince William* spent most of the war, except for a few aircraft transport missions in both the Pacific and the Atlantic, in a training role.

(It should be noted that several sources differentiate between the *Bogue* and *Prince William* classes. Actually, the only difference was the arrangement of the 40-mm guns.[15])

Only twenty C-3 hulls were available for the 1942 escort carrier program; so four *Cimarron*-class fleet oilers were chosen to bring the program up to the twenty-four authorized conversions. These ships had been built in 1939 as mercantile tankers and taken over by the Navy in 1940–41 for use as fast

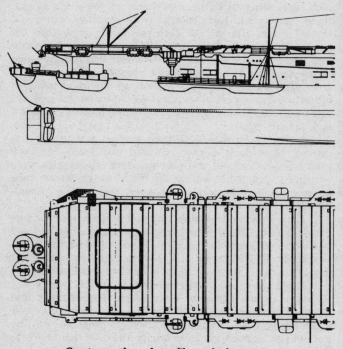

Croatan outboard profile and plan view.

fleet oilers. They were considerably larger than the *Bogue*-class vessels. Their size made them extremely valuable and useful, and work was rushed on them so they could be used in the invasion of North Africa in November of 1942.

The name ship of the class was the *Sangamon* (AVG-26, later CVE-26). The other three ships were the *Suwannee* (AVG-27, CVE-27), the *Chenango* (AVG-28, CVE-28), and the *Santee* (AVG-29, CVE-29). Under full load they displaced 23,250 tons. They were 553 feet long overall, with a beam of 75 feet. Their flight decks were 503 feet by 85 feet. Initially, one catapult was fitted, but a second was installed in 1944. Two small squadrons of aircraft could be carried.

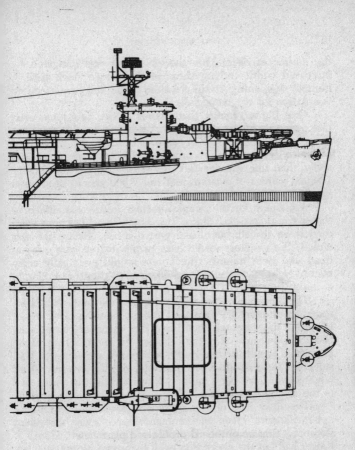

The *Sangamon*-class ships had their geared-turbine engines grouped aft in a single engine room driving twin screws. This arrangement gave them a sustained speed of approximately 18 knots and a maximum speed of over 19 knots. However, because the engines were in the same engine room, these carriers were vulnerable to a single torpedo hit. Exhaust stacks were located on either side of the flight deck near the stern.

The *Sangamon*-class ships were much more stable than the *Bogue*-class vessels because they had lower flight decks—42 feet versus 54 feet. These vessels also had two elevators, but the hangar deck distance between them was shorter than in

the earlier carriers. This shorter length was mitigated by
increased width and no shear in the hangar deck area. A
number of openings in the flat sides of the hull gave excellent
ventilation for the hangar deck.

One big advantage that vessels of the *Sangamon* class
had over the *Bogue* class was in the amount of fuel oil the
former could carry. The *Bogue* could carry only 3,290 tons,
whereas the *Sangamon* could carry 5,880 tons. Over and
above this, too, was the fact that these ex-oilers could carry
100,000 gallons of aviation fuel and 7,000 gallons of aviation
lubricants.

Armament for the *Sangamon*-class vessels was similar to
that of the *Bogue*-class ships. Two 5-inch/38-caliber guns were
carried on the starboard and port quarters. Before the war
ended, the ex-oilers would have twenty-two 40-mm guns in
quad and twin mounts (the *Santee* would eventually carry
twenty-eight 40-mm guns) and nineteen to twenty-one 20-mm
mounts.[16]

The *Sangamon*-class ships were very efficient, with more
speed, greater range, increased stability, and the capability of
operating more aircraft than the earlier escort carrier classes.
However, because of a critical need for more oilers, these
four ships would be the only such vessels converted. "Had
sufficient tanker hulls been available, the Kaiser-class CVEs
might never have been built."[17] Nevertheless, this design led
to the ultimate escort carrier class, the *Commencement Bay*.

The next class of escort carriers came about through a
not-so-standard chain of command. Once again President
Roosevelt was involved. The shipbuilding magnate Henry J.
Kaiser had got the ear of Roosevelt by proposing the quantity
production of a type capable of speeds up to 20 knots. On 8
June 1942 Roosevelt called to the White House members of
the Bureau of Ships and the Maritime Commission. At this
meeting he told the assembled group that he desired the
immediate construction of the Kaiser design (actually a design
by the naval architect firm of Gibbs and Cox).

Following the conference, a number of meetings were
held by the Maritime Commission and naval planners to
discuss the Kaiser design. It was generally agreed by all
parties that the design was unsatisfactory though capable of
being useful as an aircraft transport and auxiliary carrier.
However, considering the president's known desires, the
design obviously was going to be built.

It was finally decided to adopt the S4-S2-BB3 type merchant hull with modifications. These would be constructed according to standard merchant marine practice with naval specifications as necessary. Fifty ships were ordered from the Kaiser Company to be built in its Vancouver, Washington yard. Kaiser built all the hulls and supplied most of the installations. Certain parts were built by the Navy and added to the carriers at the fitting-out yard at the Astoria, Oregon Naval Base.

The name ship of this class was the *Casablanca* (CVE-55), but the type was also known as the Kaiser-class. Hull numbers ranged from CVE-55 to CVE-104. First delivery of the type was planned for February 1943, but various problems caused the program to fall behind schedule, and the *Casablanca* was not commissioned until 8 July. Nevertheless, using prefabricated sections and mass production methods, the program was completed by 8 July 1944. This was a tremendous achievement for the U.S. shipbuilding industry.

The *Casablanca*-class ships had an overall length of 498 feet. The flight deck was 477 feet long and 80 feet wide, with two elevators and the usual nine wires and three barriers. A single catapult was located forward on the port side. A distance of 257 feet between elevators without shear or camber gave more room for handling planes on the hangar deck.

Uniflow reciprocating engines of 9,000 horsepower driving two shafts provided the propulsive power for these carriers. Maximum speed was about 19 knots though the *Casablanca* raced through a measured mile at 20.75 knots during her trials. The engines were located in widely separated spaces, and this design, plus improved compartmentation throughout, gave the type better protection against a single torpedo hit.

The *Casablanca*-class ships were the first all-welded carriers. Much lighter than the *Bogue*- and *Sangamon*-class vessels, they displaced only 10,900 tons at full load. They were extremely maneuverable because of the way the propeller race acted on the large balanced rudder, and had a tactical diameter of only 540 yards. Armament was very much similar to the other escort carrier classes except that only one 5-inch/38-caliber gun was carried at the stern. Antiaircraft armament included sixteen 40-mm guns in twin mounts and twenty 20-mm guns.[18]

For all the shortcomings the Navy saw in the *Casablanca*-class carriers, they turned out to be very useful ships during their relatively brief lifespan. Rear Admiral Daniel V. Gallery would say later, "They were just barely good enough, but they were good enough."[19] Still, the Navy wanted something better. What emerged was the last escort carrier type of the war, the *Commencement Bay* class.

This type was based on the *Sangamon*-class vessel and incorporated into the design all that had been learned since the *Long Island*. The oiler-type vessel had been chosen on 24 October 1942 and the design officially approved on 1 December 1942. In January of the next year the contract was awarded to the Todd-Pacific yards in Tacoma, Washington.

Outwardly this new class bore a great resemblance to the earlier *Sangamon*-class ships, but the design of these vessels was much more refined. Overall length was 577 feet 1 inch. The flight deck and elevators were stronger, designed to handle 17,000 pounds instead of the 14,000-pound limit of the earlier classes. In response to many complaints, the elevators operated faster. Two catapults were installed, the second located on the starboard side of the flight deck parallel to the centerline and partially overlapping the forward elevator. To handle new equipment, the island was made a foot wider. For additional strength two more transverse bulkheads were installed. Full-load displacement was up to 23,000 tons. This class retained the twin-screw configuration but reverted to steam turbine engines of 16,000 horsepower. The listed maximum speed of these ships was 19 knots though the *Commencement Bay* exceeded 20 knots in her trials.

Armament was greatly increased in these vessels. Once again two 5-inch/38-caliber guns were installed on each quarter. Antiaircraft armament included twelve 40-mm guns in quad mounts, twenty-four 40-mm guns in twin mounts, and twenty 20-mm mounts. An interesting feature of the type was the fitting of two 40-mm twin mounts forward of the island.

Twenty-three ships of the *Commencement Bay*-class were approved, but only nineteen (hull numbers CVE-105 to -123) were completed. The *Commencement Bay* was commissioned on 27 November 1944, and only a few of these ships saw any action in the war.[20]

Born of necessity for aircraft transport, convoy escort, and antisubmarine operations, the escort carriers proved to have amazing versatility and stoutness. Six of the CVEs would be lost in World War II, one of these in the Atlantic. But the rest stood up to punishing seas, typhoons, Kamikazes, and other assorted dangers to fulfill their roles in aircraft ferry missions, air support for numerous invasions, pilot and crew training for their "big sisters" (the fast fleet carriers), and countless other tasks. Considering the scope and hazards of their operations, it can truly be said that "the Lord looks after drunks, little children, and CVEs."[21] But, aside from one memorable clash at Leyte Gulf, it is in the role of submarine hunter that the escort carriers really left their mark. Numerous U-boat skeletons moldering at the bottom of the Atlantic provide mute testimony to their effectiveness.

2

THE CVES GO TO WAR

Though the C-3 hulls had been slated for conversion to the *Bogue*-class carriers first, the *Sangamon*-class ships would be the first to see action. (The *Long Island* was used in a transport role to Guadalcanal in August 1942, but was involved in no combat action.) The four ex-oilers would be in the thick of things off the coast of Africa during Operation Torch in November 1942.

The invasion of North Africa had first been considered in January 1942, but was soon rejected in favor of a cross-channel attack planned for April 1943. However, with Stalin screaming for a second front by his Western Allies and it becoming increasingly clear that a cross-channel attack would not be possible for some time, it was decided (reluctantly by the Americans) to launch an invasion of North Africa. D Day was initially set for 30 October, later changed to 8 November.

Planning began in earnest, for there was not much time between when the decision was finally made and when the invasion would take place. Torch would eventually comprise three major forces—the Center and Eastern Naval Task Forces (which would operate inside the Mediterranean and be primarily composed of British ships and, thus, be beyond the scope of this history) and the Western Naval Task Force, under the command of Rear Admiral H. Kent Hewitt. Hewitt would also command TF 34. The mission of this force would be to land the troops of Major General George S. Patton, Jr. on the Atlantic coast of French Morocco. Patton's force would then capture Casablanca and Port Lyautey.

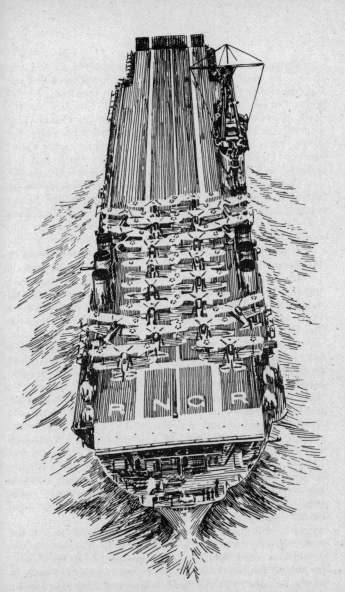

U.S.S. *Ranger* (CV 4)

The planning for Torch was somewhat haphazard and rushed, for there was little time, and an operation of this size and complexity was something new to the Americans. Nevertheless, it was carried out with great skill. Nowhere was the press of events felt more than in TF 34's Air Group. Rear Admiral Ernest D. McWhorter had under his command the "large" carrier *Ranger* and the four *Sangamon*-class escort carriers. Only the *Ranger*'s Air Group 9, which had just reported on board on 3 October, was considered well trained.[1]

The *Sangamon*, *Santee*, *Suwannee*, and *Chenango* were rushed to completion, as they were greatly needed for air support during the landings. It was estimated that the French had almost 170 planes operational, and the Germans also would probably be active. Gibraltar was available only for the Center and Eastern Task Forces, so the five carriers would be the only air support the Western Task Force would have.

The *Sangamon* was commissioned as an aircraft carrier in August 1942, followed by the other three vessels of the class in September. Owing to the nearness of the Torch invasion date, their shakedown training was curtailed considerably. The *Santee* later reported: "During that first month the *Santee* returned to the Yard twice and was never free of the Yard workmen. The completion of the ship continued while the fitting out and shakedown were proceeding together and during the few days underway almost every conceivable machinery casualty was experienced. At the end of the month the air group had operated aboard only a day and a half and guns had been fired only for structural tests but the crew had learned to know their ship, their duties and each other well enough to put to sea as a combatant unit. The Navy Yard had done an almost impossible task in getting the ship out in time for the pending operations but, in so doing, only the essentials had been completed and it was then necessary for the ship to install, adjust, calibrate and repair until the ship could use her battery and her equipment."[2]

The *Santee* was not alone in her predicament. All the escort carriers were going through the same tribulations. The *Suwanee*, commanded by Captain Joseph J. ("Jocko") Clark, by dint of hard work was commissioned two weeks early in hopes that she would be able to take part in Torch. Clark's and his men's, efforts were rewarded. The *Suwannee* (because she could carry more aircraft and fuel) was ordered to replace the smaller *Charger* in the upcoming operation.[3]

Time was definitely against the carriers, however, and early in October the *Santee*, *Suwannee*, and *Sangamon* left the East Coast for Bermuda and some sorely needed training. As the *Santee*'s skipper, Captain William D. Sample, commented: "With only five experienced aviators in the air group, and a bare handful of officers and men who had previously seen salt water, the training began from scratch. The first antisubmarine patrol took off the second day out with a 45-knot wind over the deck and a pitch that would have kept seasoned carrier squadrons aboard in peace times. This was learning the hard way but was effective and the air group and ship's crew alike speedily got their sealegs."[4]

Left behind when her sister ships sailed for Bermuda was the *Chenango*. Captain Ben H. Wyatt's ship was destined not to operate offensively during Torch. Rather, her task was to transport the Army Air Force's 33rd Fighter Group to North Africa. After airfields had been secured ashore, the group's P-40Fs would be launched from the carrier. Between 13 and 15 October the *Chenango* embarked eight P-40s for handling familiarization, deck spotting checks, and a test of the ship's catapult. Following these tests, the full cargo of seventy-eight P-40Fs were loaded on 21 and 22 October. On 24 October the *Chenango* sailed to join TF 34.[5]

After too little time in Bermuda waters for training, Admiral McWhorter's Air Group (organized as TG 34.2) sortied on 25 October for the invasion of North Africa. The course that TG 34.2 took toward the rendezvous with the rest of TF 34 "resembled the track of a reeling drunk in the snow."[6] Rendezvous was planned for 28 October.

"The day set for the rendezvous was sunny with a slight mist on the horizon," Admiral McWhorter said later. "Everybody strained their eyes to sight the convoy. At last, out of the haze loomed a ship, then another, and another, until it was no use counting them. We swung into place in the formation with the signal lights blinking from halfway around the horizon. When darkness fell the lookouts had a tough job. It's not easy to keep formation in a group of any size, and this was probably the largest fleet that had ever sailed the Atlantic; 25 miles long and 25 miles wide."[7]

Following the rendezvous, the task force set course for Dakar to throw off any inquisitive observers who might be nearby. En route all the carriers operated their aircraft only in essential activities, such as antisubmarine patrols, and

even these flights were severely limited in their scope. For
example, the *Santee* flew only one antisubmarine patrol
during the crossing, and that almost turned into disaster. As
the last plane was being catapulted on this patrol, one of its
depth bombs was jarred loose and rolled up the deck and
over the bow. Somehow the hydrostatic fuze on the bomb
became armed. Shortly after the bomb entered the water, it
went off. The *Santee* was shaken from stem to stern. Her
mast area just above the bridge took a beating—her two radar
and YE homing beacon antennas, the RDF loop, range
finder, and all searchlights were carried away. "It proved
to be a very realistic damage control exercise but too close
to the real thing for comfort."[8]

On the evening of 2 November, TF 34 turned back to
the northeast to give the impression that the force was
headed for the Straits of Gibraltar. So far the weather had
cooperated with the Americans. But on the 4th the Atlantic
turned ugly, with heavy seas creating problems for the task
force. The weather forecast for D day, 8 November, was also
gloomy. Very high surf was believed possible for that day.
Admiral Hewitt, considering the predictions of his own aerol-
ogist that surf conditions would moderate, decided to go
ahead with the landings on the 8th. It turned out the surf did
moderate somewhat, to everyone's relief.

On 7 November, TF 34 broke up into its various attack
groups. The *Sangamon* and the *Chenango* headed for the
Port Lyautey area with the Northern Attack Group; the
Ranger and the *Suwannee* were part of the Center Attack
Group bound for Casablanca; and the *Santee* and the South-
ern Attack Group took up station off Safi. Besides the fifty-
four Wildcats and eighteen Dauntlesses from the *Ranger*, the
Air Group was able to furnish the following aircraft from the
escort carriers: the *Sangamon*—nine Avengers and nine
Dauntlesses of VGS-26 and twelve Wildcats of VGF-26; the
Suwannee—eleven Wildcats of VGF-27, twelve Wildcats of
VGF-28, a further six F4Fs of VGF-30, and nine TBFs from
VGS-27; the *Santee*—fourteen F4Fs of VGF-29 and eight
Avengers and nine SBDs of VGS-29.

The Americans were hoping that the French would offer
no resistance. But in the event this did happen, they were
ready. The code words "Batter Up!" would indicate that the
French were fighting in that immediate area, and "Play Ball!"
would place the general attack plan into effect. In the dark-

ness of the early morning hours of 8 November, army troops landed through still fairly heavy surf. For a short time there was relative silence; then a spattering of gunfire came from the defending troops. "Batter Up!" came the signal, followed shortly by "Play Ball!"

The carriers took no part in these initial actions. But as the sky lightened in the east, their planes began leaping off the decks to help support the troops ashore. The *Santee* fliers would have more than their share of difficulties during Torch, as "the carrier experience of these squadrons was so limited that the long layoff in flying before D-Day had more than the usual effect on the pilots."[9] Thus, in the *Santee*'s colorful words, "the pilots were definitely on the seedy side as fliers."[10]

The *Santee* fliers had their work cut out for them, not the least of which was just getting off the carrier's deck in the predawn blackness. "The spotting of the [*Santee*'s] flight deck was unique and made the few experienced pilots wonder if a successful takeoff could be made. Along the starboard side stretching from the island to the stern was a row of TBFs headed aft, while inboard of them was a row of F4Fs likewise headed aft. As the fighters were taxied to the takeoff spot, the left wheel came about four feet from the port side of the deck. The main idea seemed to be to use only the port side of the flight deck, avoiding the catwalk to the left and the parked planes to the right, executing a neat right turn after passing the island, dropping the flaps, and then proceeding straight off the deck a couple of knots above stalling speed."[11]

Surprisingly, the takeoff by the Wildcats went smoothly, with the exception of one plane that clipped a 40-mm mount during its takeoff roll. It was still able to stagger in the air, but the collision must have weakened its fuselage, for when the fighter landed later, its tail was pulled off when the tailhook engaged the arresting wire. The takeoffs by the Avengers did not go as well. Two of the big planes settled into the water and were lost, though their crews were saved.[12] (It should be noted that the *Santee* reverted to catapult launchings for the remainder of her stay off Safi.)

VGF-29's skipper, Lieutenant Commander John T. ("Tommy") Blackburn, with tongue firmly in cheek later praised his pilots, saying, "The excellent performance of some of the VGF-29 pilots is commented on herewith:

"(a) All pilots for completing takeoff."[13]

The *Santee* launched forty-four sorties during the day. Little activity was noted by the pilots in the Safi area, though thirty-five French aircraft were seen at the Marrakech airfield. Since they seemed to be no threat, they were left alone. Lieutenant Commander Joseph A. Ruddy, VGS-29's leader, meanwhile was serving as a one-man air force spotting for the army ashore. Ruddy spent over eight hours in the air doing this chore. Built like a bull moose, Ruddy was prepared for any eventuality and "was loaded down like a porter starting on a long safari. Extra equipment included a murderous looking knife, pistols, a rifle, a shotgun, a garrot, a special knapsack of home comforts, a small camera and 7 × 50 binoculars later exchanged for 7 × 35 binoculars."[14]

During the morning several photo reconnaissance flights were made over the Safi area, and a fruitless search for cruisers reported fleeing from Casablanca was also made. While returning from the latter search, Ensign R. F. Richmond saw a surfaced submarine about 15 miles distant. She was the *Meduse*, one of eight French subs that had sortied from Casablanca that morning. Richmond turned toward her and flew along the boat's port side as she stayed on the surface. He then turned across her bow, and the *Meduse* dived. Richmond racked his Avenger around to make a beam attack (not an ideal angle for an attack) from 300 feet. He dropped only one depth bomb, which exploded about 40 feet abeam of the submarine's swirl. Although traces of oil appeared on the surface, the submarine escaped. The *Meduse* was later beached near Mazagan.

The Atlantic Fleet's Antisubmarine Warfare (ASW) Unit considered Richmond's attack to have been poorly executed, but the Americans were still in the learning stage regarding aircraft attacks on submarines. The *Bogue* and her cohorts would soon show how effectively they learned their lessons.[15]

Meanwhile, the flight of fighters led by Tommy Blackburn had some problems. The five planes had been returning from their patrol, but the pilots were unable to find their carrier. Because of wind conditions, the *Santee* was much farther west than had been anticipated. The fliers could not raise the ship on radio and could not home in to the ship because her YE homing beacon was still out of service.

Blackburn was rapidly running out of gas because he had not been able to fully retract his landing gear. Realizing he would have to ditch, Blackburn ordered the other four pilots to head for shore and land before they ran out of fuel themselves. The four fliers headed for Mazagan airfield as Blackburn ditched his plane in the cold waters of the Atlantic. Blackburn floated around on his liferaft for about fifty-six hours before the *Rodman* found him.

The other four pilots (Ensigns R. W. Peterson, W. P. Naylor, U. L. Fretwell, and E. Van Vranken) had some exciting moments of their own as they "landed" on and around Mazagan. Peterson ran out of fuel 3 miles short of Mazagan and "dead-sticked" his Wildcat onto a convenient straight stretch of road. His landing was good. His rollout was not so good as he sideswiped a tree, flipping his plane over on its back. Peterson scrambled out unhurt and tried to set his plane afire. However, with no fuel in his plane and only a book of matches, this proved to be a fruitless task. A number of Arabs had gathered around to cheer Peterson on when he suddenly heard a sharp command to "Stop that!" He looked around "to find a gleaming bayonet uncomfortably close aboard."[16]

While Peterson was being whisked off to jail, the other three fliers were landing at Mazagan. The field appeared to be in good shape but was actually pretty soggy. Only one of the trio was able to land safely, the other two turning over. Van Vranken was stuck in his plane, head buried in the mud, while his friends scurried about trying unsuccessfully to destroy their planes. Van Vranken was silently cursing his buddies for not pulling him from the plane when a native suddenly appeared and slowly passed a huge knife across his throat—and cut his harness loose.

The three fliers joined Peterson in jail. They spent three days there, eating "Camel or Dog" and delivering, alternatively, descriptive or abusive language to their captors. After their release by American troops, they were taken to the *Philadelphia* for transport back to the United States.[17]

The *Santee* lost one more plane during the day. Lieutenant (jg) George N. Trumpeter's plane developed an oil leak over Safi. He headed back for the carrier but, apparently, couldn't find her and flew off. Several days later his body was found in the wreckage of his plane about 100 miles north of Safi.[18]

Off Casablanca things were going much better for the

Suwannee and her aircraft. Numerous sorties were launched throughout the day. The main problem that the *Suwannee* encountered throughout her stay off North Africa was a lack of wind. Catapult launchings helped get her planes off, but stronger winds would have been even more helpful.

The carrier's fighters spent virtually all their time on Combat Air Patrol (CAP) over the Center Attack Group and were not involved in any action throughout the stay off Casablanca. The torpedo planes, however, saw plenty of action. Shortly before 0800 on the 8th a force of seven Avengers led by Lieutenant Commander Milton A. Nation joined forces with *Ranger* planes to attack French warships in Casablanca Harbor. Heavy antiaircraft fire greeted the Avengers as they dropped down in 45-degree dives. The partially completed battleship *Jean Bart*, with her dangerous 15-inch guns, and three submarines moored in the harbor were the favorite targets. One hit was seen on the *Jean Bart*, as was another hit on one of the subs. Dense smoke rising from explosions and antiaircraft fire obscured the harbor, and the attackers couldn't see if any other bombs had hit their targets. The Avengers also went after gun batteries on Table d' Aoukasha overlooking the harbor.

In the afternoon four depth-bomb-armed Avengers joined with *Ranger* aircraft again to attack the cruiser *Primauguet* and the destroyer leader *Albatros* in the outer harbor of Casablanca. These two vessels had been involved in a morning sortie against the Center Attack Group and had already been damaged in gun battles with the battleship *Massachusetts* and U.S. cruisers. These ships took another beating in these attacks and eventually had to be beached. These attacks against the French warships led the aviators to overoptimistically report that the *Jean Bart* had been put out of action. She was not knocked out and came close to inflicting severe damage on the U.S. ships a couple of days later.[19]

Farther north, Captain Charles W. Wieber's *Sangamon* was also having problems with the lack of wind. All of her planes had to be catapulted. During the entire operation the *Sangamon* catapulted 109 sorties, and only 39 sorties were made by normal deck takeoffs.

On the 8th the *Sangamon* planes encountered the most opposition that the escort carriers had. Ten of the VGF-26 Wildcats attacked five Martin 157 bombers, five Dewontine

520 fighters, and a LeO 45 bomber in the Port Lyautey area. The French aircraft, flying between 100 and 3,000 feet, put up "standard but not vigorous" defensive tactics.[20] In the ensuing battles three of the bombers and one fighter were shot down and three more planes probably destroyed. Pressing on to the Port Lyautey airfield, the *Sangamon* fliers bagged another bomber and five fighters on the ground.

While the fighters were tangling with their adversaries, eight SBDs and seven Avengers were pounding the airfield with bombs and strafing attacks. The French put up a heavy antiaircraft fire, holing several of the planes, but lost three more planes on the ground and had several antiaircraft batteries silenced.[21]

The escort carriers had got off to a pretty good start in Torch, though the *Santee* lost some planes that probably should not have been lost. The next day *Santee* aircraft flew fifty-two sorties and were involved in attacks on everything from a submarine to aircraft to trucks. Lieutenant William R. Staggs was flying an early-morning reconnaissance in his Dauntless when he came across a submarine as she surfaced. Staggs dove through a light rain shower to drop a Mk. 17 depth bomb from 100 feet. The bomb was off the mark, however, and the sub dove. Staggs was able to pepper the boat's conning tower with .50-caliber fire before the sub disappeared and escaped.[22]

Joe Ruddy was back out during the day, seemingly appearing everywhere and earning the sobriquet "The Galloping Ghost of the Moroccan Coast." Under a seventy-five-foot overcast, Ruddy zoomed over the Marrakech airfield and noted several aircraft landing or warming up. As he flew over the field, antiaircraft fire punched several holes in his plane. Considering this very rude of the French, Ruddy pulled up into the overcast and dropped his two bombs, which failed to explode. He then headed back to the ship to get another plane.

Meanwhile, Lieutenant H. Brinkley ("Brink") Bass (a veteran of the Pacific with two Japanese planes to his credit) led two other Wildcats east of Bou Gedra to attack a group of trucks reported there. Continuous strafing passes by the three planes reportedly left numerous trucks in flames, but in actuality only dispersed the vehicles.

Ruddy's report of activity at Marrakech had resulted in a

strike being launched against the airfield. En route the target
was changed to include more truck concentrations east of
Bou Gedra, and the eight SBDs and two Wildcats bound for
Marrakech bombed and strafed more than forty trucks in the
Bou Gedra area. Returning to the airfield, the *Santee* planes
were joined by Ruddy (who had jumped out of one plane on
the carrier and into another), who led an attack on the airfield
that destroyed or damaged twenty or more planes parked
there.[23]

For the *Suwannee* pilots operating off Casablanca, the
next few days would be frustrating. The fighters remained on
CAP, never seeing an enemy plane, and the bombers spent
most of their time on fruitless antisubmarine patrols. However, on the morning of the 11th four of the TBF "Turkeys"
came across a target worthy of their attention. A submarine
(identified as German, but actually the French *Sidi-Ferruch*)
was seen hugging the shore about 18 miles west of the major
French gun battery El Hank. Lieutenant Commander Nation, by dodging from cloud to cloud, was able to get his
planes close enough to surprise the submarine. The Avengers
glided in toward their quarry, and before the French were
aware of what was happening, depth bombs began erupting
around the boat.

Nation's four Mk. 17 depth bombs exploded about ten
feet left of the submarine and over her entire length. The
next four bombs were near-misses to starboard. The *Sidi-Ferruch* was diving when the last four bombs exploded directly over her. The conning tower bobbed back up, and pieces of
the vessel were flung into the air. The conning tower then
submerged vertically. Violent explosions and a "boiling" of
the water disturbed the surface for about ten minutes. Seeing
the obvious death throes of the submarine, the fourth pilot
held his bombs. A light boiling of the water, accompanied by
some oil, continued for forty-five minutes. There was no
doubt that the VGS-27 fliers had destroyed the sub.[24]

Farther north, *Sangamon* fliers were busy flying support missions for army troops ashore. On the 9th a group of
fourteen French tanks were threatening to break through a
thin line of resistance put up by some U.S. tanks. A call for
help went out, and the *Savannah* obliged with some fine
shooting that destroyed several of the French tanks. Planes
from the *Sangamon* were also on hand to chase the remaining

British Hudson Bomber

tanks into a eucalyptus grove and finally disperse them. Lieutenant Rhodam Y. McElroy, Jr. led the VGS-26 planes against the tanks and carried his attack so low that pieces of eucalyptus trees were snagged in his plane. (McElroy could tell they were eucalyptus trees by the smell!) In these attacks his plane was ventilated by thirteen hits from various guns, but no real damage was done by gun or tree.[25]

Not all operations turned out as well as the attacks on the tanks. On the morning of 9 November there occurred one of those tragic mistakes that occasionally happen during wartime. Several *Sangamon* fighters on CAP came across a British Hudson bomber on an antisubmarine patrol. Not recognizing the tubby aircraft, the VGF-26 fliers shot the patrol plane into the sea.[26]

By 10 November the Americans were beginning to get the upper hand, though fighting would continue for another day. Shortly after 1000, U.S. troops captured the Port Lyautey airfield, and the *Chenango*, which had been anxiously awaiting this moment, was ordered to launch her P-40s for the airfield. Catapulting of the army planes went smoothly, though one P-40 crashed into the water shortly after takeoff and another fighter flew off into some fog and was never seen again. On the landing end, however, things were not going well. The field was soft, and numerous planes were damaged during their landings. After some forty-three P-40s landed, the launchings were stopped. The catapultings resumed the next day, with the remainder of the fighters landing at the airfield.[27]

The *Sangamon*'s planes were out in force during the day. American troops were being held up by heavy fire from the Kasba (an old fortress overlooking the river leading to Port Lyautey), but an attack by three TBFs helped break the resistance, and the defenders of the Kasba soon surrendered. A group of six Avengers, six Dauntlesses, and ten Wildcats broke up a formation of fifteen to twenty tanks and several antiaircraft guns with bombing and strafing attacks. Twelve Wildcats capped the day's performance with attacks on scattered troops in the area.[28]

The planes from the *Santee* were very busy on the 10th. French forces were again advancing toward Bou Gedra. Three Wildcat pilots located an enemy concentration about 20 miles east of Bou Gedra. The three fliers dove on the enemy troops with guns blazing and inflicted a good deal of damage on them. As the planes pulled out, a Bloch 174 twin-engined bomber was observed scooting east at 200 feet above the ground. This being the first enemy plane seen in the air by the *Santee* fliers, they were eager to get a shot at it. Ensign Bruce D. Jaques "got there first and destroyed it much to the chagrin of the other two pilots."[29]

Many missions were flown throughout the day in attacks against small groups of French troops, vehicles, and guns. Although antiaircraft fire was encountered on most missions, and this fire damaged several planes, it did not deter the *Santee* fliers. Four Dauntlesses found some guns and troops hiding in the foothills and dispersed them with repeated attacks.

Lieutenant Commander Ruddy was airborne again with two other Avengers looking for targets of opportunity. Earlier in the day, Ruddy had been delivering some photographs to the *Ranger* when he came across a surfaced submarine. Carrying no bombs, Ruddy had had to be content with spraying the sub with machine-gun fire before she submerged, but now he was carrying bombs, which he used with great effect against the enemy troops. However, ground fire shattered his cockpit enclosure and seriously wounded his gunner. Ruddy headed for Safi and landed safely on the muddy and wreck-strewn airfield. His gunner received prompt medical attention, but Ruddy was unable to take off because of the condition of the field.[30]

Lieutenant Donald C. Rodeen's Avenger was holed by antiaircraft fire during a low-altitude attack, and Rodeen was painfully wounded in both legs. However, he was able to get his plane back inside friendly lines, where he landed and then destroyed the plane with the help of army troops.

Rodeen was typical of many of the *Santee* fliers, having only two and one-half hours of flight time in the Avenger when 8 November dawned.

There was much enemy air activity around the Chichaoua airfield, south of Marrakech, during the day. Several attacks by the fighters destroyed five American-built Douglas DB-7 bombers and another plane on the ground. Ensign D. D. Pattie, flying a Dauntless, caught a DB-7 taking off and sent it crashing in flames with several bursts from his cowling guns.

The *Santee*, in the meantime, was fueling the *Philadelphia* and also replenishing the cruiser's aviation gas supply. A submarine that fired a couple of torpedoes from long range at the carrier delayed this fueling and caused Captain Sample to order the planes still airborne to land at Safi. Like the landings there on the 8th, these landings didn't turn out well. Of the three fighters, five SBDs, and three Avengers that eventually landed at Safi, five planes were damaged in landing accidents. Two other planes were destroyed, one being ditched near Safi and the other lost when its crew bailed out.

The next day saw the end of hostilities in Morocco. The *Santee*'s planes were again out in force (to the extent possible after so many planes were lost in landing accidents at Safi), but saw little action. A Wildcat and two SBDs assigned to support of troops near Mazagan were given credit by the army for the surrender of the garrison there: "Your airplanes arrived at the psychological moment and caused hasty precipitation of enemy resistance which was threatening to become ugly. They gave up immediately. The credit for the surrender of Mazagan should be given to the *Santee* and her squadrons."[31]

Actually, the French garrison had already received word from their headquarters to cease fire, and the sight of the planes (and a gathering of U.S. tanks) only reinforced their desire to stop fighting.[32] The armistice had already been declared when Lieutenant Bass, with an SBD for company, found a number of French planes parked on the Marrakech airfield. The two planes attacked, and Bass was later credited with thirteen planes destroyed on the ground. With this action the combat phase of the escort carrier's operations came to a close.[33]

With the end of hostilities, the escort carriers undertook general reconnaissance and antisubmarine patrols until they departed for the United States. The *Santee* and the *Suwannee*

left on 13 November. The *Sangamon* was also to leave then,
but a deck crash carried away all her radio antennas, and she
did not receive the word to leave for several days. She finally
left on the 16th. The *Chenango*, meanwhile, had been ordered to anchor in the harbor at Casablanca and provide fuel
for many of the ships anchored there. She also provided
aviation gas and ammunition for the supply dumps being
established ashore. Finally, she sailed for Norfolk on the 17th.
A detachment of aircraft from the *Sangamon* was attached to
the ship for the trip home.

The voyage back was very uncomfortable for many of the
ships and their crews. A heavy gale swept through the area
and caused some damage to the ships. The *Chenango* and the
Sangamon were the hardest hit. The *Sangamon* had her
forward flight deck damaged and her forward catwalks carried away. The *Chenango* lost a gun director and two 20-mm
mounts, and had the forward portion of her flight deck curled
up.[34]

Torch was now history for the escort carriers. In spite of
their lack of experience, the "jeep" sailors and airmen had
acquitted themselves well. The three carriers involved in
combat operations had flown 582 sorties, dropped 399 bombs,
and fired over 111,000 rounds of ammunition. In return they
had lost twenty-nine planes, twenty-one of these from the
Santee alone. Most of the *Santee*'s losses had come when the
aircraft were landed on the poorly conditioned field at Safi.[35]

The fliers of the Air Group received lavish praise for
their efforts in the operation. One report stated that "the
splendid performance of the Air Group was a main contributing factor to [the] success [of Torch]."[36] Nevertheless, it was
quite obvious that the escort carrier crews and aviators still
had much to learn. More training for all involved (which is
not surprising, given the short period the carriers and their
squadrons actually had for training) was a constant theme in
all reports.

One sore point mentioned in various reports was the
composition of the carrier air groups. Most aviators and CVE
captains preferred a mix of sixteen to eighteen Wildcats and
the same number of Avengers. The SBDs, with their nonfolding
wings, were to be removed from the carriers. Admiral Royal
E. Ingersoll, Commander in Chief Atlantic Fleet, did not
concur in these recommendations, however, and the Dauntlesses

U.S.S. *Yorktown* (CV 5)

would remain on the decks of the *Sangamon*-class carriers for a few months more.[37]

The operations of the escort carriers in Torch made a great impression on naval planners. "ACVs are valuable additions to the fleet at this critical time when every effort is being made to augment the number of carriers available," one report stated. "They can handle a potent air group and can operate under most weather conditions. Their speed is insufficient, but the fact that they are independent of fuel worries is a great asset in this war of long distances."[38]

The CVEs had proved themselves under combat conditions. It had not been a perfect operation, but initial operations rarely are. The officers and men of the escort carriers still had a lot to learn, but they would, much to the dismay of the enemy. A number of the men on the escort carriers went on to bigger jobs. "Jocko" Clark became captain of the *Yorktown* and then an admiral commanding a task group in

the famous TF 58. Captain Sample became head of the
Operations Division of Tenth Fleet, then commanded the
Intrepid and the *Hornet*, and later became a rear admiral
commanding various escort carrier divisions. Tommy Blackburn
would lead the soon-to-be-famous Corsair squadron VF-17
("Skull and Crossbones") into combat in the Solomons.

The *Sangamon*, *Santee*, *Suwannee*, and *Chenango* had
shown that escort carriers could do the job in the demanding
role of air support for an invasion force. Now it was up to
another CVE to show what she could do with an equally
demanding task—that of hunting and killing submarines.

3

ENTER THE *BOGUE*

In the spring of 1943 the tide of battle in the Atlantic slowly, painfully, began to turn in favor of the Allies. One of the major reasons for the increasing success of the Allies was that they were once again reading the Germans' Atlantic U-boat cipher. Some time before the war the German armed forces had adopted a machine cipher for their codes. They used a machine with a typewriter-like keyboard called an Enigma. Electrically powered, this machine used a set of rotors for encipherment and decipherment. The number of possible combinations that various settings and positions could total was astonishing. The Germans believed that with this machine their cipher system was unbreakable. Alas for them, in time this would prove to be untrue.

The British had been aware of the Germans' use of the Enigma machine for some time, and had been working on the Enigma ciphers shortly before the war broke out, but they were having a difficult time trying to break these ciphers. However, the Luftwaffe was not very security-conscious with its Enigma ciphers, and the British were able to gain valuable knowledge from their adversary's lack of signal discipline. The German Navy was another story. Though using the same type of machine, the Kriegsmarine modified it so it was more secure. The navy was also more aware of security discipline than its air force counterpart.

Then, in 1941 the British got lucky. On 23 February 1941 the armed trawler *Krebs* was captured during a raid on the Lofoten Islands. Her Enigma machine had been destroyed, but several spare rotors and secret papers were recovered.

33

This find prompted the British to plan an operation to recover an intact Enigma machine. On 7 May the British captured the weather ship *München* in a carefully planned operation. Though the Enigma machine had been destroyed, enough Enigma information and ciphers were recovered to be of great value.

In themselves the ciphers were not that important, but they helped the British to formulate a plan of attack on the German cipher system. Just a few days after this coup, though, the British had another stroke of luck. Kapitanleutnant Fritz-Julius Lemp's *U-110* was forced to the surface during a fierce battle with British surface forces. The U-boat's crew, believing their vessel was going to be rammed and sunk, abandoned the boat. But the British did not ram the submarine, and she lay wallowing in the water, still carrying an undestroyed Enigma machine, along with some high-grade ciphers and papers.

When Lemp (who had fired the first shot of the war for the U-boats when he sank the liner *Athenia*) realized his boat was not sinking, he tried to reboard and scuttle her. He was shot and killed making this vain attempt. The remainder of his crew were hustled below decks of the British ships and did not know that *U-110* had been captured. Though *U-110* sank the next day while under tow, the vital Enigma machine and ciphers were safe. The U-boat's capture was to be a well-kept secret for thirty years, and the Germans kept on believing that their codes were unbreakable.

The British were not finished with their attacks on the Enigma apparatus. On 25 June they surprised and captured the *Lauenberg*. More vital ciphers and documents were found. The British were now able to begin an all-out attack on the Enigma ciphers. Fortunately, *U-110*'s ciphers had been current and the British, almost immediately, were able to begin reading the U-boat cipher "Hydra."

Until February 1942 the British were able to read "Hydra." Then, that month the Germans introduced the "Triton" cipher, and the British were cut off from important information about the activities of the Atlantic submarines. (It should be mentioned that although the British had been reading "Hydra," all the German plans were not an open book. There were the inevitable gaps, delays in decrypting, and occasional misreadings. But the breaking of the cipher had provided an incredible cornucopia of information.)

Still, with the advent of "Triton," the British were not completely bewildered about German activities. There were other ciphers that could be read and cross-referenced (including "Hydra" which was in effect for the Far North U-boats until June 1944, and for other types of vessels), photo reconnaissance, a vastly improved and enlarged high frequency direction finding (HF/DF or "Huff-Duff") network, and other forms of intelligence to be used in painting a picture of U-boat operations in the Atlantic. But if "Triton" could be broken, it would be of enormous value.

The Germans, meanwhile, were also hard at work on codebreaking and radio intelligence. The German Naval Staff's intelligence department was B Dienst (*Beobachtungs Dienst*). B Dienst had broken the British convoy code (British Naval Cipher No. 3) early in the war, and for some time used the information gained with lethal effect. In fact, B Dienst had been reading Royal Navy traffic for some time prior to the war. Though the Americans had a more secure cipher system available, they chose to use their Allies' code, so that their ships also became vulnerable to U-boat attacks. Not until well into 1943 would the British and Americans become aware of German eavesdropping and change the code.[1]

In late 1942 and early 1943 a number of important events took place on both sides. On the Allied side "Triton" (called "Shark" by the British) was finally broken, and U-boat operations again became susceptible to attack. In Germany Doenitz replaced Grand Admiral Erich Raeder as Commander in Chief of the Navy on 30 January 1943. Doenitz still retained his post as Flag Officer U-boats, though his chief of staff, Rear Admiral Eberhard Godt, handled B.d.U.'s (*Befehlshaber der Untersee-Booten*'s) day-to-day activities.

In March 1943 the Allies took several steps to smooth out their antisubmarine operations in the Atlantic. Up until now the Allies' antisubmarine effort had been marred by a conflict between the British and Americans over who would control the antisubmarine war in the Atlantic. A Supreme Commander Atlantic Theater had been proposed, but with two equal allies having different ideas on command, tactics, etc., this plan just wouldn't have worked. At the Casablanca Conference in January it was reiterated, however, that the destruction of the U-boats was to remain a top priority.

To this end several committees were formed to study and improve antisubmarine operations in the Atlantic. Two of these committees began meeting about the same time during the first half of March. The Allied Antisubmarine Survey Board was organized on 8 March and dissolved in September 1943. During its short existence, however, a number of its recommendations were adopted by both navies.

At the same time another committee put together a number of important recommendations that the Combined Chiefs of Staff eventually accepted. This group was the Atlantic Convoy Conference. From these discussions, held over a twelve-day period in March, came plans for new convoy schedules, an expansion of the HF/DF network, increases in the number of long-range aircraft available for convoy support, the use of escort carrier groups as soon as possible, and, most important, a division of responsibilities between the Allied navies in the Atlantic. The British and Canadians were to handle the North Atlantic convoys, whereas the Americans were to be responsible for the convoys in the Central Atlantic. However, it was left up to each country to organize its own antisubmarine forces in the most efficient and productive manner. To this end Admiral King set up one of the most unique organizations in the U.S. Navy.[2]

On 20 May 1943 Tenth Fleet came into being just as the Battle of the Atlantic reached its climax. "It was essentially a reshuffle and regrouping of units rather than of the new creations that pullulated in wartime Washington."[3] King took personal command of this unit, which in itself shows the importance he placed on the war against the U-boats. However, he made Rear Admiral Francis S. Low his chief of staff for Tenth Fleet and, for all intents and purposes, Low ran Tenth Fleet. But King's presence and influence pervaded the atmosphere, and he was always aware of Tenth Fleet's operations.

Tenth Fleet had a rather ambiguous relationship with Admiral Ingersoll's Atlantic Fleet. Because Tenth Fleet had no ships of its own, it had to use those of the Atlantic Fleet. Early in the existence of Tenth Fleet, Admiral Low had studied closely the *Bogue*'s operations, and had concluded that several chances had been missed by the carrier because of the defense-oriented attitude of the escort commanders. In his opinion, better results would be obtained by the escort carriers if Tenth Fleet took operational control of them. He based this opinion on the belief that his command (with its knowledge of probable German moves through the breaking of Enigma) had a better grasp of the "big picture" than had CinCLant.

His idea had merit, but because Tenth Fleet had no knowledge of local conditions that might exist in the operational areas, Admiral King decided to leave operational control of the carriers in the hands of Ingersoll. However, he told both commands to get together and work out ways for the skippers of the CVEs to get more information, so they could plan their operations more efficiently. This was accomplished by Tenth Fleet's subtle use of "recommendations" or "suggestions" instead of orders to Atlantic Fleet, and it worked. It is a tribute to the intelligence, skill, and conscientiousness of King, Low, and Ingersoll (and their ability to work together) that such an arrangement worked so well.[4]

Tenth Fleet was made up of five major sections: the Civilian Scientific Council; the Convoy and Routing Division; the Antisubmarine Development Unit Atlantic Fleet (AsDevLant); the Antisubmarine Measures Division; and, most important, the Operations Division. Captain William D. Sample, late of the *Santee*, commanded this latter unit. Its most important section was the Combat Intelligence Division under Commander (later Captain) Kenneth A. Knowles. Actually, this division had been lifted bodily from CominCh's Combat Intelligence Division Atlantic Section. It remained a part of CominCh's headquarters while also operating with Tenth Fleet.[5]

Knowles's section operated in a similar manner to the Submarine Tracking Room of the British's Operational Intelligence Center. It was later stated that these two British and American units cooperated more closely than any other Allied organizations during the war.[6] And this close cooperation brought rich dividends to the Allies in their war against the U-boats. Both sections used Ultra (now a generic term for information gained from cryptanalysis, but used here in the context of Enigma intercepts) reports, HF/DF fixes, and myriad other intelligence sources to provide the operational units the information they needed to seek out and destroy the enemy submarines.

The tide was turning in favor of the Allies, but the spring of 1943 was still one of high points and low points for both

sides. For a time Allied shipping losses became almost unbearable. From just over 180,000 tons of shipping sunk by
U-boats in January, losses soared to about 576,000 tons in
March. The British felt that defeat was staring them in the
face. Then, almost miraculously, losses dropped to 211,929
tons in May with a corresponding increase in U-boats sunk.
The Germans began pulling their submarines out of the
North Atlantic.[7] What had happened to cause this astonishing
reversal, and what part had the American escort carriers
taken in this?

Probably the most important cause of this reversal was
the breaking of "Triton." But codebreaking (to be effective)
can't exist in a vacuum. Just having the information doesn't
help unless the means to utilize it is available. This was
finally coming to pass in the spring of 1943. Tenth Fleet had
come into existence. More and better escort vessels, new and
improved tactics and weapons, and more aggressive action by
all hands were also appearing on the scene. Among the
vessels now or soon to be available were American escort
carriers.

As mentioned in Chapter 2, American escort carriers
had been used in the North African landings. Though
submarines had been attacked and one sunk in that operation, the CVEs had not really been operating in an antisubmarine role. Plans had been made, however, for their use
against the U-boats. On 25 January 1943 Admiral Ingersoll
wrote to Admiral King: "Air coverage by land-based planes
cannot be furnished the African convoys except at the two
terminals and for a brief interval from Bermuda. The present protection of the slow convoys from submarines is
woefully inadequate owing to the limited number of escort
vessels available, the large size of the convoys and the
impossibility of air coverage by land planes during the
middle part of the passage. I intend to extend air coverage
to the African convoys by ACVs when the other ACVs
assigned to this Fleet are ready."[8]

From the outset it was Ingersoll's intention to use the
U.S. escort carriers in the Central Atlantic covering the
U.S.–Gibraltar convoys, as the weather in the North Atlantic
could be rough.[9] The British escort carriers would operate in
the North Atlantic. The first of the new American escort
carriers to appear was the *Bogue*.

Name ship of the class of eleven carriers converted from C-3 merchant hulls, the *Bogue* was launched at Tacoma on 15 January 1942. Named after Bogue Sound in North Carolina, the *Bogue* would have been just a merchant ship, the *Steel Advocate*, if war hadn't broken out. Escort carriers in general were not particularly attractive, and the *Bogue* most certainly was not just another pretty ship, but Captain Giles E. Short and his crew (of whom many had served aboard the old *Lexington*) instilled in her a personality and toughness that more than made up for any lack of aesthetics.[10]

She was packed (too tightly, some said) with 97 officers and 921 men. Approximately 495 feet long, she was shorter than the *Sangamon*-class vessels, but could carry up to twenty-eight aircraft. Her single-screw geared turbines of 8,500 horsepower could drive her through the water between 16 and 18 knots, though her engineering gang occasionally coaxed her a bit faster.[11]

So the *Bogue* wasn't a pretty ship, and she wasn't a fast ship, but she packed quite a punch as the U-boats found out, and she wound up the war with an outstanding record and a Presidential Unit Citation.

Captain Short commissioned the *Bogue* at the Puget Sound Navy Yard on 26 September 1942. The ship then spent the next month and a half undergoing sea trials and the usual modifications as problems cropped up. Finally, she was ready and left Puget Sound on 17 November bound for San Diego. Here the *Bogue* took on her first squadron, VC-9. The squadron, under the command of Lieutenant Commander William M. Drane, had nine TBFs and twelve F4Fs assigned. Here in San Diego there was opportunity for the ship's crew and the aviators to get used to working with each other, and extensive training was accomplished.

On 11 December the *Bogue* left San Diego bound for the Panama Canal and the East Coast. This shakedown cruise was uneventful, and she arrived in Norfolk on New Year's Day 1943. However, if the carrier's crew thought that action was right around the corner, they were greatly disappointed, as they learned they would have to undergo six more weeks of training. Finally the training was over, and the men were itching for action. Alas, their first missions were not to be too exciting.[12]

The *Bogue* was to be the U.S. Navy's first escort carrier

used in support of convoys. Notwithstanding Admiral Ingersoll's desire to use the "jeeps" in the Central Atlantic, the *Bogue*'s first missions were in the North Atlantic. On 24 February 1943 she left Norfolk in company with the "flush-deck" destroyers *Belknap* and *George E. Badger*, bound for Argentia, Newfoundland. (Many of the *Bogue*'s escorts on her early missions were "flush-deckers" that had been converted to seaplane tenders and converted back to destroyers. However, the *Belknap, Greene*, and *Osmond Ingram* retained the designation AVD.) The carrier and her two escorts formed TU 24.4.1 Mid-Ocean Escort Group on 5 March and joined the eastbound convoy HX-228 the next day.

About this time an event occurred that could have had grave consequences for Allied convoys. The Allies had known for some time that the Germans were planning a changeover from their three-rotor Enigma machine to a four-rotor machine. This change took place at midnight on 8 March, and the Allies were once again in the dark as over sixty U-boats prowled the Atlantic. By dint of tremendous exertion, though, the British broke into "Triton" again by the 19th. But the blackout had serious consequences for HX-228. The convoy had been able to evade one submarine patrol line before the changeover, but then its luck changed. B Dienst deciphered a signal in the compromised convoy code giving HX-228's new course and speed. Thirteen boats of the *Neuland* Group were ordered to intercept the convoy, with five more submarines to join the attack later.[13]

For the *Bogue* the next few days were uneventful, but on the 10th the VC-9 aviators had their first U-boat sighting. Ensign Alexander C. McAuslan was patrolling through misty skies when he saw a submarine only 2 miles away, heading in the opposite direction. McAuslan "poured the coal" to his Avenger and pounced on the sub. He was doing 180 knots and only fifty feet above the sub when he pressed his bomb release. Nothing happened! The two Mk. 17 depth bombs he was carrying failed to release. McAuslan yanked on his stick and swerved back toward the U-boat. The boat, which had obviously been surprised by the first attack out of the rain, was diving.

McAuslan's second run was as unsuccessful as the first. Once again his bombs failed to release! Frustrated and running out of gas, he flew to the nearest destroyer to summon her to the scene. By the time the destroyer reached the area, however, the U-boat had made good her escape.

The attack had not been an auspicious start for the *Bogue* and VC-9. The bomb rack failures (which happened several more times) were a source of concern to higher headquarters, as was the *Bogue*'s practice of fitting only two depth bombs in her Avengers. But these were problems that could be, and would be, overcome.[14]

Because of low fuel, the *Bogue* was detached from the convoy on 10 March to proceed back to Argentia. Her detachment came at an inopportune time. That evening the first U-boats struck the convoy, and the *Bogue* was too far away to give assistance. Before the battle was broken off two days later, HX-228 had lost four ships plus the British destroyer *Harvester*. In exchange, the escorts sank two U-boats.[15]

On the 11th, en route to Argentia, *Bogue* planes made a possible contact very near the carrier. Bomb rack failures again made the attacks unsuccessful, but the porpoises (which the attack analysis concluded were the target) didn't mind. The same day the carrier picked up twenty-one lucky survivors from the earlier-torpedoed *SS Jonathon Sturges*. The *Bogue* group arrived in Argentia on 14 March.[16]

The flattop's first mission was now history, and, though no subs had been sunk, all involved had received valuable experience that would stand with them in good stead later. The *Bogue*'s stay in Argentia was short, as she left again on the 20th with her two "little friends" to escort convoy SC-123; and whereas the weather on the first mission had been bad, on this cruise it was atrocious.

Task Unit 24.4.1 rendezvoused with SC-123 on the morning of 21 March. The *Bogue* took up station inside the convoy, with the *Belknap* and the *George E. Badger* on either side of her bow. Bad weather hampered flight operations considerably. On the 23rd a serious accident was narrowly averted when Ensign Harry Fryatt's Avenger bounced over the barrier during a landing on the carrier's pitching deck. The big plane staggered off the bow barely airborne, but Fryatt eased his plane along until he regained flying speed. His next landing was quite normal.

The rough seas prevented the "tin cans" from being fueled, and the continuing bad weather forced the cancellation of most flights; so TU 24.4.1 left the convoy on the afternoon of the 26th to head back to Argentia. Just thirty-two minutes after the *Bogue* left the convoy, a pack of U-boats attacked SC-123. They were finally driven off by the convoy escorts, but the *Bogue* and her screen took no part in the action as communication problems deprived Captain Short of meaningful information.[17]

Though the *Bogue* was out of the battle, she had been spotted by *U-663*. The U-boat's skipper reported the sighting on the evening of the 26th, although he took the *Bogue* to be an *Illustrious*-class carrier. Doenitz replied that "the sinking of the aircraft carrier is particularly important for the progress of the convoy operation. Do not on that account, however, let any other chances slip."[18] The real and implied threat of an escort carrier operating with a convoy appears to have been lost on Doenitz.

What was not lost on him was that the convoy battles in March had depleted his forces considerably. On 16 April he reported: "A large number of boats have returned owing to fuel and torpedo exhaustion and damage. The gaps thus produced must be filled as quickly as possible, if the monthly sinking figures are to be increased."[19]

The *Bogue* arrived in Argentia on 30 March. She would not be going back out on convoy duty soon, though, as catapult problems forced her to return to Boston for repairs. However, these repairs were not serious, and she was back at Argentia by 20 April. There she was joined by her old friends the *Belknap* and the *George E. Badger*, plus the new additions *Greene*, *Lea*, and *Osmond Ingram*, to form TG 92.3. As can be seen, it had been found that two destroyers were not enough to screen an escort carrier.

The task group left Argentia on 23 April and joined HX-235 two days later. The convoy was routed a bit farther south than earlier convoys, which gave the VC-9 fliers better weather for operations. The voyage was uneventful until the afternoon of the 28th, when at 1641 Lieutenant Roger C. Santee caught a fully surfaced submarine 50 miles from the convoy. Santee attacked immediately, but his depth bombs ricocheted before exploding, and the submarine escaped. The next night the *Bogue* and her escorts proceeded ahead of the convoy on the assumption that more U-boats were in the path of the convoy. Nothing was found, and TG 92.3 was detached on 30 April to head for Belfast.[20]

During these early operations it was often the policy of the *Bogue* to have her planes observe strict radio silence while on patrol. Message drops were to be made when reporting any unusual activity. During one such patrol a TBF "Turkey" was seen approaching the ship with its gear up and flaps down in preparation for such a message drop. With mounting excitement, those topside took position to receive the message. The plane's run was perfect, and the radioman dropped the message pouch right in the middle of the flight deck. Eager crewmen rushed to open the pouch. The message read, "Testing! Testing!"[21]

Catalina Flying Boat

As the *Bogue* set course for Belfast, what is now considered the turning point in the Battle of the Atlantic was in the first throes of a cataclysmic action. The westbound convoy ONS-5 was involved with a mass attack of some forty to fifty U-boats. Doenitz hoped that his submarines would overwhelm the defenders (who never had more than nine vessels, and usually fewer, throughout the convoy's passage). But events showed that the escorts were a tough, hard-working team, and Doenitz's submariners were unable to destroy the convoy. When the battle finally ended, thirteen cargo vessels had been sunk, but five submarines had been sunk by the escorts, one by a Catalina flying boat, and two more had gone down after colliding with each other in bad weather. And that was not all the bad news for Doenitz. Seventeen more U-boats had been damaged to varying degrees. These were losses that U-boat Command could not afford. Nevertheless, Doenitz was determined to stick it out a while longer in hopes the losses suffered in the attacks on ONS-5 were just an aberration. Unfortunately for him, they were not.[22]

The *Bogue* arrived in Belfast on 2 May as ONS-5 was undergoing its agony. The carrier and her escorts remained in the area for two weeks for training at the British antisubmarine facilities in Northern Ireland and Liverpool, and it was during this stay that the *Bogue* had an indispensable piece of equipment installed—an HF/DF set.[23] It was also during this period that VC-9 had its quota of Avengers increased to twelve. This led to cramped conditions aboard ship, and the fighter complement was subsequently reduced to nine.

Task Group 92.3 (also known as the Sixth Escort Group for this voyage) left Belfast on the afternoon of 15 May escorting the SS *Toltec* to Iceland. A Royal Navy officer was on board the *Bogue* to supervise the operation of the new "Huff-Duff" set. After dropping the *Toltec* off at Iceland, the task group joined convoy ON-184 on the morning of the 19th. Upon joining, the *Bogue* took station outside the convoy.

Captain Short later said, "The ship's aircraft must be flown and safely recovered to justify even an ACV gamboling about in the playgrounds of the U-boats."[24] The previous procedure of having the carrier operate within the convoy was supposed to have created a very safe place for the *Bogue*, but this had just not worked out. Operating within the convoy imposed some severe limitations on the flattop. The *Bogue* had a tactical diameter of between 690 and 750 yards. To fly off a fully loaded Avenger required a wind over the deck of 31 knots; a fully loaded Wildcat needed 27 knots. With a catapult launch these same aircraft required 16.5 knots and 6 knots, respectively.[25]

Thus, working in the confines of the convoy severely restricted the *Bogue*'s flight operations. Also, a collision with one of the merchantmen was always a possibility, which put a greater strain on the *Bogue*'s crew. So, for this mission the *Bogue* and her screen took station astern of the convoy, a position that gave her more freedom of action.[26]

In the path of ON-184 was a just-coalescing group of forty-two U-boats called Group *Donau-Mosel*. This group of boats would be the first test for Tenth Fleet. Using Enigma intercepts and "Huff-Duff" plots, the chessmasters at Tenth Fleet planned their strategy to counter the moves of their opponents on the Atlantic chessboard. Word of the impending onslaught on ON-184 was flashed to the *Bogue*.

The *Bogue* fliers first spotted enemy submarines on 21 May. VC-9's skipper, Lieutenant Commander Drane, was patrolling at dusk when he caught *U-231* on the surface. Drane piled in from dead ahead to evade any antiaircraft fire (which did not develop, as he had surprised the crew). Just before he released his four bombs, Drane dropped his gear so as to slow down and avoid the ricochets that had plagued Lieutenant Santee a few weeks before. Drane's flat-nosed Mk. 44 bombs straddled the U-boat, and the explosions obscured her from view. Though the sub's bridge was damaged badly, her commander was able to dive and escape more attacks. The *Osmond Ingram* and HMCS *St. Laurent* arrived in the area around midnight, but *U-231* had already pulled out for home and repairs.[27]

The VC-9 fliers were busy the next day. At 0535 Lieutenant (jg) Roger C. Kuhn, flying in and out of clouds and occasional rain squalls about 55 miles southeast of the *Bogue*, saw the bow of a submarine break the surface some 3 miles away. She was *U-468*, and if she kept heading the same direction, she would soon intercept the convoy. Kuhn climbed to 3,000 feet to take advantage of the clouds. When he broke out of the clouds, the sub's alert gunners saw him and took him under fire immediately with their 20-mm guns. Kuhn accidentally switched on his VHF radio instead of his intercom, and his surprised comment to his crew, "Well, I'll be damned! They're shooting at us!" was received on board the *Bogue*.[28] The return fire didn't deter Kuhn—it just angered him.

Kuhn pushed his big Avenger over into a 50-degree dive and returned the Germans' fire with his own .30-caliber cowl gun. Just before he pickled out his four depth bombs from 150 feet, Kuhn apparently hit the U-boat's gunners, for their

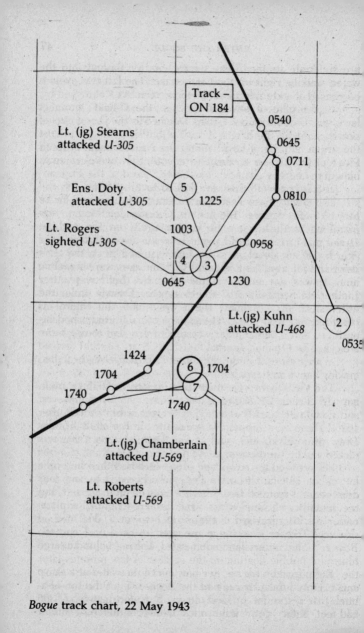

Track –
ON 184

0540

0645

0711

Lt. (jg) Stearns
attacked U-305

0810

Ens. Doty
attacked U-305

5

1225

1003

0958

Lt. Rogers
sighted U-305

4 3

1230

0645

Lt.(jg) Kuhn
attacked U-468

2

0535

1424

6 1704

1704

7

1740

1740

Lt.(jg) Chamberlain
attacked U-569

Lt. Roberts
attacked U-569

Bogue track chart, 22 May 1943

fire suddenly stopped. The depth bombs splashed into the water, walking right up the boat's wake. The last two exploded just aft of and underneath *U-468*'s stern. As Kuhn sped by, a line of fireflies followed his plane, the U-boat's gunners having returned to action. Kuhn watched as the vessel circled slowly, down by the stern. A trail of bluish oil began to coat the water. Twice a spray of compressed air or steam erupted fifty feet into the air as though the sub's crew were trying to blow her tanks.

The U-boat continued to circle for over an hour after the attack, but Kuhn was powerless to inflict more damage, for he had no more bombs. He had reported his sighting to the *Bogue* but had made an error in plotting his position, and the carrier was unable to get a radar fix on his plane. Half an hour after his attack Kuhn saw an intense flash of light on the sub's stern and for a moment thought the Germans were signaling him. It was never determined what this light was. After another thirty minutes, *U-468* disappeared slowly under the water stern first. By now Kuhn was wondering where his relief planes were. A call to the *Bogue* finally established his position, and a pair of convoy escorts were sent to comb the area, but *U-468* had escaped.[29]

A little over an hour after Kuhn's attack a Wildcat pilot looking for him saw another submarine, *U-305*, 35 miles ahead of the convoy. The boat dove before the fighter could get within range. *U-305* didn't stay down very long, however, and Ensign Stewart E. Doty caught sight of her shortly after 1000. The sub's skipper, Kapitanleutnant Rudolf Bahr, saw Doty also and broadcast an aircraft sighting report that was picked up by the *Bogue*'s HF/DF.

Doty glided in toward the sub, which was throwing up a lot of flak. This didn't bother Doty, who bored in to drop four depth bombs from 60 feet. There were well off to the left, but the fourth had a mind of its own. It veered right to explode under the boat forward of the conning tower. *U-305* lurched sideways and for a moment appeared to be out of control. Bahr regained control and submerged, leaving behind a large bluish oil bubble floating on the surface. A few minutes later the boat popped back up, her bow out of the water at a sharp angle. Doty jubilantly radioed the *Bogue:* "I got the son-of-a-bitch. He's straight up and down."[30] Unfortunately, *U-305* had not been "got." Bahr once more got his boat under control and took her back down. The *Osmond Ingram* (which came boiling over from the convoy to get a piece of the action) failed to find *U-305*.[31]

She was still in the area, however, and Bahr surfaced a little after 1200. When he came back up, Bahr found still another of the pesky Avengers [this one flown by Lieutenant (jg) Robert L. Stearns] buzzing around. Stearns saw a "large dark object" five miles ahead and immediately began a run from 1,200 feet. Bahr's crew were not surprised and filled the air around the Avenger with black puffs of flak. Their shooting was poor, though, and Stearns dropped his four depth bombs from 125 feet. The bombs, with their usual fuze settings of 25 feet, exploded close aboard *U-305*. Bahr changed his mind about staying surfaced and dove. Giving up trying to attack the convoy, Bahr took his boat back to Brest.[32]

The day's activities were not over yet for the *Bogue*'s fliers. *U-569* was also snooping around the convoy. The carrier's "Huff-Duff" pin-pointed her only 20 miles away at 1623. The U-boat had already been forced to submerge a number of times by aircraft and destroyers. Her crew should have been more alert, but they weren't. At 1704 Lieutenant (jg) William F. Chamberlain found *U-569* cruising unconcernedly on the surface. Taking advantage of puffy cumulus clouds, Chamberlain pounced and surprised the enemy. (Pictures taken after the bombs had been released show men in the conning tower apparently still unaware they are under at-

Swardfish

tack.) Four depth bombs straddled U-569's conning tower and drove her under.

Chamberlain circled the scene for twenty minutes, waiting for U-569 to resurface, until he was relieved by Lieutenant H. S. Roberts. The U-boat came back up at 1740 only to find Roberts waiting. The submarine was almost directly under Roberts's Avenger. He quickly made a dive bombing attack, releasing his four bombs from 600 feet. Yanking back on his stick, Roberts zoomed back up to 800 feet, where his plane was hanging on its prop and barely moving.

As he leveled off, Roberts saw that all of his bombs had exploded near U-569's stern. The submarine disappeared from view. She plunged 350 feet before her crew could gain control, blow her tanks, and resurface. Her bow came out of the water at a 30-degree angle. The boat slid under and back up two more times, and it was obvious to Roberts that she was in trouble. When the boat finally remained on the surface, Roberts's gunner began shooting at the conning tower in an effort to keep the Germans below so they could not scuttle their submarine.

This was successful for a time, but during a lull when ammunition cans were being changed, twenty or thirty Germans spilled out of the conning tower (some waving white cloths in surrender). An attempt to drive them back below with more gunfire resulted in most of these Germans jumping overboard. Meanwhile, Chamberlain came charging back to add his guns to the party after hearing Roberts's report of the fight.

The two pilots and their gunners kept taking potshots at the U-boat as they waited for the *St. Laurent* to reach the scene. When the destroyer arrived, she nosed up to within a few yards of the submarine. But the enemy vessel could not be boarded. Her flood valves had been opened, and U-569 was soon gone. The sea was very rough, and only twenty-four of the U-boat's crew were rescued.[33]

Meanwhile, south of the *Bogue* and convoy ON-184, the British carrier *Archer* and the Fourth Support Group were escorting HX-239. The day after the VC-9 planes had got U-569, a Swordfish aircraft from the *Archer* caught U-752 on the surface. The plane was carrying rockets and used them with such effect that the U-boat had to be scuttled by her crew. U-752 was the first U-boat to be sunk by aircraft rockets. It would be some months, however, before U.S. carrier aircraft would also be equipped with rockets.[34]

U-569 was the first victory for the *Bogue* group, but it would not be the last. What was more important than this one kill, though, was the fact that ON-184 had sailed on unmolested. To the Germans this operation "showed again clearly that it (was) not possible (at that time) to attack, with available weapons, a convoy escorted by strong air cover."[35] And more and more convoys would now have air cover from escort carriers. From this point more convoys would be getting through relatively free of submarine interference. The tide of battle had surged, irretrievably for the Germans, in favor of the Allies.

The *Bogue*'s one kill, of course, had little effect on the Battle of the Atlantic during these decisive months. With only two or three escort carriers available (the others were the Royal Navy's *Biter* and *Archer*), and these not always at the same time, there was no way they could have had a great effect. The escort carrier's full potential was still to be reached, as the Germans soon discovered.

The months of March through May 1943, when the Battle of the Atlantic reached its climax, saw a number of events occurring on both sides that had a profound influence on the war in that ocean. On the Allied side, as the Americans and British cryptanalysts were able to burrow deeper into "Triton," more and more of its secrets were revealed. As mentioned earlier, the information gained proved of immense value because convoys could be routed around known U-boat concentrations, and even individual submarines could sometimes be singled out for attack. This latter point was proved later many times as the American escort carrier groups were sent on successful offensive sweeps based largely on this Ultra information.

This cipher intelligence, along with a highly efficient HF/DF network and improved radar and sonar, took away the U-boat's greatest strength, her invisibility. Without it the U-boat's chances of success were virtually nil.[36] When the Germans realized that their submarines were losing their invisibility, they undertook highly detailed studies of the problem but invariably came up with the wrong solution.

Such was the case with radar, "Huff-Duff," and cipher intelligence. Both sides had done radar research prior to the war, but much of the German effort had led to a dead end, whereas Allied efforts had taken a more profitable direction. Early radars had proved their value at locating ships (including surfaced submarines), but German scientists stubbornly clung to their belief that this was an impossibility. This stubbornness cost them a number of U-boats.[37]

Enough of the early long-wave radar sets had been installed in escort vessels and aircraft by mid-1942 to be used with great success on unsuspecting U-boats. Airborne radar, coupled with a powerful searchlight, was used with devastating effectiveness. One of the last sights some submariners saw was a brilliant light swooping down on them out of the night sky.

It was only around October 1942 that the Germans came out with an operational radar warning device, *Metox*. It was an unwieldy but somewhat portable unit that did provide some warning of the early radar signals. Though *Metox* was a help, it wasn't a cure-all, as will be seen later. Though the Allies had temporarily lost the advantage of early detection because of the advent of *Metox*, they were already at work on an improved radar, the ten-centimeter microwave set. This radar appeared in quantity in late 1942–early 1943. Once again in this deadly game of one-upmanship, the Allies were on top. It would be some time before the Germans countered with the *Naxos* receiver, and even then, U-boat commanders would remain leery of using it, lest its "radiations" be picked up by the ever increasing number of enemy searchers.

Throughout the war, radar would continue to be the "bogeyman" for U-boat Command. On 5 March 1943 Doenitz stated that "the most important revelation—confirmed almost without a doubt—was, that the enemy was able, with the help of aircraft radar, to intercept U-boat dispositions with great accuracy." To minimize the effects of radar, Doenitz issued an order for his boats to dive as soon as they became aware of radar transmissions and to stay submerged for at least thirty minutes.[38] This order was inhibiting, to say the least, to a group whose aggressiveness was already, slowly, beginning to wane.

Two months later, on 3 May, the theme of the radar "bogeyman" was reiterated in a message from Doenitz to his U-boat commanders. In this message he said, "In his efforts to rob the submarine of her most valuable characteristic

(invisibility) the enemy is several lengths ahead of us by
virtue of his radar location."[39] In the B.d.U. War Diary for
that date a lengthy discussion of the use of radar in submarine
warfare followed Doenitz's message. It is obvious that the
enemy's use of radar was a matter of grave concern to the
Germans.

Doenitz's concern with radar blinded him to another
weapon his enemies were using with good effect—HF/DF.
This is surprising, as the U-boat Command was one of the
most loquacious (or "gabbiest," as Ladislas Farago colorfully
puts it) organizations of World War II. Doenitz kept a tight
rein on the operations of his submarines. "The constant and
close personal direction of the U-boat from shore necessitated
complete reliance on radio communications. U-boat radio
traffic constituted in effect a system of operational bookkeep-
ing which required daily posting if the U-boats were to
function as Command intended."[40]

Between the U-boats and U-boat Command flowed the
following information: heading points and operational plans,
passage reports, position reports, requests to return to base,
fuel on hand (including comprehensive reports by supply
boats), reports on new equipment, general orders, situation
reports, and more.[41] All these messages, along with Doenitz's
tight control of operations from ashore via radio, put the
U-boats in a very vulnerable position regarding "Huff-Duff"
position fixing and radio intelligence. "U-boat logs . . . [had]
frequent entries recording the sending of signals and the
subsequent appearance of an escort ship steaming straight for
them at high speed."[42] Nevertheless, the Germans believed
that shore HF/DF stations were not accurate enough for good
fixes, and they seemed to be unaware that ships were now
carrying HF/DF sets for close-range work. Radar continued
to be the Germans' obsession.[43]

Even more astonishing in hindsight than their "tunnel
vision" about radar, was the Germans' smug satisfaction about
the security of their codes. Several times during the war the
Germans became suspicious when it appeared that Allied
vessels were too often on the scene following an exchange of
messages between various U-boats and U-boat Command.
For example, on 8 May 1943 Doenitz was concerned with an
obvious detour that a convoy had made around a pack of his
boats. Mulling over the reasons for this detour, he stated, "It

is also considered unlikely that the enemy has cracked our ciphers unless he has captured one of our boats." (He was, of course, unaware of the capture of *U-110* in 1941.) He continued, "The possibility of his having cracked our ciphers has been cancelled out by an immediate change in the cipher setting. Other possible sources of leakage are again being checked."[44]

Again and again, when U-boat Command's suspicions were aroused about their ciphers being decrypted, the German naval intelligence service was asked to investigate. And again and again, the intelligence people just could not believe that such compromises were possible with their "unbreakable" ciphers, and they refused to take seriously the possibility that the Allies had the ability or the means to break the ciphers. Treachery and espionage were much more reasonable explanations of any cipher compromises.[45]

The Germans never knew how deeply the Americans and British had burrowed into their ciphers. Even after the war, Doenitz in his memoirs was not sure if his codes had been read by the Allies.[46]

In June a source of valuable information dried up for the Germans. For some time B Dienst had been deciphering signals pertaining to Allied convoy routings. Some sources have considered that this achievement gave Doenitz the equivalent of fifty more U-boats.[47] The Americans had for some time been aware that all was not right with the convoy code, but it was not until May of 1943 that its compromise could be proved without a doubt. CominCh's Atlantic Section pinpointed problems with the cipher in late May when it, in turn, read U-boat messages of attacks against convoys HX-237 and SC-129. With this proof CominCh and the Admiralty approved a change in the cipher that went into effect on 10 June 1943. Almost immediately the Germans were operating in the dark.[48]

Even before this change took place, another event of far more importance had occurred. Faced with the loss of at least thirty-one of his boats (the actual total was forty-one) during May, Doenitz pulled his submarines out of the North Atlantic on 24 May. Though it was not known to either side at the time, on that date the Allies had finally gained the upper hand over the U-boats and would never relinquish it. The Germans had lost the Battle of the Atlantic.

In the B.d.U. War Diary for 24 May were the following stark details: "Losses, even heavy losses, must be borne when they are accompanied by corresponding sinkings. But, in May in the Atlantic the sinking of about 10,000 GRT had to be paid for by loss of a boat, while not long ago there was loss only with the sinking of about 100,000 GRT. The losses in May have, therefore, reached an impossible height."[49]

In a series of messages to his U-boats, Doenitz explained why he was pulling them out of the area:

1. Our heavy submarine losses in the last month are to be traced back predominantly to the present superiority of enemy location instruments and the surprise from the air which is possible because of that. More than half of all losses have occurred through this surprise, and indeed on advances and returns as well as in the operational area in attack dispositions. The losses in battle against the convoys themselves were in comparison slight except for one case, in which particularly unfavorable conditions prevailed. A part of these losses, too, resulted from aircraft.

2. The monetary situation as concerns enemy aircraft and enemy radar must be bridged over by special precautionary measures en route and in the waiting disposition, meanwhile making the best of other disadvantages. Orders for this have been issued. In that connection I will bring about further results in the choice of the attack areas.

3. My whole energy is engaged in the improvement of our own *ortung* [literally "location," but generally applied to radar], defense against *ortung*, and A/A arms. This task is being worked on with maximum application at all our stations. Practical results will come forth in a very short time. The time until then must be passed with cunning and caution on cruise and while waiting, but with your old inexorable severity in the battle itself.[50]

In further messages he exhorted his commanders and men that "it is essential that the *morale* of the men should not be affected by these temporary defensive measures, a task which requires full cooperation of the Commanding Officers, as well as the personal touch of the Commander in Chief of the Navy," and that "we will then be the victors, —my faith in our boats and in you convinces me of this."[51]

Doenitz hoped to relocate most of his boats to areas, particularly the Central Atlantic, where the Allies were not so aggressive. He did not know, of course, that escort carrier groups would soon be roving throughout the Atlantic, seeking the U-boats wherever they were, and would no longer be tied down to a passive defense of convoys. As he shifted his boats elsewhere, Doenitz left behind in the North Atlantic a few submarines to conceal the movement with spurious radio traffic. This ruse didn't last long, as knowledgeable listeners at Tenth Fleet and O.I.C. soon discovered what was up.

The Germans had lost the Battle of the Atlantic, yet the fighting would go on for two more bloody years. Doenitz would never regain the initiative, for when his submarines finally returned to the offensive, their operations were "firmly mirrored in Ultra intelligence. Unable to find and strike [their] main target, [the U-boats] moved cautiously, never free from the constant fear of surprise attack."[52]

Meanwhile, following her bouts with the *Donau-Mosel* Group the *Bogue* put in to Argentia on 26 May for supplies. On 31 May she, with the *Clemson, Greene, Osmond Ingram,* and *George E. Badger,* sortied as TG 21.12 to support the North African convoys. Captain Short and the *Bogue* were now operating under a new set of orders. Admiral Ingersoll had "decided that close air support of central transatlantic convoys was a waste of effort; that it would be better to leave the commanders of escort carrier groups complete discretion to hunt down submarines where HF/DF fixes indicated, or to transfer their support to another convoy that needed close protection."[53] Thus, Short was given virtually a free hand to conduct operations as he saw fit.

Short planned to keep his somewhat short-legged destroyers topped off whenever possible, using convoy tankers when available. He also wanted his destroyers always to have enough fuel to be able to reach port or a convoy if the *Bogue* were sunk. When the carrier arrived on station on 1 June, Short received a report of a possible U-boat concentration in the area of 35°00′N, 45°00′W. Three convoys, GUS-7A, UGS-9, and Flight 10, would be threatened by this concentration.

The reported concentration was quite accurate, as the number of U-boats and their general position had been known to Tenth Fleet since 24 May, when a message directing the subs to head for that spot had been read.[54] Group *Trutz*, a pack of seventeen boats, had initially formed a patrol line along the 43rd meridian between latitudes 32° and 39° North. Because of an apparent compromise of Flight 10's routing dispatch and also because he was aware of GUS-7A's progress, Doenitz shifted his boats south to catch the convoys.[55]

Short had a couple of options to counter any U-boat attack. He could head right for the center of the reported concentration, but be able only to support UGS-9, or he could head toward the southern part of the concentration and support all the convoys. Fueling of his escorts would be more favorable with the latter plan, and Short chose it.

GUS-7A was diverted south of the *Trutz* line and appeared to be in the clear on the morning of 3 June. Captain Short decided to take the *Bogue* eastward and scour the area ahead of UGS-9. During the night the carrier steered northeasterly.[56] The fourth of June came up a fine day, with just a few puffy clouds and a bit of sea haze. The morning passed without incident, but the afternoon was another story entirely.

Oberleutnant Erwin Christophersen was on the bridge of his *U-228* enjoying the beautiful afternoon sun when he was surprised by a pair of Avengers. Lieutenant (jg) Fryatt and Lieutenant E. W. Biros had been flying at 2,500 feet on the trail of a "Huff-Duff" bearing when they saw *U-228* at 1642. The sub was a mile and a half to their right. Fryatt peeled off toward the boat with Biros right behind.

Fryatt came roaring in from astern of the dull brownish-gray painted submarine. He glimpsed a group of surprised faces (which were probably paling rapidly) turning toward him. He salvoed his bombs from fifty feet, and they exploded near the conning tower, sending towering plumes of spray into the air. The boat shuddered and turned violently to the right.

Biros had to bank sharply to keep the submarine in his sights when she slewed around. He also salvoed his bombs from fifty feet. Debris flew through the air as they exploded. *U-228*'s bow came out of the water a few feet, then settled. Christophersen quickly took his boat down stern first. Though she had been damaged, *U-228* was able to escape.[57]

A short time later two more U-boats were jumped by VC-9 aircraft. At 1715 Ensign Edward R. Hodgson was returning to the *Bogue* at 2,500 feet when he saw *U-603* cruising on the surface some 3 miles ahead. The U-boat was about 50 miles north of the carrier, but only 10 miles south of the convoy of nineteen British LCI(L)s called Flight 10. If the sub found these vulnerable vessels, they would be decimated.

Hodgson dove immediately on the submarine. At 200 knots he raced up the vessel's track and dropped four depth bombs across her bow. One of these struck the U-boat's jumping wire and bounced off before exploding. Hodgson circled back to strafe the sub. The now-alert Germans met this pass and a second strafing run with heavy antiaircraft fire. They continued to fire as Hodgson scurried out of range. Before Hodgson could make another pass, *U-603* dove and escaped.

While Hodgson was sparring with *U-603*, Lieutenant (jg) Wilma S. Fowler had run across *U-641*. Fowler's radioman, ARM2c C.J. Wojcik (buried deep in the belly of the Avenger and poorly positioned to see much of anything), actually saw the U-boat first. (This was a first for an Avenger radioman.) The battleship-gray-colored sub was pushing through the water, fully surfaced, 5 miles away. Fowler dove out of the sun toward his quarry. He had the Germans dead to rights when he reached his release point. Then he made an unfortunate decision. Thinking the 200 knots he was doing was too fast, Fowler pulled up to make another run. This gave the Germans the chance to man their guns.

Fowler didn't have much better luck on his second run. Though he was doing 165 knots this time, only two of his depth bombs released. These exploded close aboard the sub's starboard side midway between the bow and conning tower, causing only minor damage. *U-641*'s commander, Kapitanleutnant Horst Rendtel, suspected that his attacker had not dropped his full load. He remained on the surface, continually swinging to starboard to keep Fowler from making a straight-in run, and all the while filling the sky around Fowler's "Turkey" with the deadly flak.

At 1728 Lieutenant Commander Drane arrived to join the attack. Rendtel, no expert on aircraft identification, believed the two planes to be a "Curtiss" and a "Hurricane." While Fowler came in from the opposite direction, Drane darted in from the starboard quarter to deliver four Mk. 17s from sixty-five feet. Accurate antiaircraft fire greeted the attackers, with Fowler's TBF taking a hit in the engine (which, fortunately, caused little damage), while tracers zipped by Drane on both sides. As U-641 swung right, Drane laid his bombs barely twenty yards off the sub's port quarter. The explosions raised her stern out of the water. When a third plane put in an appearance, Rendtel (whose vessel was still relatively undamaged) decided it was time to dive. His dive was so steep—about 40 degrees—that the Americans thought they had got a sure kill.[58]

The *Bogue* fliers had attacked three U-boats but had not yet scored a kill. The next day, however, there would be no doubt about a kill. After recovering his aircraft at dusk, Captain Short thought it might be a good idea to see if the enemy patrol line extended south toward UGS-9. During the night TG 21.12 headed west, and then back east on the morning of the 5th toward the area of the previous afternoon's actions. The task group then turned south toward the convoy. In the path of the task group lay an unlucky submarine.

Lieutenant Richard S. Rogers and the newly promoted Lieutenant (jg) McAuslan were returning from a regular antisubmarine patrol at 0650 when they came upon U-217, cruising placidly on the surface about 7 miles away. Rogers darted in to clear the decks with his six .50-caliber machine guns. The sub's gunners returned the fire, but this stopped when Rogers's bullets knocked six men into the sea. A blaze started in the conning tower that persisted until Rogers's third run. After his Wildcat partner had eliminated any defensive fire, McAuslan eased his tubby Avenger out of the sun to drop four depth bombs from 100 feet. Mortally hit, the U-boat went down in a steep dive only thirty-three seconds after the bombs exploded. Rogers helped send her on her way with one last strafing.[59]

U-217 had been the southern end of the *Trutz* line. After her sinking, U-boat Command made a bad decision on the morning of 5 June to contract the line, in the belief that GUS-7A would try to slip through the line on the night of the 6th. With *Trutz*'s southern anchor now gone, it became that much easier for the convoy to edge away from the U-boats. When it became evident that the convoy had slipped past, an angry Doenitz (who had not been informed of the decision to shorten the line) ordered the *Trutz* boats to break off and fuel to the northeast from *U-488*. He told his staff officers that a proper plan would have sent the boats eastward "so as to prevent at all costs the convoy passing the patrol line."[60]

The *Bogue* turned back west on 7 June. Nothing was encountered, and Captain Short turned again to the east, suspecting that the U-boats might have got around him to attack UGS-9. On the afternoon of the 8th enemy radio activity was picked up by the *Bogue*'s HF/DF. At 1508 Lieutenant (jg) Letson S. Balliett was returning from an unsuccessful "Huff-Duff" bearing search when his radioman spotted a fast-moving submarine only 2 miles away. The enemy boat was Kapitanleutnant Helmut Manseck's *U-758*. The 769-tonner was en route to the Caribbean and was not part of the *Trutz* Group. Manseck had come upon UGS-9, and his sighting report was apparently the signal the *Bogue* had picked up.

U-758 was the first boat to be outfitted with a quadruple mount of 20-mm guns. The necessity to improve the U-boat's armament had grown since the summer of 1942 when the boats began to encounter greater numbers of aircraft. After a few false starts it was decided to equip the majority of the U-boats with the quad 20-mm guns beginning in July 1943. Heavier armor plating for the bridge was also to be fitted at the same time.

But "the ever-increasing danger from air activity and the growing losses caused by enemy aircraft made it necessary in the middle of May 1943 . . . to push forward the completion of quadruple-mounted guns and appropriate turrets and their installation on operational U-boats on a large scale without waiting for the reports of performance in action."[61] *U-758* was the result, and her crew were itching for a chance to use the new weapons.

U-boat Command had originally planned for *U-758* to refuel on 9 June (initially from *U-118*, later changed to *U-460*) and then head for Trinidad. Then *U-758* found UGS-9. However, the submarine was herself discovered before she could attack the convoy or rendezvous with the fueler.

Balliett circled the submarine so as to get the sun behind him. This took some time, as he went the wrong way and turned almost 300 degrees before starting his attack. The sub's gunners were waiting as Balliett roared in at 200 knots.

Tracers streaked by his Avenger but none hit. Dropping down
in a 45-degree dive, Balliett toggled out his four depth bombs
at 200 feet. The bombs exploded around the after part of
U-758, raising her stern 15 feet out of the water. Several men
were blown overboard and could be seen swimming back to
the submarine.

The U-boat slowed to about 5 knots and began circling to
the right. Balliett returned to strafe the boat, his turret
gunner's fire silencing the enemy. *U-758* straightened out and
picked up speed to around 18 knots. Balliett radioed the
carrier, which heard his transmissions, but Balliett "couldn't
hear [the] ship until [his] radioman disconnected relay and
held receiving antennae in hand."[62]

Lieutenant (jg) Fowler arrived on the scene at 1547 and
bored in immediately. The 20-mm guns on the "bandstand"
aft of the conning tower were again in full cry as Fowler
jinked his way in. And the Germans were on target. Shells
ripped into the Avenger's engine, right wing, and bomb bay
area, and tore off part of the left horizontal stabilizer. Fowler's
radioman, Wojcik, was wounded, also. Nevertheless, Fowler
pressed on to drop three depth bombs (the fourth hung up)
close aboard the U-boat's stern. The submarine shook all
over, another man fell into the water, and *U-758* almost
stopped. Fowler couldn't stay around to see what was happening, as his engine was smoking badly and Wojcik needed
medical attention. He reached the *Bogue* safely.

Meanwhile the carrier had launched Lieutenant (jg) Frank
D. Fodge's Avenger and Lieutenant (jg) Phil Perabo's Wildcat
to aid in the attack. Like the other VC-9 pilots, they would be
"confused by the enlarged bridge, [believing] they were
dealing with a 1,600-ton supply submarine."[63] Fodge arrived
before Perabo and circled until his fighter support got there.
Manseck was still on the surface circling slowly, hoping to
"sucker" an attacker into making a foolhardy attack. Fodge
didn't take the bait, but his gunner fired on the boat from
time to time, receiving replies in kind from *U-758*'s gunners.

When Perabo arrived, Fodge signaled him to strafe the
U-boat and put her guns out of action. This Perabo did with
alacrity, clearing the decks with a hail of .50-caliber fire. Two
more times he returned to strafe the ship. With his guns now
out of action, Manseck decided it was time to "pull the plug."
As *U-758* slid under the waves, Fodge rushed in to drop his

depth bombs from seventy feet. These did not destroy the submarine, but many valves were broken, and a compartment was flooded.

Manseck resurfaced about ten minutes later, and a reconstituted crew got the guns back in action. Perabo made another pair of strafing runs, but was met each time by heavy fire from the still-full-of-fight Germans. The attackers called the *Bogue* for more help, but they would not be getting any. Captain Short had decided to withhold his last four Avengers for use in covering the convoy the next few days. Three destroyers had been sent, but overly optimistic reports from his fliers had led Short to recall the ships. The lull enabled Manseck to make a leisurely dive and escape. The *Clemson* finally arrived around 1715 but could not ferret out the U-boat.[64]

U-758 had escaped, but this encounter had a greater impact on future operations for both sides than such an action would generally signify. In the long run, Manseck's success with his "fight-back" tactics led the Germans to make a grievous tactical error. In his report of the engagement, Manseck radioed: "Eight carrier planes warded off; one shot down, four damaged." A delighted Doenitz replied: "Well done. Long live your quadruple."[65]

Heartened by Manseck's report, proponents of the "fight-back" tactics believed that such tactics would be the salvation of the U-boats in their war against aircraft. They were wrong. A major problem with the increased armament was that its installation increased crash-diving time.[66] And, while these tactics initially could be successful, the Germans didn't seem to take into account that the Allies just might come up with countermeasures. An order to use the "fight-back" tactics was in effect for ninety-four days. During this period U-boats shot down fifty-seven aircraft. At the same time, however, twenty-eight submarines were lost, and twenty-two more damaged by aircraft.[67]

In the short run, the damage to Manseck's boat necessitated changes in plans for U-boats in the immediate area and gave the *Bogue* the opportunity for more kills. Manseck's *U-758* had originally been planned to rendezvous with *U-118* and pick up fuel and a *Metox* receiver before heading on for Trinidad. This refueling was later changed to a rendezvous with *U-640* a bit farther west. *U-118* was then to provide fuel

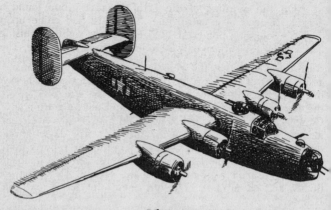

Liberator

to two other submarines. When *U-758* was damaged, the plan
had to be revised again.

U-118 and *U-460* were ordered to go to Manseck's aid.
Unfortunately for the Germans, the order giving *U-118*'s
rendezvous point was read by Tenth Fleet. Several other
messages were read when the two rescue vessels radioed
U-boat Command that they could not find *U-758*. HF/DF
plots also fixed the area of their operations. Captain Short was
notified of the area of U-boat activity.

On the afternoon of the 9th *U-118* finally met *U-758*, and
the next day *U-460* also rendezvoused. *U-460* transferred
extra fuel to *U-118* (which also took on some wounded from
U-758), and then *U-460* shepherded Manseck's boat safely
back to port. *U-118* headed back to her original station at
30°45'N, 33°40'W. Here she was to stand by to fuel four
outbound submarines between 12 and 18 June.[68]

Meanwhile, fearing that Manseck's sighting report on
the night of 8 June was just the first indication of a mass
attack on UGS-9, Short continued escorting the convoy eastward until the afternoon of the 10th, when a Morocco-based
Liberator assumed the escort chores. The *Bogue* now put
about and headed west along the 30th parallel toward a newly
reported U-boat concentration. In the evening TG 21.12
retired to the east so as not to be in the center of any
submarine concentration at night.

On the morning of the 12th the task group found a target. Instead of a patrol line, TG 21.12 had come upon *U-118*'s refueling point. At 1145 *U-118* was sighted cruising placidly on the surface only 20 miles astern of the *Bogue*. The U-boat didn't really have a chance. Eventually eight planes pounced on the 1,600-tonner and sank her.

Lieutenant (jg) Stearns and his Wildcat partner, Lieutenant (jg) R. L. Johnson, were patrolling when they saw *U-118* only a mile away. Johnson led the way, firing his guns from 3,000 feet down to 15 feet and raking the boat from stern to bow. Stearns was close behind. He had to drop his landing gear and raise it again to slow enough to drop his depth bombs. The four bombs landed on both sides of the sub. *U-118* had been diving, with only her conning tower visible, when Stearns attacked but popped up again almost immediately. She was heading at right angles to her original course, and oil was streaming behind her. She dove again, and Johnson chased her under with gunfire.

Lieutenant (jg)s Fowler and Raymond J. Tennant, having seen the attack from an adjoining sector, arrived a few minutes later. *U-118* was surfacing once again, obviously in difficulty. Fowler dropped his four bombs off the sub's starboard side, one hitting just abaft the bow. Tennant made a pair of strafing runs, then circled away to wait for someone to try to man the guns. Finally, Tennant and Fowler joined forces to make coordinated attacks from each side, chasing men back and forth across the U-boat as they sought cover from the attacks.

Tennant and Johnson then teamed up to give the U-boat a .50-caliber massage. By this time the Germans were virtually helpless. Any attempt to man a gun brought instant retaliation. Many men could be seen putting on life jackets. Johnson had to return to the *Bogue* when he ran out of ammunition, but his place was taken by Lieutenant (jg) Fryatt. Fryatt ran in to drop two depth bombs that straddled the conning tower. *U-118* listed to starboard and began sinking slowly by the stern.

Fryatt was going to make another run, but so many planes were circling the sub (four more had shown up as he finished his attack) that he couldn't get near the boat. The three remaining fighters made several strafing passes, and Lieutenant (jg) Chamberlain dropped two bombs that exploded under *U-118*'s conning tower. A few diehards on board the

submarine fired his way, but Chamberlain put a stop to this
when he dropped two more bombs underneath the sub.
Large pieces of metal and debris, along with globs of oil,
fountained into the air. One more attacker had been waiting a
turn, but now there was nothing left to attack. A few miles
away *U-172* lay submerged, waiting to rendezvous with *U-118.*
A little earlier she had reported to U-boat Command of
constant aircraft activity over the rendezvous point. *U-172*'s
report didn't help *U-18.* As they waited underwater, *U-172*'s
crew could hear the explosions that spelled the death of
U-118.[69]

When the spray subsided, both dead and live men could
be seen floating in the water. Fryatt zoomed low over them to
drop his raft. Several of the Germans clasped their hands
above their heads or waved thanks to the American. The
attack on *U-118* had been devastating. Fourteen 325-lb
depth bombs, 4,410 rounds of .50-caliber, and 800 rounds of
.30-caliber ammunition had been used. All of *U-118*'s officers
had been killed in the conning tower, four other dead were
left in the water, and seventeen sailors (one of whom died
later) were picked up by the *Osmond Ingram.* Some of the
rescued turned out to be wounded transferred from Manseck's
U-758.[70] Perhaps trying to impress or scare his captors, one of
those rescued told his interrogator, "We have been chasing
you [the *Bogue*] for fourteen days."[71]

These actions during the first half of June had not gone
in the Germans' favor. The *Trutz* boats had not sunk a single
ship, and an angry Doenitz finally repositioned them in hopes
they might find something. Two U-boats had been lost and
one damaged by carrier aircraft, yet U-boat Command seemed
unable to grasp the offensive character of TG 21.12's assignment. Messages had been sent to *U-118* and *U-460* warning
them of carrier aircraft operating in conjunction with the convoys, but nothing was mentioned about the possibility of
offensive operations against the submarines by the *Bogue.*
When U-boat Command finally awoke to the danger, it was
too late for *U-118.*

After the loss of *U-118,* U-boat Command finally felt it
necessary to stress to the boats the possible appearance of
enemy carrier aircraft. On 13 June the B.d.U. War Diary
stated that "the aircraft which are equipped with excellent
location gear, carry out antisubmarine hunts.... All boats

have again been reminded that aircraft must always be expected even in the most remote areas."[72]

(It is interesting to contemplate what Doenitz would have thought if he had known that the "excellent location gear" that the VC-9 fliers used in these attacks was their own eyesight.)

As mentioned earlier, there were a number of repercussions from these actions, including some other specific events involving *U-118* and *U-758*. Manseck had originally been ordered to get a *Metox* receiver from *U-118* for delivery to another submarine. (This, in itself, shows the concern Doenitz had about radar.) When *U-118* and *U-758* were put out of action, two more subs had to rendezvous to get the *Metox* receiver. This meeting, in effect, canceled one of the U-boat's patrols and caused valuable fuel to be burned by both vessels. This vividly illustrates "the intricately interrelated character of Command's plans and the extent to which these could be disorganized by the failure of a single U-boat."[73]

The *Bogue*'s crew knew nothing of these events, of course, but they did know that they had put a good dent in U-boat operations in their area. With no more contacts after *U-118* was sunk (and with his escorts low on fuel, his planes running out of depth bombs, and the *Bogue*'s catapult damaged), Captain Short took his force back to the United States. The group arrived at Norfolk on 20 June. It had been a successful cruise, with two submarines to the *Bogue*'s and VC-9's credit. However, it had not been a perfect cruise, as the Atlantic Fleet's Antisubmarine Warfare Unit pointedly reminded all concerned, for the VC-9 fliers had relied almost exclusively on eyesight instead of radar for U-boat contacts and also had a tendency to salvo their bombs instead of dropping them in train.[74]

Still, Admiral Ingersoll understood what went into *Bogue*'s success when he sent the following message to the ship upon her arrival in Hampton Roads: "Well done. Results indicate hard work and thorough training."[75] The "hard work and thorough training" that all the escort carrier groups would experience would be the basis for many future successes.

4

CUTTING THE CVES LOOSE

Antisubmarine activity in the Atlantic increased in the summer of 1943 as more escort carriers were sent into action. Eventually the *Santee* would be involved in that type of task, but before then she would operate in a much different role. After the North African landings the *Santee* had returned to the United States for further assignment. But instead of following her sister ships to the Pacific, the *Santee* was sent in a different direction—south.

The *Santee* (still commanded by Captain Sample) left Norfolk on 26 December 1942 escorted by the destroyer *Eberle*. The two vessels anchored at Port of Spain, Trinidad, on New Year's Day and were joined by the destroyer *Livermore*. Two days later the trio left Trinidad and continued south. Arriving in Recife, Brazil, they became TU 23.1.7 of Rear Admiral O. M. Read's TG23.1 of the South Atlantic Force. (This force became the Fourth Fleet on 15 March 1943.)[1]

The South Atlantic Force, operating out of Recife, was not awesome—a few older light cruisers and the more modern cruiser *Savannah*, plus a sprinkling of destroyers and smaller vessels. The composition of the South Atlantic Force was not particularly geared for antisubmarine warfare, but it was well-suited to hunt the German blockade-runners. It was for this purpose that the *Santee* and her two consorts joined Admiral Read, flying his flag in the *Savannah*.

Hunting was poor at first (the *Livermore* had one sound contact on 24 January, but nothing developed), and the *Santee* fliers saw little except some occasional debris or, perhaps, a whale.[2] But on 10 March Admiral Read's little group hit the jackpot. Patrolling about 650 miles east of Recife, TG 23.1 was alerted by a *Santee* plane that a ship flying a Dutch flag was only 17 miles away from the task group. The force immediately went to general quarters, and the *Savannah* and *Eberle* cranked up 31 knots and headed for the unidentified vessel. The *Livermore* remained behind with the *Santee*.

As the cruiser and destroyer neared the supposedly Dutch ship, Admiral Read recognized from the vessel's distinctively painted masts that she was a blockade-runner. He quickly radioed the *Eberle*, "Never mind Dutch flag, pile in there, this is a runner."[3]

Warning shots were fired across the enemy's bow, and the *Eberle* readied a boarding party. The Germans abandoned ship with alacrity, but not so quickly as to forget to set demolition charges. The now-abandoned ship was burning extensively when the *Eberle* boarding party reached her. The fires didn't deter them, however. Lieutenant (jg) Frederick L. Edwards, followed by SM3c William J. Pattison and S1c Alexander J. Bisheimer, were able to board the blockade-runner by way of a Jacob's ladder. The others in the boarding party had to wait while their boat circled for another attempt to grab the ladder.

On board the blockade-runner, Edwards, Pattison, and Bisheimer found the fires were out of control despite their efforts in heaving numerous incendiary units overboard. Edwards also took the time to gather up a number of documents that were found lying about. Meanwhile, the *Eberle*'s boat had returned, and the remainder of the boarding party were beginning to climb the ladder.

Suddenly an explosion almost directly beneath the whaleboat blew it to pieces and killed most of the men in that area. Several men who were on the ladder were able to hold on though buffeted about by the explosion. The ship began to sink rapidly, and the survivors of the boarding party retreated back into the water. Before help could reach the men, Pattison drowned. Eight more of the *Eberle* sailors had been killed and two injured in the explosion. Five others were uninjured.

The enemy vessel was identified as the 7,300-ton runner *Karin*, formerly the Dutch ship *Kota Nopan*. Though the

SBD Dauntless

Allies had tried to keep track of the German blockade-runners through Enigma intercepts, nothing was known of the *Karin*'s movements until about two weeks later, when a message telling some U-boats where to meet her was decrypted on 27 March. It was not long before the Germans became aware that the *Karin*'s cargo of tin and rubber from Malaysia would not be arriving. For their heroism during the boarding of the *Karin*, Edwards, Pattison (posthumously), and Bisheimer were later awarded the Navy Cross.[4]

    The *Santee* had taken no part in the action after the initial sighting of the *Karin*, but it would not be too long before her planes would get their chances against a U-boat.

    The South Atlantic Force became the Fourth Fleet on 15 March, and the *Santee*/*Savannah* group became TG 41.7 on the same day. On the 16th the *Santee*'s fliers finally saw some action. Ensign E. M. Koos was on a routine search in his SBD-3 when he saw a surfaced submarine about 12 miles away. The sub was leaving quite a wake in the choppy sea, and Koos first thought she was the *Savannah*. Drawing closer, he finally saw the vessel was a submarine. The Germans saw the *Dauntless*, and Koos was unable to make a surprise attack. Accurate antiaircraft fire greeted Koos as he dove from 900 feet. He tried to drive the gun crew away from their guns by strafing, but his guns wouldn't work. Just before he released his depth bomb, Koos was wounded in his left leg and hand by the antiaircraft fire. Still he was able to drop his bomb about 25 feet off the sub's port beam. The U-boat slid broadside about 8 feet and heeled over about 20 degrees as the bomb exploded. The antiaircraft fire had also smashed his radio, and Koos had to race back to the *Santee* and make a couple of message drops to inform Captain Sample of his attacks.[5]

Because of a TBF crash earlier in the day, the *Santee* had only one aerial operative for ship-to-aircraft transmissions. In conjunction with the time lost in the message drops from Koos, the delay in transmitting instructions to airborne aircraft caused almost an hour to pass before another attack could be made.

At 1734 Ensign W. R. Taylor found the U-boat and attacked. As Taylor bored in, the submarine began a hard left turn. Taylor released his first 325-lb depth bomb from 300 feet. Neither Taylor nor his crewmen saw where this bomb landed, because they were busy returning the German fire as they pulled out. Taylor made two more strafing runs, then dropped another depth bomb with an instantaneous fuze just 15 feet to the left of the U-boat. The sub "appeared to be sliding over water sidewards to starboard for 100 feet, then made continued tight circle to port, not straightening out again."[6] Taylor then returned to make eight more strafing passes.

While Taylor was making his strafing runs, Ensign Jonathan Oster showed up in his SBD. His first two attacks were unsuccessful as his depth bomb failed to release. Using his manual release, Oster's third attack was successful, and his bomb hit 20 feet aft of the submarine. The boat began to leave a trail of oil. Oster followed his bombing attack with six strafing runs.[7]

Taylor and Oster eventually had to leave because their

fuel was running low. The U-boat, despite the several near-misses, was apparently only slightly damaged. Two more TBFs and two Wildcats (plus the *Eberle*) were dispatched to catch the submarine, but they were unable to find her. Admiral Jonas Ingram, commander of the Fourth Fleet, was "not satisfied with this attack, as it showed inexperience and lack of punch in getting on the enemy with speed and determination."[8] But the *Santee* fliers were still learning, and not many months later they were performing like "old pros."

The *Santee/Savannah* group had been in the process of being dissolved just prior to the attacks on the enemy submarine. When the later searches turned up nothing, the *Santee* (accompanied by the destroyer *Kearny*) was finally detached and headed back to the United States and a new assignment. She would now join in convoy escort and antisubmarine operations in the Central Atlantic.

Before the *Santee* undertook any convoy runs, however, another "jeep" had begun operations in the Atlantic. The *Card*, commanded by Captain Arnold J. ("Buster") Isbell, had been only a week behind the *Bogue* in leaving Puget Sound. She was fresh from her shakedown cruise when she was ordered to escort Convoy UGS-8A, bound for Gibraltar. This convoy, one of the largest of the war, eventually comprised 129 merchant ships and 19 escorts, plus the *Card* and her escorting destroyers, the *Bristol*, *Ludlow*, and *Woolsey*.

UGS-8A would have supplied many tempting targets to any nearby U-boat, but, fortunately, none was present, and the trip over was uneventful. Isbell took the opportunity to exercise his fliers in both day and night operations. As the *Bogue* had done before her, the *Card* remained inside the convoy, dropping astern only for air operations.

After seeing UGS-8A safely across, Isbell took his ships into Casablanca for supplies. On 9 June the *Card* left Casablanca to escort Convoy GUS-8 back to the United States. But this time the *Card* would be operating under a new set of orders. "It was not necessary to keep a continuous umbrella over the convoy," Isbell said later, "and ... we could operate independently against any reported concentration [of U-boats] within striking distance, as long as we could get back to the convoy before the concentration could reach it."[9]

The first hesitant steps of the U.S. escort carrier groups were rapidly becoming surer. Now the carriers would no longer be tied closely to the convoys, but could roam farther afield yet still be able to support the convoys. In the not-too-distant future lay the final stage of the escort carrier group's evolution—the independent hunter-killer group.[10]

Convoy GUS-8 carried a number of German prisoners, and they were apprehensive about crossing the Atlantic, since German propaganda had claimed that few Allied ships were making it across the sea. Some prisoners tried to jump ship as the convoy passed through the Straits of Gibraltar, and a few others were shot to squelch any plans some might have had to do the same. The prisoners were both relieved and depressed when they reached the United States—relieved that they made it across the Atlantic, depressed when they saw that the United States had not been scarred by war.[11]

As the *Card* escorted her charges westward, the *Santee* (now under the command of Captain Harold F. Fick) and her escorts, the *Overton*, *Bainbridge*, and *MacLeish*, were bringing Convoy UGS-10 from the East Coast, bound for Casablanca. The *Santee*'s TG 21.11 operated in close proximity to the convoy most of the time, with the carrier often taking a position in one of the convoy columns.

Doenitz had rearranged his *Trutz* boats in hopes of catching a convoy such as USG-10. These fifteen boats were located about 850 miles east of Bermuda in three north-south lines approximately 25 miles apart. But in getting into position, the German submariners once again broke radio silence to transmit their intentions to U-boat Command. These transmissions, some of inordinate length, enabled Allied "Huff-Duff" stations to roughly gauge the positions of the U-boats.[12]

With the position of Group *Trutz* known with some certainty, UGS-10 was routed south of the U-boats and should have made it all the way across the Atlantic without incident. However, the convoy was not well led, with poor night discipline and stragglers commonplace. On the afternoon of 22 June a mysterious signal was intercepted by the *Santee* and several other vessels in the convoy. This signal was heard the next two days, also. It was obvious that it was coming from a ship in the convoy and indicated that an enemy agent may have been on board that vessel.[13]

One of these mysterious transmissions was picked up by Oberleutnant Günther Kummetat in *U-572*, and he homed in on the convoy. A few hours after the signal had first

appeared on the 22nd, *U-572* penetrated the convoy screen.
At that time the *Santee* was occupying a position in the
convoy, but had twelve planes in the air on antisubmarine
patrols. Her three escorts were operating with the convoy
screen.

The ease with which Kummetat got inside the convoy's
screen may have been helped by an accident on the *Santee* as
U-572 closed in. A Wildcat pilot taking off from the flattop
lost control of his aircraft, and the fighter veered over the
side of the ship, smashing into the sea. The plane sank almost
immediately, and the pilot was not recovered. Perhaps this
tragic accident diverted the attention of some of the ships of
the screen at a most inopportune time and allowed Kummetat
to slip by.

In any event, despite the escorts and aircraft, Kummetat
was able to put two torpedoes into the French tanker *Lot*.
The ship went down quickly, taking twenty-three officers and
men with her. Although held down for five hours by the
now-aroused screen, *U-572* escaped to live until 3 August,
when she was sunk off Trinidad by a Liberator.[14] Fortunately,
the remainder of the voyage was uneventful except for the
sighting of another submarine that escaped before an attack
could be made. The *Santee* docked at Casablanca on 3 July.[15]

The day before Kummetat sank the *Lot*, Doenitz, disgusted
by the *Trutz* group's failure to sight anything, ordered these
boats eastward to form a new line south of the Azores. As
Doenitz was transmitting these new orders, Captain Isbell
and the *Card* were also receiving orders, to head for the
supposed *Trutz* concentration. Needless to say, the *Card* did
not find anything, as the U-boats had moved east before she
reached the area. The *Trutz* boats were broken up on 29 June
into three packs of four boats each (collectively named *Geier*),
but only eight of these eventually made it back to port.[16]

It was not long before the "jeeps" began to score heavily
against the U-boats, however. As Dr. Philip K. Lundberg has
written: "The peculiar significance of Admiral Doenitz's decision to shift the focus of U-boat operations to the Central
Atlantic in June 1943 was that it enabled CinCLant, with full
justification, to bring no less than five American-manned
escort carriers into waters under his operational responsibility
by early August and, with the aid of the newly-created Tenth
Fleet, to mount an anti-submarine offensive off the Azores

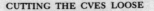

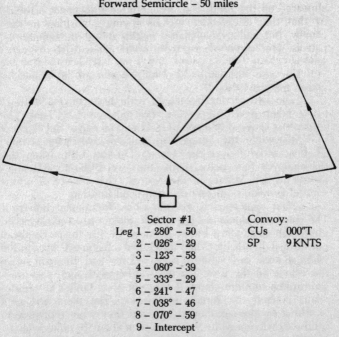

Forward Semicircle – 50 miles

Sector #1		Convoy:	
Leg 1 – 280° – 50		CUs	000"T
2 – 026° – 29		SP	9 KNTS
3 – 123° – 58			
4 – 080° – 39			
5 – 333° – 29			
6 – 241° – 47			
7 – 038° – 46			
8 – 070° – 59			
9 – Intercept			

Typical search pattern used by CVEs in the Atlantic. *Santee* scouting patrol, June–July 1943

that was unique for the rapidity with which tactical innovations were introduced."[17]

The fourth of these carriers to enter the Atlantic arena was the *Core*, a *Bogue*-class vessel that had been launched 15 May 1942 in Seattle. After the usual trials, the ship proceeded down to San Diego where she picked up her air group. VC-13 boarded the *Core* on 24 March 1943 with its nine Avengers and six Wildcats. The *Core* arrived in Norfolk on 12 April, and was soon readied for her first operational cruise. On 27 June Captain Marshall R. Greer took his carrier out from Hampton Roads to escort Convoy UGS-11. She was screened by the "flush-deckers" *Bulmer, George E. Badger,* and *Barker*.[18]

While the *Core* and UGS-11 plodded eastward, the

Santee and her three "tin cans" left Casablanca on 7 July to
accompany GUS-9. The carrier lost one of her planes almost
right away. Shortly after the flattop left port, the normal
antisubmarine patrols were launched. One of her Avengers
didn't return from its patrol, and it was later learned that the
pilot became lost and had to land in Spain, where he and his
crew were interned.[19]

The two carriers remained with their convoys until 11
July, when new orders were received from CinCLant. The
Core was ordered to leave UGS-11 and take over the escort of
GUS-9, while the *Santee* was sent to investigate possible
U-boat activity near the Azores. On the 12th, when this
changeover took place, both ships were 600 to 700 miles
south of Sao Miguel in the Azores. This change of orders
would provide both carriers with good hunting.

First to get a kill was the *Core*. Lieutenant Robert P.
Williams and Lieutenant (jg) Earl H. Steiger had been launched
from the carrier just before noon on 13 July to search ahead
of GUS-9. Tenth Fleet had developed a fix on a U-boat in the
Core's area just a short time before, and the pair were
searching for this prey. The day was fair, with some scattered-
to-broken cumulus clouds dotting the area. Only a few white-
caps marred the surface of the sea. The fliers had seen
nothing on their outbound leg, and they were returning to
the ship when a white wake was seen about 10 miles away by
Williams's turret gunner. The time was 1421. Just a few
minutes earlier the TBF's radar had been secured (nothing
had disturbed the blankness of its scope anyway), and both
planes had descended to 5,500 feet to keep under some
clouds.

The wake was off to the left, and both planes turned that
way, using the clouds to cover their approach. As they neared
the object, the Americans could see that it was a dirty brown
or black-looking submarine. Oberleutnant Konstantin Metz,
believing his *U-487* was in no danger, had let his crew on
deck to sun themselves and to play with a floating bale of
cotton. The playing stopped suddenly as Steiger whipped by
in his F4F. His bullets chased many of the submariners below
while others headed for the guns. Right behind Steiger came
Williams.

Williams glided in on the boat and dropped four Mk. 47
depth bombs from 250 feet. Spaced about 70 feet apart, the

first two bombs straddled the sub's bow while the last two exploded off her port side. Williams and Steiger pulled up to 3,500 feet and watched as the U-boat began to circle slowly to the right. Oil began to ooze from her hull. The Germans finally had their act together and were filling the air near the aircraft with deadly puffs of flak.

The report of the attack was radioed quickly to the *Core*, and five more planes led by the squadron commander, Lieutenant Commander Charles W. Brewer, were soon on their way. (Brewer would later distinguish himself, and tragically lose his life, leading the *Essex*'s VF-15 during the Battle of the Philippine Sea.) The destroyer *Barker* also headed toward the scene. Before these reinforcements reached the area, however, Williams and Steiger made another pass over the U-boat to take some pictures. Though the pictures did not turn out, as they passed the submarine, Williams thought he saw white water astern of the U-boat and the sub beginning to pick up speed.

Williams asked Steiger to make another run and put some more holes in the boat's pressure hull. Though only one of his guns was now working, Steiger immediately began his run. As he neared the U-boat, Steiger's Wildcat suddenly swerved to the left, then dove into the sea just off the submarine's port bow. Steiger was killed instantly.

The other VC-13 planes were now on the scene. They saw Steiger crash and heard Williams report that the sub "had gotten one of our planes."[20] Angered by this loss, Lieutenant Commander Brewer brought his Wildcat screaming down from astern of the submarine in a strafing run. In this one pass Brewer used some 1,200 rounds of ammunition. Another F4F, which had just arrived from an adjacent search sector, also began a strafing run but pulled up when a pair of Avengers darted in to bomb the U-boat.

Lieutenant (jg) James F. Schoby glided in at 245 knots from off the sub's starboard bow to drop four Mk. 47 depth bombs from 100 feet. These did the trick. The first exploded on the boat's starboard bow, the fourth just off the port quarter, and the middle two directly underneath the boat. The force of these explosions drove the submarine upward a few feet before the plumes of water covered her. When the water subsided, only about 30 feet of the stern (sticking up at an acute angle) could be seen. Five seconds later *U-487* slid under the water. Several men could be seen in the water swimming toward two liferafts. Another pair of half-sunken rafts could also be seen.

By 1535 all planes had left except for two that guided the *Barker* to the survivors. A large oil slick, combining with the characteristic brownish scum left by the explosions of the depth bombs, spread over the water. A small light apple-green area was the tombstone of the 1,600-ton *U-487*. She had gone down about 720 miles south–southwest of Fayal, Azores. The *Barker* soon arrived to pull thirty-three very wet, very discouraged Germans from the oil-covered water. Oberleutnant Metz was not among those rescued.[21]

U-487 had been one of the so-called milch cows (large U-boats used primarily for supply and fueling purposes) supporting the ill-fated 1st Monsoon Group headed for the Indian Ocean. Doenitz had long been interested in this area and the Cape of Good Hope, and had sent several independent patrols almost to the cape in 1940 and 1941. However, it was not until the summer of 1942 that a larger operation near Capetown was planned. This operation was very successful, with twenty-four ships sunk in October of the year. Doenitz was now ready to move around the cape.

The Indian Ocean, with its many unescorted vessels scurrying here and there, was a juicy arena. Doenitz, obsessed with his "tonnage warfare" theory of sinking as many merchantmen as possible wherever they might be, could see the Indian Ocean as a new "happy hunting ground." An initial operation in that ocean was quite successful, and the U-boats began using the Japanese submarine base at Penang, Malaya, to extend their time on station.

Doenitz planned more operations for his U-boats in the Indian Ocean and dispatched several Monsoon groups to that area beginning in June of 1943. But, unknown to the Germans, Tenth Fleet had been reading U-boat Command's messages and thus had a pretty fair idea of what was happening and where to look for the U-boats. So it was that the U-boat refueling area for the Monsoon boats was "infested as never before with U.S.N. CVEs."[22]

This infestation was the result of the Navy's increased emphasis on the *offensive* use of Enigma information. The *Bogue*'s operations against the *Trutz* boats in June had been one of the first instances of this offensive use. Now the Navy was zeroing in on the U-boat fueling point. There were two related reasons for these operations. First, the sinking of the milch cows would greatly inhibit further actions of the combat U-boats. Second, because of the huge amount of information that was needed by both the submarines and U-boat Command, there was a great deal of radio traffic relating to the rendezvous. Thus, "the refueling rendezvous was a kind of center from which combat U-boats could be tracked to their attack areas on the edges of the ocean."[23]

The British were not too keen on the American use of Enigma information for offensive purposes, fearing (with good reason) that these operations would alert the Germans to the fact that their "mail" was being read. But fortune favors the bold, and, to the relief of the Allies, the Germans never caught on.[24]

Another U-boat was spotted the day after U-487 was sunk. Lieutenant Williams was out again early on the 14th scouting to the north side of GUS-9. An oil slick was seen 9 miles to the north, and Williams turned to investigate. It was an even nicer day than the day before, with no clouds and a visibility of 25 miles. At 0854 a periscope wake was spotted. Then a submarine was seen surfacing slowly. Williams pushed his portly TBF over and dove toward the vulnerable target. From 150 feet he toggled out four depth bombs.

The first bomb hit the water on the U-boat's starboard quarter close aboard. This bomb may have ricocheted across the boat, or the second bomb may have hit the sub's deck and bounced off to port. The other bombs hit farther off to port. Water from the explosions completely covered the submarine. When they subsided, the U-boat could be seen disappearing on a relatively even keel. An oil slick formed that slowly dissipated over the next hour.

Two more Avengers and an F4F were catapulted from the *Core*, but they found nothing until 1200, when a fresh oil slick was seen about 7 miles from the original attack site. The *Bulmer* and the *Ericsson* were also sent to the area, but nothing was found, and the U-boat escaped.[25]

The VC-13 fliers were not getting all the action. About midnight on 13–14 July the *Santee* received a special "Huff-Duff" report from Washington. A sub had been plotted about 200 miles northwest of the carrier. This report was the first in a series of such reports that would lead directly to sightings and attacks. The *Santee* would later make "a deep bow of appreciation" to those at Tenth Fleet who supplied this information.[26]

On the morning of the 14th, Lieutenant (jg) John H. Ballantine, in an Avenger, and Lieutenant "Brink" Bass, in a Wildcat, were patrolling about 145 miles north of the *Santee*. Shortly after 0800 Ballantine caught the reflection of the sun off a submarine about 21 miles away. Ballantine rocked his wings to get Bass's attention and pointed out the light-gray-painted sub. The U-boat was *U-160*. Commanded by Ober-leutnant Gerd von Pommer-Esche, she was on her maiden voyage.

When Bass picked out the U-boat, he streaked ahead to strafe the boat with his deadly 'fifties. Pommer-Esche started his boat down as Bass came around again to strafe. Ballantine was still a short distance away when *U-160* crash-dived. This maneuver would not save the boat, for Ballantine was carrying a new and deadly weapon that the *Santee* was introducing to combat. This was the Mk. 24 mine—a homing torpedo known colloquially as Fido.

Ballantine zoomed in from the opposite direction of Bass's last pass. Dropping his landing gear to slow and steady his corpulent aircraft, he then made a 180-degree turn for his attack. He sighted the sub's swirl left from the dive and dropped his Fido 200 yards ahead and 100 feet to the right of the turbulence. As he circled back, Ballantine saw a pronounced shock wave form in the water, followed by a ring of foam and the characteristic brown depth bomb discoloration. Nothing else was seen, but *U-160* made no more reports to U-boat Command.[27]

It was several days before the Germans were aware of the loss of both *U-487* and *U-160*. *U-487* was finally considered lost on 18 July. The day before she was lost, *U-160* had been detailed to act as an emergency tanker for the 1st Monsoon Group. On the 21st U-boat Command had to conclude that *U-160*, too, had been lost. The unexplained loss of these boats mystified the Germans until they received a Spanish steamer's report of a "large aircraft carrier" in the U-boat's last known positions. Based on this information, the Germans rerouted their boats west of the Azores in an attempt to escape the clutches of the carrier.[28]

On the afternoon of the 14th a pair of VC-29 Dauntless

pilots found another sub leaving a periscope wake. A depth bomb dropped by one of the SBDs was seen to explode directly over the conning tower, but no damage was noted. Malfunctioning bomb racks prevented the other dive bomber from dropping its bomb. Lieutenant (jg) John W. Padberg joined the other planes in his Avenger and took over the responsibility of destroying the U-boat. About two hours after the initial attack, Padberg saw the sub surfacing 6 miles away.

Padberg began a strafing run, but was met by a hail of 20-mm fire. Nevertheless, he continued his run, peppering the U-boat with his .30-caliber nose guns. Darkness was approaching rapidly, and Padberg made three more passes before the sub began to dive. Turning about quickly, Padberg dropped a Fido from 200 feet. No explosion was seen, however, and the U-boat (probably *U-168*) escaped.[29]

The VC-29 fliers struck again on the morning of the 15th. At 0818 Lieutenant (jg) Claude N. Barton, flying an Avenger, saw a surfaced sub 14 miles away. The boat was painted in a blotchy gray, brown, and green pattern. Barton's fighter partner, Ensign Jack D. Anderson, tightened formation momentarily, then dove for an attack across the sub's port beam. He followed this with another strafing from the opposite direction, meeting some inaccurate gunfire that he did not notice, and then made two more passes that were "notably accurate." In the meantime, Barton was "dirtying up" his plane by dropping his gear and flaps, and was waiting for his chance to attack.

During Anderson's third pass the U-boat began evasive maneuvers and on the fourth strafing, submerged. This was Barton's chance. He jumped the disappearing sub and dropped his Fido from 225 feet. The homing torpedo entered the water 250 feet ahead and to the right of the swirl. A shock wave was seen in the water a few seconds later, followed by a heavy bubbling swirl, a large discharge of oil, and the Fido's brownish residue. The grave of the 1st Monsoon Group's *U-509* was some 180 miles south of Santa Maria. There were no survivors.[30]

Upon their return to the *Santee*, Barton and Anderson told the story of the action to Captain Fick. When Barton related how much antiaircraft fire had been directed his partner's way, Anderson's face reflected his amazement. As the pair left the bridge, Anderson could be heard asking

Barton in a rather hurt tone, "Did you say they were shooting at me?"[31]

Yet another submarine (probably *U-532*) was attacked by a VC-29 Wildcat Avenger team on the afternoon of 15 July. Three strafing runs by the Wildcat pilot forced the U-boat to submerge. Unfortunately, subsequent attacks by the Avenger were unsuccessful because the selector switch for the Mk. 24 mine was in the wrong position. When the Fido was finally dropped, it entered the water too far from the sub's swirl to be effective, and the boat escaped.[32]

The *Core* got back into the act on 16 July, tracking down another Tenth Fleet fix. And once more Lieutenant Williams was "Johnny-on-the-spot." Williams had been on patrol for about two hours when he saw a submarine cruising on the surface. The boat was about 842 miles west–southwest of Flores and only 27 miles from GUS-9. Using cloud cover, Williams was able to sneak up on the sub. He was on the boat before her crew knew what was happening. Four Mk. 47 depth bombs, fuzed for 25 feet and set at 70-feet intervals, were dropped from 400 feet. One apparently exploded 50 feet aft of the conning tower and beneath the boat. The others exploded off the port side. The U-boat's bow angled sharply out of the water, and iridescent blue oil gushed from fatal gashes in her hull. In only five seconds the submarine had disappeared from sight. An area of pale green water lying just under the surface of the ocean contrasted strongly with the deep blue of the Atlantic.

The destroyer *McCormick* arrived on the scene at 0630 and found three survivors, two others having disappeared less than half an hour earlier. These men had been on deck when bombed and had been thrown into the water by the explosions. Their boat had been *U-67*, under the command of Kapitanleutnant Gunther Muller-Stockheim. She had been returning from an unproductive patrol of the Caribbean and the southeast coast of the United States. Now she no longer needed the fuel she had been hoping to get from *U-648*.[33] For his energetic efforts over the last few days, Williams would receive the Navy Cross.

Four U-boats sunk in four days was good hunting for the two escort carrier groups. The remaining boats south of the Azores (about twelve), warned by U-boat Command from Spanish merchantmen reports, decided that the presence of the carriers was too dangerous and headed for safer waters to the west and north.[34]

The *Core*'s TG 21.12 did not have any more luck finding submarines. However, the group had a fairly exciting time on the evening of 21 July when one of the VC-13 aircraft got lost. Ensign Doyle W. Hall was on an antisubmarine patrol when a small fire wrecked his interphone system. The fire apparently put his radio receiver out of operation, also, for he could transmit to the carrier but could not receive any of the *Core*'s transmissions.

Hall became lost after flying through several showers. Actually, the *Core* had radar contact with his plane most of the time, but Hall couldn't hear the ship reporting this fact. For almost three hours the men on board the *Core*, unable to help, watched the radar screen and listened to Hall on the radio vainly trying to establish contact with the ship.

Finally, Hall radioed, "I'm going to ditch while I still have enough gas for a power landing." Then, "Stand by!" followed by a crunching noise and silence.[35] Hall and his crewmen, RM2c Ray S. Hansen and AMM2c Robert H. Meyer, were able to get out of their sinking plane without too much difficulty and clambered into their raft.

As he dragged himself into the raft, Meyer exclaimed, "Gosh, Mr. Hall. We've got our own ship now. You're the captain and we both the execs."[36] The trio then settled down in the raft for a possibly long, cold, and wet stay.

The *Core*'s radar had pinpointed the ditching site, however, and the probable drift of the raft was plotted. The next morning one of the destroyers found Hall and his crew, all uninjured, right where they were supposed to be. With no more excitement in the offing, the *Core* headed for Norfolk, where she arrived on the 30th.[37]

The *Santee*, meanwhile, was having just as little success in flushing out U-boats south of the Azores. For the next several days no U-boats were seen, but the search missions took their toll. Two Dauntlesses and their crews were lost during these necessary flights.[38] The *Santee* would be getting some help, however. The *Bogue* left the Chesapeake Bay area on 12 July to escort Convoy UGS-12. The ship was now commanded by her former executive officer, Captain Joseph B. Dunn. VC-9 was still aboard, and the *Bogue* was now screened by the *George E. Badger*, *Clemson*, and *Osmond*

Ingram. Organized as TG 21.13, for the major part of the journey the group remained out of sight of the convoy chasing down "Huff-Duff" fixes unproductively.

Previous experience had shown that many U-boat skippers tended to be careless about their own rears when making a stern chase on a convoy. Captain Dunn hoped to take advantage of this by coming in behind the reported concentrations of enemy submarines. On the 21st the *Bogue* left the company of UGS-12 to make an offensive sweep toward a U-boat concentration reported 600 miles south of the Azores. These boats were reported moving southwest.[39] Two days later the *Bogue* group struck paydirt. The weather was not particularly good, with intermittent rain squalls and low-lying clouds, but the VC-9 fliers took advantage of it.

Around 0600 an Avenger/Wildcat team spotted a surfaced submarine. The boat was only 11 miles ahead of the *Bogue* and was steering a course that would have closed with the convoy in about two hours. The team jumped the sub and drove her under with strafing and depth bombs. An oil slick showed that the U-boat was damaged, but she was able to escape. The action for the day was not yet over, however.

At 0906 the *Badger* got a sonar contact on a submarine (possibly the one attacked earlier) 1,100 yards away. At the time the destroyer was 4,000 yards off the *Bogue*'s port bow. The *Badger*'s skipper, Lieutenant Thomas H. Byrd, ordered full left rudder, but the target was inside the "tin can's" turning circle. No attack was made, and the contact was temporarily lost, but the sub was soon picked up again by the hard-working sonar operator. An eight-charge pattern set for 600 feet was dropped, but nothing except seawater came up. A second attack with the same pattern and depth settings brought the same results.

Byrd was not about to give up, however. It appeared that the sub was first trying to keep her stern to the destroyer, then fish-tailing and turning in one direction, followed by a turn in the opposite direction to get behind her wake. A third attack was begun, and the U-boat was tracked moving slowly to the right. Contact was lost at 400 yards and another eight-charge pattern was dropped. The results were disappointing as the sub evaded once again.

Depth charges were reset once more as the *Badger* regained sonar contact. The sub was inside the flush-decker's turning circle, but Byrd skillfully countered this with hard left rudder and engines. One more run was made by the *Badger*. This time the roar of the depth charges exploding had a different sound—the sound of a U-boat being ripped open. Evil-smelling diesel oil, with the gruesome debris of splintered woodwork, clothing, and mutilated corpses, spewed to the surface of the ocean. A stream of bubbles resembling carbonated water rose from the depths.

The *Badger*'s sonar operator reported hearing a "loud howling noise which increased in intensity for a few seconds, followed by intermittent bubbling and hissing sounds."[40] As the *Badger*'s crew searched through the ghastly flotsam, one ironic piece of evidence was found—a German translation of Poe's *Murders in the Rue Morgue*. Postwar evidence would show that the unlucky submarine had been the 769-ton *U-613*, bound for Jacksonville on a minelaying mission.[41]

The *Bogue* and her planes were not yet done for the day. Shortly after 1200, when the *Bogue* and her escorts were about 55 miles from UGS-12, an Avenger flown by Lieutenant (jg) Stearns came across a pair of U-boats. Stearns was flying at 300 feet, just below the clouds, when he saw a few oil patches. A few minutes later Stearns's gunner saw two wakes about fifty yards apart. These wakes were being left by the 1,144-ton *U-527* and the 769-ton *U-648*, then in the process of fueling.

U-527, commanded by Kapitanleutnant Herbert Uhlig, was on her second patrol. She had just returned from the Gulf of Mexico and had been directed to meet with *U-67* and *U-648* and take fuel from the latter vessel, which was acting as a relief supply boat. *U-67*, of course, would not be making the rendezvous, as she had been sunk earlier by *Core* aircraft. *U-527*'s crew were already nervous, having "sensed an ill omen in the farewell ceremony, when the commanding officer of the flotilla, Korvettenkapitan Kuhnke, concluded his address with 'Aufwiedersehen, Kamaraden.' The men, apparently expecting the customary 'Heil Hitler' stood in awkward silence and did not respond until Kuhnke repeated his words."[42] Now they had been caught in the vulnerable process of fueling.

The Germans were very surprised when the Avenger suddenly was on them. The crew of *U-648* were quicker than their comrades, and their boat was under before Stearns could attack. Uhlig headed for a nearby fogbank at 15 knots, firing at Stearns all the time with the new 20-mm guns recently mounted aft of the bridge.

Stearns was on the U-boat too soon for any accurate defensive fire, however. Four depth bombs, fuzed for 25 feet, were dropped from dead astern. *U-527*'s stern was covered with water, and her pressure hull torn open aft of the conning tower. One man was blown into the air, and several others were seen to jump overboard. The explosions were so severe that everyone on board was stunned or completely disabled. The boat began to turn slowly to the right as smoke rose aft of the conning tower. *U-527*'s bow rose higher in the water until it was almost vertical; then she sank stern-first. The *Clemson* was soon on the scene and pulled thirteen survivors, including Uhlig, from the water.[43]

That same day the *Santee* was also running into U-boats again. At 0819 on the 24th an Avenger/Wildcat team spotted *U-373* about 130 miles west of Madeira. The sub was bound for Port Lyautey to lay mines in the Wadi Sebou. Several strafing attacks and a Fido drop only damaged the boat, but she had to return to France without sowing her mines. As a rendezvous with GUS-10 was scheduled for the next day, an intensive search by VC-29 planes and the *Bainbridge* for the U-boat was finally called off near sunset.[44]

On the 26th the *Bogue*'s TG 21.13 left UGS-12 to

Fw 200

proceed for Casablanca. The *Osmond Ingram* was having boiler problems and needed repairs before the task group could efficiently escort any more convoys. En route to Casablanca, Captain Dunn received information that long-range Fw 200's might be in the area. Until the *Bogue* entered Casablanca on 1 August, Dunn kept a constant daylight fighter patrol over the ship—one of the few times in the Atlantic that an escort carrier had to do this.[45]

Meanwhile, the *Santee* was heading westward with GUS-10. All was quiet until the afternoon of 30 July, when Lieutenant (jg)s Richmond and Van Vranken (searching north of the convoy) saw two wakes about 10 miles away. As the two pilots closed in through puffy cumulus clouds, they could see two subs—a small type (the 769-ton Type VIIC *U-403*) ahead of a larger one (the 1,032-ton Type IXA *U-43*).

Van Vranken climbed to 1,500 feet and charged ahead of the two boats, while Richmond kept his "Turkey" just hidden in the base of the clouds. When Van Vranken got into position, he pushed over toward the enemy vessels. His .50-caliber guns cleared the leading sub's deck; then he ruddered his Wildcat slightly to rake the second boat with his shells.

Immediately behind the fighter came Richmond. *U-403* was turning sharply to port as he attacked. Two Mk. 47 depth bombs fell fifty feet to the right of her conning tower. Some oil trickled from the boat as she dove to escape the onslaught. *U-43* was also turning to port and submerging when Richmond dropped a Fido. The torpedo sniffed around and ferreted out the U-boat. "Two minutes following the drop an underwater explosion occurred, causing a mushroom, boiling effect on the surface." *U-43*'s load of mines that she had been carrying for use off Lagos had exploded, and only oil, brown water, and small pieces of the boat came to the surface.[46]

The loss of so many submarines in so short a time alarmed Admiral Doenitz. A number of milch cows had been among these losses. On 4 August he noted grimly, "As at present no further supply is possible, all boats now in the operation area must start on their return passage so that they can reach port without refueling or taking over provisions."[47]

Over the next few days Doenitz returned continually to the supply problems. Statements like "the supply situation has already had its effect on operations . . ." and "there are no more reserve tankers" reflected growing concern by U-boat Command of the seriousness of the situation.[48]

Crew morale also worried Doenitz. On 6 August he told his skippers, "Do not report too much bad news, so as not to depress the other boats; every radio message goes the rounds of the crew in every boat. If necessary report matters which ratings do not need to know by officer's cipher."[49]

Casting about for a reason for these losses, U-boat Command once again took a hard look at the Metox receiver. It had been known that Metox did emit some radiation, but recent tests had shown that these radiations extended a much greater distance than was earlier realized. It appeared to the Germans that the Allies were using these radiations to home in on U-boats. Therefore, on 31 July U-boat Command ordered all boats to cease using Metox except under certain conditions.[50]

This suspicion was "further confirmed" about two weeks later when a British flier being interrogated at the Oberursel transit camp told his captors a tall tale that Allied aircraft were using radiations from Metox to home in on the U-boats. This story was a hoax, but the Germans, wanting to believe it, bought the tale hook, line, and sinker. Doenitz once more reiterated his order to stop using the Metox receiver.[51]

Doenitz was also concerned that his crews were not taking the threat of escort carriers seriously enough. Many of his commanding officers derided the carriers as "tired crows." Wishing to dispel this notion, Doenitz told his captains that "the sinking of an aircraft carrier is of greatest importance. If a boat sights a carrier she should attack at all costs; the carrier is always the most important target."[52]

Unaware of what was transpiring in the enemy camp, the U.S. escort carriers continued on their missions. The Santee returned to Norfolk on 6 August, followed by the Bogue (which had an unproductive cruise back from Casablanca) on the 23rd. Taking the Santee's place in the Atlantic was the Card, still commanded by "Buster" Isbell. The carrier left Hampton Roads on 27 July, accompanied by a screen of the old flush-deckers Barry, Borie, and Goff. Still aboard the flattop were the six F4F-4s and eleven TBF-1s of VC-1 skippered by Lieutenant Commander Carl E. Jones. During this cruise the opportunity was taken to try several camouflage schemes on the Card's aircraft. The final result was a dull milky white smeared with a little oil. "The result, while not pretty, [made] the planes almost invisible."[53]

After fueling in Bermuda, the *Card* group (organized as TG 21.14) joined Convoy UGS-13 on 1 August. The three old destroyers were topped off by a tanker in the convoy; then the task group pulled away from the convoy to look afield for U-boats. Isbell was eager to catch some of the underwater killers, and he had a very simple plan to accomplish this. He would take his force right through the center of any reported concentration, while his planes flew 100 miles ahead and to either side. It wasn't long before Isbell's plan had some effect.

On 3 August Lieutenant (jg) Richard L. Cormier and his Wildcat escort, Ensign A. S. Paulson, were out patrolling when they came across *U-66* some 457 miles west–southwest of Flores. Kapitanleutnant Friedrich Markworth's boat had been out almost fourteen weeks but had sunk only two ships off the United States during that time. Now Markworth was heading home, cruising slowly on the surface. Cormier saw *U-66* from about 11 miles away. Because there was no cloud cover, he elected to attack immediately. Paulson raced ahead to strafe the boat.

Once again a U-boat crew was caught flat-footed by an attack out of the sky. Paulson's first attack fatally wounded the officer of the deck, and the men in the conning tower quickly sounded the diving alarm. Markworth just as quickly rushed topside, belayed the order to dive, and prepared to follow the current doctrine of "fighting back." Cormier's initial attack was unsuccessful, as his depth bombs failed to release. Paulson braved the fire from the now-alert Germans for another strafing pass, while Cormier came in for another run.

This time Cormier pressed his electrical release and also pulled his emergency release as he passed over the U-boat. Both depth bombs and the Fido fell from the Avenger's bomb bay. About forty seconds later a shock wave was seen to form about ten feet to the right of the sub and slightly forward of the conning tower. "This wave swept out not only to starboard but also over on the port side of the submarine. The U-boat seemed to be lifted from below and then listed to starboard. Then a heavy column of water about 125 feet high obscured the submarine from view."[54]

Markworth had been seriously wounded in these attacks, and his second in command had to take the boat down. *U-66* was able to escape, and that night surfaced to radio U-boat Command for assistance. As *U-117* was the nearest milch cow, *U-66* was ordered to rendezvous with her. Shortly before midnight on the 6th the two submarines met, and Oberleutnant Frerks relieved Markworth.[55]

The U-boats were still in great danger, for the stream of messages between *U-66*, *U-117*, and U-boat Command had been read by Tenth Fleet. Though the exact point of the rendezvous was unknown, its general area had been narrowed considerably. The *Card* was notified of the area of the rendezvous.[56]

On the morning of 7 August Lieutenant (jg) Asbury H. Sallenger was west of the carrier looking for the U-boats when he saw a "large white object" off to his right and about 12 miles distant. Investigating, he discovered that the "object" was, in fact, two submarines—*U-66* and the milch cow *U-117*. The boats were slowly cruising 200 feet apart. Though it was a bit hazy, there was no cloud cover to hide Sallenger.

Nevertheless, Sallenger positioned himself for an attack out of the sun. The German sailors, busy with their duties, did not see him until he was just 400 yards away. Both boats opened fire (*U-117* had the newly increased armament), but though their fire was intense, it missed Sallenger's plane. He later remarked, "Their firing was rotten. It was all around me, but no hits."[57]

Sallenger released two depth bombs from 125 feet. These straddled the big milch cow, one exploding 8 feet off the sub's starboard quarter and the other 18 feet out and just ahead of the conning tower. As Sallenger pulled up, his radioman snapped pictures of the wounded vessel, and his turret gunner fired at the boat. *U-117* began to smoke heavily and began making "erratic turns in a crazy quilt pattern."[58] She was badly hurt and unable to submerge.

Before attacking, Sallenger had radioed the *Card* (then 82 miles away), and reinforcements were on the way. Before they could reach the scene, however, *U-66* (which had been trying to assist *U-117*) began to submerge. Sallenger immediately attacked her. He had to brave the fire of *U-117* as he skimmed by her conning tower at only 130 knots and 200 feet. But her fire was again inaccurate, and Sallenger dropped his Fido 50 yards to the right and 150 yards ahead of *U-66*'s swirl. Fido lost the scent, however, and the U-boat escaped once again.

Sallenger climbed to 6,400 feet to vector the other planes in. A few minutes before the reinforcements arrived, U-117 tried to submerge, but she came back up almost immediately. Two Avengers and a pair of Wildcats arrived shortly after 0730. Lieutenant Norman D. Hodson and Lieutenant (jg) Ernest E. Jackson strafed the submarine "unmercifully." Lieutenant Charles R. Stapler and Lieutenant (jg) Junior C. Forney pushed over from 3,000 feet to make their attacks. Although the gunners on the U-boat were still putting up a considerable amount of flak, this had little effect on the attackers.

Stapler's depth bombs landed close aboard the submarine's port side forward, and the geysers of water from the explosions almost completely engulfed the U-boat. Forney followed close behind, his bombs going off about 25 feet from the sub's starboard quarter. Hodson and Jackson returned with more strafing passes. U-117 was mortally hurt. She slowed down and began turning to the right, then began to submerge. Stapler and Forney, who had been waiting for this moment, darted in. Just before they reached the drop point for their Fidos, U-117 struggled back to the surface.

For about five minutes the sub wallowed on the surface; then her bow came up, the conning tower disappeared under the water, and her bow went under. Stapler and Forney were back in seconds. Stapler's Fido went in on the starboard side of the swirl, while Forney's entered on the port side. Five minutes after the Fidos were dropped, an area of light blue water filled with bubbles suddenly appeared. There was no doubt now; U-117 had made her last dive.[59]

The loss of U-117 was a serious blow to U-boat Command, as she was "urgently needed." Another milch cow, U-489, had been sunk off Iceland, and it was to be up to U-117 to fuel some fourteen U-boats returning home.[60] Not until 13 August would the Germans be aware of the loss of U-117. Once again the loss of a tanker had thrown a monkey wrench into U-boat Command's carefully laid plans. The escort carriers were quickly showing their influence on operations in the Battle of the Atlantic.[61]

The morning after the sinking of U-117, Sallenger was back out on patrol. He was not alone this time, being escorted by Ensign John F. Sprague. The pair were flying in and out of low-hanging clouds and through occasional rain squalls when, at 0611, they popped out of a cloud and found

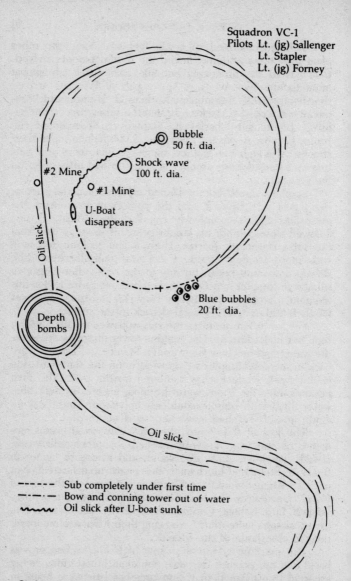

Squadron VC-1
Pilots Lt. (jg) Sallenger
Lt. Stapler
Lt. (jg) Forney

Bubble
50 ft. dia.

Shock wave
100 ft. dia.

#2 Mine

#1 Mine

U-Boat
disappears

Oil slick

Blue bubbles
20 ft. dia.

Depth
bombs

Oil slick

- - - - - - Sub completely under first time
- · - · - · Bow and conning tower out of water
~~~~~~~ Oil slick after U-boat sunk

Sinking of *U-117*, August 1943.

themselves almost on top of two U-boats. The submarines were making only about 3 knots, and their decks were awash. Sallenger had no time to inform the *Card* of the sighting but attacked immediately.

Sprague barreled in, raking the nearest submarine with effective machine-gun fire. But the Germans were firm believers in the "fight back" tactic and quickly filled the air with lead. Sallenger's TBF was the unfortunate recipient of most of this fire. As he raced in, his plane shuddered from several hits that started a fire in the bomb bay and knocked out the radios and the electrical system. Because of the damage, Sallenger was unable to release his bombs on this pass. Nevertheless, he doubled back to once more face the antiaircraft fire.

The enemy fire again ripped into the Avenger, this time starting a fire in the left wing root. Sallenger's plane was in bad shape. His crewmen were also having problems. AMM3c James H. O'Hagan said later, "Our electrical system was shot up and I could not work the turret or get in contact with Mr. Sallenger. I called to [ACRM(a) John D.] Downes, our radioman, to ask him to help me turn my turret around as it was stuck. I looked down in the tunnel and he was lying on his face. The radio equipment was on the deck by his feet, the camera by his side smashed up."[62]

Sallenger dropped his two depth bombs manually, and they exploded near one of the submarines, *U-664*. He next jettisoned his Fido and prepared to ditch his crippled plane. Because the hydraulic system had been shot out, the flaps were up and the bomb bay doors were open when the TBF touched down; so the ditching was pretty rough. Sallenger and O'Hagan popped out of their plane quickly and began inflating their raft. Discovering that Downes was not with them, Sallenger swam under the plane in an attempt to extricate his radioman through the tunnel door. However, the plane began to settle and went under in less than thirty seconds. Downes was lost with it.

Sprague, meanwhile, was continuing his strafing runs, but the other submarine, *U-262*, shot his Wildcat down, and Sprague was killed. Thus the "fight back" tactics had proved very effective in this instance; but continued reliance on these methods would be more dangerous to the U-boats in the future.

When Sallenger and Sprague did not return, Captain Isbell turned the *Card* toward the missing aviators' search sector. The *Barry* was sent ahead to look for the men, as were several aircraft. Six hours after they had climbed into their raft, Sallenger and O'Hagan were found by the planes, which guided the *Barry* to the rescue. A wet and discouraged Sallenger, who had claimed the enemy fire was "rotten" the day before, had no comment on the accuracy of the German fire this day.[63]

The attack by Sallenger and Sprague had so damaged *U-262* that she had to return to base. Before leaving the area, however, the sub was to turn over any extra fuel and provisions she had to *U-664* and *U-760*. *U-664* was then to head for the American coast. But the *Card* would once again disrupt U-boat Command's plans.[64]

U-664 was still hanging around on the 8th as the *Card* combed the area for submarines. Dusk was falling as the watch officer of *U-664* saw what he identified as a large tanker. The sub's commander, Oberleutnant Adolf Graef, was called to the bridge. Graef was not well liked by his crew, who described him as a "martinet, as a man lacking all the skills necessary to a U-boat skipper, as a poor shot and as being totally unable to understand any of the problems of his crew. His passion was playing chess and his capacity to sleep and lazy around was surpassed only by his ability to curse and mistreat his men."[65]

Graef showed his shooting prowess by firing three torpedoes at the "tanker." All missed, and the target—the *Card*—steamed away unscathed, blissfully unaware that she had been attacked. On board the carrier "Buster" Isbell and VC-1's skipper, Lieutenant Commander Jones, were huddling together to devise some new tactics to use against the now more aggressive U-boats.

Instead of the previous Avenger/Wildcat team, they devised a plan to use one Wildcat and two Avengers as an attack team. One of the TBFs would be armed with two instantaneously fuzed 500-pound bombs, while the other would carry depth bombs and Fido. This new plan would get a good workout on the afternoon of 9 August when the VC-1 planes would again meet their nemesis, *U-664*.[66]

That afternoon a three-plane team was flying at 1,500 feet and had just popped out of a cloud when all three crews saw *U-664* just off to the left. The boat, decks awash, was less than 2 miles away. Lieutenant (jg) Gerald G. Hogan, carrying the 500-pounders, was to be the first to attack under this new plan; so he climbed 1,000 feet to get set for his attack. At the same time he radioed the *Card* of the sighting. Hogan then pushed over in a 50-degree dive toward the U-boat.

Lieutenant Hodson, flying the Wildcat, was a bit closer to *U-664* than Hogan and actually beat his teammate to the punch, strafing the sub just seconds before Hogan released one bomb from 750 feet. At this time only part of the conning tower (bearing the blue sawfish emblem of the 9th Flotilla) and the stern were visible. Hogan's bomb hit about 20 feet off *U-664*'s port bow.

Lieutenant (jg) Forney was only ten seconds behind Hogan, making his own attack. He zoomed in from the rear starboard quarter and dropped his two depth bombs, set for 25 feet, from an altitude of approximately 100 feet. As Forney roared past the sub, he looked back and saw his bombs explode beneath the sub. These bombs effectively stopped the U-boat's dive, and she bobbed back to the surface.

Inside the submarine pandemonium broke loose as a number of the crew panicked. The engineering officer in the conning tower yelled to Graef, "Permission to abandon ship?" Many of the crew took this as an order to leave the sub, and fourteen of them popped out of the conning tower hatch onto the bridge. This move was fatal to several men, as Hodson came back to clear the bridge with his 'fifties and also to start a fire aft of the conning tower. It was a few more moments before Graef decided to take his boat down again.

Hogan hastened the dive with a 500-pounder 55 feet off the port quarter. *U-664* was badly hurt, with much of her precious oil gushing to the surface. Forney, believing the sub to be sinking, disdained the use of his Fido. About twenty minutes later more planes arrived to find the submarine struggling to resurface with little way on. Two Avengers dropped 500-pound bombs that exploded 30 feet astern and 75 feet ahead of the submarine. A second Wildcat strafed the terribly mauled boat, and yet another Avenger came in to attack but accidentally dropped its bombs 200 yards ahead of the U-boat.

By now the Germans had had enough. The crew came pouring out of the sub and leaped into the sea. Eleven rafts

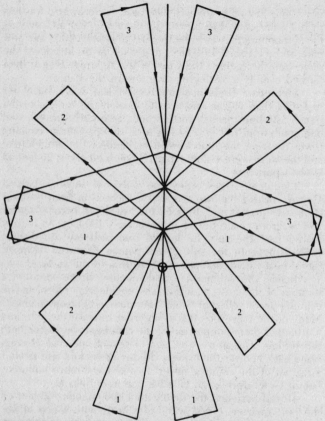

Instructions:

One plane flies sectors 1, 2, and 3 in each quadrant.

Planes begin at "0" and fly six consecutive legs as indicated.

Relative sector search. Total distance 592 miles. Total time 3 hours and 48 minutes.

If only two planes are used the port and starboard forward sectors will be searched.

Typical search pattern used by CVEs in the Atlantic. *Card* two- or four-plane geographic search, July–September 1943.

could be seen strung out behind the U-boat. *U-664*'s bow came higher and higher out of the oil-fouled water, and at 1420 she sank stern first. Seven hours later the *Borie* plucked forty-four of the waterlogged Germans from the sea. The destroyer had to stop rescue operations when another U-boat sent five torpedoes her way.[67]

The *Borie* transferred her prisoners to the *Card*, and TG 21.14 headed north of the Azores. "Huff-Duff" traffic had indicated that U-boats were in that area, and it didn't take long for the *Card*'s fliers to discover the submarines. On the afternoon of 11 August Lieutenant (jg) Charles G. Hewitt and Ensign Jack H. Stewart were patrolling as an Avenger/Wildcat tandem. The weather was clear with only a bit of haze. Suddenly Stewart saw slightly to his left and about 15 miles away a brilliant white wake. A few moments later the dark-gray *U-525* (a 1,144-ton supply boat) stood out from the ocean background.

Stewart pointed out the submarine to Hewitt, then dove at full throttle for a strafing pass. No one appeared to be on deck as Stewart flashed by, machine guns blazing. Large red flashes sparkled on conning tower, and dark smoke erupted aft of it. The sub was starting to settle as Hewitt came in. His two depth bombs exploded close aboard the port beam, midway between the conning tower and the stern.

Her stern rose slightly out of the water, and the U-boat began to dive, leaving a trail of oil. Stewart chased her down with another effective strafing. He then pulled up and circled the spot where the sub had dived. This position would give him the rare experience of actually seeing Fido at work.

Though *U-525* was leaving a trail of oil, the water over her was still clear. Stewart could see her about 30 feet under the surface. He watched as Hewitt dropped his Fido about 20 feet to the right and just ahead of the sub's swirl. Stewart saw the Fido swing toward the sub and hit her halfway between the stern and conning tower. A brownish plume of water erupted 150 feet into the air, and large quantities of oil spread 200 feet outward. A large air bubble marked *U-525*'s last gasp. She went down 376 miles west–southwest of Corvo. There were no survivors.[68]

Finding no more submarines and badly in need of replenishment, the *Card*'s TG 21.14 put into Casablanca on 16 August. Her planes and crews had turned in an excellent

performance. One reason for this was the effectiveness of the
Mk. 24 Mine. In his report of this operation, Isbell had
several comments on the use of Fido and the 500-pound
bombs. In his view the main purpose of the 500-pounders
was to force the submarines down so that the Mk. 24's could
be used effectively. But the bombs also had other effects:
"500-pound bomb breaks enemy's morale and at same time
improves ours," Isbell said.[69]

Discussing Fido, Isbell said, "It is believed that the Mk.
24 Mine is far more effective than commonly given credit. It
is acknowledged that our eggs are in one basket. However,
when the mine functions as it is supposed to,—the show is
over, and there is no further argument by either the enemy
or ourselves."[70]

Some more good hunting for the CVEs was in the offing.
While the *Card* was waiting for a convoy to form to escort
back to the United States, the *Core* (under Captain Marshall
R. Greer) was back in action south of the Azores. The carrier,
now carrying six F4Fs and twelve TBFs, took up station
ahead of Convoy UGS-15 and began extensive patrols.

One submarine, Kapitanleutnant Horst Uphoff's *U-84*,
was spotted 750 miles southwest of Fayal on 23 August. She
got away, but not for long. Meanwhile, another submarine,
U-185, skippered by Kapitanleutnant August Maus, was
also in the area. *U-185* was returning from off Brazil, where
she had been patrolling with *U-604*. The latter boat had
been incessantly hounded by U.S. aircraft and ships and
finally scuttled on 11 August, following a rendezvous with
U-185 and *U-172*. This meeting was crashed by a VB-107
Liberator, but *U-185* shot the plane down with all its crew.
A few days later *U-185* and *U-172* met again, and twenty-
three members of *U-604*'s crew were transferred to *U-172*.
U-604's commander, Kapitanleutnant Horst Höltring, remained
with *U-185*. The crewmen transferred to *U-172* had no idea
how lucky they were.[71]

On the morning of 24 August two sections, each with an
Avenger and a Wildcat, were launched from the *Core* to
search the area where *U-84* had been seen the day before. It
was a clear day, visibility about 11 miles, with a few cumulus
puffballs where a plane could hide if necessary. By 0705 the
first section of Lieutenant Williams and Lieutenant (jg) Martin G. O'Neill was 100 miles east of the *Core*. (It is amazing
how Williams was always present when there was any action!)

At this moment Williams's radioman caught the glint of the sun reflecting off a fully surfaced submarine 4 miles to the right. She was unlucky *U-185*, looking for a drink of fuel from the supply boat, *U-847*.

Both planes headed for nearby clouds and darted out of them astern of the sub. O'Neill strafed the boat, wounding *U-185*'s entire bridge watch on this one attack. He was followed immediately by Williams, boring in on the boat's starboard quarter. In his excitement, Williams forgot to open his bomb bay doors, but his observant radioman noted this and opened them himself. He then scrambled back to his station fast enough to take some excellent action photos.

Williams dropped both his Mk. 47 depth bombs from 250 feet. One exploded aft of the conning tower underneath the boat, and the other hit the 105-mm gun forward. Spray almost completely enveloped *U-185*. When next seen, she had turned almost 90 degrees to port. Dense black smoke trailed from the conning tower. Soon she began settling by the stern and listing to port. O'Neill strafed the boat one more time.

Inside the submarine was utter chaos. The bombs had ruptured the pressure hull and crushed tanks on the port side. Chlorine gas from damaged batteries began to fill the submarine. Several men in the engine room died at their stations as the gas seeped into their compartment. As the crew began to abandon ship, a "strange drama was being enacted" in the bow compartment.[72] Höltring (*U-604*'s skipper) had been lying down when the attack began. He rushed into the bow compartment where a *U-185* sailor, wounded in an earlier action, was lying. The youth, unable to walk and knowing he would die from the chlorine gas, begged Höltring to shoot him. Höltring obliged, then shot himself in the head.

Maus, seeing that his boat was sinking, ordered it abandoned. Meanwhile, Lieutenant Commander Brewer and Lieutenant R. F. Neely (hearing Williams's contact report) had arrived and begun attacking the mortally injured vessel. Brewer strafed the boat twice, but a "popped" circuit breaker prevented Neely from dropping his bombs. As he banked around for a second try, Neely could see that *U-185* was going down; so he held his bombs. The U-boat was still doing 9 knots, but her stern was sinking rapidly. Finally, the bow angled in the air about 60 degrees; then it, too, disappeared.

U-185 went down about 700 miles southwest of the

Grumman TBF Avenger

Azores. The *Barker* arrived several hours after the sinking
and plucked thirty-six survivors (of whom nine were from
U-604) from the water. Four of these survivors, however, died
later from the effects of the chlorine gas.[73]

Around noon of the 24th Lieutenant (jg) William A.
Felter saw *U-84* (which had escaped the day before) come out
of a rain squall 10 miles from the spot where *U-185* had been
sunk. The U-boat submerged as Felter bored in, but she
didn't escape this time. A Fido finished off *U-84*.[74]

Two more "jeeps" went sub-hunting during the time the
Card and *Core* were having all the fun, but neither of these
carriers had any luck. The *Santee* didn't see anything but the
Card on the cruise that lasted from 26 August to 12 October.
The ship, though, had a number of flight deck accidents that
had everyone's adrenaline flowing. Two pilots who had accidents were restricted from any further flying duty for the
duration of the cruise. One of these fliers was only 5 feet, 5
inches tall, and following his third accident in sixty days, it
was decided that an aircraft other than the Wildcat would be
more suited to his stature.[75]

To break the monotony of this cruise, a number of jingles were composed to alert the crew to the dangers of whirling propellers and slippery decks. Examples of this deathless doggerel (which was announced over the loudspeakers each morning) include:

> If you want to get home to kiss that girl,
> Stay well clear of the propeller's whirl.
>
> That old prop is tougher than you or I,
> If one ever hits you it's just, bye, bye.
>
> If you want to go back to those Norfolk maids,
> Keep well clear of those whirling blades.[76]

The *Bogue*-class *Croatan*, meanwhile, was making her first operational cruise, and if her fliers didn't sink any subs, at least they saw some. The *Croatan*'s air component was the twelve TBFs and six FM-1s (a modified version of the F4F-4 with only four .50-caliber guns) of VC-6. Actually, the squadron designation was VC-25 until 1 September, when it was changed to VC-6. (A new VC-25 went on to operate in the Pacific.) The squadron moved aboard Captain John B. Lyon's *Croatan* on 5 August. The next day the "Old Crow" left Hampton Roads to provide roving support for Convoy UGS-14. She was screened by the old flush-deckers *Belknap*, *Paul Jones*, and *Parrott*.

The Coast Guard cutter *Menemsha* had a run-in with *U-760* on the night of 11 August, and Captain Lyon was ordered to search for the U-boat. Leaving the convoy, the *Croatan* and her escorts (organized as TG 21.15) headed for the scene of the confrontation. Squally weather helped to hide the U-boat, and though they tried, the VC-6 fliers could not find her. TG 21.15 rejoined the convoy on 15 August.

On the 19th Lyon received more orders to hunt for submarines operating northeast of the Azores. Two days later an Avenger/Wildcat team ran across one of these boats. Lieutenant (jg) Morris L. Nelson saw the U-boat about 5 miles away and immediately radioed the *Croatan*, "Tallyho, Pig, Pig, Pig." The ship was only 82 miles away, but radio problems prevented the carrier from sending reinforcements. Nelson and his fighter escort attacked the submarine, *U-134*, alone but were unable to damage her. When the *Croatan* finally was able to send help, two deck crashes delayed the attack group's departure even longer, and *U-134* escaped only to be sunk three days later by British aircraft.[77]

This unsuccessful attack depressed the squadron, who now realized that it wasn't easy to sink a submarine, but they vowed to bag one soon. Meanwhile, the *Croatan* was having problems of her own. The two deck crashes had reduced her already limited supply of aircraft; a main fuel pump failure lowered her speed to only 10 knots; and her surface radar conked out. Finally, the catapult broke down, and Captain Lyon decided it was time to head for Casablanca and repairs. The *Croatan* docked at Casablanca on 26 August, where "the pilots were ordered to shore patrol duty, much to their chagrin."[78]

Task Group 21.15 left Casablanca on the 30th. Three days later the *Croatan*'s planes sighted the *Card* group. The "Old Crow" spent another three days supporting Convoy GUS-13, then headed south of the Azores to look for subs. One was found on 9 September, and the VC-6 fliers almost had cause for a victory celebration.

Lieutenant (jg) Joseph W. Steere was on a solo patrol in his Avenger when he came across *U-214* heading westward on the surface. Steere made his contact report, and then climbed into some clouds and used his radar to keep track of the U-boat's position. When he was about 1,000 yards from the submarine, Steere darted out of the cloud for his attack. *U-214*'s crew saw him and began firing at him, while the boat began turning to the left.

Steere had got within 700 feet of the submarine when the enemy fire struck telling blows. His engine air intake took a hit, and the cowling opened, blocking Steere's vision. Just as he released his depth bombs, the bomb bay took a shell. This hit jarred the plane just as the bombs were being released, and they missed. The explosions shook the sub but caused no great damage, and *U-214* submerged unhurriedly. Having no Fido to use on the U-boat at this vulnerable moment, Steere had to watch helplessly as she disappeared. Several planes finally showed up, but Oberleutnant Ruprecht Stock had his boat safely away.[79]

To the VC-6 pilots this attack proved that an Avenger should always be accompanied by a fighter. The fighter could be used to suppress any defensive fire and "two heads [were] better than one" when it came to navigation and searching.[80]

Captain Lyon also commented in a report to Admiral King that the attack emphasized "the fact that if the submarine [was] not disabled by the first attack there [was] small chance of reinforcements effecting a kill."[81] The *Croatan* and her escorts returned to Norfolk on 22 September. It had been an unproductive cruise, but the invaluable training that all had received would prove its worth in the future.

Meanwhile, the *Core* was on her way home—shakily, to say the least. Her turbines were vibrating so much that it was a chore to maintain even 12 knots. The *Card*, fresh from her visit to Casablanca, took her place in the Atlantic, to search for a concentration of U-boats that Tenth Fleet had reported to be north and east of the Azores.

On 27 August Lieutenant (jg) Hogan (who had helped sink *U-664* on the 9th) met another U-boat cruising fully surfaced. She was *U-508*. Instead of depth bombs, Hogan was carrying a combination of one 500-pound bomb and one homing torpedo. The sub was about 10 miles away when Hogan turned toward her. As he closed with the enemy boat, Hogan sent his contact report to the *Card*. *U-508*'s crew had seen Hogan, also, and were filling the air around his plane with deadly bluish-white puffballs of flak. However, their aim was bad, and the Avenger was not hit.

Hogan maneuvered to come up the sub's stern, but just before he released his 500-pounder, *U-508* made a sharp turn to the left, followed by another hard turn to the right. This threw Hogan's aim off, and his bomb hit 200 feet to the left of the sub. *U-508* crash-dived, and Hogan made a sharp turn to bleed off airspeed so he could drop his Fido. A distinct swirl marked the U-boat's dive, and Hogan dropped his Fido near this swirl about a minute after the sub had disappeared. Though it appeared that Fido was on the right track, it lost the scent, and *U-508* escaped.[82]

Meanwhile, Lieutenant Ralph W. Long and his two fighter escorts, Lieutenant (jg) Frederick M. Rountree and Ensign Stewart, had been vectored from the *Card* to assist Hogan. Arriving on the scene of the initial attack shortly after 1100, they did not see Hogan but did see a submarine cruising at 12 knots on a southeasterly course. Not seeing Hogan, the trio figured they had found another U-boat. They had—the 1,616-ton *U-847*. This big boat had been the last of the 1st Monsoon Group to leave for Penang. However, de-

spite the fact that the Germans were eager to get *U-847* to
Penang, the loss of both *U-117* and *U-489* had forced them to
change their plans once again. Now, instead of heading for
the Far East, *U-847* was to act as a supply boat for a number
of submarines operating in the middle Atlantic.[83] The submarine had already supplied several other boats with fuel and
provisions since 19 August (including five boats earlier on the
27th).

Long ordered the fighters to strafe and try to force the
U-boat down so he could use his Fido. Rountree, followed by
Stewart, darted ahead to come up the submarine's wake.
Several men could be seen firing from the conning tower, but
a blast of 'fifties quickly stopped that. What looked like the
figure of a man could be seen falling into the water. Rountree
and Stewart racked their Wildcats around and gave *U-847*
another dose of fire from the opposite direction. Another man
was seen to fall, and then the U-boat began to submerge.

Long told the fighters to pull clear; then he spiraled
down in a tight circle to release his Mk. 24 mine. Fido
entered the water 100 feet to starboard and ahead of the
swirl. The homing torpedo could be seen making a gradual
turn toward the sub before both disappeared from sight.

"About fifteen seconds later... there was an instantaneous dark circular disturbance (about 50 feet in diameter) in
the water ahead of the swirl. This was followed by a mound-
shaped mass of water rising above the surface several feet,
accompanied by bubbling and agitation. Immediately, considerable quantities of oil started coming to the surface.... then
after another 20 seconds, [Long] saw a terrific flash in the
water, quick as lightning, and at least 300 feet wide. Again it
was dark in color, but it was not followed by any boiling or
agitation."[84]

This explosion was so intense that men on *U-508*, several
miles away, heard it. *U-847*'s grave was plotted at 28°19′N,
37°58′W.[85] *U-847* was the sixteenth submarine that the U.S.
"jeeps" had gotten since the *Bogue* sank *U-569* on 22 May—
an average of approximately one U-boat a week. Half these
boats were the very important milch cows. For some time the
Germans had had things pretty much their own way in the
Central Atlantic, with milch cows refueling almost 400 U-boats.
But the appearance of the escort carriers changed things
drastically.

"In concentrating on refueling R/Vs in the summer of 1943," the Tenth Fleet/Op-20-G history stated, "Allied airpower was in truth striking at the heart of Doenitz's system. For without refuelers, neither prolonged independent cruise nor extended convoy operations were possible to the [smaller boats] that made up the vast majority of the U-boat fleet."[86]

By mid-June of 1943 only one of four tankers in the Azores was still operating, and two months later only three out of twelve milch cows remained in the Azores area. Because of this lack of milch cows, Doenitz had to abandon his operations in the Central Atlantic much earlier than had been planned. The "jeeps" had put a big dent in Doenitz's plans.[87]

5

THRUST AND PARRY

The escort carriers had good hunting in August, but the sinkings dried up in September as Doenitz redeployed his U-boats for *Zaunkoenig Blitz* against the North Atlantic convoys. The initial success of this acoustic torpedo was not particularly great (six merchant vessels and three escorts actually lost against German claims of thirteen escorts sunk or probably sunk and eleven cargo ship sunk or probably sunk in attacks between 20 and 24 September). The threat this weapon presented, however, was quite real, though not unbeatable.[1]

(After the war Professor Dr. Jürgen Rohwer estimated that the Germans used slightly over 700 acoustic torpedoes during World War II. Only seventy-seven of these were definite hits. This indicates only about a 10 percent success rate for this vaunted weapon.[2])

Doenitz was hopeful that the *Zaunkoenig* ("Wren," also known as "Gnat" to the British) torpedo and a variety of other weapons would help turn the tide for his underwater fleet. He was also anxiously awaiting the arrival of his first snorkel-equipped boats (which only became operational in early 1944) because the presence of escort carriers in the Atlantic had inflicted a running sore on his U-boat operations that could only be cured with the aid of a snorkel bandage.

One of Doenitz's worrisome problems was back out scouring the Atlantic in September. The *Bogue*, this time with the VC-19 planes of Lieutenant Commander Claude W. Stewart aboard, was on the prowl again. Unfortunately, this cruise was quite unproductive, although Captain Dunn and Lieutenant Commander Stewart tried to "sucker" the U-boats into revealing themselves. Their plan was to send an Avenger/Wildcat team out at 5,000 feet following known HF/DF bearings. It was hoped that a U-boat would transmit a sighting report, for thirty minutes behind the first section would be a second team flying at only 50 feet. The plan didn't work, however, and the *Bogue*'s TG 21.12 put into Casablanca on 26 September in a rather foul mood.[3]

Task Group 21.12's mission back to the United States was equally unproductive. The force left Casablanca on the 29th. On leaving port the *Clemson* damaged a propeller and had to be detached for repairs. The *DuPont* replaced her on 6 October. Convoy GUS-16 was escorted until 2 October, when the *Bogue* left the convoy to sweep possible refueling areas east and northeast of the Azores. The task group then continued west and south of Flores. Only one submarine was seen (that on the 8th), but she dove before any attack could be made. To add insult to injury to the disappointed VC-19 fliers, a Canadian merchant ship fired on the *Bogue* aircraft, fortunately without any damage to the planes. The *Bogue* returned to Norfolk on 20 October.[4]

The *Card* was also out during this time, but she had much better luck than her sister ship. The *Bogue*'s old squadron VC-9, now under the command of Lieutenant Commander Howard M. Avery, would be the *Card*'s strike force. In September the *Card* had been undergoing overhaul in Norfolk. During this time her escorts, the *DuPont*, *Borie*, *Barry*, and *Goff*, were fitted with some new gear that had been developed following the interrogation of a talkative torpedoman from *U-487*, which the *Core* had sunk in July. This gear was designed to make noise that would attract the new *Zaunkoenig* acoustic torpedo. Called FXR or "Foxer," it worked fine except that its noise drowned out the sonar gear at speeds of 10 knots or more. Some of the "tin can" skippers decided to place a sailor armed with an ax on the fantail. The sailor had orders to cut away the "Foxer" when the destroyer got a sonar contact on a submarine.[5]

"Buster" Isbell led his force, TG 21.14, out of Hampton Roads on 25 September. His mission was to support Convoy UGS-19. The *Card*'s group first headed for Bermuda (where the *DuPont* was detached to join the *Bogue*), and then it

turned into the deep Atlantic. At this time Isbell didn't favor
the use of Wildcat/Avenger search teams. Instead he was
recommending that the CVEs carry twenty Avengers and no
fighters. His view would change in time, however. For the
present, VC-9 would fly single bomber searches, with each
plane "armed with one 500-pound bomb to force sub down,
and one Mk. 24 Mine to kill."[6]

Task Group 21.14 forged deeper into the Atlantic. The
only excitement for the first few days was the loss of an F4F
during refresher landings. (The pilot was recovered.) Then,
on 4 October the *Card* hit paydirt. Lieutenant (jg) Stearns
(who had been involved in the sinking of *U-118* in June) was
on the last leg of his dawn antisubmarine patrol shortly after
1000 when he saw something on the surface about 15 miles
ahead. He called to his crewmen, "I think we have something
here." A few seconds later came the excited cry, "There are
four of them!"[7]

Indeed, there were four of them! The 1,688-ton milch
cow *U-460* had just finished fueling *U-264* and was getting
ready to fuel *U-422*. *U-455* was waiting her turn. The big
fueler and the three Type VIIC boats were only about 500
yards apart, cruising slowly northwestward. About 7 miles
ahead of this group of boats Stearns thought he could see
another formation of submarines also heading northwest.
Stearns's radioman sent a contact report, but the transmission
was garbled, and Captain Isbell did not know that *four*
submarines had been found.

The *Card* launched a killer group of one TBF (armed
with four Mk. 47 depth bombs) and two Wildcats. In the
meantime, Stearns was circling the Germans, picking out his
target. *U-460*, the milch cow, was under orders from Doenitz
to dive when attacked. However, her commander (Kapitanleutnant Heinrich Schnoor) was embroiled in an argument
with *U-264*'s Kapitanleutnant Hartwig Looks over who would
dive first, and neither boat dove. This argument would be
costly to the Germans.[8]

Stearns circled the formation one time at 5,000 feet,
then pounced on the quartet in a steep dive. All four boats
immediately began firing at the TBF. Their aim was not good
but getting better when Stearns released his 500-pounder
from 1,700 feet. The bomb exploded between *U-460* and
U-264, but too far away from either to do any damage. As
Stearns darted out of range, the four U-boats tightened their

formation, but they still were weaving and zigzagging radically as a group. With only his Fido left, Stearns had to wait for reinforcements to arrive.

The reinforcements soon appeared. Lieutenant (jg) D. E. Weigle arrived at 1032. He quickly radioed the *Card* that four U-boats were involved. Three Avengers that were returning to the ship were vectored to the scene, and five more Avengers and two Wildcats were launched to join in the action. With the arrival of Weigle (who was awaiting some fighter support before attacking), the Germans decided they had better dive and get out of the area.

U-455 submerged just before Lieutenant (jg)s Elbert S. Heim and David O. Puckett arrived in their Wildcats. The remaining trio of submarines put up a "solid curtain of fire about 150 feet high by 300 feet wide and about 25 feet deep, filled with black and white puffs."[9] Nevertheless, the two pilots pressed home their attacks, raking the U-boats with gunfire. Heim's plane was untouched, but Puckett's took several hits, one of which knocked his port outboard gun off the trunion. The flak gradually died down as the fighters' guns took their toll. A sailor could be seen lying face down, arms outstretched, on one of the submarines.

U-422 now dove, leaving the milch cow *U-460*, and *U-264* surfaced. This was a good setup for the Americans— one sub each for the Avengers, while the fighters strafed to beat down the remaining antiaircraft fire. Unfortunately, the plan didn't quite work. Puckett dove on *U-264*, closely followed by Weigle. Puckett's attack had some effect, for Weigle was not bothered by much antiaircraft fire. But in his zeal to add the force of his two .50-caliber wing guns to his attack, Weigle pressed the wrong switch. Instead of the gun trigger, he pressed the bomb release switch. All four of his depth bombs dropped, the nearest one falling 750 feet short of the U-boat.

Stearns, meanwhile, was positioning himself for a run on *U-460* when she submerged. When he saw that *U-264* was undamaged and diving, Stearns flipped his TBF around and started for that U-boat instead. (It should be noted that all the fliers thought *U-264* was the milch cow and *U-460* a standard sub.) By the time Stearns reached his drop point, there was no indication of *U-264*'s position, and he was reluctant to waste his Fido when another vulnerable sub was present.

He pulled up and turned back toward *U-460*. She had been battered by the repeated strafings of Heim and Puckett, and Kapitanleutnant Schnoor finally decided, too late, to dive. As Stearns approached, the big boat started under. Her stern was still above the water as *U-460* turned sharply to port. She didn't leave a definite swirl as she disappeared, but a trail of green water 90 degrees to her original course could be seen.

Stearns dropped his gear to slow down, and followed the trail of green water around. From 200 feet he dropped his Fido. The acoustic torpedo struck the water about 50 feet in front of the point where *U-460* submerged. It traveled ahead a short distance, then turned sharply to the left. About twenty-five seconds later a well-defined shock wave could be seen to form.

A brown slick came to the surface, followed shortly by a large amount of oil and debris, including three steel-colored cylindrical objects. Fido had found *U-460*, and Doenitz was without the services of another milch cow. For their part in this action Puckett and Stearns would be awarded the Navy Cross. (This would be the second time that Stearns had received this decoration.)

"Buster" Isbell and the VC-9 crews were somewhat depressed at the outcome of this action, however, believing that the milch cow had escaped. The amount of flak the four U-boats had thrown up caused concern, also. They thought that "the fact that four submarines were seen on the surface at one time might indicate the possible existence of AA U/Bs, the sole purpose of which would be to protect other U/Bs during vulnerable periods, such as those presented by fueling operations."[10]

Isbell was not far off the mark. Doenitz had lost too many of his milch cows for comfort. Thus, the protection of these vital vessels was of extreme importance. He told his crews: ". . . during supply operations the most important thing is to protect the tanker. On her depends the fighting efficiency of numbers of operational boats and thus the continuation of convoy operations with as many forces as possible.

"In case of surprise aircraft attacks on supplying boats, the main object of all defensive action must be to protect the tanker, to provide her with a good opportunity to dive and to screen her diving."[11]

Card planes kept the area of the attack under surveillance into the afternoon. A pair of whales that wandered by were attacked by a Wildcat and Avenger, but the results of this attack were not reported. Then, at 1538 U-422, possibly damaged during the morning encounter, surfaced about 3 miles away from the point of the original attack. Four thousand feet above her, hidden in some scattered clouds, were Lieutenant (jg) Stewart B. Holt and Ensign Joseph D. Horn.

The pair saw the U-boat, and Horn immediately pushed over and roared in toward the sub. Starting from 3,000 feet, he fired almost continuously down to 50 feet. The conning tower "seemed to be alive with tracer bullets" from his guns. U-422 dove, but Holt was right there. Just seconds after the sub had gone under, Holt dropped his Fido. Horn could see the Fido under the water move forward a few feet, then take off directly for the submarine. He saw it explode midway between U-422's conning tower and stern. A small plume of water rose into the air, followed by oil and debris (including a raft). There was no doubt—another U-boat had made her last voyage.[12]

The weather now turned bad, and flight operations became even more hazardous than usual. On the 7th an Avenger flown by Ensign C. H. Goodchild was attempting to land on the Card when a squall overtook the ship. Goodchild lost control of his plane and spun in. He and his radioman were lost, but his gunner was picked up by one of the escorts. A Swordfish from HMS Fencer was also lost during this period. A search by the Card group for this plane was unsuccessful.[13]

Flight operations on an escort carrier could be dangerous and sometimes tragic, as the above passage and other events described in this book illustrate. But occasionally incidents occurred that had a lighter side, such as this one on board the Bogue.

The Wildcat was in the groove for landing. The landing signal officer's talker reported, "Wheels and flaps down. . . . Hook not down."

The LSO, not paying much attention, said, "Roger." and gave the cut.

The Wildcat touched down and sailed right into the barrier. As the LSO watched the accident open-mouthed, he felt a tug on his pants leg. Glancing down, he saw his talker looking up innocently at him. "Sir, that hook still isn't down."[14]

*   *   *

Captain Isbell tried to find smoother seas, but the weather remained atrocious for a while longer. Flight operations continued, though, and the VC-9 fliers ran into U-boats again on the 12th. The Americans had come across another fueling rendezvous. *U-488* had been ordered to fuel several U-boats of the *Rossbach* Group about 600 miles north of Flores. The VC-9 fliers would break up this rendezvous.

The 12th was a foggy day, with some mist and drizzle and a very rough sea. A little after 1100 Lieutenant (jg) Balliett's radioman saw a submarine surfacing just a mile and a half away. Balliett immediately broke hard right to make a Fido drop. The U-boat, *U-488*, was fully surfaced by now, however, and Balliett had to climb to get into position to drop his 500-pounder instead. The U-boat's crew apparently saw the Avenger, for the sub began to turn right and submerge. Balliett had to change plans again and armed his Fido. The U-boat was already under as Balliett roared in from astern; the Fido was released about twenty seconds after the submarine had disappeared. However, Fido apparently lost the scent in the rough water, and *U-488* escaped.[15] A few hours later Lieutenant (jg) Fowler also found *U-488*, but his Fido attack was equally unsuccessful.[16]

On the afternoon of the 12th yet another sub (*U-731*) was spotted on the surface. Ensign Doty was about 50 miles from the task group when he saw a "peculiar white cap" 3 miles away. The weather had improved considerably, although it was still quite hazy and the ocean very rough. Doty circled *U-731* twice at 1,000 feet, but the U-boat's crew must have been napping, as they gave no indication they had seen the Avenger. Doty climbed to 2,000 feet before pushing over for a glide bombing attack. The Germans didn't see Doty until his bomb exploded 175 feet off the boat's port beam.

U-731 swung left as antiaircraft fire began hunting for the Avenger. Doty circled away, waiting for the U-boat to dive. When she didn't, Doty made a number of strafing runs hoping to force the submarine down. The German skipper refused to play Doty's game and, instead, headed for a nearby rain squall. The squall kept moving ahead of the sub, so she never reached its safety.

A little over half an hour after Doty's attack, Lieutenant (jg) Holt arrived. At first Holt thought *U-731* was not the same submarine, but Doty assured him she was. Holt piled in from dead ahead, and though he encountered no defensive fire, his bomb hit 250 feet astern of the submarine. As he jinked away, Holt's plane was surrounded by many black puffs of flak, none of which hit. Shortly after Holt's attack, Ensign Hodgson arrived to make a depth bomb attack. Hodgson forced his way through a tremendous wall of fire being put up by the sub's gunners to drop four Mk. 47 bombs just off the U-boat's port side. He then pulled around to strafe the boat.

With three pesky flies buzzing around him and more probably on the way, U-731's skipper decided it was time to dive. As the U-boat submerged, Doty darted in to deliver a Fido. About six seconds after it entered the water, an explosion that threw a small plume of water into the air was seen. Although the Americans believed they had bagged another sub, U-731 escaped—though she had to head home for repairs.[17]

VC-9 had better luck the next day. Shortly after 0800 Lieutenant (jg) Fowler spied U-378 plowing through the rough seas. Fowler couldn't tell if the sub was diving or not, but when she threw a burst of flak his way, Fowler figured a 500-pounder would take care of her. Unfortunately, his bomb failed to release, and Fowler had to climb back up. The U-boat took this opportunity to dive. Fowler saw her going under and "dove down with wheels down, whipping the plane all over the sky trying to lose speed and altitude."[18]

Fowler was in a bad position at his drop point and had to yank his plane around in a tight circle for another run. This time his position was okay, and a minute after the U-boat had disappeared, he dropped his Fido about 450 feet ahead of her swirl. Fowler's torpedo missed, but U-378 had less than a week of life left anyway.[19]

Meanwhile, VC-9's skipper, Lieutenant Commander Avery, was launched from the Card to help Fowler. When Avery reached the scene, the U-boat was gone. He combed the area, hoping she might pop back up again. Shortly before 1100 Avery saw a fully surfaced submarine about 12 miles southeast of the spot of Fowler's attack. The boat wasn't U-378, but Korvettenkapitan Baron Siegfried von Forstner's U-402.

Because of the heavy seas breaking over the submarine, Avery thought she was diving. He raced in toward his target and prepared to drop his Fido. As he got closer, Avery could see that the U-boat was not submerging, but he was now too low to drop his 500-pound bomb. Nevertheless, he continued in, strafing with his wing guns. The surprised Germans didn't take the Avenger under fire until it was already past. Avery remained at a distance, waiting for the submarine to dive, while the Germans threw an occasional shell his way.

The Germans were so busy with Avery that they didn't notice the arrival of Ensign Barton C. Sheela, who pushed over in a steep dive from astern the sub. Just as he released his bomb, *U-402* turned left, and the bomb hit wide of the mark. The explosion caught the submariners' attention, though, and they quickly "pulled the plug." The U-boat's stern rose high out of the water as she dove.

This was the moment Avery had been waiting for. Going to full power to quickly close the distance, he then chopped his throttle and dropped his gear to steady his TBF for the Fido drop. Twenty-five seconds after the conning tower had disappeared, the Fido entered the water. It began its run and turned left. A few seconds later an explosion was seen in the water 200 feet up track. A few minutes later the Fido's brownish residue appeared on the surface, along with a big oil slick and three cylindrical objects. VC-9 had another U-boat to add to their scoreboard.

An interesting aspect of all these attacks by the *Card* fliers was the fact that radar was not used on any of these attacks for "security reasons," perhaps because it was thought the Germans were picking up the radar impulses. This restriction on the use of radar was lifted a short time later, however.[20]

The day's excitement was not yet over. In the afternoon Lieutenant (jg) Fryatt jumped another sub. The Germans put up a heavy barrage, with a "steady stream of red tracer" passing just beneath the Avenger. Not all shells missed. One tore out a hydraulic line, a hit that would cause a lot of trouble later. Fryatt kept boring in to drop his 500-pounder just off the conning tower. The U-boat began to submerge, and Fryatt racked his big plane around to drop his Fido. It missed, however; so Fryatt headed back to the *Card*.

When Fryatt arrived over the carrier, he discovered that he could not get his right landing gear down. To complicate matters, high winds and rough seas were making landings aboard the "jeep" treacherous. Darkness was also approaching, and Isbell had to land all the other planes aloft before bringing in Fryatt.

Fryatt made two passes before he got a cut from the landing signal officer. The Avenger hit the deck and ballooned past the arresting wires and over the barrier. The plane's right wing hit the island, and then the Avenger bounced into another TBF parked on the right side of the flight deck. The Avenger finally came to a stop about fifteen feet from the end of the flight deck, and Fryatt and his crew clambered out of their battered plane unhurt. But this spectacular accident had caused one casualty.

Watching Fryatt's dramatic arrival had been his roommate, Roger Kuhn. Kuhn had landed earlier, and it was his plane that Fryatt hit. Kuhn had been standing next to his TBF and was knocked overboard, along with his plane, by the collision. He was fortunate not to drop the flashlight he was carrying and used it to signal the *Barry*, which picked him up out of the darkness a short time later. A slight leg injury and a drenching were all that Kuhn received.[21]

Isbell took the *Card* into Casablanca for supplies on 18 October. Taking the *Card*'s place in the hunt for U-boats was the *Core*, now commanded by Captain James R. Dudley. The *Core* had left Hampton Roads on the 5th, but it was not until the 20th that the ship's squadron, VC-13, saw any action. That afternoon Lieutenant Commander Brewer and Lieutenant (jg) Robert W. Hayman flushed out *U-378* north of the Azores. Brewer led the way with a devastating strafing attack that exploded ready ammunition stored in the boat's conning tower and blew several gunners into the water.

The exploding ammunition fascinated Brewer. "Right in the middle of my run," he said later, "that sub had my mouth hanging open. The whole conning tower and after-gun platform burst into a pink flame."[22] Hayman followed up with a brace of bombs that ended *U-378*'s sailing days.[23]

The next morning a pair of Avengers pounced on *U-271* (at the time only 35 miles from the *Core*) and damaged the submarine. The *Belknap* was sent to the scene but was unable to find the U-boat.[24] The *Core*'s group had no more luck and put into Casablanca on 27 October. "This gave [VC-13] its first chance to set foot on foreign soil. All hands made the most of their opportunity, returning to duty with Moroccan headaches, evil-smelling leather goods, and heightened morale."[25]

The *Core*'s voyage back to the United States was fairly routine except for one incident that could have been disas-

trous. Around 0200 on 15 November the *Core*'s crew heard
and felt a distinct explosion near the ship. Two lesser explosions followed, and then four more faint shocks. The carrier's
screen combed the area without success. A short distance
away Oberleutnant Richard von Harpe took his *U-129* deep
after taking four potshots at the *Core*. He had come close, but
not close enough to sinking the carrier.[26]

Meanwhile, the *Card* was back out again providing cover
for GUS-18 until the convoy was past the Azores, then
breaking off to look for a reported U-boat fueling concentration 500 miles north of Flores. But a brand-new escort carrier
had beaten her to the scene. The *Block Island* had already
been across the North Atlantic once ferrying aircraft to England,
but this was her first combat mission.

Commanding the *Block Island* was Captain Logan C.
Ramsey. Ramsey had already made a name for himself in the
war. He had been on the staff of Patrol Wing Two at Pearl
Harbor on that fateful December day. It was he who had
ordered sent the famous message, "Air raid Pearl Harbor!
This is no drill!"

This "jeep" had her own jeep. This vehicle was not
standard issue, though. It seems that a soldier had parked his
jeep near the carrier when he was delivering a message to a
nearby ship. The *Block Island*'s deck gang swung their crane
around and lifted the jeep on board. It was hustled into the
paint shop and quickly painted gray. It is not known how the
soldier explained the loss of his jeep.[27] Captain Ramsey
finally traded the jeep because he was afraid his crew would
kill each other driving it around the flight deck.[28]

The *Block Island* and her three escorts set out from
Norfolk on 15 October. On board the flattop were the nine
FM-1s and twelve TBF-1cs of VC-1. Initially, the *Block
Island*'s group (TG 21.16) covered UGS-21. Then the task
group was ordered to proceed northeast to operate against
the fueling concentration stationed behind the boats of Group
Siegfried. Numerous radio intercepts of enemy transmissions
confirmed that U-boats were in the area. On the night of 25
October "Huff-Duff" bearings indicated that one or more
submarines were very near the task group. The *Parrott* and
the *Paul Jones* found *U-488*, but their attacks were poorly
organized, and the submarine escaped.[29]

Three days later the fliers of VC-1 got their own chance

for action. On the morning of 28 October, Lieutenant Franklin M. Murray and Ensign Harold L. Handshuh were patrolling north of the carrier when two submarines were sighted 20 miles distant. Murray radioed a contact report, then closed the distance. The U-boat crews were taken by surprise when the Americans pounced on them. Both planes strafed the nearest boat, *U-220*, and Murray dropped depth bombs that exploded on either side of her conning tower. The submarine slowed and skidded around 180 degrees. As she began to settle, her stern rose steeply out of the water, hung there briefly, and then slid under the water. The 1,763-ton minelayer *U-220*, returning from a mining mission off New-

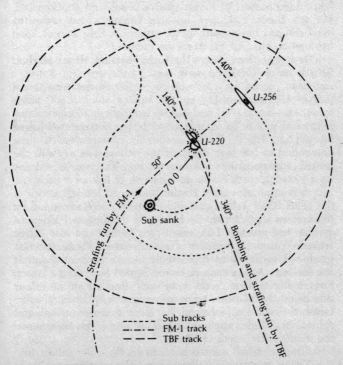

Sinking of *U-220*, 28 October 1943.

foundland and looking for a supply boat, made no more
transmissions to U-boat Command.

The second sub, *U-256*, was in the meantime putting up
a heavy curtain of antiaircraft fire. Murray and Handshuh
kept feinting at the sub, hoping to keep her on the surface
until reinforcements arrived. None appeared, however, and
the U-boat finally submerged. Murray raced in to drop a Fido
and a sonobuoy (an underwater listening device just recently
delivered to the escort carriers), but there was no indication
that the homing torpedo scored. The sinking of *U-220* would
be the only one made by the *Block Island* fliers during this
cruise.[30]

The *Card's* group had now arrived in the area and was
also searching for more submarines. On the afternoon of the
30th, Lieutenant (jg) Fryatt spotted a sub and attacked her,
but the U-boat's skipper, heeding Doenitz's new orders to
dive instead of remaining on the surface to fight aircraft, took
his boat down, and Fryatt's Fido missed.[31]

It was not long before the *Card's* aviators struck paydirt.
Shortly after 1600 the next day, Lieutenant (jg) Fowler's
radioman picked up a blip on his radar. Fowler soon saw a
pair of U-boats cruising on the surface about 1,000 yards
apart. The boats, *U-91* and *U-584*, were about 18 miles ahead
of the task group. In accordance with the doctrine established
by Captain Isbell, Fowler made his contact report, then
descended to 500 feet astern of the submarines to await the
arrival of more planes before attacking. The two vessels put
up a heavy, though inaccurate, curtain of flak for a time.

A few minutes after Fowler positioned himself astern of
the boats, *U-91* submerged and escaped. *U-584* remained on
the surface although she had stopped shooting at Fowler. In
another few minutes Lieutenant (jg)s Balliett and MacAuslan
arrived. With the appearance of more Avengers, Kapitanleutnant
Joachim Deecke decided belatedly to take his boat down. It
was too late. As the conning tower dipped beneath the water,
Fowler and Balliett raced in to each drop a Fido on either
side of the submarine. A few seconds later, plumes of water
broke the surface, followed by large amounts of oil and
debris. Both Fidos apparently had hit, and *U-584* went down
about 580 miles north of Flores.[32]

"Buster" Isbell wanted badly to get the other submarine,
U-91, as he mistakenly believed her to be a milch cow. So, at

sunset he sent the *Borie* after her. This was the beginning of what would turn out to be one of the most dramatic actions in the Battle of the Atlantic. Thirty-year-old Lieutenant Charles H. Hutchins took his old flush-decker through heavy seas to the scene of the late afternoon attack. *U-91* was long gone, but Oberleutnant Wilhelm Brauel's *U-256* (fresh from her encounter with the *Block Island* planes) had crept into the area.

When the *Borie* arrived in the area, her radar picked up a target 6,500 yards away. It was the 769-ton *U-256*. When she was 1,700 yards away, the *Borie* fired starshells to illuminate the U-boat. As the first shells burst, Brauel "pulled the plug," and the *Borie* lost radar contact. Sonar contact was quickly gained, however, and Hutchins used this information to make three attacks that damaged the sub. A heavy underwater explosion was heard after the first attack. This explosion rattled the *Borie* and knocked out some of her equipment.

Following the second run, *U-256* was seen to come to the surface, her bow high in the air. She bobbed up and down a couple of times, then submerged stern first. Hutchins was sure his ship had made a kill and signaled the *Card*, "Scratch one pig boat. Am searching for more."[33] Though *U-256* did leave behind quite a bit of oil that could be smelled on the *Borie*, she had not been sunk. Brauel was able to get his boat under control and escape.[34]

Hutchins spent the next three hours crisscrossing the area making sure the sub was not playing dead. The *Borie* wound up about 26 miles east of the original attack. Shortly before 0200 another radar contact was made at a range of 8,000 yards. The *Borie* cranked up 27 knots and pounded closer to the target through waves fifteen to twenty feet high. When the range had dropped to 2,800 yards, the sub (*U-405*, commanded by Korvettenkapitan Rudolf Hopman) submerged. Hutchins switched to sound search. His sound man, SoM2c Lerten V. Kent, quickly picked up the U-boat again.

The *Borie* slowed and closed in. When she was over the submarine, a standard depth charge pattern was ordered released. Something went wrong with the release mechanism, and every depth charge ready in the racks tumbled over the stern. But this plethora of charges had the right effect. *U-405* popped to the surface, astern and to port of the *Borie*. In the sickly gleam of a float light, the whitish-colored

U-boat looked as big as the *Borie*. (Actually, the 220-foot Type VIIC U-boat was about 100 feet shorter than the destroyer.)

Hutchins brought his ship hard right and had his 24-inch searchlight switched on. The *Borie* sped up to 25 knots. Germans could be seen swarming out of the conning tower and manning the 20-mm guns mounted there. Though they would score some hits in the *Borie*'s engine room and bridge area, these Germans would soon be dead. During the *Borie*'s turn her No. Four 4-inch gun got off a shot that missed, but the next shells would be extremely accurate.

The Germans had no chance to use their own deck gun. The *Borie*'s second or third salvo struck just under the gun, and when the smoke cleared, it had disappeared. The *Borie* closed with *U-405*, and Hutchins prepared to ram. The "tin can's" crew could see clearly the German sailors pouring out of the conning tower. Their appearance, some clad only in underwear, many with long hair tied with brightly-colored bandannas, "offended [the] bluejackets' sense of propriety."[35]

Hutchins boresighted the U-boat, and everyone on board the old destroyer prepared for the ramming. But just before the impact, Hopman swerved hard left, and a big wave lifted the *Borie*. The destroyer slid up and over the U-boat about thirty feet aft of her bow and settled on her forecastle. The impact had been so gentle that the *Borie*'s "black gang" was unaware there had been a ramming.[36]

For about ten minutes, angled about 30 degrees apart in the heavy seas, the two vessels were locked in a deadly embrace.

From only a few feet away the men of the *Borie* poured a torrent of gunfire on the hapless U-boat. The No. Two four-incher slammed shells into the after part of the submarine, while the No. Four gun did the same to the area just aft of the conning tower. Three of the 20-mm batteries were able to keep *U-405* under fire, but the crews of two of these batteries had difficulty depressing their guns far enough without hitting their own screens. This didn't stop them, however. They fired right through the thin metal screens!

The *Borie*'s gunfire (which also included pistols, shotguns, and tommy guns) was taking a terrible toll of the Germans, who were still bravely trying to get topside and defend their boat. A burst of 20-mm fire literally tore one German to pieces. Another's head was blown off. Fireman 1st

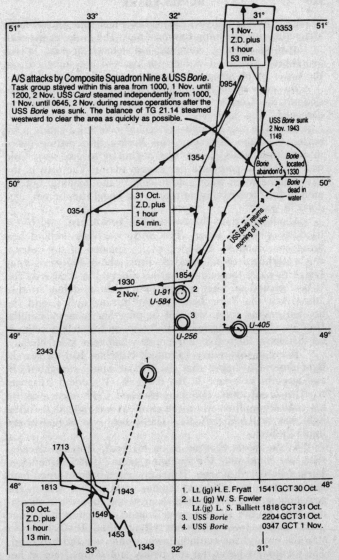

A/S attacks by Composite Squadron Nine & USS *Borie*.
Task group stayed within this area from 1000, 1 Nov. until
1200, 2 Nov. USS *Card* steamed independently from 1000,
1 Nov. until 0645, 2 Nov. during rescue operations after the
USS *Borie* was sunk. The balance of TG 21.14 steamed
westward to clear the area as quickly as possible.

1 Nov.
Z.D. plus
1 hour
53 min.

31 Oct.
Z.D. plus
1 hour
54 min.

30 Oct.
Z.D. plus
1 hour
13 min.

USS *Borie* sunk
2 Nov. 1943
1149

Borie
located
1330

Borie
abandon'd

Borie
dead in
water

USS *Borie* returns
morning of 1 Nov.

1930
2 Nov.

1854

1354

0954

0353

0354

2343

1713

1813

1549

1453

1343

1943

U-91
U-584   2

U-256   3

U-405   4

1

1. Lt. (jg) H. E. Fryatt   1541 GCT 30 Oct.
2. Lt. (jg) W. S. Fowler
   Lt.(jg) L. S. Balliett 1818 GCT 31 Oct.
3. USS *Borie*   2204 GCT 31 Oct.
4. USS *Borie*   0347 GCT 1 Nov.

Card track chart, 30–31 October, 1–2 November 1943.

Class David F. Southwick threw his 5-inch-long sheath knife
at a submariner running toward a gun. The knife hit the man
in the stomach, and, clutching his stomach in pain, he fell
overboard. Another German was brained and knocked into
the water by an accurately thrown empty 4-inch shell case.

But even as the *Borie*'s men were inflicting such destruction on the Germans, the *Borie* herself was being gravely
damaged. The high seas were pounding the two vessels
together. The sub's tough skin could take the beating a bit
better than the destroyer; the *Borie*'s thin plating (worn
thinner from years of use) was beginning to give way. Cold
water began to pour into her engine rooms. The men in the
after engine room were able to control the flooding, but the
men in the forward engine room soon found themselves neck
deep in water.

About this time the two vessels broke free, and *U-405*
tried to open the range. The *Borie* was right behind her,
firing continuously. A 4-inch shell exploded in the submarine's starboard diesel exhaust. From about 400 yards away
Hutchins had a torpedo fired at his quarry, but it missed. The
U-boat turned hard left and began to circle. Hutchins tried to
follow, but the *Borie* had a larger turning radius, and the
flooded engine room was not helping her maneuverability.
U-405 was still taking many shell hits, and Hutchins estimated that about thirty-five of the enemy had been killed already.

Tiring of this merry-go-round, Hutchins had his searchlight doused in hopes that the U-boat would straighten out
and attempt to escape in the darkness. It worked. Hopman
tried to break away. Hutchins watched *U-405* ease away on
his radarscope; then when the moment was right the searchlight was switched on again. The U-boat was pinned in the
light's beam.

As the *Borie* charged in on his boat, Hopman decided
that two could play the ramming game. *U-405* turned into
Borie's starboard quarter. Hutchins immediately turned hard
left, stopped the starboard engine, and backed full on the
port engine. The destroyer's stern swung toward the oncom-
ing sub. As the stern slewed around, Hutchins had three
depth charges (with thirty-foot settings) fired. It was a perfect
straddle around the conning tower—one over and two short.
The explosions lifted the sub bodily and stopped her in her
tracks. "Men on [the *Borie*] said that if there had been

another coat of paint on either ship there would have been a collision."[37]

But *U-405* was amazingly tough. As the *Borie* picked up speed to open the distance, so did the submarine. But now she was moving sluggishly. One more torpedo was fired at the submarine, missing the boat. A 4-inch shell didn't miss, however. The starboard diesel exhaust was hit once more, and the U-boat slowed to 4 knots.

The Germans were finally abandoning their battered boat, firing red, green, and white starshells as they did so. The *Borie* ceased firing, but one last 4-inch shell had blown most of the conning tower, along with several men clustered on it, into the sea. *U-405*'s bow came out of the water, then she slipped under and exploded. From the *Borie*'s crew came a yell that "probably could be heard in Berlin."[38]

When the Germans had fired their starshells, an answering signal was seen to the southwest. As the *Borie* eased in to pick up the estimated fifteen survivors, the sound operator heard a torpedo racing in from the direction of the signal light. The *Borie* came hard left, and the torpedo whizzed by only thirty yards off her port side. Unfortunately, this maneuver caused the ship to run down the group of survivors, and they were not picked up.

The *Borie* slowly and painfully pulled out of the area. She was in serious trouble. Her entire port side had been mangled, and her forward engine room flooded completely. Machinist Mate 1st Class Irving R. Saum, Jr. volunteered to go into the flooded compartment to close the secondary drain suction. This action would enable all pumps to be placed on the after engine room's suction to prevent that compartment's flooding. Saum had to spend quite a bit of time under the cold and debris-filled water, but he finally accomplished this hazardous task.

Hutchins radioed the *Card*, "Just sank number two in combined depth charge attack, gun battle and ramming. May have to abandon ship."[39] This message was garbled when received on board the carrier, and Captain Isbell remained unaware of what happened to the *Borie*.

In an effort to save his ship, Lieutenant Hutchins had all nonessentials thrown over the side. The remaining torpedoes were fired and the torpedo tubes cut off; all the machine guns went over, and only ten rounds per gun were saved for the four-inchers; all unessential top hamper was discarded. A storekeeper came up to Hutchins carrying the "Title B Book," which contained the list of items on the *Borie* that Hutchins had to sign for as his personal responsibility. The seaman asked, "Sir, who's going to take responsibility for all this Title B stuff we're throwing away?"[40] Hutchins took the book and threw it overboard, too.

At 0900, with seawater contaminating the fuel oil and the turbine blades finally blocked, the *Borie* went dead in the water. What gasoline remained was needed to run the pumps; so lighter fluid, alcohol, and kerosene were used to power the generator so that the radio could be used. The *Card* had her planes out, but they could not locate the *Borie* in the poor visibility until 1100, when the *Borie* sent an ominous message, "Commenced sinking." The *Card* was able to get a bearing on this message. At 1129 an Avenger found the destroyer dead in the water only 14 miles from the carrier.

The *Card, Barry,* and *Goff* arrived a short time later to find the *Borie* in grave condition. She was wallowing heavily in the high seas and was down by the stern. The *Goff* tried to close with her sister ship to pass over handy-billies and hose for pumping purposes. The Atlantic had built up to forty-foot swells, however, and the *Goff* could not get near enough. Hutchins did not want to abandon ship, but late in the day Captain Isbell thought it best to get the crew off before darkness came.

Hutchins finally gave the word to abandon ship at 1644, and his men reluctantly began to leave their beloved "flush-decker." The water was cold (only 12 degrees above freezing) and very rough. The *Barry* and the *Goff* moved in to pick up the men while the *Card* roamed skittishly about, aware that she was now unprotected. The high seas prevented the rafts from getting close to the rescue ships, and men were thrown into the water and dragged under the ships. No one had been killed during the battle with *U-405,* but three officers and twenty-four men were lost in the cold waters as they tried to reach the *Barry* and the *Goff.*

During the night a submarine tried to sneak in on the *Card,* but radar picked up the intruder's approach. The two destroyers were sent after the U-boat and frightened her away. When dawn broke on 2 November the *Borie* was still there, though she was lower in the water. An erroneous

Lockheed P-38

report of some fifty submarines within 300 miles of the *Card* prompted Isbell to call off any more attempts at rescue or at salvaging the *Borie*. The *Barry* tried to sink her with three torpedoes, but they missed. Finally, an Avenger dropped four depth bombs. These did the trick, and a gallant lady went down at 0954 on 2 November 1943.[41]

The loss of the *Borie* reducing his already slender supply of escorts, Isbell decided to cut short his mission and head for Norfolk. The *Card* arrived there on 9 November. Both Hutchins and Saum would be awarded the Navy Cross for their actions during this dramatic battle with *U-405*. Several other men of the *Borie* would also receive well-deserved awards. Despite the sinking of the *Borie*, the *Card*'s group had had good success. But even better hunting for the escort carriers was just around the corner.

The *Santee* and the *Croatan* had also been out escorting

convoys and looking for submarines during October and
November, but had no luck on their missions. The only
excitement noted by either ship was the "forced landings" by
the *Santee's* Lieutenant Bass and Lieutenant (jg) B. D.
Jaques at Lagens Field, Terceira, Azores, on 6 November.
Ostensibly made because of bad weather, the real purpose of
the landings was to determine the Portuguese reaction to the
presence of American military personnel in the Azores. The
two pilots returned to the *Santee* the next day.[42] This cruise
of the *Santee* was just about her last in the Atlantic. Following a ferry trip with a load of P-38s to England in December
and January, she headed for the Pacific where she found her
share of excitement.

But if the *Santee* and the *Croatan* were drawing blanks
during their missions, the *Bogue* was finding plenty of action.
The flattop (still with VC-19 and her old friends the *George
E. Badger, Osmond Ingram, Clemson*, and *DuPont*) left Norfolk
on 14 November to escort Convoy UGS-24. Task Group 21.13
stayed with UGS-24 until east of Bermuda, leaving the convoy on 17 November to head southeast toward some U-boats
reported near the Azores.

On the 22nd the *Clemson* got a couple of contacts that
kept her busy until the next day, but nothing developed. Five
days later, as the *Bogue* was topping off the *Osmond Ingram*,
the *Badger* reported a sound contact and raced over to make
several depth charge attacks. Though some oil rose to the
surface, the U-boat escaped.

Several more submarines were in the area, as evidenced
by radio transmissions over the aircraft frequency. One pilot
heard a heavily accented English voice calling "VC-1 from
(numerals), how do you receive me?" for about ten minutes.
Then, the *Bogue's* listening watch heard a German voice say,
"Blow water ballast 1, 2, 3, 4." Finally, toward evening of the
28th as planes were circling a sound contact, another German
voice was heard to say, "Watch your step. Aircraft still
overhead."[43]

It was not until 29 November, however, that the *Bogue's*
group would be able to record a kill. That afternoon the
DuPont and the *Badger* were investigating a sound contact
when Lieutenant (jg) Bernard H. Volm caught *U-86* on the
surface 50 miles west of the task group. Kapitanleutnant
Walter Schug did not seem in a hurry to dive, and Volm

remained astern of the U-boat to await reinforcements. Six more planes were sent, and *U-86* dove for the last time 385 miles east of Terceira.[44]

The next day Lieutenant (jg)s James E. Ogle III and Carter E. Fetsch saw Oberleutnant Horst Hepp's *U-238* slicing through the black waters of the Atlantic. Hepp was one of Doenitz's best submariners, and his crew were well-trained. They put up a heavy barrage that frustrated the attackers' efforts, but Ogle and Fetsch were finally able to break through and damage the U-boat seriously enough that Hepp had to head for Brest.[45]

Following this action, the *Bogue* put into Casablanca on 5 December. She would remain there until the 8th. By this time it was apparent to Tenth Fleet that the Germans were shifting their submarine effort back to the North Atlantic. Several U-boats were still in the immediate area, and the *Bogue* was ordered after some of these boats concentrating about 770 miles south–southwest of Madeira.

"It is evident that [Admiral Ingersoll] was combing his area of responsibility with a fine-toothed comb, for the object of his interest was a brief fueling rendezvous of a 1,763-ton supply boat, *U-219*, with a submarine outward bound for operations in the Indian Ocean."[46]

The *Bogue* sortied on 8 December, escorting Convoy GUS-23 for a time, then heading for the area of the rendezvous. On the morning of 12 December, Lieutenant (jg) E. C. Gaylord was on a routine antisubmarine patrol when he saw the fully surfaced *U-172* 4 miles away. This U-boat was the one that was to rendezvous with *U-219*. Gaylord immediately sent a contact report and turned toward the submarine.

Unfortunately, a broken hydraulic line prevented Gaylord from opening his bomb bay doors automatically. The sub's skipper was slow in spotting Gaylord racing in, though, and didn't begin to dive until Gaylord was only 2 miles away. Gaylord was able to open the doors manually and selected a Fido for the drop instead of the 500-pound bomb. Because of the hydraulic problem, Gaylord couldn't use gear or flaps to slow down, so he went through a series of violent maneuvers to lose speed.

These maneuvers did the trick, and Gaylord was able to drop his Fido about thirty-five seconds after the U-boat had disappeared. He followed this with a sonobuoy drop. It took the sonobuoy almost fifteen minutes to start working, however. One minute after the Fido entered the water, Gaylord and his crew saw a shock wave. The U-boat had been damaged by the Fido, but her captain, Oberleutnant Hermann Hoffmann, was able to bring his boat under control for the time being.

In the meantime, three more planes and the *Badger* and the *DuPont* had been sent to help. One of these planes dropped a large pattern of sonobuoys around the scene, but they all remained unusually quiet. As the aircraft circled the oil slick left when *U-172* dove, the submarine broached suddenly about 400 yards ahead of the slick. The fliers were caught out of position, and the U-boat had once again disappeared before they could make an attack. By this time the two destroyers were just racing over the horizon.

Hoffmann lay quiet for the time being while, one by one, the planes left because of low fuel. Unfortunately for him and his boat, however, the *Badger* and the *DuPont* had been ordered to remain in the area to try to smoke out the enemy boat. The *DuPont* made several depth charge attacks on promising sound contacts, but the submarine escaped again.

The "tin cans" were persistent, though, and kept the U-boat under. About 2120 *U-172* surfaced and was picked up by the *Badger*'s radar at a range of 9,000 yards. The destroyer crept in, hoping to surprise the sub. When the range had dropped to 6,000 yards, it appeared to the *Badger*'s crew that the submarine was dead in the water. A spread of starshells was fired, but nothing was seen. Then, the radar reported the target moving again. Finally, the submarine was seen visually 3,000 yards away. Three rounds of 3-inch shells were fired which missed, and the U-boat retaliated with an acoustic torpedo which also missed.

U-172 dove at 2218, but the destroyer quickly had a sonar contact. Two more depth charge attacks did more damage to the U-boat. Despite the loss of most of his gauges and the disabling of one diesel engine, Hoffmann was still able to keep his boat down. The two destroyers were finally recalled by Captain Dunn about 0600 on the 13th, but *U-172*'s ordeal was not over yet.

A little over an hour later one of the *Bogue*'s planes saw a moving oil slick about 7 miles from the spot of the last attack. The *Clemson* and the *Osmond Ingram* were sent to investigate. The *Badger* soon followed. At 0907 the *Clemson* loosed a nine-charge pattern that inflicted still more damage to the grievously wounded submarine. A pair of Avengers dropped sonobuoys, and another pair of Wildcats were also on the scene ready to pounce when the sub surfaced. The aircraft were able to keep the destroyers informed of the U-boat's movements.

The *Clemson* and the *Osmond Ingram* made four more runs, and at 1016, unable to take any more attacks, Hoffmann brought *U-172* up. As the U-boat surfaced, she was strafed by the aircraft and taken under fire by the three destroyers. Lieutenant Commander Roger F. Miller wanted to take his ship, the *Osmond Ingram*, in to ram the submarine. Captain Dunn was not enthusiastic about this tactic, and it also appeared that the Germans were abandoning their stricken boat.

Some men were, but not all. Several manned the deck gun and exchanged gunfire with the *Osmond Ingram*. A shell hit the destroyer, killing one sailor and injuring several others. But the duel was a mismatch. All three of the "flush-deckers" raked the submarine with 3-inch fire. Soon a heavy explosion rocked the U-boat, and a sheet of flame rose from her conning tower. *U-172* began circling to the right, then sank and exploded underwater.[47]

Oberleutnant Hoffmann and forty-five of his crew were rescued. Hoffmann had been thoroughly disliked by his crew, and this may have been the reason "the morale of the boat on this last patrol was anything but desirable."[48] But the morale problem could have been caused by the persistent efforts of the attackers. Doctor Lundeberg summed up the situation neatly, saying: "This action, which lasted a full twenty-seven hours from the time of first contact, demonstrated that by the end of 1943 the United States Atlantic Fleet had succeeded in combining the salient features of British surface support group tactics with the rapidly developing technique of carrier warfare, in which American success was pre-eminent. The prolonged 'hunt to exhaustion' illustrated better than almost any other operation a proper coordination between planes and ships, between two or more ships engaged in sound search and depth charge attacks, a correct choice of weapons and a high degree of individual proficiency."[49]

U-219, the boat that Hoffmann had been looking for, was still hanging around, and the *Bogue* group spent most of the

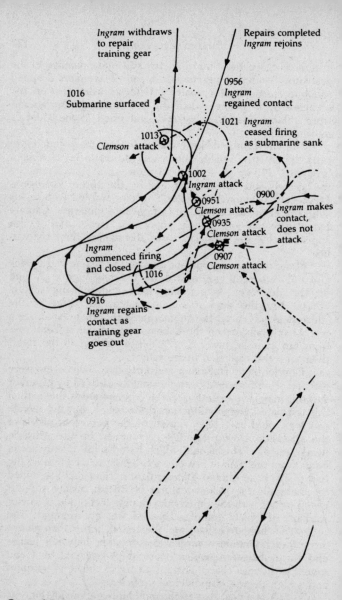

Osmond Ingram and Clemson track chart, 13 December 1943.

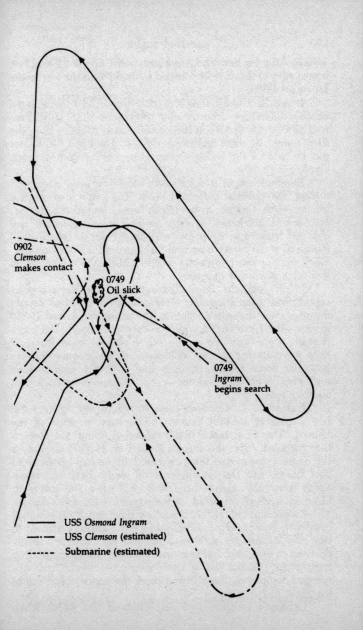

0902
Clemson
makes contact

0749
Oil slick

0749
Ingram
begins search

——— USS *Osmond Ingram*
—·—·— USS *Clemson* (estimated)
------ Submarine (estimated)

14th looking for her. The Americans were unable to find her, however, and the U-boat escaped to finally end the war as the Japanese *I-505*.

It was not until the 20th that the VC-19 fliers found another submarine. Shortly after 1300 Lieutenant (jg) Wallace A. LaFleur saw *U-850* on the surface some 70 miles from the *Bogue* and 530 miles southwest of Fayal. The big 1,616-tonner was headed for the Indian Ocean as part of the 2nd Monsoon Group.

Kapitanleutnant Klaus Ewerth's lookouts must have been dozing, for LaFleur surprised them. LaFleur's first run was unsuccessful, though, as his depth bombs would not release. He racked his heavy Avenger around in a tight turn and charged back in to drop his two Mk. 47 depth bombs. The Germans were awake now, and LaFleur met a hail of gunfire. His drop was short, with the second hitting about 200 feet off the sub's starboard quarter.

Meanwhile, the *Bogue* (having heard LaFleur's contact report) was catapulting four more aircraft to aid him. Twenty minutes after the initial sighting, the other planes had *U-850* in view. The Germans, devoting all their attention to LaFleur's aircraft, were unaware of the other planes' approach until they were strafed by two Wildcats, but the enemy gunners got over their surprise quickly and took the new arrivals under fire. This fire died out as the Wildcats came back with another pass.

Ensign G. C. Goodwin came in behind the fighters and laid a perfect straddle across the forward position of the U-boat. The first depth bomb exploded about ten feet off the starboard bow; the second landed on *U-850*'s deck near the conning tower; the third exploded fifteen feet off the sub's port beam; and the fourth went off about forty feet away. Spray completely covered the boat, and when she emerged, huge amounts of oil could be seen pouring from her flanks.

Lieutenant (jg) H. G. Bradshaw then began his run, but his depth bombs fell short. The brace of fighters returned to lace the submarine with machine-gun fire. Ewerth finally decided to dive, and LaFleur and Bradshaw darted in to drop their Fidos. Just a few seconds after the U-boat had submerged completely, both Fidos struck the water ahead and to the right of her swirl.

LaFleur's weapon had just entered the water when

U-850 resurfaced, her bow breaking the water at a sharp angle. Just thirty seconds after the first Fido hit the water it struck the submarine's starboard side near the stern. A split-second later the other Fido hit the same side midway between the conning tower and stern. The two blasts became one huge explosion rising 150 feet into the air. Her stern blasted off, *U-850* sank, bow up, at a vertical angle.

The *George E. Badger* and the *DuPont* were dispatched to the scene and reported picking up "dismembered bodies, pieces of clothing, life jackets, and broken pieces of wood."[50] *U-850* was the *Bogue*'s last score for this cruise. She put in to Bermuda on Christmas Day, where her crew enjoyed a well-earned Christmas dinner.

As the *Bogue* was drawing close to Bermuda, the *Card* was taking her place near the Azores. The *Card* had left Norfolk on 24 November with a new set of escorts, the *Decatur, Leary, Schenck,* and *Babbitt* (the latter detached later when she had engine problems), and a brand-new squadron, VC-55. Although the cruise to Casablanca was uneventful, the passage back was to be anything but routine. The *Card*'s escorts would once again discover that U-boats didn't like destroyers.

The carrier spent a couple of days in Casablanca, leaving on 17 December to escort Convoy GUS-24. While in port the task group's crews had their Christmas dinners, which was fortuitous, as the weather on the return voyage was horrendous. VC-55 had little opportunity to fly because of the weather. On one day (the 23rd) "an attempt was made to launch planes . . . ,but the sea was found to be so rough that the planes could not even be taxied to the catapult."[51]

Shortly after departing Casablanca, the *Card*'s TG 21.14 was ordered toward a submarine concentration gathering around 45°00′N, 22°00′W. This was Group *Borkum*—thirteen U-boats placed to cover the return of the blockade runner *Osorno* from Japan. For a short time on the 23rd the seas finally calmed enough to launch one plane to scout the area, and it spotted an unidentified merchantman plowing north through the heavy seas. The vessel was flying the red ensign of the British merchant marine.

The pilot challenged the ship and received no reply. He radioed the carrier that there was something suspicious about the vessel. "Buster" Isbell couldn't send any of his destroyers

to look the ship over, however, because the weather had
made it impossible to fuel, and his escorts were running low
of the precious stuff. Still, Isbell contacted Gibraltar about
the ship and also studied photos of her taken by his plane.
There was no doubt—she was the *Osorno*. The weather
precluded launching any planes to attack her, and the *Osorno*
completed her three-month journey from Kobe to Bordeaux.[52]

The sea remained rough. On the afternoon of the 23rd
one of the *Card*'s aircraft (with its pilot strapped in his seat)
was thrown over the side as the flattop took a heavy blow
from a wave. The pilot went down with his plane. Because of
the state of the ocean, TG 21.14 had to run before the sea to
the east and southeast instead of almost due south toward
Horta where Isbell planned to fuel his destroyers. It was only
at 0849 on 23 December that the task group had been able to
take up a course of 220 degrees for Horta.

That afternoon Isbell received the disturbing news that
"ten or more [submarines] estimated patrolling within 100
miles 45-00N, 22-00W."[53] This put the center of the concentration only 85 miles dead ahead of the task group. Isbell was
not especially impressed by this report, as Tenth Fleet estimates had sometimes been wrong in the past. Anyway, he
had to get to Horta or his escorts would be dead in the water.
Isbell decided to press on toward Horta and the reported
submarine concentration. Unfortunately for TG 21.14, the
U-boats were where they had been reported. On the 22nd a
roving Luftwaffe aircraft had seen the *Card* and passed the
word on. Doenitz ordered the boats of Group *Borkum* to
head for the carrier's position at the "highest possible speed."[54]

Another aircraft sighting further narrowed the search for
the carrier by the Germans, and they moved in for an attack
on the night of the 23rd. Shortly after 2100 that night, both
forces ran head-on into each other. At 2120 the *Card* began to
pick up radio transmissions from nearby U-boats. Then, the
Schenck got a good sound contact and attacked, but with no
results. About the same time Kapitanleutnant Rudolf Bahr
saw the *Card* from the bridge of his wind- and spray-tossed
U-305. Bahr began stalking the carrier and coaching in his
comrades.

Bahr was unable to get in an attack, however, as the
Schenck picked up his boat on her radar and charged in to
drive him down with 20-mm and 3-inch gunfire. *U-415* was

also nearby, and Kapitanleutnant Kurt Neide was able to get his boat within 3,700 yards of the *Card* before firing three F.A.T. (*flachenabsuchender torpedo*—zigzag or pattern runner) "fish" at the carrier. The torpedoes missed, fortunately, as the *Card*'s crew did not see *U-415* until after the torpedoes had been fired. The carrier zigzagged away, and the *Decatur* (having to be steered by hand because of a flooded steering room) was sent to investigate. *U-415* dove, and the *Decatur* and the *Leary* were unable to gain contact.

Isbell recalled the *Decatur* and sent the *Leary* to help the *Schenck*, still sniffing around for *U-305*. The two destroyers were told to "keep subs down during night. We will be over in the morning. Good luck."[55] Radio problems on the *Schenck* forced the *Leary* to use a combination of TBS, aircraft frequencies, and blinker to maintain contact with her partner. The two destroyers quickly picked up several radar contacts to the north, and the *Leary* went ahead to attack the most distant contact, while the *Schenck* moved in on the closer targets. The two ships became separated by about 5 miles.

As the *Schenck* closed in on her quarry, contact was lost at 2,500 yards. Then the U-boat was seen submerging, her stern pointing right at the destroyer. Lieutenant Commander Earl W. Logsdon took his ship through a quick change of course, evading a torpedo in the process. Logsdon slowed his ship to make a deliberate depth charge attack on the now-vanished U-boat. At 0145 a nine-charge pattern rolled over the side. The depth charges apparently damaged the submarine, for thirty minutes later she surfaced.

The *Schenck* was only 4,000 yards away when the U-boat's "pip" appeared on the destroyer's radar. Logsdon immediately headed for the contact. The sub again dove, but sonar contact was regained at 1,900 yards. As the *Schenck* passed over the spot where the sub had dived, a shallow pattern was dropped. These depth charges did the trick. About two minutes after the last charge was dropped, a deep thundering explosion was heard and felt by the *Schenck*'s men. A surge of oil came to the surface—*U-645*'s tombstone. But before a sample of oil could be taken, an urgent call came from the *Leary*. She had just been torpedoed!

After the two destroyers had separated, the *Leary* had continued north. She was heading right into a group of

U-boats. At 0158 a radar contact was made on an object about 6,500 yards distant. Commander James E. Kyes ordered the object illuminated with starshells, even though the *Leary*'s crew had not caught sight of the object. It was a disastrous decision. The starshells had no effect except to call attention to the destroyer's position. And one gun kept on firing the shells because of a misunderstanding.[56]

The object (Oberleutnant Helmut Bork's *U-275*) dove and turned toward the *Leary*. The bright light cast by the starshells gave Bork a perfect view of the destroyer, and he wasted no time in sending two acoustic torpedoes speeding toward the "tin can." Kyes's sonar crew, meanwhile, were bedeviled by the noise of the ship's "Foxer" gear and the gunfire and lost *U-275* until she was only about 750 yards away. Then, the ship's intercom chose that moment to malfunction. Precious time was lost before Kyes could get any information. At 0210, before Kyes could take any action, Bork's two torpedoes slammed into the *Leary*'s starboard side.

One torpedo exploded in the aft engine room and the second slightly farther aft. The two explosions were so close together that they blended into one terrible roar. The *Leary* staggered like a punch-drunk fighter and slowed to a stop. The "entire rear of [the] ship was jagged, twisted iron, with arms, legs, and other carnage in all directions."[57] Only five men would be recovered from the after part of the ship. All power was lost on board the ship, and only by use of an auxiliary generator could a call for help be sent to the *Schenck*, then unaware of her sister ship's predicament.

As the *Leary*'s crew gathered on deck, many thought they saw three subs surrounding the stricken ship. The *Leary* was listing 25 degrees and settling rapidly by the stern when Commander Kyes ordered "Abandon ship!" The men had just begun to go over the side into the cold, choppy water when *U-382* sent a torpedo crashing into the forward engine room. The *Leary* went down fast. Commander Kyes was last seen in the water giving his life jacket to a mess attendant who had none.

Of the *Leary*'s crew of approximately 150 men, about 100 were able to abandon ship, but only 59 would be picked up by the *Schenck*. Two rafts and a few cork-float nets were all that was available to the *Leary*'s men. When Lieutenant

Commander Logsdon arrived, the *Schenck* picked up three radar contacts and a sound contact in the immediate area.[58]

Logsdon had to be very careful in case the Germans were waiting to ambush the rescuer. Nevertheless, as the *Schenck* steamed past the survivors, Logsdon lowered his gig and a boat crew to pull the men from the water. He continued searching for the U-boats (which pulled out rapidly to the northwest), stopping occasionally to pick up survivors from the gig. By 1000 on the 24th the last *Leary* sailor was on board the *Schenck*, and the destroyer was heading back toward the *Card*.[59]

While the *Schenck* had been going about her lifesaving mission, the *Card* had been in a very uncomfortable position. Just 15 miles from sinking and escorted only by the steering-hampered *Decatur*, the *Card* was a tempting target. But Isbell kept his ship zigzagging and sent out a call for help to CinCLant and the *Block Island* group operating nearby. The *Block Island*'s help was not needed, however, as the Germans let a "bird in the hand" get away. Unable to regain contact with the *Card* and with new orders from Doenitz, Group *Borkum* moved north to concentrate on the convoys moving between the United States and Gibraltar. U-boat Command was quite pleased with the performance of the *Borkum* boats. Though both *U-275* and *U-382* had attacked the *Leary*, the Germans thought they had sunk two different ships. They also thought that *U-415* had got another destroyer.[60]

The seas finally abated somewhat, and the *Schenck* and the *Decatur* were able to be fueled from the *Card*. No further contacts were made by the task group, and the downcast force anchored in Hampton Roads on 2 January 1944. For the next few months the *Card* would be used primarily in aircraft ferry and personnel transport to North America, and the carrier would not score another kill until July.

The escort carriers, with the *Card* leading the way, had piled up an impressive list of scores since the *Bogue* had entered combat in March. At the end of 1943 the *Card*'s planes and escorts were the top scorers with ten U-boats. Close behind was the *Bogue* with eight submarines, followed by the *Core* with five, the *Santee* with three, and the *Block Island* with one. The British carriers *Tracker* and *Biter* each had two U-boats to their credit. The top squadron was VC-9, which had sunk eight U-boats while flying from the *Bogue* and the *Card*.[61]

By the end of 1943 the escort carrier groups had shown themselves to be outstanding exponents of offensive warfare. They had also shown they could operate under the most adverse conditions. Their presence in the Atlantic had forced the Germans into changing certain operational procedures and tactics. Now, "the disposition and habits of USN CVE groups were pressing concerns which necessitated revisions of current orders on the defense situation in an effort to determine where and when U-boats might safely surface."[62]

But there were few places left where a U-boat might surface undisturbed. To combat the ever increasing numbers of carrier and land-based aircraft, the Germans had increased the antiaircraft armament of the submarines. Such changes were not always to the betterment of the U-boats. Also, by the latter part of 1943 patrols were often ineffective because of the time the U-boats had to spend underwater to escape the attention of the seemingly omnipresent aircraft. This constant threat even caused one nighttime encounter.[63] Despite the coming appearance of snorkel-equipped boats, the situation was one the Germans could only ponder with growing dread.

6

GRINDING THEM DOWN

While the *Card*'s TG 21.14 was undergoing its ordeal
with the *Borkum* boats, two more escort carriers were in the
Central Atlantic searching for U-boats. The *Core*, carrying
the nine FM-1s and twelve TBMs of VC-6, had been at sea
since 5 December. Her mission turned out to be nonproduc-
tive, but it was not without excitement. Shortly before noon
on 22 December the *Core*'s radar picked up an aircraft 16
miles away and closing. The weather was not good because of
rain showers and low clouds, but two Wildcats were, none-
theless, readied for launching as soon as the weather lifted.

The *Core* ran into a clear area, and Lieutenant (jg) H. G.
Hyde was catapulted. (The other fighter also took off, but the
pilot's earphones were knocked off during the catapulting,
and he took no part in the ensuing action.) Two minutes after
he took off, Hyde saw what appeared to be a Do 217 only 200
feet off the water and heading directly for the *Core*.

The German pilot saw Hyde at the same time, and he
racked his twin-engine plane sharply to the left. As Hyde
closed in from astern and to the left, the enemy gunner
began firing at him, but his aim was poor. Hyde could see
these bursts exploding off his right wing. From 400 yards
Hyde sent several bursts into the bomber's cockpit. His fire
seemed to have little effect, however, and the Do 217 began
to open the distance. Hyde made two more runs but steadily
lost ground. The German plane finally disappeared into a rain
squall.[1] This action was notable for being the only air-to-air

137

Do 217

battle by an American CVE plane in the Atlantic during antisubmarine operations.

On 2 January two of the *Core*'s escorting destroyers plus several TBMs made a number of attacks on a possible submerged U-boat. Although an oil slick was seen, no submarine was discovered, the boat apparently having escaped with only slight damage.[2] The *Core*'s cruise ended on 17 January 1944 without further action.

Meanwhile, the *Block Island* was also out scouring the waters of the Central Atlantic. Logan Ramsey's ship had left Norfolk on 15 December accompanied by the *Paul Jones*, *Bulmer*, *Parrott*, and *Barker*. VC-58 provided the force's (TG 21.16) air power. Initially, cover was furnished for Convoy UGS-27. On the 23rd Ramsey received orders to proceed on other duties and then head for a reported submarine concentration near 45°00′N, 20°00′W. (This was the *Borkum* boats, which would soon be giving the *Card* and her escorts such a hard time.)

Hardly had the *Block Island* started on her assignment when an urgent CinCLant message was received. Task Group 21.16 was to head immediately toward the submarine concentration! "Buster" Isbell's call for help had been heard, and the "USS F.B.I." (Fighting *Block Island*) was being sent to the rescue.

However, before the carrier reached the scene, the U-boats had skulked out of the vicinity. Then, on the 27th a message was received from the Admiralty giving the position of the blockade runner *Alsterufer*. The enemy vessel had passed through an Allied aircraft barrier patrol area several days before it had been established and was now only about 240 miles north of TG 21.16. Four TBF-1s carrying depth charges and a new armament of rockets were sent to sink the ship. Unfortunately, the pilots blew their assignment, and Logan Ramsey blew his top. In the words of the *Block Island*'s action report:

> As proof of the adage that "you can lead a horse to water, but you can't make him drink," [the Avengers] arrived at the locality of the blockade runner and discovered that it had already been attacked by shore-based planes from the Azores and was on fire. Despite very positive orders given the flight commander and each individual pilot before their takeoff from *Block Island* to sink this blockade runner, the group, probably fascinated by the fire, circled the blockade runner for some forty minutes but did not attack. At 1507, plus two zone time, a very weird transmission was received from the flight leader, "Sighted enemy ship 45°42′ 19°04′. Am returning to base." He was immediately asked, "Did you attack enemy ship?" and replied, "Did not attack enemy ship. Ship was burning when we arrived." He was then ordered to sink this vessel but did not acknowledge this transmission. Five minutes later, another plane in the formation replied, "Ship was sunk when we arrived. Do not know if it was enemy ship." This last transmission was incorrect. The ship was *not* sinking, and it was later necessary for the British to dispatch a Czechoslovakian squadron from the Azores to complete this mission.[3]

Captain Ramsey was furious over the mishandling of this mission. When three of the Avengers landed well after dark, the crews found themselves being chewed out royally by Ramsey. The flight leader temporarily missed this experience when he became lost and had to set down in the sea. He and his crew were picked up two days later by the *Barker*. Upon arrival back on the flattop he discovered that Ramsey had recommended him for a general court-martial for "failure to exert himself to the utmost against the enemy, and for deliberate disobedience of orders."[4] It is not known if this court-martial was ever carried out.

The same day that the Avenger was rescued, the *Block Island* stumbled across several of the *Borkum* boats. Numerous radar and sonar contacts were made with presumed submarines, but though several attacks were made by the destroyers, little damage was done to the enemy vessels.[5] Ramsey believed that eight or nine U-boats were present, but it is possible that only a couple were actually on the scene.

The following day a surfaced submarine was seen by an

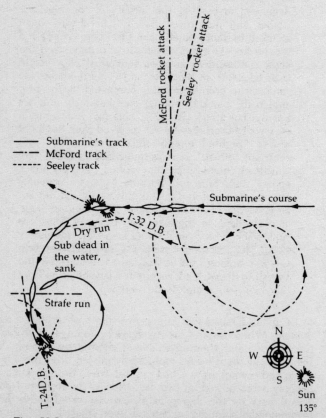

McFord rocket attack

Seeley rocket attack

——— Submarine's track
—·—· McFord track
------ Seeley track

Submarine's course

T-32 D.B.

Dry run

Sub dead in
the water,
sank

Strafe run

T-24 D.B.

N
W   E
S

Sun
135°

First U.S. CVE aircraft rocket attack, 11 January 1944.

Avenger pilot, but she submerged before the aircraft could close. The next few days were quiet, and TG 21.16 put into Casablanca on 4 January. The force remained in port four days, then sortied to cover two British convoys (north- and southbound) which were to pass close to each other.

The *Block Island* suffered the first loss of her career on 11 January when a Wildcat crashed on takeoff and sank with its pilot. A first of a different nature also occurred on the 11th. On a morning antisubmarine patrol Lieutenant (jg)s Leonard L. McFord and Willis D. Seeley caught a U-boat on

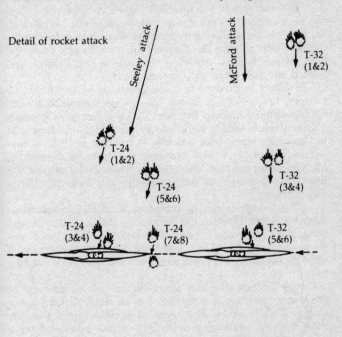

First U.S. CVE aircraft rocket attack, 11 January 1944.

the surface. Besides the usual two Mk. 47 depth bombs, the two Avengers were each equipped with some new armament—eight Model 5 3.5-inch rockets.

McFord led the way, gliding in from the sub's starboard beam. At 1,500 yards he let loose with two rockets, followed by more pairs at 1,100, 600, and 500 yards. McFord thought his third salvo hit just short of the conning tower. Seeley was not far behind and let loose with rockets in pairs at 1,200 yards and between 600 and 350 yards. He also thought he had got a pair of hits.

The sub was not defenseless, however. Her crew filled the sky with quite a bit of, fortunately inaccurate, antiaircraft fire. As Seeley pulled out, McFord was coming back for a depth bomb attack. He dropped his two bombs from 450 feet. These bombs straddled the U-boat, exploding close aboard and just aft of the conning tower.

Seeley's next run was unsuccessful, as he had forgotten to open his bomb bay doors. The U-boat remained on the surface making a sharp left turn. To keep the sub's gunners occupied while Seeley got his doors open, McFord charged in to strafe. He carried his attack in so low that he came within twenty feet of the U-boat's conning tower. As he zoomed by, McFord observed that "there were certainly a lot of guns [on board the U-boat], so many that the sub looked... like a picket fence."[6]

The U-boat began to submerge as Seeley returned to drop his depth bombs. The submarine had just disappeared when the two Mk. 47's were released. The first bomb was short by about thirty-five feet, but the next one exploded right on the sub's track and just a few feet aft of the conning tower.

Just seconds after this attack the sub's bow came out of the water, pointing sharply into the air. Her conning tower soon was also visible. She began an erratic turn to the left, then stopped, wallowing unsteadily. A few minutes later a large puff of yellow-green smoke erupted aft of the conning tower, and the U-boat then sank slowly by the stern. Sonobuoys were dropped, but nothing was heard for over five minutes. Then, a loud "crunching" noise was picked up over the sonobuoy circuit.[7]

The U-boat was believed to have been sunk, but as happened so many times throughout the war, she escaped.

This attack was noteworthy, however, for the use of rockets. It was their first such use by the U.S. Navy's escort carrier aircraft, and would not be their last.

The use of rockets and other new weapons by the Allies worried Doenitz. In an "admonitory radio message" to his skippers on 15 January he said, "In the race to overtake the enemy after his spurt ahead in developing efficient antisubmarine measures, every single experience must be used to discover new enemy defense weapons and methods, so as to be able to counter-balance them by tactics and new weapons of our own. The flood of constantly changing orders and instructions will not cease until we have achieved a decisive advance."[8]

The *Block Island* continued searching for U-boats, but results were negative. On the 14th the task group came upon a cluster of forty-three survivors from *U-231*, which had been sunk by an unidentified aircraft the night before. These men were picked up to become the only Germans to be seen close up on this cruise. With the *Croatan* group coming on station near the Azores, the *Block Island* returned to Norfolk on 3 February.

Despite Ramsey's belief that his force had sunk several submarines, no U-boats had actually been destroyed. Still, "significantly enough, despite the failure of either the *Core* or *Block Island* groups to secure kills northeast of the Azores during this tempestuous interlude, the pressure they exerted was so great that on 3 January, the U-boat Command broke Group *Borkum* up into subgroups of three boats each and abandoned plans for surface attacks on Gibraltar-bound convoys during daylight."[9]

The Americans kept up the pressure, as the *Croatan* sailed from Norfolk on 14 January. With daylight sightings of U-boats becoming rare, the Navy had decided to look into night flying off the "jeeps." As early as August 1943 (with further thoughts on the subject in October) the *Santee* had recommended that the escort carriers begin night operations.[10] The *Croatan* was to be the first escort carrier to test the value of night-flying Avengers.

The *Croatan*'s cruise turned out to be unproductive. Nevertheless, one of the "Old Crow's" night-flying Avengers was credited with the first authentic night attack on a U-boat following a radar contact. Early on the morning of 15 February an Avenger got a radar contact on a target. A flare revealed a U-boat cruising on the surface. The submarine dove before an attack could be made, but sonobuoys were able to keep tabs on the boat. A Fido was dropped when noises increased in volume near one of the sonobuoys, and an explosion was noted by the Avenger crew listening to the sonobuoys, followed a short time later by "metallic, clanking noises" and the sound of escaping air bubbles. The *Croatan*

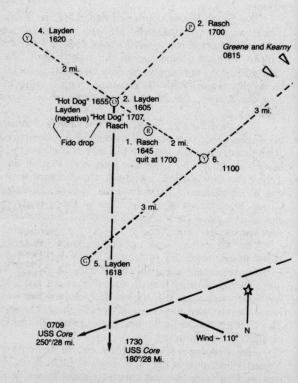

Typical sonobuoy pattern. This U-boat escaped.

fliers believed they had sunk the submarine, but she escaped. Nevertheless, this attack indicated to both sides that the U-boats could no longer rely on the blackness of night to mask their activities.[11]

Just as unproductive a cruise was that of the *Mission Bay*, the first Kaiser-class carrier in the Atlantic. After the usual shakedown in the waters off San Diego, the *Mission Bay* sailed for Norfolk, arriving on 5 December 1943. After a

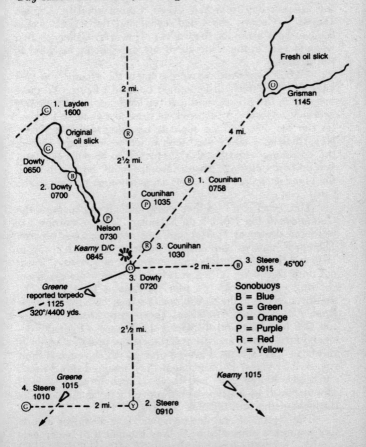

Fresh oil slick

(O) Grisman
1145

(R)

4 mi.

1. Layden
(G) 1600

Original
oil slick

(G)

Dowty
0650

(B)

2. Dowty
0700

2½ mi.

(B) 1. Counihan
0758

Counihan
(P) 1035

(P)
Nelson
0730

Kearny D/C
0845

(R) 3. Counihan
1030

3. Steere 45°00′
(B) 0915

2 mi.

3. Dowty
0720

Greene
reported torpedo
1125
320°/4400 yds.

Sonobuoys
B = Blue
G = Green
O = Orange
P = Purple
R = Red
Y = Yellow

2½ mi.

Greene
4. Steere 1015
1010
(G)

2 mi.

Kearny 1015

(Y) 2. Steere
0910

short stay, she left Norfolk on 26 December with the veteran VC-9 on board. Her initial mission to Casablanca and back covering a number of east- and westbound convoys turned up just radar contacts, which served to keep everyone alert. The *Mission Bay* didn't score this time, but her presence would be felt before the war was over.[12]

Another Kaiser-class ship joined the Atlantic Fleet at the end of 1943. She was the *Guadalcanal*, which had sailed with the *Mission Bay* from San Diego. Commanded by Captain Daniel V. Gallery, the *Guadalcanal* and her escorts would soon make a name for themselves. However, Gallery at first was not very enthusiastic about his ship's being assigned to the Atlantic.

"When I got word we were going to the Atlantic," he said later, "I was bitterly disappointed because I figured I'd done my stint in the Atlantic and that the battle of the Atlantic was won now anyway. So I figured we were just going to backwater the war now, and we ought to be going to the Pacific."[13] Nevertheless, Gallery was determined to make the best of the situation. When the *Card* returned to Norfolk, he spent several hours picking "Buster" Isbell's brain, hoping to make the *Guadalcanal* as outstanding an antisubmarine ship as the *Card*.

The "Can Do" (as her crew quickly nicknamed the *Guadalcanal*) left Norfolk on 3 January 1944. Escorting her were the destroyer *Forrest* and four new destroyer escorts. Though a massive shipbuilding program was under way in 1943 and the DEs were beginning to pour off the ways, it was not until December of that year that these new vessels began showing up as convoy escorts and screens for CVEs. The destroyer escorts in the *Guadalcanal*'s screen were the *Pillsbury*, *Pope*, *Flaherty*, and *Chatelain*. These were *Edsall*-class vessels 306 feet long and displacing 1,200 tons. Originally designed for 24 knots and using turbines, because of machinery shortages this class used geared diesels, which reduced their speed to 21 knots. For armament they mounted three 3-inch and eight 40-mm guns and three 21-inch torpedo tubes.[14] The destroyer escort type would prove their value repeatedly throughout the remainder of the war.

The screen of one destroyer and four destroyer escorts was somewhat unusual, but Gallery thought it to be an ideal setup. "The DD can be rushed to the scene of a contact at high speed," he commented later, "and has plenty of striking power when it gets there. The four DEs, with their long cruising range, relieve the carrier from the burden of constantly refueling escorts."[15] The *Guadalcanal*'s group kept this formation for its next cruise also, but the strictly destroyer escort screen soon became the standard.

The *Guadalcanal*'s air group was the veteran VC-13, now led by Lieutenant Commander Adrian H. Perry. The squadron started out with nine FM-1s and twelve TBF-1cs, but the "combination of a new type carrier and bad weather proved costly" in both planes and aircrews.[16] The losses began soon after the *Guadalcanal* left Norfolk, when TG 22.3 ran into very heavy weather. Two Wildcats were so damaged that they had to be put ashore when the carrier put into Bermuda. VC-13 was now down to seven fighters.

There were other losses for the *Guadalcanal*. One evening, as the ship was being bounced about by the violence of the sea, someone realized that a couple of the forward lookouts had not reported for some time. A sailor was sent forward to see what was wrong. All he found was a pair of headsets and phones. The heaving sea had swept the lookouts away.[17]

But just as a coin has two sides, this storm provided the men of the *Guadalcanal* with time for a little laughter as well as tragedy. It seems that the ship had a medical officer who was always insisting that there was no such thing as seasickness. One afternoon, while the ship was twisting and turning in the pitching seas, one of the crew came upon the doctor hanging over a railing and looking decidedly green. Unable to resist, the sailor asked, "Feeling a bit seasick, Doc?" Still hanging over the side, the officer replied shakily, "It's all my state of mind."[18]

The losses continued as the "Can-Do" headed through the stormy seas toward a reported U-boat fueling rendezvous some 500 miles west of the Azores. On the 10th Lieutenant (jg) James F. Schoby (who had received the Distinguished Flying Cross for his part in the sinking of *U-487* in July of 1943) was trying to land on the pitching deck when his big TBF went over the port side. Only the turret gunner was rescued. Just two hours later another Avenger landed in the catwalk. Because another plane in the air was low on fuel, the TBF had to be jettisoned. The *Guadalcanal* was left with ten bombers.[19]

Paydirt was struck on the 16th, but the cost was almost too high for the gain. Late that afternoon Ensigns Bert J. Hudson and William M. McLane came across *U-544*, *U-516*, and *U-129* at the fueling rendezvous, which had been accurately plotted by Tenth Fleet. The 1,144-ton *U-544* was fueling *U-516* and was making ready to send some *Naxos* gear to both boats when the Americans appeared. *U-129* "pulled the plug" and submerged, but the other two U-boats were caught with fueling lines still attached.

As sailors on both subs frantically tried to uncouple the fueling lines, Hudson raced in on their starboard beams at 250 knots. He fired two rocket salvos in quick succession at a

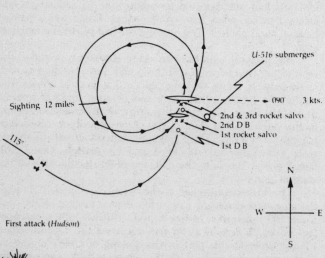

U-516 submerges

Sighting 12 miles

090   3 kts.

2nd & 3rd rocket salvo
2nd D B

115°

1st rocket salvo
1st D B

N

W — E

S

First attack (*Hudson*)

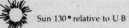
Sun 130° relative to U B

VC-13 rocket attacks on *U-516* and *U-544*, 16 January 1944.

distance of 500 to 800 yards. The first two rockets hit just short of *U-516*, whereas the next two slammed into *U-544*, with one going through the hull and out aft of the conning tower. Hudson pressed in until he was only seventy-five feet high when he fired his last rockets and dropped two depth bombs simultaneously. These last rockets penetrated *U-544*'s hull, causing extensive damage. The first depth bomb exploded about fifty feet short of *U-516*, while the second landed between the two boats. *U-516*'s bow came out of the water at a sharp angle, and she slowly went down by the stern. As she disappeared, men on *U-544* began to jump overboard.

Close on Hudson's heels, McLane fired his rockets in three salvos. The last two rockets hit the water about fifty feet short of the submarine. Just as he fired his last two rockets, McLane released his two Mk. 47s. The first bomb exploded

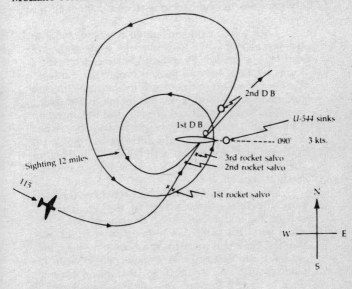

VC-13 rocket attacks on *U-516* and *U-544*, 16 January 1944.

close aboard, while the other landed too far away to do any great damage. Nevertheless, *U-544* was done for. Her bow rose to about 45 degrees as she sank by the stern. Twenty to thirty-five men could be seen in the water as an oil slick began to form around them. Though two of the destroyer escorts were sent to search for them, no survivors were recovered.

Hudson and McLane had put in a well-executed attack that paid off. Nevertheless, because of the difference in trajectories of the two weapons, the simultaneous use of rockets and depth bombs was a tactic frowned upon by CinCLant and the tacticians in the antisubmarine schools.[20]

Now dusk was falling, and Gallery had to get his planes (eight of them on patrol) back aboard the *Guadalcanal*. This turned out to be quite a chore. The masterful storyteller Dan Gallery provides the best picture of what happened next:

> Each pilot in the air figured it was essential to the war effort for him to fly over the scene of the kill and take a gander. Despite urgent recall messages from the ship, they all flocked over to have a look. By the time we got them back to the ship, the sun had gone down, and it was beginning to get dark.
>
> The first four got aboard okay. But they used up a lot of time because of wave-offs for bad approaches in the gathering dusk. The fifth landed too far to starboard and wound up with both wheels down in the gallery walkway and his tail sticking out into the landing area.
>
> This is the sort of thing that separates the men from the boys—three planes in the air, darkness closing in, and a foul deck. We turned out to be small boys that night. We were a new ship; this was the first time real pressure had been put on us, and we got butterfingered. We simply couldn't clear the landing area. We couldn't get that plane back on deck to drag it forward. We couldn't even heave it overboard. After ten minutes of futile fumbling, it was pitch dark, and the boys in the air were getting low on gas.
>
> The planes that had landed reported seeing a fourth submarine in the area of the kill. It's not a

good idea to show bright lights when you think there are U-boats breathing down your neck. But in this case we had no choice. To have any chance of getting our boys aboard, we *had* to turn on the lights. You might as well go for broke in such a spot, so we lighted up like a saloon on a Saturday night.

Then I got on the voice radio and made the following pitch to the boys in air—"That tail sticks out only about 15 feet into the landing area. If you land just a little bit to the left of the center line, everything will be lovely."

It didn't work. By this time everybody had the jitters. The boys came in too high, too fast, and too far to port. Finally one of them took a desperate "cut," hit the deck, bounced high in the air, rolled over on his back, and plunged into the sea to port. The plane guard destroyer fished all three of the crew out of the water unhurt.

But that was enough of that. I had all ships turn on searchlights pointed at the water. We ditched the other two planes and picked up the crews. Then we blew out the lights and got the hell out of there.[21]

Gallery's and the *Guadalcanal's* first experience with night air operations had not been a great success. But he was determined that the next time the "Can Do" sailed, his aviators would be well versed in night operations. And he made sure his deck crew became very proficient in clearing a foul deck. The bent "Turkey" that went into the catwalk that night was used every day by the deck crew in practice crash removals. The crew was "damned well fed up with that daily chore," Gallery said, "and our poor old 'Turkey' was so badly battered it wasn't worth repairing. I let our jubilant deck crew give it a decent burial at sea."[22]

The finding and sinking of *U-544* just where Tenth Fleet had said she would be impressed Gallery greatly. Of course he did not know how Tenth Fleet came up with their estimates, but Gallery commented later:

"There was a Commander Ken Knowles in Washington who ran this submarine estimate thing. He was just a sooth-sayer. He could put himself in the position of a German skipper and just figure out what that guy was going to do, and where he would go. He was absolutely uncanny in his predictions.

"I treated the Cominch daily estimate as Bible truth every day, and we based our operations on it completely."[23]

Just a couple of days after the carrier's wild landing experiment, the *Guadalcanal* had some more unplanned excitement. A Wildcat coming aboard made such a hard landing that its belly tank ripped off. The tank skittered across the deck, trailing its volatile fuel—which a spark quickly ignited. Soon a large column of black smoke and flame covered the ship's stern. The "Can Do's" escorts moved in to pick up survivors, believing the flattop was done for.

Actually, there was more "sound and fury" to this fire than danger to the ship, as much of the fuel drained through scuppers and over the side. The *Guadalcanal's* crew quickly brought the fire under control. The only casualties of the fire were three rather red-faced (or, possibly, red-fannied) sailors who were "doping off" in the head underneath the flight deck. Flaming fuel draining into the head's flushing system interrupted the trio's reading time.[24]

Although this incident had a relatively happy ending, another incident did not. On the 20th Lieutenant (jg) Bert M. Beattie became lost while on a routine patrol. He was unable to contact the ship, and his Avenger was last seen on the carrier's radar heading for the Azores. Inhabitants of the island of Flores saw a plane ditch off the island's north coast that evening, and then three men were observed struggling in the surf for two hours before they were carried out to sea. The body of Beattie's radioman was later recovered, but Beattie and his gunner were never seen again.[25]

The *Guadalcanal* finally anchored in Casablanca for a well-earned rest. When she put to sea again, the weather was still bad, and weather conditions, coupled with the shortage of aircraft, limited the "Can Do's" operations considerably. The bad weather inevitably caused more accidents. When VC-13 flew ashore on 16 February, only three Wildcats and three Avengers were operational out of the twenty-one aircraft that had begun the cruise.[26] Despite the sinking of *U-544*, the loss of so many aircraft had made this mission a most inauspicious way to inaugurate operations. But Dan Gallery and his crew were fighters, and the future would be much brighter for them.

The *Card* (screened like the *Guadalcanal* by a destroyer and four DEs) was now back out on offensive operations, but, as related earlier, she would run into a string of unproductive patrols and not score again until July. Nevertheless, this cruise was not dull. Along with the *Croatan*, the *Card* became one of the first escort carriers to implement night flying procedures.

Actually, the *Card*'s procedure called for takeoffs at dusk and landings after sunrise, with no flight deck operations at night, but Captain Gallery and his squadrons from the *Guadalcanal* would soon refine this idea with true nighttime deck operations. The *Card* stripped two TBFs (duly christened "Owls") of all unnecessary weight, including the gunner, armor, and armament. Two 58-gallon wing tanks and one 275-gallon bomb bay tank were added, along with flame dampeners, parachute flares, extra batteries, and other equipment. All these changes reduced the aircraft's weight by 451 pounds. These Avengers were now capable of flights of up to sixteen hours. The actual duration of flights for the *Card*'s two VC-55 Avengers ranged up to thirteen hours. With the help of coffee, sandwiches, and benzedrine pills, the crews handled the long flights well.[27]

The rough weather prevalent in the Atlantic at this time of year caused a number of accidents aboard the *Card*, but a spectacular one on 27 January was not weather-related. Lieutenant (jg) John H. J. Pearce was landing on the carrier when his big Avenger began to settle rapidly. The landing signal officer gave a waveoff, and Pearce pulled up sharply. The Avenger's nose rose too high and the plane stalled, and it then began to roll and spin. As the Avenger spun in, it hit a 20-mm splinter shield and its left wingtip was sheared off. The plane slammed into the water next to the ship, its engine ripping loose upon impact. Pearce was badly injured and was only saved when his radioman, ARM2c Charles W. Foster, pulled him clear of the sinking plane. Lieutenant A. R. McGonegal, a radar expert making tests of the TBF's radar set, was trapped and went down with the plane. Shortly before the plane sank, two strong underwater explosions were felt on the carrier. These were evidently caused by depth bombs which had been torn from the plane by the impact. Foster was later awarded the Navy and Marine Corps Medal for the rescue.[28]

The *Card* returned to the United States on 9 March. No fewer than three more of the industrious "jeeps" would be operating in the Atlantic before the *Card* anchored at Norfolk. First out was the *Block Island*. The "USS F.B.I." was operating with a new team. The carrier's screen was now composed of the destroyer *Corry* and the *Cannon*-class destroyer escorts *Thomas*, *Bostwick*, *Breeman*, and *Bronstein*. VC-6 had replaced VC-58 and was equipped with a new version of the Wildcat, the FM-2. This version, built by Eastern Aircraft, had been developed specifically for escort carriers. The fighter was lighter, with a more powerful engine and a taller fin to counteract the extra torque from the engine. Instead of six .50-caliber guns, the FM-2 carried four. The aircraft was a perfect selection for the escort carriers.[29]

It was planned that the *Block Island* would operate in the vicinity of the Cape Verde Islands, off the bulge of Africa. This area was thought to be a refueling and rendezvous point for U-boats going to and from the Indian Ocean. However, the carrier was quickly shunted north to the Azores to search for submarines operating against convoys in that area.

Things were quiet for the *Block Island*'s group until the evening of 29 February (1944 was a leap year). Just before sunset a TBF/FM-2 team caught a glimpse of a periscope "feathering through the water" only 20 miles from the carrier.[30] As darkness settled over the ocean, the fliers lost sight of the periscope, but sonobuoys picked up unusual and irregular sounds close by. No attack was made, but the evening's activities had only begun.

Around 2100 the *Thomas* picked up a contact, and she and the *Bostwick* raced after it. As they sniffed around on the scent, what was thought to be a second target appeared on the task group's radars. Lieutenant Sheldon H. Kinney took his ship, the *Bronstein*, toward this contact. When he got within range, Kinney ordered starshells fired to illuminate the scene. The brilliant light revealed a rather surprised group. The crews of the *Thomas* and the *Bostwick* were surprised as they now saw a surfaced U-boat sneaking in on them. And the captain of *U-709*, Oberleutnant Rudolf Ites, was just as surprised, as he had been concentrating on the two DEs and was unaware of the *Bronstein*'s approach.

Kinney's guns were trained on the submarine, and he had them firing immediately. A hail of gunfire surrounded the

U-boat as she went deep. The *Bronstein* charged in to fire a couple of hedgehog patterns, and the *Thomas* and the *Bostwick* followed with more hedgehogs and depth charges. For *U-709* there would be no escape. The *Thomas* and the *Bostwick* kept after the U-boat into the early-morning hours of 1 March, harrying and tormenting their quarry. Finally, Lieutenant Commander David M. Kellogg brought the *Thomas* in for one more run. A deep-set pattern of depth charges was laid. For what seemed an interminable time there was nothing; then came the unmistakable sound of a U-boat being ripped apart. *U-709* was gone—the first victim to fall to a destroyer escort.

U-709 had not been the only submarine in the area, however. Oberleutnant Hans Joachim Bertelsmann's *U-603* had been moving in on the *Block Island* as *U-709* was being worked over. The situation probably looked pretty good to Bertelsmann until the sudden appearance of Sheldon Kinney and the *Bronstein*. Although Kinney's ship had only been commissioned on 13 December 1943, he had already whipped into shape a smooth-running team. Amid the explosions surrounding *U-709*, Kinney's sonar operator had picked up the sound of *U-603* sneaking in.

When *U-603* was first discovered, the destroyer escort was very close to the submarine. Kinney's crew had depth charges rolling off in good time, however. More patterns were laid. Then, about 0122 on 1 March, the *Bronstein*'s crew both heard and felt a tremendous explosion. It was *U-603*'s death rattle. The brand-new *Bronstein* and her rookie crew had quickly become old hands at the game of sinking submarines. Kinney would receive a well-deserved Legion of Merit for this day's exploits.[31]

The *Block Island* group put into Casablanca on 8 March, and when the flattop came back out on the 11th, she had a new skipper, Captain Francis M. Hughes. The carrier and her escorts headed toward a point west–northwest of the Cape Verde Islands where Tenth Fleet believed a refueler would be arriving about 16 March. This estimate proved to be accurate.

On the morning of the 15th the *Block Island* picked up a target on her radar only 8 miles away. It was Kapitanleutnant Hans-Joachim Brans's *U-801*. The sub was tracked for about forty-five minutes, but a heavy haze caused by dust blown from the Sahara prevented aircraft from spotting her. The *Corry* and the *Breeman* were sent after the U-boat, but they were also unable to find her. However, the U.S. ships kept getting tantalizing returns on their radars indicating that a U-boat was still hanging around.

The next afternoon Brans surfaced to get in some gunnery drill (even though this was a generally forbidden practice). It was a beautiful day, and the ocean was glass-smooth. After this practice about fifteen of the crew were topside changing watch, and the subs's 37-mm gun was partially dismantled for servicing. Suddenly an aircraft alarm was sounded. The crew was slow to react, as several false alarms had been given earlier in the day. This was the real thing, though, as two VC-6 planes were boring in from astern.[32]

Lieutenants (jg)'s C. A. Wooddell and Paul Sorenson were on the return leg of their patrol when they saw a submarine off to their left about 10 miles away. The pair immediately banked toward the U-boat and, taking advantage of some clouds, closed in. Sorenson (in his FM-2) led the charge. He was on the U-boat before the Germans could react. His gunfire scythed across the deck, cutting sailors down where they stood.

Wooddell was close behind but was not satisfied with his position, so delayed his attack. Sorenson banked around to rake *U-801* once more. His fire wounded nine men, including Brans, and killed one. "The barrel of one 20-mm was shot to pieces and the after part of Platform II in the vicinity of the ammunition containers was burning fiercely."[33] The Germans scrambled into the conning tower, and Brans took her down. Before the U-boat could submerge, Wooddell returned to drop two Mk. 47s, which exploded about fifty yards to the right of the boat. *U-801* had disappeared before he could make another attack, so Wooddell released a pair of sonobuoys.

Submarine sounds could be heard over the buoys, and a Fido was dropped near one of the color-coded buoys. The weapon made a sharp left turn, but no explosion was heard. However, reception from the buoys ceased for about fifteen seconds, and when the submarine noise resumed, Wooddell described the sound as "clanky" and "banging." The noise finally faded away. Wooddell believed the sub had been damaged.[34]

Two more Avengers were launched to relieve Wooddell

and Sorenson. More sonobuoys were dropped, and *U-801* could again be heard, but another Fido drop was unsuccessful. Shortly after this drop a fire broke out in the bomb bay of one of the TBFs. Though the fire was soon extinguished, the plane's depth bombs had to be jettisoned. These two aircraft, low on fuel, finally had to return to the *Block Island*.

It was now night. Hughes, unlike Gallery, did not believe that "all-out night flight operations [were] practical for CVEs."[35] However, he was willing to launch aircraft to develop a contact, provided enough moonlight was available for them to operate. These conditions were met, so a MAD-equipped TBF was launched to take over the search. (This was one of the first operational uses of Magnetic Airborne Detection equipment by a carrier aircraft.) Unfortunately, the MAD gear didn't indicate anything present, and problems with sonobuoys canceled the use of that equipment.

Brans was still in the area, though, and had already surfaced once that night to radio U-boat Command that he needed a rendezvous with a supply boat to transfer casualties and to obtain needed supplies. A meeting with *U-488* was arranged for the 20th.[36] These transmissions were heard by other listeners. The *Corry* was sent to investigate, as was Lieutenant (jg) Norman T. Dowty. Shortly after 0100 the *Corry* had a radar contact at 6,800 yards. Subsequently the destroyer discovered a pair of radar decoys (called *Thetis* by the Germans), which she destroyed with gunfire.

At 0141 Dowty got a radar contact with an object only a mile away. Dropping down to 200 feet, Dowty headed for the contact. A minute later Dowty's eagle-eyed radioman, ARM1/c Edgar W. Burton, spotted *U-801* heading west at about 18 knots. The Germans heard and saw the Avenger also and dove before an attack could be made. Dowty circled the area dropping sonobuoys. The buoys weren't putting out very well (not an unusual situation for the equipment of the time), but a little over an hour later another brief radar blip was noted. Brans just wouldn't stay down, and it would cost him dearly.

Dowty turned toward the contact and dropped more sonobuoys. Before he could tune in a buoy, Dowty saw *U-801*'s periscope slicing through the moonlit water. Dowty racked his Avenger around to come up the periscope's wake. At 0302 he dropped his Fido from 150 feet. The buoys Dowty had dropped were defective, and he was unsure if his weapon had caused any damage. It had. The Mk. 24 had shaken the boat violently and smashed a hole in the diesel compartment machinery space. Oil began to flow from the boat.

When daylight came, Dowty could see a large oil slick starting at the spot where he had dropped the Fido. The slick continued for over 2 miles to the north, then veered northwest. At 0600 Dowty was relieved by Lieutenant (jg) Elefter in another TBF. Elefter's search was routine until shortly before 0800 when he discovered that the oil slick was moving. Several sonobuoys were dropped (most of which didn't work), and submarine sounds could be heard over them. The *Corry* was then about 10 miles away, and Elefter radioed her to come over and take a look. He then laid a string of smoke floats up the track of the slick.

The *Corry* came racing over, as did the *Bronstein*, which had also been sent to help search. At 0842 both ships made simultaneous sonar contact. For over two hours the two DEs battered *U-801* with eight depth-charge attacks. Machinery was knocked out in the submarine, and Brans found it increasingly difficult to keep his boat in trim. He prepared to fight it out with torpedoes, only to discover his periscopes had been damaged. Seeing he was in a hopeless position, Brans decided to surface and abandon ship.

At 1118 *U-801* broke the surface at a sharp angle, stern down. The *Corry* immediately opened fire with her 5-inch guns and made a number of hits on the helpless U-boat. "At this time, the Task Group was seven miles off and in plain sight of the whole proceedings. The *Block Island* flight deck was crowded and cheering *Corry* and *Bronstein* on. *Corry* made quite a picture with all her automatic weapons and 5-inch guns firing while she was closing in at 28 knots."[37]

Inside the sub was chaos. "The order to abandon ship never reached the bow compartment where members of the crew only realized that the end had come when they saw the telegraphists destroying their secret equipment."[38]

Brans led the way topside, followed by the quartermaster and two other officers, who began hoisting the wounded up. When the rest of the crew scrambled topside, they discovered a horrifying sight. Brans was dead, hanging limply over the railing. At his feet was the headless body of the quartermaster. Several more dead were scattered about. The other two officers had leaped overboard, leaving the wounded where they lay. *U-801*'s engineer took charge, making sure the wounded were evacuated and everyone was off the submarine. Then he calmly went below to await the end. At 1124 the U-boat sank by the stern. Forty-seven survivors were plucked from the water by the *Corry* and the *Bronstein*.[39]

The sinking of *U-801* had been a good way to start Captain Hughes's initial cruise on the *Block Island*. In his action report Lieutenant Kinney placed this operation in perspective. "The entire task group contributed to the sinking of this submarine," he said. "The result was the product of teamwork that realized fully the mission of CVE groups by combining every weapon, air and surface."[40] The hunter-killer groups built around the escort carriers had come of age.

There was still more excitement—and tragedy—just around the corner for the *Block Island*'s group. Tenth Fleet knew that *U-488* was in the area waiting to rendezvous with the now-departed *U-801* and the Penang-bound *U-1059*; so the task group was keeping its eyes open looking for this juicy target. On the morning of the 19th VC-6 fliers found, not the milch cow, but something just as juicy. It was the 1,084 ton *U-1059* carrying a load of torpedoes to Penang.[41]

Lieutenant (jg) Dowty was out again, accompanied by Lieutenant (jg) William H. Cole in his FM-2. At 0726 the pair were about 50 miles from the carrier when Cole saw the big sub lying motionless in the water some ten miles away. *U-1059*'s commander, Oberleutnant Gunter Leupold, in a terrible error, had given permission for his crew to have a short swim just a little while earlier. He had cautioned his men, "Watch out for planes in this fine weather!"[42] About eighteen men, including Leupold, were swimming when Dowty and Cole zoomed in.

As the Americans attacked, all except one of the swimmers (who, ironically, was one of the few survivors) clambered back on board the boat. They were unable to get their boat under way, however, and were able to get off only a few rounds of 20-mm and 37-mm fire. Cole led the way, peppering the submarine with .50-caliber shells and severely wounding Leupold.

Dowty followed about twenty seconds later to drop two depth bombs "squarely astraddle" the conning tower.[43] Survivors of *U-1059* later stated that one of these bombs actually exploded aft on deck and the other just below the surface

near the torpedo storage compartment. Cole and Ensign
Mark E. Fitzgerald (riding as Dowty's gunner on this flight)
saw the explosions lift the submarine bodily out of the water
and break her back. "Perfect hit, skipper," Fitzgerald heard
radioman Burton yell to his pilot. Dowty then ordered his
crew to get ready for a Fido drop.

As Dowty pulled out, Cole returned for another strafing
run. *U-1059* was sinking rapidly stern-first, and a fire was
raging in her ready ammunition lockers. Cole could see that
the submarine had not moved from the slick left by the
explosions. Cole finished his run and saw Dowty's TBF, its
wheels down and making a sharp turn back toward the
U-boat, suddenly plow into the water.

Fitzgerald first knew that his plane had crashed when he
"felt the plane shudder and the next second found himself in
the water."[44] All that could be seen of the plane was a piece of
the tail section. Dowty and Burton were nowhere in sight.

Cole saw about fifteen men in the water, but because
they had had no chance to don life jackets, only eight of these
men would be recovered. Sharks could also be seen circling
the area. Five of the survivors clung to pieces of wreckage,
while the other three (including Leupold) congregated around
Fitzgerald's raft. A little over two hours later the *Corry*
picked up the survivors. The loss of Dowty and Burton was a
heavy blow to VC-6. Dowty was one of the old-timers in the
squadron, and he and his radioman were considered two of
its most outstanding individuals. Dowty would be awarded a
posthumous Navy Cross for this action.[45]

But the war went on, and many more individuals were
destined to die in the frightful and bloody battles yet to
come. VC-6 aircraft made another submarine contact on the
23rd. Though several attacks were made using MAD-equipped
Avengers and sonobuoy information, these attacks were unsuccessful. Equally unsuccessful were the efforts of the *Corry*
and the *Bostwick* to sniff out the submarine. After some
eighteen hours with no results, the ships called off their
search.[46]

While this search was on, two other ships of the *Block
Island*'s screen were detached to undertake an unusual mission. The *Breeman* and the *Bronstein* were sent to Dakar to
transport gold to New York. The Bank of Poland had (by
various means) got $60,000,000 in gold ingots to French West

Africa. The Polish government in exile now needed this gold, and it was up to the two destroyer escorts to deliver the gold safely. They accomplished this task with no problems, but the crews on both ships must have been very wistful as they watched the gold being carted away under heavy guard.[47]

The *Block Island*'s group had no further contacts and returned to Norfolk on 31 March. Here the aviators of VC-6 received a surprise greeting from numerous high-ranking officers, including Logan Ramsey. A band played, and a huge sign proclaimed, "Welcome Home, Champs." The ceremonies and the tumultuous party that followed etched the day forever in their memories.[48]

There was no band and no party when the *Bogue* sailed from Norfolk on 26 February. Indeed, that was the usual lot of the escort carriers; they would steam out, do their job, and steam back in with no fanfare, no brass bands to greet them. But King, Ingersoll, and Low (and Doenitz) knew how well they were doing their jobs.

Between the time the *Bogue* got back to the United States in late December and her departure on this mission, the carrier had made a trip to England—not an antisubmarine patrol, but an aircraft ferry mission. In mid-January she delivered a load of P-47s to Glasgow, Scotland. The weather on the trip over was atrocious, with mountainous seas causing the ship to roll 32 degrees to port at one point, but the voyage back was even worse. The heavy seas caused the carrier to roll and pitch severely. One roll to port was logged at 40 degrees.

This rough weather didn't seem to bother the *Bogue* sailors too much. In fact, they may have been hoping the weather would cause some slight damage. Occasionally, after the flattop had taken a very hard shot from the surging sea, a yell could be heard on the hangar deck. "Yahoo! Another three days in the yard!"[49]

Ralph Hiestand recalls that "the storm turned us every which way but loose. The foc'sle and well-deck joists and girders giving up the good fight, twisted and buckled. The forward starboard corner of the flight deck peeled up like a toboggan, and some welds on the hangar deck bulkhead seams cracked. At some time we actually took water over the flight deck rolling down the deck like the surf at Coney Island."[50] However, the *Bogue* was a tough ship, and less than

P-47

two weeks after she anchored at Norfolk, she was out at sea
again.[51]

The *Bogue* had finally bidden farewell to her long-time
flush-deck associates, and now she had a fresh screen of the
destroyer escorts *Haverfield, Swenning, Willis,* and *Janssen*
and the destroyer *Hobson.* Also new to the carrier were the
aircraft and men of Lieutenant Commander John F. Adams's
VC-95. This squadron had only been commissioned on 1
February. The ships were formed into TG 21.11, under the
command of Captain Dunn.

After leaving Norfolk, the task group rendezvoused with
Convoy USG-34 to fuel the escorts from a tanker in the
convoy. After this was completed, TG 21.11 broke away to
search for a submarine reported northwest of the Azores.
Heavy seas, which caused the *Bogue* to pitch and roll (plus
very bad weather), prevented the VC-95 planes from operating for several days. On 8 March the task group began
receiving indications of U-boat activity. Numerous sound
contacts were reported by the escorts for the next four days,

but all searches turned up nothing. Then, on the 13th, the force struck paydirt.

At 0650 that morning the *Bogue* got an HF/DF bearing on a submarine estimated to be at 45°20′N, 26°08′W. Though the *Hobson* and a plane found nothing at that point, a U-boat was lurking in the area. The submarine was *U-575*, and the 13th was to be her unlucky day.

Lieutenant Commander Adams had been launched shortly after the "Huff-Duff" bearing was obtained, and at 1015 sighted a suspicious oil slick northwest of the original HF/DF plot. The sonobuoys he dropped picked up faint tantalizing noises that Adams thought merited more investigation. The *Haverfield*, along with another plane, was sent to the scene. More sonobuoys dropped by the relief plane indicated that a submarine was indeed present.

When the *Haverfield* arrived, it didn't take long for her to make sonar contact. At 1419 she began a series of hedge-hog and depth charge attacks. Her attack at 1447 brought a surge of oil bubbling to the surface. Just before the *Haverfield* made her last attack, surprise reinforcements appeared. HMCS *Prince Rupert* had been heading northeast when she came upon TG 21.11. Captain Dunn signaled the Canadian ship to join the *Haverfield* in more attacks, and the Canadians were only too happy to oblige.

The two ships made several coordinated attacks, with the *Prince Rupert* coaching the *Haverfield* in on several of them. Oberleutnant Wolfgang Boehmer's *U-575* was taking a terri-ble pounding from the deep-set depth charges. This pounding was to increase as the *Hobson* joined the attack at 1759, along with the Avenger of Lieutenant Donald A. Pattie. *U-575* was trapped in the invisible web of the attacking vessels' sonars and Pattie's sonobuoys.

At 1833 the *Hobson* delivered a very deep depth charge attack that was *U-575*'s undoing. Two minutes later the U-boat's bow broke the surface, angling steeply into the air. The three ships immediately took her under fire, while Pattie dove in to deliver a rocket attack that punched two holes completely through the submarine. The Germans fired a few ineffectual shots at their tormentors, but this stopped when the ships lashed the U-boat with their own gunfire, and Pattie dropped two depth bombs that enveloped the submarine in spray.

Realizing the end had come, Boehmer sent one last

message to U-boat Command reporting the attack; then the submariners abandoned ship. *U-575* began to settle rapidly. At 1843 her bow suddenly reared skyward and she sank stern-first. Many survivors were in the water and thirty-eight, including Boehmer, were eventually rescued. *U-575* had been fitted with a snorkel and was the first of this type of submarine to be lost to American ASW units.[52]

U-575 was the only kill the *Bogue* group would score this cruise. Though several more contacts were made, nothing turned up. After a short stay in Casablanca, TG 21.11 swept the area west of the Cape Verde Islands, then headed for Trinidad and fuel. The *Bogue* finally arrived in Hampton Roads on 19 April. VC-95 had put in a lot of flying time on this mission and had only *U-575* to show for it. But this was becoming typical as more snorkel-equipped U-boats became operational. The CVE squadrons would discover it increasingly difficult to locate and sink a U-boat. But their job would not be any less dangerous or tiring because of this; in fact, their mission would become even more hazardous and exhausting. The following passage from the VC-95 History shows how this squadron saw their job.

> The mere report of "so many" searches and "so many" flights with no success cannot begin to portray the arduous and dangerous work that is the life of a squadron engaged in antisubmarine warfare above a CVE in the Atlantic.
>
> A routine day aboard such a CVE would start with the dawn hop—four pairs of planes (VT and VF) doing relative sector searches on a radius of up to 80 miles from the carrier, duration four hours. The forenoon and afternoon hops repeating the process. The sunset hop normally is composed of three VT planes doing geographic "barrier" searches with roughly the same length of legs. Depending on the proximity or the probability of an enemy submarine in the area, hops will continue throughout the night, ending with the pre-dawn hop—thus affording continuous twenty-four hour operations until a kill is produced or until search for a particular U-boat is abandoned. This writer knows of no aviation activity more exacting or more fatiguing for flying personnel than that engaged in by the VC Squadrons based in

the Atlantic aboard the escort carriers. Long hours of monotonous and difficult patrol in all kinds of weather, normally with no tangible result for their efforts—some pilots will spend as much as twenty-four months at sea without sighting a submarine—is a heart-breaking, thankless job that seasons and ages pilots as no other activity can. When opportunity for action comes, these pilots must have considered judgment, ability to make the correct tactical decision, and above all to act quickly. Since it takes but thirty seconds for a submarine to submerge, and another thirty seconds to get beyond lethal range, every second is precious. Their skills have to be varied. In addition to flying their planes, they must be superlatively proficient in glide bombing, low-level bombing, rocket firing, searchlight runs, strafing, and in other specialized antisubmarine warfare skills such as the use of the sonobuoy—this last of itself a sufficient field for the normal person.

With the development of night flying, a totally new field has been opened for the pilot. First came the use of parachute flares to provide illumination for night attacks on radar contacts. Later, peak efficiency was to be provided by the adoption of the 55,000,000 candlepower searchlight as an illuminant. Requiring low-level flying (100 feet maximum ceiling), a shift from instrument to contact and back to instrument flying, and all this while developing a radar contact requires infinite skill and judgment by the pilot—not to mention the important part he must play in the actual bombing. Meanwhile, the plane must be kept oriented so that a safe return to the carrier may be assured. Small wonder, therefore, that the pilots of Composite Squadrons are a breed known only to the United States Navy.[53]

While the *Block Island, Bogue,* and *Guadalcanal* were operating against the U-boats, two other "jeeps" were seeing some new territory. The *Mission Bay* and the newly arrived *Wake Island* had been assigned the task of delivering badly needed aircraft and troops to India. Leaving New York on 20 February as TG 27.2, the two flattops and their screens were routed via Recife and Capetown, South Africa (where they received an impressive welcome) to Karachi. On the return trip they put into Durban, South Africa and Bahia, Brazil.[54] Aside from the bumps and bruises suffered by the "pollywogs" as they were initiated upon crossing the equator, the mission was quite tame. But it was typical work for these "jacks-of-all-trades," the escort carriers. From hunting submarines and escorting convoys to ferry missions carrying troops and aircraft, there was always something for the "jeeps" to do.

Dan Gallery's *Guadalcanal* was the next carrier to leave Norfolk, steaming out on 7 March. Accompanying her were her usual screen of the destroyer *Forrest* and four destroyer escorts. For air operations the carrier now had on board Lieutenant Commander Richard K. Gould's VC-58. After the fiasco on the earlier mission, Gallery was itching to see how his plan for true night-flying operations would work. Unfortunately, the weather wouldn't cooperate on the way to Casablanca, and night flying would have to wait until the return trip.

The trip over to Casablanca was remarkably routine; the U-boats were lying low during the day and only coming up at night, so Gallery's fliers were not finding anything. One of the few "sightings" reported provided a few chuckles later. On the 19th a TBF reported an unidentified warship near the task group. This ship answered the recognition signal incorrectly, and the *Chatelain* was sent to investigate. When the aircraft returned, it was discovered that the "unidentified" ship had been the *Chatelain*. "An error of approximately 15 miles in pilot's navigation plus incorrect reception of recognition signals by both plane and ship resulted in sending the USS *Chatelain* to investigate herself."[55]

After a short stay in Casablanca, the *Guadalcanal* put to sea again on the 30th. It was not until 8 April, though, that the VC-58 fliers got into the swing of night flying and, in the process, bagged a submarine. At sunset on the 8th four Avengers were launched to patrol 60 miles ahead and 100 miles on each beam of the carrier. After this launch two of the ship's arresting cables became inoperative, so Gallery decided to cancel any more flights that night after the four "Turkeys" had been recovered. A dramatic report from one of the returning pilots quickly changed his mind.

After the planes were recovered around 2115, the crews were being debriefed by Gallery and his operations and intelligence officers. At this time one of the pilots dropped a bombshell. "Cap'n, I almost got him!"

"Wh . . . Wh . . . What do you mean?" Gallery exclaimed.

"That submarine. He barely got under in time to get away after I identified him."

"What submarine?" everyone demanded.

"Didn't you get my radio an hour ago?" came the reply.[56]

In the stir caused by this bit of information, it soon became apparent that somewhere there had been a breakdown in communications. However, when the position of the sighting was plotted, it was found that the U-boat would still probably be well within range of the *Guadalcanal*'s aircraft. Despite the inoperative arresting cables, Gallery decided the destruction of the submarine was worth any landing problems later. It was also decided to wait about an hour before sending planes out in order to give the sub a chance to surface.

Two Avengers were launched at 2215, and several others made ready. As the planes were being sent off, a friendly B-24 circled TG 21.11 for about ten minutes, then followed the Avengers to the spot where the U-boat had last been seen. "Apparently this plane's only motive was idle curiosity or perhaps a desire for company on a dark night a long way from home because all efforts to establish radio contact with him and get him to lend a hand in the search were fruitless. After he had seen all he wanted, he went on about his business and missed the beginning of the big hunt a half hour later."[57]

The submarine was still in the area. She was the 1,120-ton *U-515* under the command of Kapitanleutnant Werner Henke, who was one of Doenitz's "Aces," having sunk twenty-seven ships. Henke was tough and smart, but he met his match this day. At 2330 one of the TBF pilots saw *U-515* silhouetted in a wedge of moonlit sea. The Avenger jumped *U-515*, but the two depth bombs dropped did no damage. Henke's alert crew met their attacker with a good deal of gunfire that also did no damage. However, Henke was forced to stop his battery recharging and "pull the plug."

Without a full charge Henke was in a bad spot. The *Guadalcanal* was only 40 miles away and heading for the contact. At 0116 on the 9th the carrier launched another TBF to assist in the search, and about forty-five minutes later the *Guadalcanal* got a radar contact on an object only 5 miles distant. This contact was probably on either *U-68* or *U-214*, both of which were also in the area. Meanwhile, the *Chatelain*'s search for *U-515* was unsuccessful, as was the *Pope*'s hedgehog attack on another contact at about the same time.

Another aircraft found an oil slick in the gray light of dawn near the scene of the *Pope*'s attack. Submarine noises were heard on sonobuoys but they were probably from *U-68* or *U-214*. At 0630 the *Pillsbury* and the *Flaherty* were detached to help in the search. About ten minutes later an Avenger caught *U-515* on the surface and straddled the boat with depth bombs, Henke was able to take his boat down again with no damage. The *Pillsbury* and the *Flaherty* were directed to the scene of the last contact. As the *Pillsbury* was going about her search, a loud explosion was felt and heard close aboard the DE. It was later thought that this explosion was from an acoustic torpedo set off by the ship's "Foxer." (It is possible that the torpedo was fired by *U-214*.)

The two destroyer escorts continued to comb the area, occasionally loosing a barrage of hedgehogs, but Henke was taking his boat deeper and deeper to evade these attacks. *U-515*'s lifespan grew shorter by the minute, however, as the *Chatelain* (and then the *Pope*) joined the other two vessels. At 1030 the *Pope* obtained a dubious sound contact on an object 700 yards distant. The contact was lost, then regained, and *U-515* was caught. "Contact was maintained constantly until the sinking four hours later."[58]

For the next four hours the ocean rumbled and boiled as the four destroyer escorts laid their "ash cans." An oil slick and air bubbles that came to the surface at 1250 encouraged the hard-working crews to redouble their efforts. While their boat had been being pummeled, *U-515*'s crew were also working hard to stem a number of oil and water leaks. The boat was soon almost 30 degrees by the stern. The aft torpedo compartment was closed off, and all available men were sent forward to balance the U-boat.

Even this did little good. Henke had the aft fuel tanks blown, and this helped to return the submarine to an even keel. But soon she began to become bow-heavy from water flowing through the boat and air expanding in her aft section. Unable to vent the blown aft tanks, Henke saw that he would have to surface. At a 45-degree bow-down angle, *U-515* shot to the surface.

In the meantime, the Americans had lost sonar contact. A scouting line was ordered formed. At 1659, when the line had hardly begun moving, the *Chatelain* regained contact and immediately laid a pattern. Only four of the charges had been fired when *U-515* broached in a welter of white water and black oil only seventy-five yards abaft the *Chatelain*'s starboard beam.

Seven more charges were fired from the ship's K-guns, of which two landed on the U-boat's deck and then rolled off. Germans poured out of the hatches to man their guns. They were able to get off only a few shots before a fusillade of fire from the *Chatelain* and the *Flaherty* cleared the decks. The *Flaherty* also fired a torpedo, which missed *U-515* and took off after the *Pillsbury*. The torpedo chased the destroyer escort until an aircraft strafed the torpedo and sank it.

A few miles away the *Guadalcanal*'s crew had a ringside seat for *U-515*'s final moments. An Avenger and two Wildcats circled the U-boat, strafing and firing rockets at the doomed vessel. At 1908 the sub was shaken by an internal explosion (possibly caused by a rocket hit), and her crew began to abandon ship. Four minutes later *U-515* lifted up "like a cobra rearing its head to strike" and sank.[59] From the *Guadalcanal*'s bridge came an old whaling shout, "Thar she blows . . . and sparm at that!"[60] The U-boat went to her grave some 175 miles northwest of Funchal. Henke and forty-two of his men were fished from the water.[61]

Later, Henke and Gallery had a number of meetings that led Gallery to use some devious methods to gain information from his prisoner. It was obvious to Gallery that Henke was quite conceited and only grudgingly gave his crew any credit for *U-515*'s successes. Perhaps this could be used to his advantage, Gallery thought.[62]

Then Gallery learned that Henke had sunk the British liner *Ceramic* in December 1942. Only one person from her crew and passengers (including women and children) had survived. The British had discovered that it was Henke who had sunk their liner, and they were anxious to get their hands on him.

Gallery decided that this knowledge might also be useful. He had a fake message written that read, "British Admiralty requests you turn over crew of *U-515* to them when you refuel Gibraltar. Considering crowded conditions your ship authorize you to use your discretion."[63]

Gallery also had another statement (written on legal paper and adorned with the ship's seal) drawn up for Henke to sign. This said, "I, Captain Lieutenant Werner Henke, promise on my honor as a German officer that if I and my

crew are imprisoned in the United States instead of England,
I will answer all questions truthfully when I am interrogated
by Naval Intelligence Officers."[64]

A despairing Henke, naturally uncomfortable about what
might happen to him in England, signed. Gallery then made
sure a photostat of this note circulated among Henke's men.
Henke later repudiated this note, but many of his crew were
cooperative with their interrogators.

(It should be noted that Ladislas Farago, in his book *The
Tenth Fleet*, mentions that a German historian believes this
episode to be a total fabrication.[65] Perhaps so. Yet it does have
a certain credibility.)

Around this time another group of U-boats were heading
for the Far East. Most of them made it through, as there had
been a break in the barrier when the *Bogue* headed for
Trinidad, and the *Guadalcanal* had not yet got on station.
However, one of these boats ran afoul of the "Can Do," with
fatal results for the submarine. After *U-515* had been sunk, it
was realized that there had been more than one submarine
nearby. *U-488* had been in the vicinity to fuel *U-129*, *U-66*,
U-537, *U-68*, and the now-departed *U-515*. At 0259 on the
10th *U-214* was caught on the surface by an Avenger and
depth-bombed, but she escaped with little damage.[66]

When *U-214* reported that a carrier was in the area,
U-boat Command changed *U-488*'s rendezvous point. But it
was not changed soon enough to save *U-68*.[67] Dawn was just
breaking on the 10th when a pair of Avengers and a Wildcat
(sent to search the area of the earlier attacks) saw *U-68* on the
surface silhouetted against the slowly brightening horizon.
The fight was over quickly.

The planes swept in from the still-dark western sky and
caught the Germans flatfooted. The first Avenger slammed
home several rockets and then returned in the face of heavy
but belated antiaircraft fire to drop two Mk. 47 depth bombs
just aft of the conning tower. Oil began to stream from the
U-boat. Lieutenant Commander Gould swooped down to
rake the sub with devastating machine-gun fire. The antiaircraft fire stopped, and the second Avenger took advantage of
this pause to deliver an accurate rocket attack, followed by a
depth bomb attack. About 0535 *U-68* sank, leaving a large
greenish-colored oil slick and an enormous air bubble. One
survivor, who had been left on deck when the submarine
tried to dive, was later pulled from the oil scum, in which

pieces of cork, air flasks, clothing, and fragments of bodies also floated.[68]

U-515 and *U-68* were the only U-boats the *Guadalcanal* bagged this cruise, but Gallery was well pleased with the results and especially with the night air operations. His fliers, after their initial concern over night landings on what seemed, to them, a postage-stamp size deck, became very proficient in the demanding art. The one major problem his aircraft encountered had been with the three MAD-equipped Avengers. Though they had been present in all attacks, their equipment had been useless, and it had been sonobuoys that provided the best information to the Avenger crews. Gallery had also changed his mind on doing away with the fighter complement on the CVEs, as he had recommended after the *Guadalcanal*'s first cruise. He now found the Wildcats to be most valuable in beating down defensive fire and also in spotting submarines from a distance.[69]

Gallery's most telling point about this mission was stated in his Action Report: "The most impressive feature of this cruise was that 2,100 hours of intensive daylight operations accomplished nothing whereas 200 hours of night flying resulted in two kills."[70] From now on the aviators flying off all the "jeeps" would have to be proficient in both day and night operations.

When the *Guadalcanal* put into Norfolk on 26 April, Gallery was toying with a new idea. *U-515* had been fatally damaged, and Henke, a tough customer, had surfaced to enable his crew to escape. But what if a submarine had not been fatally damaged, but her crew (perhaps not as tough) thought she had? This vessel would be vulnerable to boarding if the attackers could be restrained from filling the U-boat full of holes. Gallery considered the possibilities with a gleam in his eye.

Three more "jeeps" had followed the *Guadalcanal* to sea in March. The *Tripoli* had been next out on the 15th, followed by the *Solomons* on 21 March (see Chapter 9) and the *Croatan* on 24 March. Captain Wendell G. Switzer's *Tripoli* was a brand-new *Casablanca*-class carrier that had only arrived at Norfolk on 16 February. There she boarded the *Core*'s veteran squadron VC-13. Unfortunately for the fliers, this cruise would be relatively unspectacular.

"Aside from awards and attacks," the VC-13 historian would report, "the only breaks in the routine of alternate

patrols and sunbaths were afforded by two water landings.
The same pilot and crew were picked up from a raft shortly
after each landing."[71]

After escorting Convoy UGS-36 for a few days, the
Tripoli and the five destroyer escorts of Escort Division
(CortDiv) 7 headed south for Recife. There TG 21.14 fueled
and provisioned on 5–7 April. Putting back to sea, the *Tripoli*
hunted unsuccessfully for U-boats until the morning of the 19th.
Shortly before sunrise Lieutenant (jg) C. B. Humphrey caught
U-543 on the surface waiting to rendezvous with her milch
cow, *U-488*. In the face of spirited antiaircraft fire, Humphrey
made three attacks—the first with rockets, an unsuccessful
run on the second when his depth bombs wouldn't release,
and a Fido drop on his third pass. None of these attacks had
any effect on *U-543*, however. She escaped despite the efforts
of two escorts and several planes to locate her.[72]

Nevertheless, this attack broke up the rendezvous and
forced the Germans once again to change a meeting place for
their U-boats. There were few places left in the Atlantic
where a submarine was safe anymore.[73]

The *Croatan*'s cruise turned out to be much more successful than those of the other CVEs. The *Croatan* had a new
skipper, Captain John P. W. Vest, and a new squadron,
VC-42. Rounding out Vest's TG 21.15 were the destroyer
escorts *Frost*, *Inch*, *Huse*, *Barber*, and *Snowden*. Embarked
on the carrier for this cruise was Escort Division 13's commander, Commander Frank D. Giambattista. This practice of
having the commander of the screen ride in the carrier
instead of one of the DEs was a new idea being evaluated by
the Atlantic Fleet's Antisubmarine Warfare Unit. Early reports indicated that this idea was worth serious consideration.[74]

After leaving Hampton Roads, the task group initially
headed east along the North African convoy routes. On the
26th Captain Vest received new orders to proceed to a point
southeast of Nova Scotia to catch two westbound U-boats that
Tenth Fleet estimated to be in the area of 40°00′N, 52°00′W.
The next day, as routine patrols covered their sectors without
results, the TBM (the General Motors version of the Avenger) of Lieutenant (jg) James B. Nelson crashed during its
search, and before any rescue attempt could be mounted, a
dense fog settled around the task group. When the fog lifted
two days later, the three crewmen had disappeared.[75]

Despite this tragedy, the search for the elusive U-boats

Destroyer Escort (DE)

had to go on. However, after several days of hunting with no success, Vest decided he needed more help, and two groups of destroyers were sent to assist on 1 April. These ships ran down several contacts during the next two days, but were unsuccessful in destroying any submarines. On the 3rd these ships were replaced by the seven destroyers of TU's 27.6.1 and 27.6.2. These destroyers had as little luck as their predecessors until they ran across *U-856* on 7 April.

The *Croatan* had launched two Avengers at 0325 on a routine search mission. The night was very black, with no moon, because of a heavy overcast. Beneath the planes as they droned through the darkness, waves up to thirty feet high surged across the ocean. About 0400 Lieutenant Wilburt A. Lyons's radioman got a blip on his radar, distance 4½ miles. Lyons was homed in to the contact by his radioman, but nothing was seen in the blackness when the target's position was reached.

Suddenly, gun flashes could be seen, and tracers zipped

by the plane. Lyons attempted to drop a flare without
success, but in the process dropped his Fido instead. (It was
the policy of the *Croatan* to carry rockets and Fido only; no
depth bombs were carried. This reliance on only two weapons may have caused VC-42 to miss several attacks on this
cruise.[76]) Lyons dropped sonobuoys, but could hear nothing.

Thirty minutes later the second plane that had been
launched earlier joined Lyons. The sonobuoys Lyons had
dropped were still operating, but *U-856* was apparently lying
quiet as there was no sound coming over the buoys. A
four-plane killer team (two Avengers and two Wildcats) had
been launched at 0600 to join in the search. They dropped
more sonobuoys, but these too were unsuccessful in pinpointing
the location of the U-boat.

At 0710 the four destroyers of TU 27.6.2 arrived to take
over the search. The "tin cans" formed a patrol line to comb
the area, with each ship about 3,000 yards from the others.
An hour later the *Boyle* had a sonar contact at 950 yards.
Because the sea was so rough, causing the sound indications
to fade in and out, the *Boyle* didn't drop any depth charges
on her first run. A strong sonar contact was then made, and
the destroyer charged in to lay an eleven-charge pattern set
for 200 to 300 feet. As these charges were being dropped, a
periscope was seen close aboard and directly astern of the
destroyer.

U-856 had popped up. Just prior to the *Boyle*'s run,
U-856's captain had brought his boat up to periscope depth to
see what was causing the noises reverberating through his
boat. (His hydrophones were not working at the time.) What
he saw was frightening. "His first look through the periscope
disclosed a shower of depth charges encompassing the U-boat."[77]
As soon as the depth charges had gone off, he took his boat
deep. The *Boyle* reversed course quickly, but lost contact
with the submarine.

The three vessels of TU 27.6.1 arrived at 0915, followed
by the DEs *Huse* and *Frost* (detached from the *Croatan*'s
screen to aid in the search). It was now planned to conduct a
box search, with the *Frost* and TU 27.6.1 scouting westward
and TU 27.6.2 and the *Huse* searching eastward from the
location of the *Boyle*'s attack. The two destroyer escorts were
operating separately so that each group would have a ship
armed with hedgehog. It was afternoon before the hunters
picked up a trace of *U-856*. At 1542 the *Champlin* got a good

sonar contact but shortly lost it again. The rough seas were giving the sonar operators fits.

The *Huse* was sent to help the *Champlin*. Finding the sub again, they made well-coordinated attacks that soon brought *U-856* to the surface. A hedgehog attack by the *Huse* had yielded two muffled explosions. Then the *Champlin* followed with a nine-charge deep attack based on the *Huse*'s calculations, and these were on target.

Inside the submarine, water was entering through the main bilge pump. During one depth charge explosion, the hand wheel of the main blowing valve was torn out of its socket and hurled across the control room. *U-856* was becoming very stern-heavy. Meanwhile, the *Huse* had regained contact only to have her hedgehog misfire. The *Champlin* took over to deliver a nine-charge medium-depth pattern, and these charges inflicted more damage. Water began to pour into *U-856*'s motor and stern compartments. There was just enough air left to blow the tanks and surface.

At 1700 *U-856* lurched to the surface where she was taken under fire by both ships. The Germans were not in any mood to fight, just trying to abandon ship. However, their exit was blocked when the conning tower hatch stuck. A crowbar finally pried it open. The *Champlin*'s skipper, Commander John J. Schaffer, brought his ship in to ram the dying sub. The destroyer hit the submarine's stern solidly (causing considerable hull damage to the destroyer), then slid off. The *Huse* also tried to ram, but missed. The attackers circled the U-boat, pouring out devastating volleys of gunfire at short range.

There was no return fire, yet the Americans suffered casualties. As the *Champlin* circled, the 20-mm gun on her port bridge was traversed to remain on target. A restricting cam broke, permitting the gun to swing too far. A shell from the gun struck a nearby ammunition ready-box and detonated it. Shrapnel hurled into the bridge, mortally wounding Commander Schaffer and injuring three others. It was an unfortunate ending to a well-executed attack by the *Champlin* and the *Huse*. A few minutes later *U-856* went down, a heavy underwater explosion announcing her demise. Three officers and twenty-five men were plucked out of the rough sea.[78]

Captain Vest's task group had more to celebrate than just the sinking of *U-856*. Following the sinking, they got some welcome news. The *Croatan* and her screen were heading to Bermuda for fueling and a short rest. After the monotony of the leaden skies and slate gray seas of the North Atlantic, the deep blue of the Bermuda waters, the green foliage, and the vivid colors of the houses brightened everyone's spirits considerably. After a few days of bicycling around the island, enjoying the beaches and the sun, and lifting a few at the taverns, they were all refreshed and ready to head back to combat.

On 12 April the *Croatan* left Bermuda bound for the Cape Verde Islands to hunt a submarine reported there. For almost two weeks nothing was found, though a transmission from the homeward-bound *U-66* was picked up by both the *Croatan's* and Tenth Fleet's "Huff-Duffs" on the night of 19–20 April. As no bearing was obtained on this transmission, she was able to escape. Her days were numbered, however, because Tenth Fleet was building quite a dossier on her based on information gathered from her numerous urgent messages to U-boat Command. Because *U-66* was badly in need of fuel and supplies, Doenitz scheduled a rendezvous for her with *U-488* on the 26th.[79] There would be other, unwelcome, visitors at this meeting place, for Tenth Fleet had put its finger on the rendezvous, and the *Croatan* would be nearby.

U-66 was sighted briefly on the night of the 25th, but dove before the plane making the sighting could attack. (The Antisubmarine Warfare Unit was quite concerned about VC-42's tactics regarding attacks on surfaced submarines at night. Four times during this cruise planes found U-boats on the surface, but failed to deliver attacks before the boats submerged. Too much time had been wasted climbing to drop flares or circling to gain an optimum attack position. Captain P. R. Heineman of the ASW Unit remarked bluntly, "Something is wrong here."[80])

More aircraft were dispatched to the scene, but sonobuoys picked up no trace of the submarine. The *Frost* and the *Huse*, followed later by the other escorts, were also sent to ferret out the enemy. At 0440 on 26 April the *Frost* obtained a sound contact on a target 1,000 yards distant. It was not *U-66*, which escaped to live a few more days, but her supply vessel, *U-488*. This veteran milch cow (which had fueled boats of the *Trutz* group back in June 1943) had already been chased from place to place by the operations of the American CVEs during the last few weeks, and her time had run out.

The *Frost's* first run was spoiled because her hedgehog was not ready to fire, but her second approach yielded three underwater explosions after the hedgehogs were fired. The ocean was so calm that the DE's sonar operators were continually thwarted by poor returns caused by the ship's own wake. Although a radar target was noted briefly a short time later, both this contact and the sonar contact were lost. Nearby, the crew of *U-66* could hear clearly the explosions and "sinking noises."[81]

In the afternoon an oil slick was seen forming in the area of the *Frost*'s attacks. This slick persisted for the next two days, growing larger until it covered a 10-mile diameter. Nevertheless, the Americans were unsure of a kill because several sonar returns had been obtained and lost during this time. On the morning of the 29th the five destroyer escorts swept through the oil slick to deliver a massive depth charge attack on a target estimated to be 560 feet down. Several explosions were noted, but, other than the oil already present, no debris rose to the surface to indicate a success. The *Croatan*'s group eventually received a Class B Assessment ("probably sunk") from CominCh on these attacks, but *U-488* had actually reached her final port.[82]

The *Croatan*'s group was relieved by the *Block Island*'s TG 21.11 on 29 April. Captain Hughes was more impressed with the possibility of a U-boat sinking than CominCh. He radioed Captain Vest, "If you don't have a sub, you've struck oil. Stake your claim!"[83]

The *Croatan*'s escorts fueled from a tanker in Convoy UGS-40 on 1 May, then spent the next several days making numerous attacks on what was thought to be a submarine. This massive expenditure of depth charges and hedgehogs brought no debris to the surface, and if there actually had been a U-boat present, she escaped. A frustrated task group finally left the area on the 6th, bound for home.

The carrier's cruise had not been a bad one. Two submarines had been sunk by the escorts and other vessels. Nevertheless, the Atlantic Fleet's ASW Unit was concerned. As mentioned earlier, VC-42's tactics were considered below average. Also, the *Croatan*'s policy of not having her Avengers carry depth charges was thought to be very questionable. Finally, and very surprisingly, the captains of the destroyer escorts had not been given any information regarding sonobuoys and had never heard of the Fido! It was a situation that displeased the ASW Unit considerably.[84]

But it was analyses like this one of the *Croatan*'s mission by Captain Heineman and the ASW Unit, and recommendations by the various ship commanders, that enabled the Navy to implement changes to increase the efficiency and coordination of all units organized into hunter-killer groups. To the dismay of the enemy, these after-action comments usually brought results.

After it became apparent that *U-488* was not going to return home, the B.d.U.'s War Diary stated grimly: "Refueling even in mid-Atlantic will be scarcely possible in future. This situation will continue until the introduction of submerged oiling.

"Until then refueling will only be carried out in urgent cases from fighting boats.

"All boats have received instructions to commence return passage in good time so that they can reach port without refueling."[85]

Two more "jeeps" were out patrolling before the *Croatan* dropped anchor in Hampton Roads. Captain J. R. Dudley's *Core* group left Norfolk on 3 April. Embarked on the carrier was Lieutenant F. M. Welch's VC-36. En route to Casablanca the task group operated against enemy submarines north of the Azores and near Madeira. After a short stay in Casablanca the *Core* searched south of the Azores, and she arrived back in the United States on 30 May.

During this cruise a number of radar, sonar, and visual contacts were made on possible U-boats, but nothing was found on follow-up. The closest the *Core* came to bagging a submarine was on 26 May. That day a boarding party from a U-boat searched a Portuguese freighter and forcibly removed a British subject. Unfortunately, this incident occurred just outside the range of the VC-36 aircraft, and, in fact, the U-boat was gone before the *Core* was aware of the incident.

One other incident broke the monotony of the daily operations. The Spanish vessel *Monte Alberta* was boarded by a party from one of the escorts after she was thought to be acting suspiciously. All her papers were found to be in order, however, and she was ordered on.

Hampering the *Core*'s operations of this mission was the fact that few of VC-36's pilots had been trained in night flying. Several pilots volunteered for night operations and were used, but a fatal takeoff crash on 20 May brought an end to these operations.[86]

Whereas the *Core* drew a series of blanks during her mission, the *Block Island*'s cruise would turn out to be one of the most exciting of the war.

TWO SHIPS

The war in the Atlantic continued though the Germans were obviously on the defensive in 1944. Atlantic area shipping losses to U-boats had decreased dramatically by the spring of 1944, as compared to the terrible losses suffered in 1942 and early 1943 (from a high of 636,907 tons sunk in November 1942 to only 7,048 tons in February 1944). Still, the submarines were always waiting, ready to pounce on unwary vessels, and there would be only one other month for the remainder of the war when losses were lower than the February figure.[1]

It was not just merchant vessels that could fall prey to the U-boats; combatant ships could also be victims, as was revealed only too clearly in May of 1944. One unfortunate vessel to be forcibly reminded of this was the *Block Island*.

Captain Hughes brought his ship out of the sheltered waters of Hampton Roads on 22 April 1944. Hughes commanded TG 21.11, which consisted (besides his flattop) of the destroyer escorts *Ahrens*, *Barr*, *Buckley*, and *Eugene E. Elmore*. Aboard the carrier was Lieutenant Commander B. A. Miles's VC-55. The task group had been ordered to relieve the *Croatan*'s group west of the Cape Verde Islands.

The *Block Island* went by way of Bermuda to give her escorts and aircraft extra training time before heading east to the operational area. On 29 April the *Croatan*'s group was sighted. After "obtaining tactful information on the operating area via VHF," the *Block Island* relieved her sister ship.[2] It was thought that a milch cow (*U-488*, which the *Croatan*'s

179

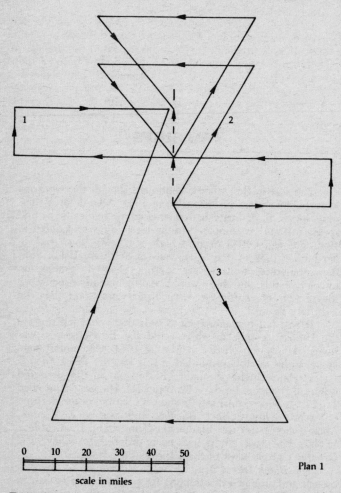

Typical search pattern used by CVEs in the Atlantic. *Block Island*
three TBM night search, April–May 1944.

group had already sunk) was operating in the area, and TG 21.11 was detailed to find her.

U-488 was gone now, but U-66 (which heretofore had led a charmed life) was still hanging around, badly in need of fuel. It had originally been intended for U-66 to take on supplies and fuel from U-488 or U-515, but both of these boats had been sunk. U-boat Command next planned a rendezvous for U-66 with U-68 and U-188. But once again the Americans had been on the scene, with the *Guadalcanal* taking care of U-68. Finally, the Germans planned for U-66 to meet U-188 and for both boats later to pick up more supplies from another pair of U-boats, because U-66 was now in

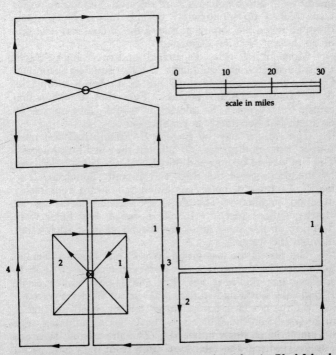

Typical search pattern used by CVEs in the Atlantic. *Block Island* typical square search patterns.

serious straits. To the Germans it must have seemed that they were always one step behind the Americans.[3]

Captain Hughes thought that *U-488* was still nearby, waiting to fuel a north-bound U-boat (*U-66*). This impression was heightened on 1 May when Tenth Fleet sent him an HF/DF fix on a boat about 50 miles west of Santo Antao. This fix put the submarine within 150 miles of the *Block Island*'s present position.

Searches were begun immediately, which before long discovered submarine activity. Late on the evening of the 1st, a TBM/FM night search team spotted *U-66*'s wake a few miles distant. The U-boat was seen momentarily, then lost in the darkness. A faint swirl where the boat had dived was finally seen, and sonobuoys were released. Submarine noises were picked up immediately on the buoys. A Fido was dropped when the sounds indicated the U-boat was near one of the buoys. Nothing happened.

More aircraft were dispatched, and they almost caught the submarine around midnight. She had surfaced again, and an Avenger was able to drop one depth bomb before she dove. Another TBM dropped a Fido, but a malfunction caused the weapon to be released unarmed. Once more *U-66* escaped, but her time was running out.

The *Ahrens* and the *Eugene E. Elmore* had also been sent to assist in digging *U-66* out, but they had little success. The sun was up by now and the U-boat was being held down by the presence of the ships and aircraft. Tantalizing fragments of submarine noises continued to be heard from freshly dropped sonobuoys. The ships and aircraft made several attacks without success. (In one instance, two Fidos were dropped at the same time and began chasing each other through the water.[4])

The rest of the task group arrived, and Hughes decided to initiate "hold-down" tactics and eventually force *U-66* to surface. For the next few days the U-boat was tracked. Periodically she would surface, but aircraft were always waiting to force her back down. These sightings enabled Hughes to keep tabs on the sub. Inside the U-boat, conditions were becoming increasingly unbearable. The air was foul, moisture was everywhere, the men were tired from their long patrol and a lack of vitamins. The crew of *U-66* were just about at the breaking point—which they finally reached on the night of 5–6 May.

Earlier in the day the *Ahrens* and the *Elmore* had been sent 60 miles ahead of the group to search along the submarine's projected track. This left the *Buckley* and the *Barr* to screen the carrier. At 2122 *U-66* popped up (much closer than expected) only 5,000 yards off the *Block Island*'s starboard quarter. The sub's captain, Oberleutnant Gerhard Seehausen, needed to get fresh air into his boat and had taken this moment to put in an appearance.

As *U-66* surfaced, the *Block Island*'s radar picked up her presence. The carrier sheered away in great haste, and Hughes ordered Lieutenant Commander Brent M. Abel's *Buckley* to go after the target. Abel found nothing, as *U-66* dove when her crew discovered where they were. For the next few hours the *Buckley* crisscrossed the area, but there was no sign of the elusive U-boat. She was to remain hidden for a few more hours until Lieutenant (jg) Jimmie J. Sellars, flying an Avenger stripped for night searches, found the sub back on the surface only 18 miles from the carrier.

Sellars radioed the flattop, and the *Buckley* was sent charging to the scene. The sea was calm, a gentle northeasterly breeze floated through the air, and the moon was almost full—too romantic a setting for the battle to come. Seehausen kept his boat moving erratically on the surface, afraid the plane buzzing overhead would bomb him when he dove. Little did he know that Sellars was armed only with a .45-caliber pistol! And he also did not know that the real danger, the *Buckley*, was approaching rapidly from the south.

While surfaced, Seehausen sent a message to U-boat Command telling of the strain his crew and boat were enduring. He also mentioned that he had attempted an attack on the *Block Island* with no success. He then noted the aircraft droning overhead and, in plaintive tones, reported the "middle of Atlantic worse than Bay of Biscay."[5]

It took the *Buckley* forty-five minutes to reach the scene, but Sellars kept Lieutenant Commander Abel fully informed of the sub's position. The DE made radar contact with the U-boat, then 14,000 yards away, at 0245. A minute later Abel brought his ship to general quarters. The *Buckley* came up the moon's path, still undetected by *U-66*'s lookouts who were concentrating on Sellars's plane. As the range dropped, Abel ordered his ship's sound gear secured, depth charges set on shallow, and the "Foxer" gear streamed. Abel discarded his earlier plan to use torpedoes.

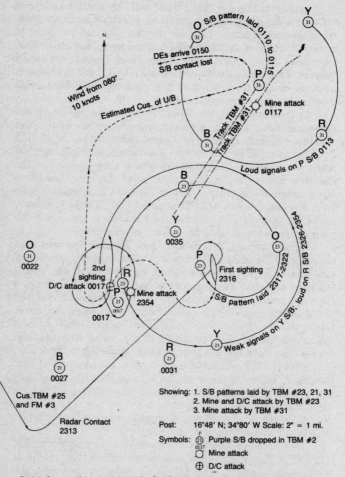

Initial attacks on *U-66* by VC-55 aircraft, 1 May 1944.

Still bothered by Sellars's persistence, the sub's gunners loosed a burst at his plane at 0308. With commendable bravado, Sellars replied with his pistol. He radioed Abel, "The s.o.b. is taking a few shots at me and I wish I had something to throw back at him."[6] The *Buckley's* crew, however, took the gunfire to be recognition flares signaling a rendezvous with a milch cow.

At 0317, when *U-66* was 2 miles away, her shape could be seen black against the silvery sparkles of the moonlit water. Abel turned left to unmask his guns and to expose his "Foxer" to acoustic torpedoes that might be sent the *Buckley's* way. About this time the Germans finally saw the destroyer escort bearing down on them. Seehausen, who was below, was called to the bridge. The U-boat opened fire inaccurately, but the *Buckley's* return fire was right on.

The *Buckley's* three-inchers opened fire at 0320. Their first salvo scored a hit at the base of the conning tower. The

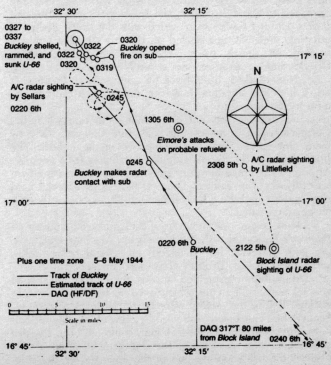

Final attacks on *U-66*, 5–6 May 1944.

40-mms and 20-mms joined in the deadly chorus, raking the sub's deck. Sellars radioed the *Block Island*, "*Buckley* has opened fire—sub is returning fire. Boy! I have never before seen such concentration! *Buckley* is cutting hell out of the conning tower."[7]

The Germans fired back, but were able only to put a small hole in the *Buckley*'s stack. The DE crossed astern of *U-66*, and the sub began to slip out of the moon's wake. A torpedo was reported approaching off the starboard bow, and Abel ordered right full rudder to avoid it. (This sighting may have been an imaginative one. Conflicting survivor statements indicate *U-66* fired no torpedoes.)

Abel maneuvered his ship to place the sub up-moon once more and began to close with *U-66*, which was cranking up speed to about 19 knots. The *Buckley* resumed fire, and *U-66*'s conning tower was covered with the firefly flashes of bursting shells. A fire started on the sub's bridge but was snuffed out shortly by a direct hit from a 3-inch shell. Oberleutnant Seehausen was severely wounded about this time. Nevertheless, he ordered his crew to keep fighting. It was a hopeless situation, however, and he soon ordered the men to abandon ship.[8]

The *Buckley* was not close enough to ram when the Germans began to leave their boat. But Abel and his crew were unaware of what was happening on the U-boat. The *Buckley* closed the distance rapidly, paralleling *U-66*'s course. At pointblank range her guns smothered the submarine with a deadly sheet of gunfire. Then, at 0329 Abel ordered hard right rudder, and the DE crunched into the U-boat, riding up on her forecastle.

"Men began swarming out of the submarine and up on *Buckley*'s forecastle with their hands up. Machine gun, tommy gun, and rifle fire knock[ed] off several before ship's company realiz[ed] U-boat's crew [was] surrendering."[9]

"Ammunition expended at this time included several general mess coffee cups which were on hand at ready gun station. Two of the enemy were hit in the head with these. Empty shell cases were also used by crew of 3-inch gun, No. 2, to repel boarders. Three-inch guns could not bear. *Buckley* suffered its only casualty of the engagement when a man bruised his fist knocking one of the enemy over the side. Several men, apparently dead, could be seen hanging over the side of the sub's bridge at this time. One German attempting to board was killed with a .45 pistol by the boatswain's mate in charge of the forward ammunition party. Man fell back over the side. Midships repair party equipped with rifles manned the life lines on the starboard side abaft light lock, and picked off several men on the deck of the submarine. Chief Fire Controlman used a tommy gun from the bridge with excellent results."[10]

This barroom brawl hardly lasted a minute before the *Buckley* backed off to keep too many of the Germans (some of whom were armed) from boarding. A group of five armed Germans, huddled together on the DE's forecastle, were disarmed and hustled aft.

Still under power, *U-66* drew ahead rapidly to port, and Abel ordered all engines ahead full. The *Buckley* closed again, and her guns swept the sub's topside. Abel had his starboard K-guns prepared to fire shallow charges. But at 0335:

"Sub, still making about 18 knots, intentionally or out of control, veered sharply to port toward *Buckley*, now alongside at distance of 25 yards with bow abreast of *Buckley*'s bridge. *Buckley* stopped the starboard engine and gave right full rudder in an attempt to swing stern clear and protect shafting. Order given to set depth charges on safe. Sub struck *Buckley* a glancing blow and the bow of the sub rode under *Buckley*'s after engine room. Sub slowly rolled over to 60 degree angle. Personnel on deck had a clear view into the conning tower, which was a flaming shambles. A man on the deck of the sub, attempting to man the gun, disintegrated when hit by four 40-mm shells. Torpedomen threw hand grenades, one of which dropped through the sub's open conning tower hatch before exploding. Twenty-mm guns continued their raking fire. Sub slowly drew aft on starboard side with bow under *Buckley*, scraping along ship's side."[11]

The U-boat staggered astern, still making 15 knots. Flames were shooting from her open hatches. The DE's aft 3-inch gun slammed three more shells into the dying sub before *U-66* slid under the waves. The battle had lasted sixteen minutes. A short time later a heavy underwater explosion was heard. *U-66* was gone.

Attesting to the ferocity of this action was the amount of ammunition the *Buckley* had used—105 rounds of 3-inch,

3,118 rounds of 20-mm and 40-mm, 390 rounds of rifle, pistol, and shotgun, two grenades, and an unrecorded amount of coffee mugs and shell cases.[12]

The *Buckley* did not come out of the battle unscathed. Her starboard shaft had been sheared off, her after engine room holed, and the side of the ship buckled in several places. But she could still steam and fight, and her hard-working crew plunged in immediately to make repairs. For the next three hours (while repair parties worked feverishly) the DE scoured the area, finally recovering thirty-six survivors of the ill-fated submarine. Sadly, two British prisoners from a sunken English merchantman had apparently been on board *U-66*, also. They were not recovered. On the afternoon of 6 May "the somewhat battered *Buckley* was given a royal welcome upon rejoining the TG," where she transferred her prisoners to the carrier.[13]

Because of her damage, the *Buckley* had to be detached from TG 21.11 and sent back to the United States. She reached New York safely under her own power. The *Buckley* had fought an outstanding battle, not necessarily a typical one for a destroyer escort, but one that proved again that the DEs were tough ships that also packed quite a punch. For his conduct of this battle, Lieutenant Commander Abel deservedly received the Navy Cross.[14]

Before the *Buckley* rejoined the task group, the *Elmore* and the *Ahrens* had picked up traces of another intruder in the area. Several attacks were made on the supposed U-boat, and for the next six days the task group carried out intensive hold-down tactics. The attackers believed they had "positively sunk" *U-66*'s refueler. This was not true, but the refueler (*U-188*) had been close enough to see and hear *U-66*'s last battle. Realizing what was going on, she beat a hasty retreat back to Bordeaux.[15]

On the 12th the task group was ordered to look for a south-bound Japanese submarine. The boat, *RO-501*, was in the area, but it was up to the *Bogue*'s group, just arriving to relieve the *Block Island*, to bag the submarine. (See Chapter 9.) After this unsuccessful search the *Block Island*'s group headed for Casablanca, arriving on 18 May. Here the *Robert I. Paine* joined the task group as a replacement for the *Buckley*.

After a five-day stay the *Block Island* put back out to sea.

She would never see another port. It had been reported that
two U-boats were moving south near Madeira, and the *Block
Island* was ordered to intercept them. Day and night searches
from the 25th to the 27th brought no results, though, and
figuring the area had dried up, CinCLant assigned the task
group a new area west of the Azores. Before heading for the
Azores, however, Captain Hughes decided to conduct one
more search on the night of 27–28 May. This last sweep did
find something.

Shortly after midnight on the 28th, a TBM searcher
made radar contact with a target 64 miles north of TG 21.11.
Communication problems and a low ceiling prevented the
pilot from making an attack, however. More aircraft were sent
to the scene, as were two destroyer escorts, but the subsequent contacts were tenuous. Nevertheless, the *Ahrens* fired
twenty-four hedgehogs at a sonar contact. Whatever was in
the area escaped. A constant surveillance was maintained by
ships and aircraft for the rest of the day.

More "Night Owls" were launched that night to search
along the U-boat's projected course. At 0255 on 29 May one
of the unarmed TBMs picked up a strong radar contact on a
target 78 miles from the task group. At this time the weather
was not too promising for a successful attack. It was a black

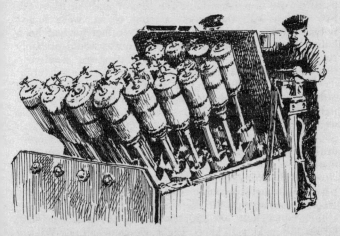

Hedgehog

night, with a solid overcast extending from 2,000 to 6,000 feet. Hughes believed that an attack could be made, and two armed Avengers were sent to help.

The three planes rendezvoused, but one of the attack planes had to retire when its radar malfunctioned. The two remaining TBMs then planned a coordinated attack. The unarmed Avenger would drop a flare and keep tabs on the submarine with its radar, while the other plane would make the attack. The two planes descended through the murky skies until they broke into the clear at 2,500 feet.

As soon as the attack plane got into position, the "Owl" dropped a flare which lit up the area with a sickly yellowish glow. About two minutes later the pilot of the attack plane saw the phosphorescent wake of the U-boat etching the blackness of the water. He dove for his attack and saw the submarine submerging less than 1,000 yards away. Suddenly the flare went out! Literally in the dark and less than 150 feet above the water, the pilot had to pull out. The U-boat disappeared, and subsequent searches could not dig her out. She was still around, however.

After daylight, expanding square searches were made, but the U-boat continued to elude her pursuers. By this time TG 21.11 was 60 miles north of the contact, and all the escorts were in need of fuel. The *Elmore* and the *Barr*, the two vessels with the lowest amount of oil, were fueled between 0800 and 1200. The submarine had not yet been found, but it was estimated that her course would probably be south–southwest. Accordingly, the task group headed in the same direction after fueling.

At 1700 six Wildcats were launched to search out to 100 miles. It was planned to launch six Avengers and a Wildcat radio relay aircraft at 2100 to search farther afield. The weather began deteriorating about 1800, though, and these plans had to be changed. The fighters already aloft were ordered to return to the carrier, but they would not get back in time.

By 1955 it was believed that the task group had proceeded past the U-boat's probable position. Hughes, therefore, decided to backtrack to the north, recover the fighters, and also launch two "Owls." At 2001 the group was steady on 020° (True) and making 15 knots. Eight Avengers and one Wildcat were spotted on the *Block Island*'s flight deck. Off the carrier's port beam was the *Paine*, with the *Ahrens* dead ahead. The *Elmore* was stationed ahead on the starboard side, while the *Barr* trailed behind her abeam the carrier. There was another vessel present, *U-549*.

There was no warning before a torpedo struck the *Block Island* on her port side near frame 12 at 2013. A laundryman below decks was opening a centrifugal dryer when this torpedo hit, and the shock of the explosion threw him into the spinning dryer. Before shipmates could pull him out, the gyrations of the dryer broke a number of his bones. (Despite his injuries, he was floated off the ship later and recovered safely.)[16]

Just a few seconds after the first torpedo hit, a second torpedo slammed into the ship. To some the blast felt "like a truck hitting a concrete wall."[17] There was a shattering blast that knocked people off their feet as this torpedo sliced through several frames of the carrier and exploded in an oil tank. This blast roared through the shaft alley and up through the 5-inch ammunition magazines.

Captain Hughes had been in radar plot when the torpedoes hit. As he rushed to the bridge, he could see that the port side of the flight deck was curled back about ten feet and that oily water covered the forward deck. It was obvious his ship had been "pretty badly hurt."[18] General quarters was sounded and men rushed to their stations, if the torpedoes explosions hadn't already got them started that way.

The *Block Island* had been seriously hurt. Though flank speed had been ordered, she was losing way. Her rudder was jammed hard left, the steering engine was wrecked, and her left engine room was taking in considerable water. These two torpedoes had been quite effective. The ship settled about nine feet by the stern, listing slightly to port. Things did not look good for the "USS F.B.I.," and Captain Hughes ordered his men to prepare to abandon ship. This order had to be passed from man to man as most communications had been lost.

A short time later a periscope was seen off the starboard quarter. An attempt to have the five-inchers fire on the periscope failed when the gunners couldn't spot it. The *Elmore* did see the periscope, however, and raced in to drop a thirteen-charge pattern. Though noisy, these depth charges missed.

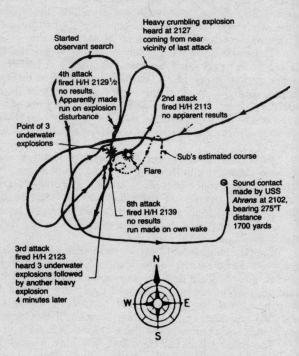

Started
observant search

Heavy crumbling explosion
heard at 2127
coming from near
vicinity of last attack

4th attack
fired H/H 2129½
no results.
Apparently made
run on explosion
disturbance

2nd attack
fired H/H 2113
no apparent results

Point of 3
underwater
explosions

Sub's estimated course

Flare

8th attack
fired H/H 2139
no results
run made on own wake

Sound contact
made by USS
Ahrens at 2102,
bearing 275°T
distance
1700 yards

3rd attack
fired H/H 2123
heard 3 underwater
explosions followed
by another heavy
explosion
4 minutes later

N
W   E
S

Note:
1906-2010 DRT scale 1000 yds. per inch
2010-2024 DRT scale 500 yds. per inch
2024-2046 estimated track of *Elmore*

The sinking of the *Block Island*, 29 May 1944.

As the *Elmore* charged in, a third torpedo hit the *Block
Island* with a tremendous shock. The ship seemed to drop
several feet in the water. A thirty-foot hole was blown in the
aft end of the hangar deck, and an eighteen-inch-wide opening near the aft expansion joint ran clear across the flight deck
and down the side to the hangar deck. Shortly afterward, the
men saw the *Barr* charging in off their port beam for an
attack on the U-boat. She had not streamed her "Foxer" gear,

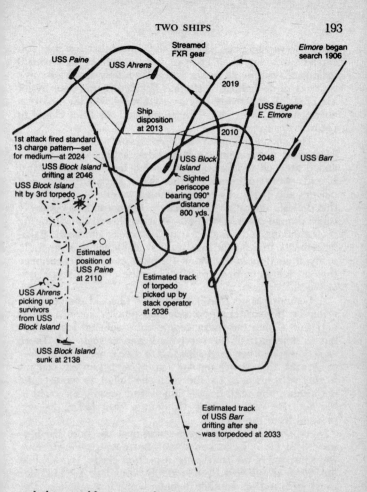

USS *Paine*

USS *Ahrens*

Streamed
FXR gear

Elmore began
search 1906

2019

Ship
disposition
at 2013

USS *Eugene
E. Elmore*

2010

1st attack fired standard
13 charge pattern—set
for medium—at 2024

2048   USS *Barr*

USS *Block Island*
drifting at 2046

USS *Block
Island*

USS *Block Island*
hit by 3rd torpedo

Sighted
periscope
bearing 090°
distance
800 yds.

Estimated
position of
USS *Paine*
at 2110

USS *Ahrens*
picking up
survivors
from USS
Block Island

Estimated track
of torpedo
picked up by
stack operator
at 2036

USS *Block Island*
sunk at 2138

Estimated track
of USS *Barr*
drifting after she
was torpedoed at 2033

and this would prove to be a serious omission. At 2030 an
acoustic torpedo struck the DE in the stern. The men on
board the carrier saw a big cloud of water and smoke suddenly appear off her stern. At first they thought the DE had
found the sub and was working her over, but cheers quickly
changed to a stunned silence as they saw the *Barr*'s stern fold
up.[19] The destroyer escort was out of the fight.

By now Hughes was aware that further damage control

efforts were hopeless. He was also aware that his ship still carried 142 depth charges in her magazines and 65,000 gallons of aviation gas in her tanks. With only about forty-five minutes of daylight left, Hughes decided it was time to get his crew off the dying carrier. At about 2040 the order to abandon ship was given. The *Ahrens* and the *Paine* closed to recover survivors.

The abandonment of the *Block Island* was very orderly. Men went down ropes on both sides of the ship or walked and floated off the fantail as it settled into the water. Most liferafts were gathered on the ship's starboard side, and officers and petty officers maintained excellent control over this delicate operation. Fortunately, the ocean was relatively calm, though covered with oil. Men swallowed the oil during their dunking and coughed it up for weeks afterward. Rafts, whaleboats, and floater nets were available for most men. To many, their time in the water was more of a "fun" experience than a frightening one—possibly because of the inexperience of youth.[20]

Gunner's Mate Third Class Wayne Lee had gone into the water on the carrier's port side and quickly found a floater net. For a time the water temperature seemed reasonable, but as time passed, the survivors began getting cold. There were several other men clinging to Lee's net, but as they grew cold, they struck out for nearby rafts. Lee was content to stay with his net. As others left, he rolled up more of the net around him until he was snugly and warmly cocooned in his net. He did not have too long a wait before he was plucked from the water.[21]

As most of the crew were going over the side, Hughes, several of his officers, corpsmen, and damage control men were inspecting the ship. This inspection clearly showed that the *Block Island* had been mortally wounded. By 2130 her stern had settled another twenty feet. Ten minutes later Hughes ordered all remaining personnel off the ship. But while these activities had been going on, an incident of even greater drama had been occurring elsewhere on the ship.

A sailor's leg had been caught between the forward catwalk and the ship's structure. The carrier's doctor and several other men had been trying for almost an hour to free the man. "Due to the spring in the catwalk, it was impossible to free the man by cutting away the metal, because after each cut was made by the acetylene torch the catwalk continued springing into the side of the ship. As the ship was settling at such a rate that it was imperative for all hands to leave immediately, it was necessary to amputate the man's leg at the knee in order to clear him. This was completed just at the last moment but the man died as he was placed in a stretcher and his body was left aboard."[22]

It was a tragic ending to a heroic effort, as the rescue party had refused to leave the man even as the ship was going down until the doctor had amputated the man's leg with a sheath knife, and they had pulled him free. Especially outstanding in this effort was Chief Carpenter Clarence M. Bailey. He had risked his life a number of times by hanging out over the wrecked port side in attempts to spring the man free. He would receive the Navy and Marine Corps Medal for his superlative efforts.

The *Block Island* was going down faster now. All men remaining on board left the ship quickly for whaleboats standing by. The carrier rolled over 60 degrees, and the aircraft on her deck broke their lashings and slid overboard. Though the planes' depth charges had been set on safe, they exploded about two minutes later. The *Block Island* came out of the water until she was vertical. Her bow pointed at the darkening sky; then, almost regretfully, she slowly disappeared under the water at 2155.

Remarkably, the loss of life in this disaster was very small. Only six men were lost aboard the carrier. The *Paine* picked up 277 survivors, and the *Ahrens* added a sardine-load of 674. The *Barr* had twelve killed and sixteen wounded. But the sinking cost more lives indirectly. The six fighters that had been launched earlier could not land, of course, and were vectored to the Canary Islands. There they had to make night water landings. Only two of the pilots survived these landings.

While the *Block Island* was going through her last fight, the *Elmore* was trying to locate *U-549*. Because the *Ahrens* and the *Paine* were recovering survivors and the *Barr* was out of the battle, it was left to the *Elmore* to avenge the *Block Island*. Several minutes after the *Barr* had been hit, another torpedo searched out the *Elmore*, but missed. Then, at 2102, the *Ahrens* obtained a sonar contact on a target at 1,700 yards. Unable herself to attack, she coached the *Elmore* in.

At 2113 the DE delivered a hedgehog attack, but without any visible results. This run was followed by another hedgehog attack.

Lieutenant Commander George L. Conkey's sharpshooters were on target. Twelve seconds after the projectiles entered the water, there were three sharp explosions. A few minutes later a heavy "crumbling" explosion reverberated throughout the water. The killer, *U-549*, had been killed.

As the darkness deepened, the *Ahrens* and the *Paine* were ordered to clear the area while the *Elmore* remained behind to screen the *Barr*. The next morning the area was scoured by the three DEs and a pair of shore-based bombers. Nothing of consequence was found, and at 0930 the task group, "less *Block Island*," headed for Casablanca. The *Elmore* had to tow the *Barr* in, but all ships arrived safely on 2 June.[23]

The *Block Island* was the only U.S. carrier to be lost in the Atlantic. It was one victory the Germans could crow about because victories like this were few and far between. The survivors of the "USS F.B.I." were taken back to the United States by the *Kasaan Bay*, *Tulagi*, and *Mission Bay*. Many of these survivors would later serve on a new *Block Island* off Okinawa and Balikpapen at the end of the war.

Before some of these men went off to fight the Japanese, however, there was some unfinished business to take care of. Before the *Block Island* had left Norfolk on her last voyage, an argument had started at one of the Norfolk watering holes between the "F.B.I." men and other patrons. During the argument a barmaid became more than a little irritated at the sailors. In an unfortunate remark, she told the *Block Island* men that she hoped their ship would go out and get sunk. Well, the carrier was, and the survivors remembered. When they got back to Norfolk, they made it a point to tear the bar apart.[24]

Just a week after the *Block Island* was sunk, another escort carrier group made history of a better kind. The carrier was the *Guadalcanal*, still under the dynamic hand of Dan Gallery. Her escorts were the ships of CortDiv 4, the *Chatelain*, *Pillsbury*, *Pope*, *Flaherty*, and *Jenks*.

Gallery had been seriously considering the possibility of capturing a U-boat after he had come close with *U-515* in April. On this cruise he planned to do what he had missed

with *U-515*. In the departure conference with his commanding officers and officers from the CinCLant staff, he made his
intentions crystal clear. All ships were told to prepare plans
for a capture and, also, to organize boarding parties.

On 15 May 1944 the *Guadalcanal*'s TG 22.3 departed
Norfolk bound for the Cape Verde Islands. Lieutenant Norman D. Hodson's VC-8 was aboard the carrier for the task
group's air strength. No stranger to escort carriers or to
action against the enemy, Hodson had flown with the *Enter-
prise*'s VF-6 at Pearl Harbor and Midway, and had twice
received the Distinguished Flying Cross for attacks on submarines while flying off the *Card*.

The first two weeks of the cruise were unproductive.
Most of the U-boats heading north or south were staying
inside the islands and close to the African coast.[25] About the
only excitement happened on the 16th, just one day out of
port. A TBM was returning from a routine patrol when its
engine sputtered to a stop. The pilot had run one of his tanks
out of fuel. Before he could switch tanks and get the engine
started again, the plane was only 500 feet above the water.
Seeing their plane going down, his two crewmen bailed out
without orders. This proved fatal to one of the men when his
chute streamed. The Avenger reached the carrier without any
further problems.[26]

On 31 May, TG 22.3 was informed by Tenth Fleet that a
submarine was near enough to be rooted out from her
undersea hole. Tenth Fleet had been eyeing this particular
U-boat for some time. She had first been picked up by the
"Huff-Duff" stations in late March, but the sub had been
plagued by slim pickings in her operational areas, and there
were no sinkings to pinpoint her exact position.

Nevertheless, Tenth Fleet deduced that this boat would
stay out until about the end of May before heading for home.
Their guess was right on the nose. This as-yet unidentified
submarine was located off Portuguese Guinea on 27 May. The
next couple of days of listening showed that the U-boat,
indeed, was heading north. On the 31st it was evident the
vessel was moving straight up the 20th meridian toward Cape
Blanco. The order went out to the *Guadalcanal*, then about
300 miles south of the sub's last position, "Get her!"[27]

This unknown boat was the later-to-be-famous *U-505*.
Her captain was Oberleutnant Harald Lange. Her previous

captain had committed suicide during her last patrol, and
Lange was trying hard to erase the memory of that bizarre
incident from his crew's minds. In spite of patrolling assiduously
and aggressively, Lange had no luck, and U-505 was returning
home empty-handed.

Task Group 22.3 began searching up the 20th meridian
on the evening of the 31st. This course was also quite handy,
as it would lead toward Casablanca. The VC-8 fliers mounted
continuous night searches 125 miles ahead and behind the
task group and 100 miles on each side. The *Guadalcanal* was
catching up rapidly with *U-505* as both ships trekked north.

Lange had been running surfaced at night during the
majority of his patrol, but with the *Guadalcanal*'s planes
beginning to breathe down his neck at night and his *Naxos*
receiver squawking out their presence, he had to spend more
and more time under water. His batteries were getting
weaker, and, unknown to Lange, TG 22.3 was drawing within
striking range.

On the night of 2–3 June, the VC-8 planes reported a
number of radar contacts and "several noisy sonobuoys" about
50 miles east of the *Guadalcanal*.[28] Gallery ordered a change
of course in that direction, but further air and surface searches
found nothing. By this time, Gallery's chief engineer, Commander Earl Trosino, was becoming worried about the
Guadalcanal's fuel state. He implored Gallery to head for
Casablanca right away or risk coasting in to port. Gallery was
concerned about the fuel also, but he was sure a U-boat was
nearby.

Gallery called his officers to a conference on the afternoon of the 3rd to analyze the situation. With assurances
from Trosino that fuel would be scraped up from somewhere,
Gallery decided that it might be worthwhile to spend one
more day probing for the submarine. That evening the Plan
of the Day for 4 June was distributed. In it was the final list of
the *Guadalcanal* sailors to be used in manning and operating
a captured submarine![29]

There were no contacts during the night, and at 1100 the
next morning TG 22.3 was steadying on a north course bound
for Casablanca. The fourth of June was the kind of day travel
agents delight in describing—a sunny tropic sky, light winds,
and a swelling but not particularly rough sea, colored a vivid
blue. The only missing ingredients were swaying palms and
the strumming of guitars.

Ensign John W. Cadle, Jr., as Frisky 1, and Lieutenant Wolffe W. Roberts, as Frisky 7, had been airborne in their Wildcats for over four hours on a close-in defensive antisubmarine patrol. Just after 1100 the duo was approaching the *Guadalcanal* for landing. As the carrier was signaling her escorts that she was commencing flight operations, the "drowsy calm was shattered."[30] At about 1109 Lieutenant Commander Dudley S. Knox's *Chatelain* picked up a sonar contact only 800 yards distant. It was *U-505*!

Lange's crew had just been sitting down to lunch when screw noises were reported. Lange brought his boat up to periscope depth to take a look, and what he saw was frightening. Bearing down on him were three destroyer escorts, with what Lange took to be a carrier farther off. Lange was having trouble keeping his boat at periscope depth and thought it advisable to dive quickly. It was too late.

The next few minutes were quite hectic, but exciting. The *Guadalcanal's* TBS Log imparts a wonderful flavor to these next minutes; so extracts from the log are quoted extensively here. The following codenames are used: Bluejay—CTG 22.3; Blondie—TG 22.3; Dagwood—ComCortDiv 4; Candy—*Guadalcanal*; Daisy—*Pillsbury*; Pirate—*Pope*; Irish—*Flaherty*; Frenchy—*Chatelain*; Jumbo—*Jenks*; Frisky—Wildcats:; Torchy—Avengers.

Time	To	From	Message
1110	Bluejay	Frenchy	"Investigating possible sound contact."
	Frenchy	Bluejay	"Roger."

Two minutes later the *Chatelain* reported that the contact was evaluated as a submarine. The *Guadalcanal* swung away immediately from the contact, streamed her "Foxer," and readied a killer team for launch. Commander Frederick S. Hall, ComCortDiv 4, took charge of the remaining escorts.

| 1112 | Friskies | Candy | "Stand by to assist on sound contact." |
| | Dagwood | Bluejay | "Take another escort and assist Frenchy; leave other escorts with me." |

| 1113 | Friskies | Candy | "Contact is 3 miles astern of us." |

When the *Chatelain* finally determined that the contact was a submarine, she was too close to make an attack. She then lost contact at 100 yards. To regain contact and to get into position for an attack, Knox swung his ship right to open the range. Contact was regained at 200 yards, but the *Chatelain* opened to about 700 yards to set up a good hedgehog pattern. The destroyer escort then turned toward *U-505* and charged in to fire her hedgehogs and drop dye marker.

| 1116 | Dagwood | Frenchy | "We are attacking contact." |
| | Jumbo | Dagwood | "You will assist Frenchy—Jumbo take position 90 degrees from Frenchy for search." |

The *Chatelain*'s hedgehogs missed, and she altered course to port slightly to open the range and prepare for a depth charge attack. It was obvious to Knox from the short distances in which sonar contact was lost and regained that the sub was near the surface. Knox had his depth charges set on shallow settings.

1116.40	Frenchy	Frisky 1	"Ship that just fired hedgehogs, reverse course."
1117		Frisky 1	"I put a shot right where he is. I could see him at 2,500 feet."
		Candy	"Roger."
		Frisky 1	"I'll put down another burst."
	Jumbo	Frenchy	"Contact bearing 042, range 300. Contact bearing 055, range 350. Contact bearing 068, range 425."
	Jumbo	Dagwood	"Your first leg southerly course."

1118	Candy	Frisky 1	"Just put down another burst. At first I could see him clearly. He is fading now; he is going deeper."
		Candy	"Call Dagwood."
	Dagwood	Frisky 1	"Do you receive me?"
		Dagwood	"Loud and clear. Did you actually sight sub and fire?"
		Frisky 1	"Affirmative."
1119	Dagwood	Frisky 1	"Are you the one that put down slick?"
		Dagwood	"Negative."
		Frisky 1	"I'll circle spot. Haven't seen him since last burst."
		Dagwood	"I bear 345 degrees from ship that dropped marker."
	Frisky 1	Frisky 7	"What was sub's course?"
		Frisky 1	"Wait."

To Cadle and Roberts circling overhead, it appeared that the *Chatelain* had lost the U-boat; hence their frantic message to the ship to reverse course. However, Knox knew all the time where the sub was because his sonar operators had *U-505* tagged most of the time. Cadle's firing at the U-boat's position only confirmed what Knox already knew.

The *Chatelain* bored in at slightly over 14 knots to drop a full fourteen-charge shallow pattern. The charges had been set to function either hydrostatically or magnetically. One of the explosions was very shallow. The *Chatelain* was jolted by the blast, and water shot fifty feet into the air. These charges proved to be *U-505*'s undoing. Inside the boat men and equipment were flung about, and a hole was punched in her outer hull. Lange ordered the tanks blown, and *U-505* lurched to the surface.

| 1121 | Jumbo | Frenchy | "We are making attack." |

		Frisky 1	"Escort dropping charges, reverse course."
	Jumbo	Dagwood	"Disregard section search. You act as asssistant ship. Frenchy is directing ship."
	Dagwood	Bluejay	"Do you want the other two escorts at scene of action?"
1121.30		Frisky 1	"You struck oil! All DE's, sub is surfacing!"
		Frisky 7	"Just took a burst; come in and have fun; it's a hell of lot of fun."
		Frisky 1 ...	"Let's get the bastard." "I wish I had 10,000 rounds."
1122		Frenchy	"We struck oil!"
		Dagwood	"Roger. Go through your procedure. We will strike oil again."
1123	Dagwood	Bluejay	"I would like to capture that bastard if possible! I would like to capture that bastard if possible!"
		Jumbo	"He's been hit several times."
		Dagwood	"Jumbo cease firing; make your turn."
		Plane to Plane	"You'd better keep going around; that baby's throwing a lot of lead!" "I'll go in again." "I'll follow you up." "I see a lot of oil."
	Frisky 1	Candy	"Has sub surfaced?"
		Frisky 1	"Affirmative. There's a lot of oil on the starboard side."

		. . .	"Keep it clear! I'm going in again, Bob!"
1124	Jumbo	Frenchy	"Stay clear while we fire torpedoes."
		Jumbo	"Wilco."
	Candy	Torchy 21	"Will you vector me out?"
		Candy	"Vector west about 5 miles."
		Jumbo	"They are all holding their hands up! They are surrendering!"
		Frenchy	"Watch torpedo in the water."
		. . .	"I got in a good burst that time. Can't see anybody."
		. . .	"There are still three men on that deck."

When *U-505* broached, the *Chatelain* was only about 700 yards away. The DE turned right to put the U-boat abeam, and Knox ordered his engines stopped. Her 3-inch, 40-mm, and 20-mm guns began firing immediately, but ceased after a couple of minutes when it could be seen that *U-505* had no deck gun and that the *Chatelain*'s 3-inch fire was having little effect.

Just then Knox noticed that the submarine was still under way and turning toward his ship. Not knowing that all the Germans were abandoning ship and the sub's rudder was jammed, Knox was concerned that his ship was very vulnerable if a torpedo was fired at the *Chatelain*. So, as his three-inchers didn't seem to be having much effect, Knox decided to fire a torpedo at *U-505*. The "fish" was fired at a range of 500 yards, but, fortunately, it missed the U-boat by a good distance.

Meanwhile, the Germans were abandoning ship with alacrity. Lange had been first on the bridge, and he saw the destroyers escorts firing at his boat from close range. Several shells hit the conning tower, and their shrapnel sliced through the air. Lange, hit in the face and in both knees and legs, was knocked to the deck. As he lay there, Lange ordered his men to abandon and scuttle *U-505*. He then lost consciousness.

When he awoke, most of his men were on deck or jumping into the water. Lange tired to raise himself to crawl aft. Just as he did, a 3-inch shell hit near the starboard machine gun. The explosion flung Lange from the first antiaircraft gun deck down to the main deck. Several of his men got him into a raft.

It had taken some time for the *Guadalcanal* to launch her killer team because of fears that *U-505* would send a "fish" into the carrier while she was heading into the wind. Finally, the two aircraft were in the air at 1124. There was little for them to do.

1127	Dagwood	Bluejay	"Is that guy surrendering?"
		Dagwood	"Cease firing! Cease firing!"
	Frisky 1	Dagwood	"Cease firing until further word."
		Frisky 1	"Roger."
	Torchy 21	Candy	"Don't attack unless sub attempts to submerge."
		Torchy 21	"Roger."
		Candy	"Don't forget pictures."
		Torchy 21	"Roger."
1128	Frisky 1	Candy	"How many men do you see?"
		Frisky 1	"Aft of conning tower there were three men and two forward on last run."
		Candy	"Keep us informed."
		Frisky 1	"Shall I stay up here or fire?"
		Candy	"Cease firing."
		Frisky 1 and 7	"Roger."
		Jumbo	"Men are abandoning ship! There are lots of men in the water."
	Jumbo	Frenchy	"Get a boat over! We'll go aboard that baby!"

		Frisky 7	"The sub . . . wait . . . looks like the sub is submerging, doesn't it, Jack."
		Frisky 1	"Seems if it is awful slow."
1129	Dagwood	Bluejay	"Do you think we can capture this guy?"
	Jumbo	Frenchy	"We lost a torpedo out there."
		Jumbo	"How long ago did you fire?"
	Jumbo	Frenchy	"Approximately five minutes ago. Stay clear of water astern. Get ahead of his beam. Submarine is abandoning ship. Submarine is sinking."
	Pirate	Dagwood	"You circle the vicinity of submarine at a distance of about two miles and search for any more submarines in the area."
1130	Dagwood	Jumbo	"Request permission to put party aboard and take submarine in tow."
		Dagwood	"We have taken care of that. We have a boat to rail."
1132	Frisky 1 and 7	Candy	"Go down to altitude and look in water for survivors."
		Frisky 1	"Roger. Several life boats and men in water. More still diving in. Leaving in yellow boats—about twenty-four."
	Jumbo	Dagwood	"Start picking up survivors. Put boat in

			water and pick up any evidence. Use boat for picking up any evidence—pick up survivors over your nets."
1133	Candy	Frisky 7	"Sub seems to be settling. They may save it—close DE—they may board it."
		Frisky 1	"Robie, look at conning tower. Sure is a mess."
	Candy	Frisky 7	"All men seem to be off."
		Candy	"Are all men off topside?"
		Frisky 7	"I believe so."
		. . .	"Not a damn one left."
		. . .	"See any, Jack?"
		. . .	"All deserted."
1135		Frisky 7	"I wish those guys would hurry—there is still time to save sub."

It was now obvious that most, if not all, of the Germans had left their boat. Commander Hall (riding on the *Pillsbury*) assigned the boat from his ship the dangerous task of boarding and securing the U-boat. At 1138 Hall gave the stirring order not heard in the U.S. Navy in years—"Away boarding parties! Lower any whaleboats!"[31]

Lieutenant (jg) Albert L. David was in command of the boarding party. Their task was not going to be easy. *U-505* was still circling slowly, her deck aft of the conning tower underwater. Boarding her would be difficult. Nevertheless, the Americans came alongside and began to clamber onto *U-505*. A dead German lying on the deck stared sightlessly at the boarders as they leaped onto the submarine. The Americans were not sure of what awaited them below—a diehard submariner, perhaps, or uncontrollable flooding. Yet David, followed by RM2/c Stanley E. Wdowiak and TM3/c Arthur W. Knispel, dove below decks without hesitation.

Fortunately, no one else was on board. The trio "immediately went to work closing valves, and replacing the cover on a strainer through which a solid stream of water, six inches in diameter, was pouring into the boat."[32] David's team then disconnected wires to several demolition bombs and gathered up all papers, charts, and code books that appeared to be important, sending them away to the *Pillsbury* by boat.

By this time the *Guadalcanal* had some boats in the water to assist David and his crew. The *Pillsbury* was also easing up to the still-circling *U-505* in an attempt to get lines secured to the submarine. Her attempts to lasso the sub elicited a hearty "Ride 'em, cowboy!" from Gallery over the radio. The *Pillsbury*'s attempts also resulted in the ship's skin being punctured in several places by *U-505*'s bow planes. With a number of compartments flooding, the DE had to pull away, and her crew had to focus their efforts on keeping their own ship afloat. (It is ironic that the only damage incurred by the task group happened during the boarding and salvage phase.)

About 1240 a salvage party from the *Guadalcanal* led by Commander Trosino and Lieutenant Deward E. Hampton arrived to help Lieutenant (jg) David's hard-working crew. "One boat literally 'arrived with a bang,' being picked up by the sea and deposited bodily on the deck of the sub."[33] This cacophonous arrival alarmed those working in the murky and fetid bowels of the sub until they realized what had happened. Trosino had brought along some handy-billy pumps to help pump out the boat, which was riding dangerously low in the water.

The salvage party was finally able to shut down the U-boat's engines, and she coasted to a stop. Trosino realized the sub needed to be towed in order to keep her afloat, and he radioed the carrier a message to this effect. The "Can Do" closed with her prize, and at 1423 a 1¼-inch wire hawser was made fast to *U-505*. She was taken under tow, but her rudder was still jammed hard right, and the tow was extremely difficult.

On board the other ships, *U-505*'s crew watched glumly as a huge Stars and Stripes was run up the boat's radio mast. The German ensign still fluttered below the U.S. flag. *U-505* also had a new name bestowed on her by the *Guadalcanal's* crew. From now on she would be known as "Junior."

Gallery now had to make some decisions. The carrier's fuel was getting low, and he was unsure if his ship could make Casablanca. Although the situation aboard the submarine appeared to be stabilizing, Gallery didn't know how long she would stay afloat. The *Pillsbury's* flooding caused him even more concern. Gallery decided to head for the nearest friendly port, Dakar.

A few hours later Admiral Ingersoll ordered the task group to head for Casablanca. (If the *Guadalcanal* had anchored at Dakar, the capture of *U-505* would have been known to the Germans within hours.) A tanker and a tug were being sent to the task group's aid. During the night the towline broke. The task group spent the remainder of the night patrolling around *U-505*, while VC-8 planes furnished continuous air cover. The *Pillsbury*, which had been left behind with the *Pope* standing by, was finally patched up, and the two DEs then caught up with the other ships.

At dawn of the 5th a heavier towline was passed between the carrier and the sub. The tow was recommenced, but it was evident that the U-boat's rudder was still jammed. Itching to look the submarine over, Gallery decided to check the boat's rudder himself. When he got to the U-boat, he found that the salvage crew had not entered the after section of the boat because they feared the compartments were flooded and that there was a possible booby trap on the door leading aft.

Gallery, who had attended some ordnance courses, thought the "booby trap" was just an open fuse box. This he closed (with no fatal effects); and cracking the door open, he found that the aft compartments were relatively dry. After some huffing and puffing, the salvage party was finally able to put the rudder amidships by hand. Towing the U-boat became much easier.

In the afternoon TG 22.3 received new orders. It was now to proceed to Bermuda. Gallery figured if he could get to Casablanca, he could get to Bermuda; so course was set west. As the task group plodded west, the VC-8 planes were up continuously, operating off the carrier with only 15 knots of wind over the deck at times.

By this time Gallery's crew had become pretty cocky over their achievement. Even the invasion of France on 6

June didn't faze them a bit. "That morning when communiques from France were posted on the bulletin board," Gallery
related later, "one of my brave young lads read over all the
historic communiques coming from headquarters about the
invasion and then shoved his hat on back of his head and said,
'Boy, oh boy, look what Eisenhower had to do to top us.'"[34]

On the morning of 7 June the oiler *Kennebec*, with the
fleet tug *Abnaki* and destroyer escort *Durik*, joined the force.
Fueling of the task group began immediately, and the
Guadalcanal passed her towline to the *Abnaki*. However, as
U-505 slowed to a stop during this process, she settled
alarmingly into the water. Her bow was still out of the water,
but her conning tower hatch was almost awash.

Trosino and David and their salvage parties reboarded
their captive and worked feverishly to restore *U-505*'s buoyancy.
As the *Abnaki* churned ahead with the submarine at short
stay, more pumps were rigged on board, and all possible
loose gear was removed. *U-505* slowly began to come out of
the water, and by 2000 she was back on the same level as
when first boarded.

On the afternoon of the 7th the seaplane tender *Humboldt*
joined, bringing Commander C. G. Rucker, an experienced
submarine commander, to take charge of the salvage operations. Task Group 22.3 had now become a rather large
organization. The next day Commander Rucker boarded *U-505*
to advise and assist the salvage parties in lightening her. By
that evening *U-505* was at a fully surfaced trim.

On 9 June the *Jenks* was sent ahead to Bermuda carrying
U-505's Enigma machine and other important documents.
The haul taken in with *U-505*'s capture was of great value to
Tenth Fleet. But not everything was useful. "When *U-505*
was captured, her volume of Current War Orders, for example, were already contained in the Atlantic Section's files and
long since in the hands of Cominch. In fact, *U-505*'s copy was
out of date, having been superseded by additions and correc-
tions which she had failed to intercept herself or which had
been transmitted after her capture."[35]

The capture of *U-505* was another indication of how the
Allies' Ultra intelligence was eating away at the U-boats like
termites in wood. Ironically, on 6 July 1944 the Germans
issued orders to the U-boats also to attempt to capture code
books by boarding vessels.

"It is of the utmost importance," U-boat Command stat-

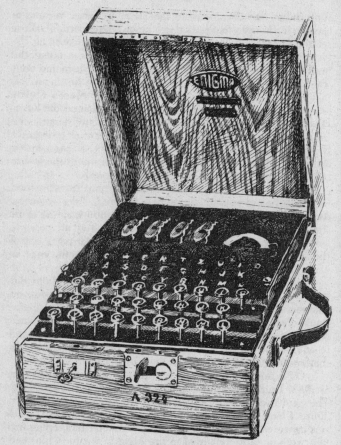

Enigma Machine

ed, "to capture English or American secret codes (code books)
and other secret material for our own Radio Intelligence
Service. The following is therefore ordered:

"If there is a chance to board sinking escort vessels
(destroyers or corvettes) or other warships, make every effort
to get these documents out of the radio room or chart house.

Otherwise do all you can to get them by other means, for instance from life boats. U-boats must take a certain amount of risk, boarding parties must be prepared for anything."[36]

Task Group 22.3's passage to Bermuda was uneventful, and on 19 June the victorious group, literally bringing home the spoils of war, steamed into Port Royal Bay. Waiting to take a look at the task group's prize was Tenth Fleet's Captain Knowles. The entire operation had been well executed—from Tenth Fleet's plotting of U-505's position to the denouement on 4 June. But perhaps the hardest task was yet to come: to keep U-505's capture secret. It was probably hardest for the men of TG 22.3 to remain quiet, bursting with pride over their achievement. But they kept quiet. And so did the other individuals involved, from the *Kennebec* and the *Abnaki* to the military personnel on Bermuda to the close-mouthed people at Tenth Fleet. The capture of U-505 was one of the best-kept secrets of World War II.

Gallery was understandably proud of his group's accomplishment. In his official report he said: "From the time we sailed from Norfolk the whole task group was determined that we would come back dragging a sub behind us. . . . and they had what it took to do it. When remarkable luck was required, we had it. When perfect cooperation between aircraft and surface vessels was required—it was there. When a clean-cut knockout punch was needed, the *Chatelain* produced it. When outstanding heroism was required, it was commonplace among the boarding parties.

"I believe every man in the task group would have volunteered for the boarding parties, and those who could not go were very envious of those who did.

"It is a great pleasure to report that all hands in the task group did their duty in an exemplary manner in keeping with the highest traditions of the U.S. Navy."[37]

Numerous honors and awards were showered on the task group and its men for this action. The Presidential Unit Citation was bestowed on TG 22.3; Lieutenant (jg) David was awarded the Congressional Medal of Honor; Captain Gallery received the Distinguished Service Medal; Commander Trosino and Lieutenant Hampton each received the Legion of Merit; Cadle and Roberts were awarded Distinguished Flying Crosses; and many other awards were given to other members of the task group. All were richly deserved.[38]

The saga of *U-505* was not over yet. The submarine, renamed the *Nemo*, spent the rest of the war acting as a "tame" submarine. In this capacity she was able to give U.S. antisubmarine forces the opportunity to get to know the characteristics and performance of the enemy boats, and to develop new or improved tactics to use against them.

After the war *U-505* finally came to rest thousands of miles from the sea where she spent her active life. Today she can be seen, and toured, at the Chicago Museum of Science and Industry. There she serves as a memorial to the thousands of men who took their vessels to sea during the Battle of the Atlantic and never returned.

8

INTERLUDE—
A TOUR OF THE RIVIERA

While the battle went on between the escort carrier groups and the U-boats in the Atlantic, a pair of American CVEs were doing their own thing in the Mediterranean. The *Kasaan Bay* and the *Tulagi* were *Casablanca*-class carriers launched and commissioned within three weeks of each other in late 1943. Their first operations were unremarkable—ferrying aircraft to Pearl Harbor in January 1944 and then doing the same chore (with the *Mission Bay*) to Casablanca in May. The *Block Island* had been sunk during their crossing, and the ships carried survivors of the sunken carrier back to New York. If anything, the task of transporting the survivors brought home to the crews of the new "jeeps" the fact that there was a shooting war going on.[1]

When the two carriers arrived back in the United States, they learned that "the endless weeks of routine training and drudgery were to be rewarded with a part in an attack on the European enemy."[2] The *Tulagi* and the *Kasaan Bay* were to be in on the invasion of southern France—Operation Dragoon.

So far in their careers the "Mighty T" and the "Sassy Kassy" had not had any air units boarded for any length of time. This was quickly remedied. Aboard Captain J. C. Cronin's *Tulagi* came twenty-four F6F-5s and two TBMs of a unique outfit. Lieutenant Commander William F. ("Bush") Bringle's Observation-Fighter Squadron One (VOF-1) had been specially trained in spotting at the Army's artillery school at Fort Sill, Oklahoma. VOF-1 would see much activity

213

F6F

in this capacity during Dragoon. Captain B. E. Grow's ship welcomed aboard the twenty-four Hellcats, three Avengers, and eight F6F-3N night fighters of VF-74. (Eight spare Hellcats were also carried by the two vessels.) VF-74's skipper, Lieutenant Commander H. Brinkley ("Brink") Bass, was no stranger to escort carriers, having commanded VGF-29 aboard the *Santee* in 1943.[3]

The carriers arrived at Quonset Point, Rhode Island on 29 June to embark Rear Admiral Calvin T. Durgin (CTG 27.7) and his staff. The next day the task group (the two carriers and six destroyer escorts) weighed anchor and left for the Mediterranean. Extensive training was carried out en route by the task group. This training was necessary, as both the ships and their air units were still very green. VF-74 felt later, however, that it received "its real carrier training in the Mediterranean during the month preceding D Day, and did not actually reach their peak in carrier efficiency until during Operation Dragoon."[4]

Task Group 27.7 reached Oran on 10 July 1944, where the formation was dissolved. Rear Admiral Durgin and his staff left for Naples to become involved in the invasion planning, while the carriers continued with still more training (including a spotting exercise for VOF-1) in the Oran area. On

Supermarine Seafire

the 17th the force, now designated TG 80.2, left Oran for
Malta. On the way the destroyer *Niblack* picked up a suspicious sound contact and attacked it with depth charges. A
VF-74 TBM pilot was aloft on antisubmarine patrol at the
time, and for nuisance value (since he could not see any sign
of a U-boat), dropped a pair of depth bombs in the general
area of the destroyer's attack. As far as can be discovered, this
was VF-74's sole submarine attack of the war. As the task
group rushed on, the *Niblack* remained behind to conduct an
unsuccessful search for the submarine.[5]

In Malta the two "jeeps" were rejoined by Admiral Durgin
who would command the task group in the operation. Also
joining were the British *Bogue*-class escort carriers *Hunter*
and *Stalker*. The two squadrons aboard these ships each had
twenty-four Seafires. The Seafires, generally excellent aircraft, were a bit fragile for carrier operations and were quite
short-legged in comparison to the Hellcats. Also, the British
carriers were a bit slower than their American cousins. Still,
the task group worked very efficiently throughout Dragoon.[6]
On the 26th the force sortied for Alexandria, Egypt, and a
"half-hearted feint to the east" and more training.[7]

Upon their arrival in Alexandria, the group designation
was changed again, this time to TG 88.2. Durgin's task group
would operate as part of TF 88 under the command of Rear
Admiral Thomas H. Troubridge, RN. Troubridge would also
command the five British CVEs and screen of TG 88.1. The
nine carriers would have ninety-six Seafires, forty-eight Wildcats, and seventy-two Hellcats available. (Besides the American carriers, one British flattop also had F6Fs). Task Group
88.2's screen would consist of the Royal Navy's antiaircraft
light cruisers *Colombo* and *Caledon*, the U.S. destroyers
Butler, Gherardi, Herndon, Murphy, Jeffers, and *Shubrick,*
and six British minelayers.[8]

Task Group 88.2 returned to Malta on 3 August, then
proceeded to Salerno on the 7th to take part in a dress
rehearsal, Preface. In the meantime, the *Tulagi's* and the
Kasaan Bay's Avengers and the VF-74(N) night fighters were
sent to Corsica to provide night cover over the task force
during Dragoon. On the 10th the ships were again anchored
in Malta preparing for the final move to the coast of France.[9]

Finally, TG 88.2 sortied from Valletta Harbor on 12
August bound for the invasion. To deceive the enemy the

force headed west until the night of 13–14 August, then turned north toward southern France. On the morning of 15 August the guns of the Allied ships opened up on the German defenses. Overhead were hundreds of aircraft—transports carrying paratroopers, bombers attacking gun emplacements, and the Hellcats of VOF-1 and VF-74. There was little aerial opposition, though antiaircraft fire was heavy at times.

Both squadrons were kept busy from the outset. A group of four coastal guns at Île de Porquerolles were attacked by both squadrons, but results were unknown because of low clouds. Spotting chores kept the VOF-1 fliers occupied for much of D day, with numerous targets sighted and ships' gunfire called in. The VF-74 fighters eventually racked up sixty sorties during the day, with the VOF-1 planes contributing another fifty-eight. Lieutenant Commander Bringle had a close call after landing on the *Tulagi* following a spotting mission. Bringle had not yet got out of his plane when the F6F landing behind him sailed through the barrier and smashed into Bringle's aircraft. Though both aircraft were demolished, neither pilot was injured. At sunset two VF-74(N) Hellcats landed on the *Tulagi* and were positioned for an immediate launch if necessary, while two more night fighters were in readiness on Corsica. The night fighters returned to Corsica the next morning after an uneventful night.[10]

Operations settled down the next day to a clockwork schedule. Each night the task group retired to the south, returning to the area the following morning. The force's "Point Option" kept moving westward, however, so that TG 88.2 was eventually operating southwest of Marseille and almost due south of the Rhone River delta. During the next two days the VF-74(N) planes patrolled over the task group without landing, returning to Corsica at the end of their patrols.[11]

On the 16th both squadrons had outstanding successes attacking enemy positions. VF-74's skipper, Lieutenant Commander Bass, scored a bullseye when he skipped a 500-pound bomb into the mouth of a tunnel between Fuveau and Brignoles. Four VOF-1 pilots also showed their accuracy when they all planted their bombs in a fifty-foot-square walled area of a four-gun emplacement commanding the entrance to Toulon.[12]

The seventeenth of August started out very well for the

Americans with a devastating attack on a gun battery on Île de Port Cros by *Tulagi* and *Kasaan Bay* planes. Then tragedy struck. The two squadrons had pretty much had things their own way the previous two days, but enemy antiaircraft fire was on target this day. Four planes were damaged, and two others were missing. Eight VF-74 Hellcats had been sent out on the last flight of the day to attack anything moving. The weather was poor, with electrical storms surging through the area. Nothing had been seen until a pair of Seafires directed the VF-74 fliers to some enemy truck convoys near Lambese.

He 114

The Americans made several rocket and strafing passes on these convoys. During this time Lieutenant Robert J. Johnson and Lieutenant (jg) John D. Frank became separated from the rest of the planes. They were never seen again, and it is not known whether they were victims of the storms dotting the area or were shot down. The remaining planes flew back to the "Sassy Kassy," where one F6F crashed into the barrier and fouled her deck. The aircraft still aloft finally landed on the *Tulagi*. This crash, incidentally, was the last flight-deck mishap the *Kasaan Bay* would suffer during Dragoon.[13]

The fighter pilots finally got some air-to-air action on the 19th. Two divisions of VOF-1 planes were heading north toward Lyon when two He 111s were seen near Vienne. The

Germans saw the Hellcats at the same time and split up, one heading north and the other south. It was too late for them. Lieutenant Rene E. Poucel (whose parents had come from the area) and Ensign Alfred R. Wood sandwiched the north-bound plane between them. Poucel's pass started the bomber smoking, and Wood finished the job with a long burst from dead astern.

Meanwhile, Lieutenant Commander John H. Sandor and Ensign David E. Robinson were going after the other He 111. Robinson tagged the bomber with a string of hits that walked along the fuselage and into the right engine. The enemy plane staggered, then crashed into a field. As Sandor and Robinson strafed the still relatively intact plane, several of the bomber's crew were cut down as they ran from their plane into the line of fire.

The Americans then continued on their mission. Just south of Vienne another He 111 was seen flying 600 feet above the ground. Wood rolled in from 6 o'clock. His shooting was accurate, and both of the bomber's engines were hit. Flames broke out; then the bomber exploded and crashed into some trees. One person was seen to jump from the stricken plane before it crashed, but his chute didn't open.

Lieutenant Poucel later damaged a Ju 88 parked in a revetment on the Montelimar airfield. The VOF-1 fliers ended the day by destroying twenty-two trucks and a train in strafing attacks.[14]

VF-74 also had some good shooting during the day. Lieutenant Commander Bass took eight planes up the Rhone River, looking for vehicles and locomotives. His pilots came in so low on some of their strafing passes that one came back to the carrier with wire wrapped around his belly tank struts. Shortly after 0800 a Ju 88 was spotted flying north at 250 feet. It was no contest as Bass's division took turns shooting pieces off the doomed bomber. Its engines hit, the plane split-essed into the ground.

When Bass returned to the *Kasaan Bay*, he dropped a message to the ship that said, "Covered Rhone valley O.K. Nothing except a few trucks, most of which we got. The western leg of hop wasn't covered well at all because of weather. The 1st Div *shot down* a Ju 88. WHOOPS!"[15]

In the afternoon six of the *Kasaan Bay* fliers caught a Do 217 northeast of Issiore. The pilots wasted a lot of ammunition in their eagerness to down the enemy, but Lieutenant (jg) Edwin W. Castanedo and Ensign Charles W. S. Hulland finally combined to destroy it. At no time did the Do 217 pilot try any evasive maneuvers other than "pouring the coal" to his plane. At 1,000 feet the Do 217 rolled over on its back and began to burn; then it smashed into the ground.[16]

The next day, 20 August, was an even blacker day than the 17th had been. The second flight of the day was particularly costly to VF-74. Ensign Thomas F. Kendrick was strafing a string of ammunition wagons near Balaruc when one of them exploded. Three feet of his starboard elevator and two feet of his starboard horizontal stabilizer were blown off. His control cables were almost completely severed, also. Nevertheless, he made two more strafing runs, though he thought his plane was acting "peculiarly." Fortunately, Kendrick (accompanied by another damaged Hellcat) made it safely back to the *Kasaan Bay.*

Not so fortunate were Ensigns William N. Arbuckle and Hulland. Following the same attacks that damaged Kendrick's Hellcat, Arbuckle was discovered to be missing. A search was begun, but he was never seen again. The three pilots remaining out of the six who had started the day continued on their mission. Near Villefranche another truck convoy was strafed. Hulland's F6F was hit by ground fire. Black smoke poured from his engine, and the oil pressure began to drop. Hulland was able to stay in formation for a time, but then reported he was going to bail out. He left his plane near the village of St. Julien (about 30 miles from the Spanish border). Hulland was seen to land safely and hide his chute, but was not seen again. However, he was later reported to be safe, apparently having escaped via Bordeaux.

In the afternoon Lieutenant Commander Bass led a flight of eight Hellcats up the Rhone Valley seeking targets of opportunity. Over the village of Chamelet, Bass suddenly dove on what the other pilots thought to be a motorcycle and sidecar. He carried his attack in too low. His belly tank scraped the ground and was torn off. The Hellcat swerved out of control and slammed into the ground, killing Bass instantly. Though the VF-74 pilots were stunned by the loss of their skipper, they continued with their mission. Near Annonay one of the pilots ran into some high tension lines and lost almost three feet of his left wing. By using full right aileron, he was able to keep his fighter level. Unable to land on the carrier, he was given the option of bailing out or attempting a landing at the Ramatuelle emergency airstrip. He chose the latter and was able to make a safe landing.

Later that afternoon five of the VF-74(N) Hellcats landed on the *Tulagi* for a briefing on an antishipping sweep off the mouth of the Rhone. The mission was routine, but one of the planes crashed on Corsica when they returned to that island.[17] The day's actions had been costly to VF-74. Besides the night fighter crash, three more Hellcats had been downed and two pilots lost, plus two F6Fs badly damaged. Fortunately, these were the last losses to the squadron during Dragoon. Lieutenant Commander Bass's loss was especially felt. Rear Admiral Durgin wrote, "His death was a great blow to the squadron which he had so painstakingly trained, and to naval aviation of which he was such an outstanding representative."[18] Lieutenant Harry H. Basore, Jr. took over command of the squadron for the remainder of the operation.[19]

The planes of VOF-1 also took some punishment on the 20th. No pilots were lost, but two had close calls. Lieutenant David S. Crockett was over Toulon spotting for the French battleship *Lorraine* when his Hellcat was smashed by flak. Smoke poured into the cockpit, and the plane fell out of control. Crockett decided it was time to leave and bailed out, landing north of Toulon. German troops were right on the spot and took Crockett prisoner. He was taken to a fort near Toulon where he spent an uncomfortable few days before his captors surrendered the fort on the 23rd.[20]

Also on the 20th, Lieutenant Commander Bringle led a flight inland on an armed reconnaissance. Several enemy truck convoys were found moving about the countryside. The VOF-1 pilots strafed all the columns that could be seen, leaving exploding trucks and wagons, dead Germans, and stampeding horses in their wake. The Germans were not defenseless, however, and several Hellcats were holed by enemy gunfire. Lieutenant James M. Alston's F6F was hit hard by antiaircraft fire, and its wing burst into flames. Alston pulled up to 5,000 feet and bailed out just as the wing broke off. Alston's chute popped open, and he floated down to the ground, where he evaded the Germans and eventually made it back to his own lines.[21]

Later in the day Bringle led another flight against a

group of armed trawlers in the Marseille area. In a series of low-altitude strafing attacks, the Americans forced four of the vessels to be beached, and heavily damaged two others.[22]

More heavy action greeted the *Tulagi* fliers on 21 August. Eight planes sortied up the Rhone River on a barge-busting mission, which was accomplished with great success. Following this, six Hellcats went off looking for enemy troop convoys, while the other two planes were sent on a spotting mission for the ships offshore. Near Nimes the sextet of fighters found and strafed numerous trucks, and then used rockets on five large groups of vehicles clustered alongside the roads. During the rocket attacks, Lieutenant (jg) J. H. Coyne's aircraft was seen to disintegrate. Coyne was thrown from his plane. His chute opened only seconds before he hit the ground, and he was never seen again. Meanwhile, Ensign John M. Denison felt a heavy jolt shake his plane and his engine misfire. The engine smoothed out again. Denison didn't find out until he landed on the *Tulagi* that an unexploded 20-mm shell had damaged two cylinders of the engine.[23]

While these actions were going on, a flight of four more Hellcats discovered that "all roads within a ten mile radius of Remouline were choked with trucks and vehicles of all types—including tanks—heading north."[24] The quartet immediately pounced on the enemy vehicles, strafing, dive-bombing with depth bombs, and firing rockets into the retreating mass. Gouts of fire and huge explosions showed how effective their efforts were. During the strafing, one of the pilots saw a Ju 88 streak eastward along the deck, but the plane had disappeared before he could go after it.

A trio of Ju 52s were not as lucky as the Ju 88. The three lumbering transports stumbled across Lieutenant (jg) Edward W. Olsezewski's and Ensign Richard V. Yentzer's paths as the pair returned from the Remouline strafing party. The Ju 52s were on the deck in a Vee formation flying north when the two Americans bracketed them. Olsezewski jumped the trailing transport from 3 o'clock and poured .50-caliber shells into its right engine and fuselage. He circled back to slam more shells into the same side. The Ju 52 skidded to the right and crashed into some trees.

Yentzer, meanwhile, was going after the number two plane. He bored in from the transport's left side (firing all the way), then pulled up in a wingover and raced back in from

Ju 52

the opposite direction. Olsezewski joined in with a run from behind the Ju 52, which had started to break formation. Olsezewski held his trigger down until a propeller was seen to fly off the enemy aircraft. The Ju 52 skidded violently, hit the ground, and ground-looped through several fences. Olsezewski strafed the wreckage for good measure.

The last transport didn't get away. Following his runs on the second plane, Yentzer went after the lead aircraft. He opened fire at a distance of 1,000 feet and continued firing until he had to pull up to avoid hitting the transport. Yentzer made two more passes before the Ju 52 crashed and exploded.[25] These transports would be the last enemy planes the *Tulagi* and the *Kasaan Bay* fliers would see in their operations off southern France.

After the recovery of planes on the 21st (which also saw the 2,000th landing aboard the *Kasaan Bay*), the carriers and destroyers of TG 88.2 retired to Maddalena, Sardinia, to take on supplies. The squadrons needed more bombs, having used a good portion of their allotment of bombs already. American-style bombs were hard to find, even though the flattops also went to Propriano, Corsica, in search of the elusive weapons. Few American bombs were found, and ordnancemen on board both ships had to grind the lugs on the bombs they were given so they would fit the Hellcat bomb racks. Needless to say, the ordnance people were given a wide berth as they did their job.[26]

The *Tulagi* and the *Kasaan Bay* were back off the coast of France on 23 August. Things had quieted considerably by now, and the next day the night fighters returned to the carriers, where they were stripped of their AIA gear, to be used thereafter only on task force missions.[27] Though there was only occasional antiaircraft fire now, what there was could be very damaging. "Bush" Bringle found this out on the 25th while spotting for the ships offshore. As he went about his chores, black puffs of flak suddenly blossomed about his Hellcat. Bringle could hear and feel the fragments smashing into the aircraft. He beat a hasty retreat, but the German fire had been too accurate. His engine began cutting out, and he was unable to reach the *Tulagi*. Bringle was able to ditch his plane safely, however, and he was soon picked up by one of the numerous vessels in the vicinity.[28]

Only one other plane was lost (also in a ditching) the rest of the time the task force was on station. Operations continued until the morning of the 30th, when both carriers retired for good to Ajaccio, Corsica.

The "Mighty T" and the "Sassy Kassy" had been in combat for thirteen days. Eleven F6Fs had been lost. In exchange, eight German aircraft had been shot down, 825 trucks and other vehicles destroyed and 334 more damaged, 84 locomotives wrecked or disabled, and innumerable rail and road cuts accomplished.

The high command was quick to praise and reward the airmen of TF 88, including the pilots of VF-74 and VOF-1. For their part in the operation, Bringle, Basore, and Hulland received Navy Crosses. A number of other decorations were awarded members of both squadrons.[29] Vice Admiral H. Kent Hewitt, commander of the Western Naval Task Force, signaled Admiral Durgin, "The support given my forces by the ships and planes under your command had been of the highest order. Your complete cooperation with the Army Air Force and gunfire support ships in this operation has been outstanding. You have left nothing to be desired. Well done to your ships and gallant pilots."[30]

Brigadier General Gordon P. Saville, commander of the XII Tactical Air Command, added, "Allow me to express my appreciation of the outstanding work which your carrier support force has done and of their splendid cooperation. I consider the relationship and cooperation of the force to be a model of perfection and a severe standard for future operations."[31]

Rear Admiral Troubridge was equally impressed, commenting, "the U.S. aircraft, notably the Hellcats, proved their superiority. The Seafire is a magnificent machine, but much too frail for operations from Escort Carriers. It is idle to pretend otherwise, in spite of the splendid performance of the squadrons equipped with the 'aristocrats of the sky'."[32]

Troubridge continued, "The high quality of their flying and aircraft maintenance, and the efficiency and sufficiency with which U.S. ships are equipped and manned, to say nothing of the superiority of their Naval aircraft, sets a standard well worthy of emulation. Once in the air, our pilots are second to none, but this must not blind us to the fact that the Royal Navy has some way to travel before it can operate home produced Naval aircraft of adequate performance with the precision and efficiency of the U.S. Navy."[33]

For the *Tulagi* the war in the Mediterranean and Atlantic was over. She headed for the Pacific where she was involved in operations in the Philippines and at Okinawa. The *Kasaan Bay* remained in the Atlantic a bit longer. She made one more aircraft ferry trip to Casablanca in October and November, then also headed west to operate in an antisubmarine role in the backwaters of the Pacific.

The war these two carriers had fought off France had been far different from the one being fought in the Atlantic. But the bleeding had been the same, the boredom had been the same, and, yes, the efficiency of the "jeeps" had been the same. The *Tulagi* and the *Kasaan Bay*, along with their sisters in the Atlantic, had proved once again that they were not just *escort* carriers, but *fighting* carriers.

9

KEEPING THE PRESSURE ON

The sinking of the *Block Island* and the capture of *U-505* by the *Guadalcanal*'s group had been important events for the U.S. Navy's escort carrier groups in the Atlantic. But both events were unique and would not again happen to the "jeeps" in that arena. What did occur was the day-to-day grind of looking and listening for, then tracking down, the (now more than ever) elusive U-boats. Many of the underwater killers were now appearing equipped with snorkels and, thus, were becoming more difficult to find. They would be found, for all the CVEs were now flying round-the-clock, but it would require a great deal of effort by the CVE groups. And the Americans would constantly be reminded that the German sailors were still tough adversaries.

But for Doenitz and his U-boat sailors, their underwater war had taken a terrible turn. They were no longer coming home full of tales of their successes against the Allied convoys. They were not coming home, period. Their fight had now turned into a fight for survival. No longer were the U-boats waging "tonnage warfare," where cargo vessels, no matter where they were sunk, contributed to a tonnage amount that the Allies could never replace. Now they were "tying down enemy forces."

Reporting to his U-boat crews on 15 June 1944 about the situation, Doenitz explained: "The job of 'tying down enemy forces' has so far succeeded, shown by observations from boats, agents' reports and radio intercept reports. The number of enemy aircraft in operation, and the number of vessels on escort duty, antisubmarine patrol and in carrier formation has increased rather than decreased.

"For the submarine men themselves the job of conducting a war for the purpose of tying down the enemy is especially difficult. More so than in any other sphere, success, till now, has been the personal reward of the whole crew, and gave them the special zest for attack, and vigour and tenaciousness in the teeth of enemy defense. Chances of success are now only slight, and the prospects of not returning from enemy patrol on the other hand very great. In the last few months only 70% of the boats which sailed per month returned from their patrols.

"That the crews managed at all in this last year of heaviest loss and smallest success to come through untouched in their morale, will to fight and desire for attack is a wonderful proof of soldierly courage, a proof of the quality of the human material involved, a reward for the thorough training, and result of the determination of the submarine weapon."[1]

These words reveal the sterility of U-boat Command's perception of the war in the Atlantic at that time. The Germans believed that by "tying down enemy forces" the U-boats were performing a great service for Germany. But they apparently did not realize, or chose not to accept the fact, that America was replacing her own and Britain's losses at an ever expanding rate. And the Germans lost sight of the fact that the U-boat *had* to sink the cargo ships carrying the men and material that would one day be used in the final assault on Germany. This the U-boats were not doing.

Meanwhile, the *Block Island* and the *Guadalcanal* had not been the only escort carriers operating during late May and early June. The veteran *Bogue* was out, as were the *Croatan* and the *Tripoli*. The *Tripoli*'s operations near the Cape Verde Islands and off Nova Scotia were unsuccessful. No submarines were sighted although VC-6 flew round-the-clock. Apparently there was some tension on the carrier during this cruise. The VC-6 history complains that the cruise "was very unsatisfactory. From almost the start to the finish the morale was low."[2] Perhaps this was so because no U-boats were found and because the squadron lost a pilot when he crashed into the water while making an emergency landing.

*   *   *

This is a good place to observe that Admiral Ingersoll was not very impressed with the Kaiser-class carriers in the Atlantic. In a message to Admiral King on 13 May 1944 he said: "Request assignment *Bogue*-class CVE . . . in lieu of Kaiser-class for following reasons:

    A) Longer radius for ASW operations due to greater fuel capacity and ability to refuel escorts.

    B) Limitations against use of Kaiser-class for ferry service in North Atlantic during winter.

    C) More suitable for all uses in Atlantic."[3]

Several ex-CVE sailors have also commented on the riding characteristics of the Kaiser carriers as opposed to the *Bogue*-class ships. Words such as "flat bottoms" and "rollers" are used to describe the Kaiser vessels.[4] In any event, of the Kaiser-class ships assigned to the Atlantic, the *Tripoli*, *Solomons*, and *Wake Island* would see relatively brief action. Only the *Mission Bay* would see combat in the Atlantic to the end of the war.

Whereas the *Tripoli*'s cruise had been unproductive, the *Bogue*'s mission was very successful. The carrier had a new skipper, Captain Aurelius B. Vosseller. "Abe" Vosseller had been the commander of the Antisubmarine Development Detachment, Atlantic Fleet (AsDevLant) at Quonset Point, Rhode Island, and this was his chance to see just how the tactics and equipment that AsDevLant devised really worked. It turned out they worked just fine.

Completing the *Bogue*'s TG 22.2 were the five DEs of Commander Theodore S. Lank's CortDiv 51 (the *Haverfield*, *Swenning*, *Willis*, *Janssen*, and *F. M. Robinson*) and Lieutenant Commander Jesse D. Taylor's VC-69 with its twelve TBMs and nine FM-2s. As U-boats were beginning to be harder to find, it was obvious that the "*Bogue* pilots would have to become owls as well as hawks, both birds of prey, to hunt Admiral Doenitz's rodents night and day."[5]

Vosseller's task group left Hampton Roads on 5 May with orders to operate against U-boats west of the Cape Verde Islands. Refresher training and gunnery practice was conducted the next week, and no contacts were made. On 13 May the *Bogue*'s group met the *Block Island*'s TG 21.11. The escorts of the latter group were a little low on fuel following the *Buckley*'s battle with *U-66* and the later U-boat contacts. The

Bogue transferred 86,000 gallons of fuel oil to TG 21.11's escorts, after which Captain Hughes took his ships to Casablanca. The *Bogue* took over responsibility for U-boat searches in the area.

It was not long before there was some action. In fact, it was the same day! As dusk was approaching on the 13th, the *F. M. Robinson* reported a sound contact 3,000 yards distant. Lieutenant Commander John E. Johansen called his crew to general quarters and charged the contact. A combined hedgehog and magnetically fuzed depth charge attack was made. The ocean boiled and roared as two hedgehog and three depth charge explosions were heard. Johansen lost contact with the target, and it was never regained. The reason was simple—the target had been destroyed.

The attack by the *F. M. Robinson* had snuffed out *RO-501*, a Japanese submarine! Actually, the submarine was the ex-*U-1224*, which had been handed over to the Japanese by the Germans. The 1,120-tonner (manned by a Japanese crew) had been on her delivery voyage to Japan. This sinking was an auspicious beginning for Vosseller's green (except for the *Bogue*) task group.[6]

What had not been so good was the loss of an Avenger that day when its wheels could not be lowered. The crew were able to get out of their sinking aircraft safely, but were in the water when the TBM's load of depth bombs went off. They received no injuries, but the explosions were very painful. The carrier lost two more Avengers later in the cruise with similar results.

The explosions of the Mk. 54 depth bombs after the planes sank concerned Vosseller. The bombs had been fitted with Mk. 230 hydrostatic fuses set on "safe" and shouldn't have exploded. Vosseller later talked with *Block Island* personnel who believed that it was faulty Mk. 230 fuses on the Mk. 54 bombs that caused the violent explosions as the flattop went down. It was just fortunate that most of the men were out of the water or too far away for the explosions to have much effect.[7]

For the next few nights the VC-69 crews were tantalized by a number of disappearing radar contacts or submarine noises over sonobuoys. No attacks could be developed, however. One of the problems that VC-69 was experiencing came in launching flares from the Avengers. None of the aircraft

had flare tubes, so it was up to the gunner or radioman to
open the entrance hatch and, on command, throw a flare out.
Needless to say, this was not an efficient method, and it
generally interfered with crew duties at inopportune times. It
was a problem VC-69 would have to put up with until their
return to the United States.[8]

On 20 May the task group was directed to proceed to
Casablanca. The trip inbound was uneventful except for the
night when an Avenger dropped a flare over the task group
by mistake. For several minutes the men of TG 22.2 felt
quite naked. They reached Casablanca on the morning of 29
May, and that evening the shocking news of the *Block Island*'s sinking was received. The *Haverfield* was dispatched
to assist in the recovery operations, and returned to Casablanca
on 2 June with two of the fliers who had ditched near Las
Palmas. (See Chapter 7.)

Captain Vosseller, ever trying to learn new lessons, met
the *Block Island* survivors when they reached Casablanca.
He had a fruitful conference when Captain Hughes and
several of his officers on damage control lessons learned.[9]

The task group left Casablanca on 2 June to search again
for submarines around the Cape Verde Islands. The *Haverfield*,
fresh from her rescue mission, rejoined the group the next
day. Very little enemy activity was noted, with bad weather
curtailing searches for several days. One of the few interesting incidents for the task group during this period was the
Swenning's recovery of eight survivors of a ditched RAF
Halifax on the 6th.[10]

On the 15th Vosseller received new orders. His group
was now to head for the area around 21°00'N, 40°00'W to
look for a pair of subs (one Japanese, one German) reported
to be in that vicinity. Tenth Fleet had found the two submarines when they talked a little too much on the radio.
"Huff-Duff" quickly tracked them down. The Japanese submarine was *I-52*. The big 356-foot-long underwater blockade
runner had left Singapore on 23 April with a load of rubber,
wolfram, molybdenum, and quinine, plus fourteen passengers, for delivery to Germany. She was to rendezvous with
U-530 to pick up some radar warning equipment and also
take on a German pilot for the hazardous trip in to Bordeaux.[11]

The two submarines had met on the 23rd, the transfer
had been made, and *U-530* had cleared the area before the

Bogue arrived on the scene. But *I-52* was still hanging around. Her presence was not noted, though, until just before midnight on the 23rd.

At 2203 that evening four TBMs were launched from the carrier. They were to scout a 360-degree arc around the ship to a distance of 75 miles. An hour and a half later Lieutenant (jg) A. L. Hirsbrunner returned over the ship to report a disappearing radar contact. (Radio problems between the *Bogue* and her aircraft plagued the force during this night's events.) Hirsbrunner was told to return to the scene and monitor the sonobuoys he had dropped without results. As he headed back, he heard Lieutenant Commander Taylor, the squadron CO, report a contact. Hirsbrunner passed the word on to the *Bogue* and was told to join Taylor and act as a radio relay. Taylor, in fact, had not just contacted a submarine, but had attacked it.

Taylor's radioman had first picked up an indication of a sub on his radarscope at 2339. He coached Taylor in until they were one mile from the target. At that point Taylor dropped a sonobuoy and two smoke lights. Immediately after the sonobuoy was activated submarine noises could be heard on it. Taylor continued to close and launched a flare when only a half mile away. Just as the flare was dropped, Taylor saw a huge submarine churning east.

Taylor turned right, then back left in a 180-degree turn. He swooped down to 300 feet and dropped a pair of depth bombs. As the bombs exploded close aboard the sub's starboard side, in the flickering light of the flare she could be seen "pulling the plug." Taylor yanked his plane around for a Fido drop. The first attempt was unsuccessful because the armament selector switch was in the wrong position.

A bit chagrined, Taylor made a tight "360" and dropped his Fido from 250 feet. The crew listened intently over the sonobuoy circuit for any indication of a hit. They could hear propeller sounds like the "rhythmic tinkling of a glass."[12] Three minutes after the Mk. 24 had been dropped, a loud explosion was heard, followed by a crunching noise. Taylor thought it sounded like a "tin can being crushed." To the other crewman it was like the "breaking of twigs or crumpling of paper but heavier and deeper in tone."[13]

All propeller noises stopped over the sonobuoy, and Taylor was sure he had bagged a submarine. However, to

make sure of a kill Lieutenant (jg) William D. Gordon was
launched to check the area. Hirsbrunner arrived on the scene
at 0024, followed by Gordon at 0100. More sonobuoys were
dropped, and these picked up increasingly loud submarine
noises. At 0154 Gordon dropped a Fido. It appeared that the
torpedo had missed; then eighteen minutes later a loud
rolling explosion that lasted almost a minute was heard.
Propeller beats continued for another two minutes, then
faded into silence.[14]

Vosseller and his airmen believed they had knocked off
two submarines in these attacks. Actually, they had only got
one, but it was a good one—the 2,564-ton *I-52*. It is doubtful
that there had been two submarines in the area. Both attacks
were probably on the same submarine, with Taylor's most
likely the killing run. Gordon's attack may have been on the
remnants of *I-52*.

The next morning the residue of *I-52* could be seen
fouling the surface of the water. An oil slick about 15 miles
square coated the ocean. Many sharks glided through the
viscous water. From this slick the escorts eventually pulled
numerous pieces of lumber and planking, bits of flesh, a
rubber sandal, and 115 blocks of crude rubber. The rubber,
needed so badly by the Germans, would be going to a new
owner.

One unique feature of these attacks had been the use of
wire recorders to record any sounds heard over the sonobuoys. These recordings proved of great value in evaluating
attacks and also in training. Another unusual facet of the
attacks was the presence of a civilian technician, Mr. Price
Fish, from the Navy Underwater Sound Laboratory. He had
wired VC-69's recorders and interpreted and evaluated the
sounds recorded. He made many flights during the cruise
and was, in fact, flying with Lieutenant (jg) Gordon during
his attack.[15]

The evening of 24 June, Captain Vosseller, thinking his
group was reaching its fuel limit, turned his force toward
Bermuda. The next day two of VC-69's Avengers were sent to
the *Wake Island* (just entering the area) for further transfer to
the *Croatan*. The pilots were ferried back by a *Wake Island*
plane later in the day. The remainder of the cruise was
uneventful, and TG 22.2 anchored in Port Royal Bay on 30
June. The stay was short, the force leaving the next day, and
by 3 July the *Bogue* was back in Norfolk.[16]

It had been a very good first cruise for Captain Vosseller. As befits the former head of AsDevLant, Vosseller's action report was full of observations and recommendations that could be of use to all escort carrier groups. Two of the most important recommendations concerned the composition of the CVE's air group. Vosseller said: "In predominately night operations, to which present indications point, the attrition of aircraft can be expected to be greater than in the past. At the same time fighters cannot be used for their principal function of strafing and in addition their rendezvous with the torpedo planes at night is out of the question unless all planes turn on running lights which is unacceptable in submarine waters. It is further submitted that the need for fighters for strafing is now reduced due to the installation of rockets on VTB aircraft. It is therefore considered that the allowance of fighters might also logically be reduced to five. . . ."[17]

Regarding the fact that his aircraft made only one visual sighting, Vosseller further observed: "It might very well be that the very unsatisfactory illumination provided by flares prevented additional sightings at night but in any event it is considered that another change in enemy submarine tactics is now established and that retention of an effective offensive is contingent upon general use of searchlight equipped aircraft from CVEs."[18]

These comments and others in a similar vein by other CVE captains and squadron commanders were taken very seriously by Admiral Ingersoll and the various antisubmarine units under his command. Before long there would be a major change in the composition of the squadrons on the escort carriers.

While the *Bogue* had been heading for Bermuda, the *Croatan's* group had been going in the opposite direction. Captain Vest's TG 22.5 left Norfolk on 3 June bound for the mid-Atlantic. Doenitz had set up a five-boat picket line between the Azores and Newfoundland to provide the Germans with much-needed meteorological information. Vest was ordered to break up this line.

Task Group 22.5 included the *Bogue's* old squadron, VC-95, and the five DEs (the *Frost, Swasey, Snowden, Huse,* and *Inch*) of Commander Frank D. Giambattista's CortDiv 13. The group met their first U-boat on 11 June. She turned out to be, not one of the weather boats, but the big 1,688-ton *U-490*. She was outbound to Penang with badly needed supplies for the U-boats that had made it to that not particularly hospitable port. She was also to supply several homeward-bound boats in the Indian Ocean.[19]

The first indication of a U-boat presence had been the receipt of "Huff-Duff" fixes from Tenth Fleet on the afternoon of the 10th. These enabled the *Croatan*'s group to narrow their search area considerably. Shortly after midnight on 11 June, *U-490* sent a brief weather report home. It would be her last message. Tenth Fleet quickly plotted the origin of this transmission as a spot some 40 miles northwest of TG 22.5. Three ships of the task group were also close enough to obtain good ground wave bearings on the transmission. The noose was drawing tight around the U-boat.

On the morning of the 11th, midway between Flores and Flemish Cap, the destroyer escorts found *U-490*. The ships began their attacks immediately. Fountains of water shot into the sky; the rumble of exploding depth charges came up from below. But—nothing! No sign of the U-boat. The DEs rolled over more depth charges. These were set for maximum depth, but there was still no indication of a kill. Commander Giambattista knew the sub was down there, below the range of his depth charges, because the sonar operators kept "pinging" off their quarry.

Oberleutnant Wilhelm Gerlach, *U-490*'s skipper, also knew his pursuers were still nearby. The explosion of depth charges could be heard, as well as an odd noise his crew called the "singing saw"—the sound caused by the DEs "Foxers." Gerlach had rigged his boat for silent running, but at one point some guinea pigs that were on board for experiments became so noisy they had to be killed.[20] *U-490* had gone deep (164 fathoms—almost 1,000 feet, Gerlach believed, but this is probably inaccurate), but he could not shake off his tormentors.

Hour after hour passed. The air in the boat became fouler. Gerlach's men were becoming edgier. When would these attacks cease? Then, about 2100, the Germans could hear the Americans leaving. Gerlach brought his boat up.

The Americans *had* left, but had not gone far. Giambattista had a plan. After almost fifteen hours of effort without results, he decided to pull a fast one. Using a tactic known as a Gambit, the *Snowden* retired at a slowly decreasing speed to the south, while the *Frost* and the *Inch* did the same to the north. The escorts moved about five miles away from the last point of contact. Then they silently and slowly eased back to take up positions around the U-boat's supposed position, and they waited.

They didn't have long to wait. At 2147 *U-490* surfaced almost directly between the *Frost* and the *Snowden*. The *Frost* and the *Inch* opened fire and illuminated the scene with starshells. The *Snowden* charged in from the south to add her guns to the fray. Oberleutnant Gerlach, when he came on deck, realized he had been duped and that there was no escape. He blinkered to his attackers, "S.O.S.! Please save us!"[21] His plea didn't help him or his crew. All three DEs renewed their fire with greater intensity.

Captain Vest had been informed of the German's strange plea and radioed Giambattista, "Don't take any of that guff. Illuminate and let him have it!"[22] The destroyer escorts were already doing this with great effect. The battle was over quickly. Gerlach ordered his boat scuttled, and at 2253 *U-490* made her last dive. The night was black, but the three escorts had no trouble in recovering *U-490*'s entire wet and shivering crew.[23]

The sinking of the cargo boat, however, had done nothing to disrupt the weather pickets' activities. Task group 22.5 again took up the job of finding these U-boats. Nothing was found for a couple of days until the inquisitive ears of the *Croatan*'s HF/DF picked up the telltale signals of *U-853* on 15 June. Kapitanleutnant Helmut Sommer's boat had been in position for about a month transmitting valuable weather reports back to Germany. She had been found on 25 May by Swardfish from two British MAC-ships, but their rocket attacks had been beaten off.

Though the VC-95 fliers flew day and night to root out the sub, they could find no trace of her. The *Croatan*'s crew began calling their nettlesome quarry "Moby Dick."[24] Then, on the afternoon of the 17th, the carrier's HF/DF picked up a transmission from *U-853*. She was only 30 miles south of the task group. Unfortunately, the *Croatan*'s Avenger complement had been depleted by crashes and material problems, and the pilots had become quite fatigued by almost continuous day and night patrols for over seventy-two hours. Therefore, Wildcat patrols were supplementing their "big brothers'" patrols on this day.

Before the standby Avenger flight could be launched, a
pair of fighters came upon *U-853*. The Wildcats attacked the
U-boat before an Avenger killer team arrived. Their .50-caliber
fire lacerated her, wounding Sommer and ten others and
killing two, but Sommer was able to take his boat down. A
subsequent sonobuoy and sonar search could not locate *U-853*.
Sommer got his boat home, but his weather-reporting duties
had been cut short after just three weeks at sea.[25]

The *Croatan*'s group had broken up a part of the weather picket line. U-boat Command warned the other weather
boats about the presence of carrier aircraft and ordered them
to dive after reporting and to change positions continuously.[26]
However, it is doubtful that the information the weather
boats provided was of any use to the Germans anyway. The
timing of the Normandy invasion took them by surprise,
coming as it did in a period of unsettled weather.

Task Group 22.5 searched for several more days without
success, then put into Casablanca for supplies on 26 June.
The brief stay "proved to be a lifesaver for the VT pilots."[27]
The group left port on the 30th to hunt for a south-bound
submarine that Tenth Fleet estimated was west–northwest of
Madeira. The boat was *U-154*, and she was actually heading
for the Cape Hatteras area. Two of the *Croatan*'s screen made
sure she didn't reach her destination.

On the morning of 3 July, while conducting a sonar
search, the *Inch* found *U-154*. Two torpedoes narrowly missed
the *Inch* as she maneuvered for her attack. The *Frost* was sent
to help her fellow escort. While the two ships scoured the
area, a British B-17 from the Azores arrived on the scene.
The *Croatan* could not launch any planes because of a
catapult malfunction; so the appearance of the British plane
should have been of use to the hunters. However, the B-17
crew must have been sightseeing, for after trading challenges
with the ships below, the bomber flew off. This was not an
uncommon experience during the war.

Actually, the *Inch* and the *Frost* did very well without
any help. After several attacks, a single explosion was heard.
Almost immediately a stream of oil and debris rose to the
surface. Among this debris were found German uniforms,
pieces of wood, and human remains. This stream of oil, 140
miles northwest of Funchal, marked *U-154*'s final resting
place.[28]

For the next two weeks the *Croatan* group searched

unsuccessfully for a submarine estimated to be passing through the area. Because of her lack of operable Avengers, the *Croatan* received two of the "Turkeys" (via the *Wake Island*) from the *Bogue*. These planes didn't help much, as the carrier's catapult broke down completely on the 14th, and the task group had to return to Norfolk.[29]

Not all of the action in the Atlantic was occurring from the Cape Verdes north. A few U-boats had slipped into the South Atlantic and into Admiral Ingram's bailiwick. No escort carriers since the *Santee* had operated with Fourth Fleet, and Ingram was glad to have the services of Captain Marion E. Crist's *Solomons* group.

The flattop had been commissioned just since 21 November 1943. She had ferried aircraft to Pearl Harbor in January 1944 and had only arrived on the East Coast in mid-February. In March she set out on her first antisubmarine mission. Actually, most of this first mission entailed training as the *Solomons* and her escorts plowed through the Atlantic toward Brazil. Upon arrival there, her group was designated TG 41.6.

The task group included the DEs *Straub, Gustafson, Trumpeter,* and *Herzog.* The carrier's air unit was the veteran and proficient VC-9, still under the command of Howard Avery. Task Group 41.6 sortied from Recife on 14 April. This cruise turned out to be quite disappointing; the only indications of submarine activity during the group's time at sea were some green flares seen early on 22 April, followed the next day by some unsuccessful hedgehog attacks on what might have been *U-196*. This was the extent of any action, and TG 41.6 put into Recife on 30 April in low spirits.[30]

On 30 May the task group put back out to sea. Everyone in the group was hoping that this mission would see more action. Their hopes would be fulfilled, though the cost would be high. A northeast-bound submarine had been reported near 13°30′S, 30°00′W, and the *Solomons* was sent after it. For the next two weeks nothing much happened, though the group also looked for three more submarines (including a possible Japanese boat). Various estimated positions were scouted with no results until 14 June. At this time there was one estimated position that had not been searched. The task group took up a northeast course to intercept the track of a submarine that HF/DF stations had plotted on 9 June. This time the group was lucky.

As the *Solomons* Action Report states somewhat tongue-

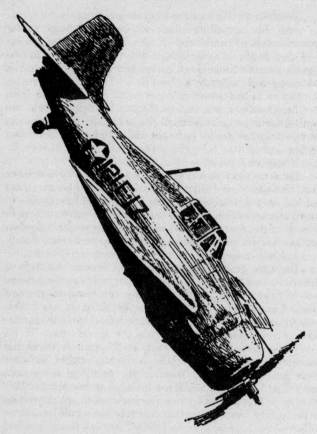

Grumman F4F Wildcat

in-cheek, "The Air Intelligence Officer had been insistent that the sub be worked over; the Executive Officer contends that contact was made in celebration of the 13th anniversary of his entrance into aviation; the Captain believes it was in honor of his daughter's birthday; in all events, contact was made with the U-boat on 15 June at 1021Z, in a position which proved the estimate to be approximately 30 miles in error."[31]

What happened next was not so amusing.

The sub, identified later as *U-860*, had been located approximately 575 miles south of St. Helena. Ensign George E. Edwards, Jr. was the first pilot to spot her. At 1021 he reported to the *Solomons* that he had a contact bearing 70 degrees and 50 miles from the carrier. There was no further word from him. It was later learned from *U-860*'s survivors that Edwards had attacked the submarine four times in the face of intense antiaircraft fire. He made one run too many, for on his last attack his Avenger was shot down. There were no survivors.

It was not until after 1400, though, that any other planes were sent to investigate Edward's contact. Lieutenant Commander Avery was dispatched to conduct a normal square search. At 1722 he caught sight of what he thought was a wake about 11 miles away. Avery turned toward it, and as he closed the distance, he could see it was a submarine heading southeast at 15 knots. A contact report was sent immediately.

U-860 remained on the surface as Avery drew closer, her only attempt at evasive tactics being a circular run to keep the aircraft at her stern. Her gunners began throwing up a heavy barrage of fire. Avery wisely kept his distance and awaited reinforcements. (It is possible that Edward's attacks had damaged the sub to such an extent that she couldn't dive.)

Ensigns Thomas J. Wadsworth and Richard E. McMahon (in Wildcats) and Moncrieff J. Spear (in an Avenger) had been launched shortly after Commander Avery to search the same general area. Their search had been unsuccessful, and they were being recovered by the *Solomons* when Avery's report came in. The three planes immediately roared off toward the U-boat.

The sun had gone down by the time these planes arrived, but there was still plenty of light left to see the U-boat. Avery, as officer in tactical command (OTC), directed the fighters to strafe the boat while he and Spear followed up with rocket attacks. Wadsworth and McMahon both piled in from the sub's starboard side as she circled. Their fire lashed the boat's deck, conning tower, and bandstand. As they pulled out only 100 feet above the sub, many bursts of flak exploded about them. Wadsworth's plane was hit in a wing tank, and he had to return to the carrier.

Avery and Spear began their rocket attacks just before

the fighters finished their passes. Spear bored in through the
black bursts of antiaircraft fire to shoot eight rockets in pairs
from 800 yards. Six of these hit slightly ahead of the conning
tower on the starboard side. As Spear zoomed away, Avery
was already releasing his six rockets from 600 yards in on the
opposite side of the sub. All of his rockets smashed into the
U-boat twenty feet ahead of the conning tower. *U-860* was
hurt.

The entire attack had taken only a few seconds. *U-860*
turned south and began to slow. Oil and billows of smoke
trailed after her. At 1751 Lieutenant (jg)s William F. Chamberlain and Donald E. Weigle arrived to continue the attacks.
McMahon made another strafing run to beat down any gunfire, and Weigle followed with another effective rocket attack.
Six of his eight rockets hit in the "lethal area" in front of the
conning tower. That particular area was receiving a terrible
beating.

U-860's speed dropped off to less than 3 knots, and an
ugly greenish-yellow scum began to coat the water behind
her. Chamberlain (with Avery running interference) charged
in from the port quarter to deliver the killing blow. He came
in too low, dropping two depth bombs directly over the
conning tower from less than 50 feet. The violent explosions
of the bombs engulfed his plane and started a fire in the
bomb bay and center cockpit. Chamberlain was able to
maintain control and "pancake" his Avenger 500 yards ahead
of the U-boat. Unfortunately, he and his crew were not
recovered. Chamberlain's loss was a particularly sad one for
VC-9. He had been a member of the squadron from the start
and had helped sink VC-9's (and the *Bogue*'s) first submarine,
U-569, back in May 1943.[32]

The loss of Chamberlain and his crew was not in vain.
U-860 had gone down, taking forty-two men with her. The
Straub and the *Herzog* were detailed to search for survivors.
It was dark now, and the two vessels had to use starshells and
flares dropped by one of the aircraft in order to locate
anyone. Their attempts to find Chamberlain and his crew
were fruitless, and they shifted their efforts to pulling the
crew of *U-860* from the sea. Only twenty-one survivors were
rescued by the *Straub* (the *Herzog* screened the operation).
One man was dead, though attempts were made to bring him
back to life. Another regained consciousness after some twen-

ty minutes of artificial respiration. Only two of the survivors were injured to any degree.[33]

The day's activities had been costly to VC-9. Besides the loss of Edwards and Chamberlain and their crews, two more Wildcats and their pilots were lost during the day. It was a somber group of airmen that flew ashore when the *Solomons* docked at Recife on the 23rd. The task group took no more part in offensive operations in the South Atlantic. There was a "show the flag" visit to Rio de Janeiro in July, and then it was back to Norfolk. For VC-9 the war in the Atlantic was over. The original CVE squadron in the Atlantic antisubmarine war was on its way to the Pacific and new tasks. For the *Solomons*, the shooting war was over, also. Except for a ferry mission to Casablanca in October, she spent the rest of the war on the East Coast in a pilot-training role.[34]

There was still U-boat activity in the Central Atlantic, and a new hunter was sent to replace the *Bogue*. She was the *Wake Island*, under the command of Captain James R. Tague. The flattop had arrived on the East Coast in January, but her only operations until this time had been the transport mission to India mentioned earlier. Now she was getting her chance to show her stuff against the U-boats.

Besides the carrier and her air unit, VC-58, the destroyer escorts *Douglas L. Howard*, *Farquhar*, *J. R. Y. Blakely*, *Hill*, and *Fiske* made up TG 22.6. The group departed Hampton Roads on 15 June headed for Bermuda. On the 17th, in the Bermuda area, a special antisubmarine exercise was held. This was the first such exercise held off Bermuda, and it was hoped that it would be of value to this new team entering the Atlantic arena.[35]

Following the completion of the exercise, TG 22.6 headed northeast to intercept a submarine south of Newfoundland. On the 20th, when the task group was almost upon Tenth Fleet's estimated position, new orders were received to proceed south and relieve the *Bogue* in her search for a Japanese submarine. (This was *I-52*, which was sunk on 24 June.) The reasoning behind this sudden change of plans was not revealed. However, "the effect on [Captain Tague] was somewhat discouraging and might have been prevented by including in the orders some of the information on which the decision was based."[36]

This change of plans was just one of many "near-misses"

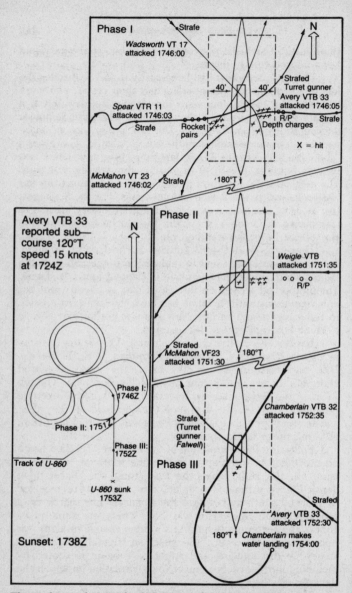

Phase I

Wadsworth VT 17
attacked 1746:00

Strafe

N

40'   40'

Strafed
Turret gunner
Avery VTB 33
attacked 1746:05

Spear VTR 11
attacked 1746:03

Strafe

Rocket pairs

Depth charges

R/P

Strafe

X = hit

McMahon VT 23
attacked 1746:02

Strafe

180°T

Phase II

Weigle VTB
attacked 1751:35

R/P

Strafed
McMahon VF23
attacked 1751:30

180°T

Avery VTB 33
reported sub—
course 120°T
speed 15 knots
at 1724Z

N

Phase I:
1746Z

Phase II: 1751

Track of *U-860*

Phase III:
1752Z

U-860 sunk
1753Z

Sunset: 1738Z

Phase III

Chamberlain VTB 32
attacked 1752:35

Strafe
(Turret
gunner
Falwell)

Strafed

Avery VTB 33
attacked 1752:30

180°T   *Chamberlain* makes
water landing 1754:00

The sinking of *U-860* by VC-9 aircraft, 15 June 1944.

that plagued the task group throughout its cruise. The cumulative effect of these incidents would lead the Atlantic Fleet's Antisubmarine Warfare Unit later to make rather strong comments about the efficiency of TG 22.6.

After it became obvious that the *Bogue*'s group had bagged the Japanese submarine, the *Wake Island* was directed to sweep the area in search of a possibly damaged submarine. On 25 June the *Bogue* sent the carrier two Avengers for further delivery to the bomber-shy *Croatan*.

The next day the *Hill* picked up a strong sonar contact. An attack run was begun but not completed because at the point where the hedgehogs should have been fired, a sailor was still removing the safety pins from the projectiles. The contact was then lost and never regained. It was the belief of the ASW Unit that the *Hill*'s sonar operator had been reading the wake of another DE.[37]

On the 28th the task group turned northeast to intercept another U-boat which Tenth Fleet had placed around 26°00'N, 20°00'W. A VC-58 pilot found the submarine on 2 July very

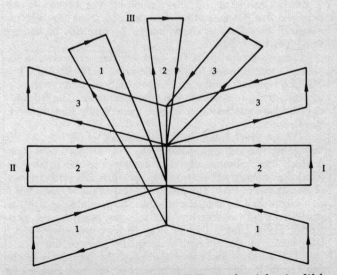

Typical search pattern used by CVEs in the Atlantic. *Wake Island* three-sector search, June–July 1944.

near the Tenth Fleet estimate. Ensign Frederick L. Moore
was on a routine search that evening when his radar operator
got a blip on his scope at 2039. The contact was 2½ miles
distant. Moore turned toward the contact and began to
descend through scattered clouds.

When he broke through some thin clouds at 1,500 feet,
Moore saw the moonlit wake of a sub almost directly under
him. Too high for an attack, Moore circled lower as his
gunner and the U-boat exchanged gunfire. Finally, he was
able to drop two depth bombs close to the submarine. As he
banked around, Moore could see that his target was submerging.
He tightened his turn to come up the U-boat's wake and
dropped a Fido. Shortly after this Moore laid a sonobuoy
pattern. These buoys were silent for about three minutes,
however.

When the buoys began operating, there was no indication of any submarine noises. Actually Fido had chased and
bitten the U-boat, and she was gone. Several more planes
were sent to help, as were two escorts, but, of course, they
could find no trace of the boat. The only evidence noted was
a slowly expanding oil slick smearing the ocean. It was
believed that Moore's attack had probably sunk the sub, but
not until after the war was it known for sure that he had got
the 1,144-ton U-543.[38]

Tague's group spent the next few days crisscrossing the
area in a vain attempt to lift up the ghost of U-543. On 7 July
TG 22.6 rendezvoused with Convoy UGS-46, and the ships of
the task group fueled from the oiler Mattaponi. The following
day the two wandering Avengers were finally transferred to
the Croatan.

Things were quiet until the morning of 12 July. As the
task group was zigzagging along, the Howard got a poor sonar
contact. Two minutes after the destroyer escort headed toward the contact, a periscope was seen just 125 yards forward
of the starboard bow. The Howard tried to run it down but it
was inside her turning circle. The DE was able to fire two
starboard depth charge projectors as she raced by the periscope. These landed too far away to have any effect, and a
later attack by the Howard was equally unsuccessful.

The Howard and the Fiske spent the remainder of the
day trying to find the submarine, but she had escaped. A
patrolling RAF B-17 wandered onto the scene and asked if it

could help. Believing the situation was under control, Tague declined the offer. Once more the ASW Unit's analysis was unfavorable to the task group. "Instances are rare in which a shore-based aircraft has volunteered assistance or even communicated with a CVE Group," the unit commented. "Even though the local air situation appeared to be well in hand it appears that the plane might well have been informed of the situation and asked to assist in the search."[39]

On the 17th another possible submarine contact was made. Throughout the day numerous sonobuoys were dropped near the spot of a disappearing radar blip. Six Fido drops were made at various times based on supposed submarine sounds coming over the buoys. Escorts were not sent to the area until late in the day, and they found nothing. In fact, nothing was turned up by anyone, and the noise indications probably had been caused by the engines of the group's own vessels or by those of a convoy passing nearby.

Following these abortive attacks, TG 22.6 headed for Casablanca. It had spent five weeks at sea with nothing to show for its efforts. (The task group did not know, of course, that it had sunk *U-543*.) It was a "down" group that docked in Casablanca. They did not know that something worse than no results was just ahead.

The task group left Casablanca on the 24th bound for the general area between the Azores and northwest Africa. Nothing was found there, though, and the task group was ordered north of the Azores to track down two west-bound U-boats. En route the *Hill*'s sonar (which had been acting up for some time) gave out completely. She was then assigned permanent plane guard duty. Her absence from the screen, however, put more of a strain on the other escorts.

The second of August was cloudy with occasional drizzles. A slight swell rolled across the surface of the ocean. The morning was quiet until 0945, when the *Howard* and the *Fiske* left the screen to investigate a sound contact. Nothing developed, and the two ships hustled back to resume their stations. Just ten minutes after they rejoined, the *Howard* saw the conning tower of a submarine break the surface 9 miles off the task group's port side.

General quarters sounded throughout TG 22.6 as the *Wake Island* and her screen peeled off to the right to clear the area. The *Howard* and the *Fiske* raced toward the con-

tact. The U-boat had disappeared as the two DEs closed in.
When they were about one mile from the sub's last position,
the two ships slowed to get better sound conditions. At 1132
the *Fiske* reported a sonar contact between her and the
Howard off her port beam.

Lieutenant John A. Comly immediately turned his ship
toward the contact and prepared for an attack. As the range
dropped, Comly was sure he had a submarine and so informed the *Howard*. The *Howard* had also turned toward the
contact, slowing slightly to ready a hedgehog attack. At 1135
the *Fiske* was holding contact at a range of 1,075 yards when
she was struck amidships on her starboard side by a torpedo.
The tremendous explosion flung men into the air or threw
them to the deck. No one had seen any wake or heard any
torpedo sounds, but this torpedo had mortally wounded the
Fiske.

The *Howard* gained sonar contact on the sub just as the
Fiske was struck, but her ensuing attack was thwarted because her hedgehogs were not ready to be fired. A hurriedly
planned depth charge attack did little but disturb the water.
Sonar contact had been lost during this run, and the *Howard*
could not regain it.

Meanwhile, the *Fiske* was in desperate straits. Her back
had been broken, and an internal explosion at 1140 only
hastened her demise. Lieutenant Comly ordered his crew to
abandon ship. The destroyer escort was slowly beginning to
sag in the middle and twist apart. Though many of the crew
had been injured, they left their ship in good order. While
the *Howard* searched vainly for the assailant, and the *Blakely*
went charging off against another suspicious contact, the
Farquhar went about the sad task of pulling the dead and
living from the water. Out of the *Fiske*'s crew of 213, four had
been found dead, twenty-six others were missing, and fifty
were wounded seriously.

Neither the ships darting about nor the aircraft flying
overhead could find any trace of a U-boat. The attack had
been so sudden and shocking that the Americans had no idea
of how many submarines were present or where they were.
Torpedo tracks were reported coming from every direction. Later it was thought that two submarines had been in
action. Actually, only Oberleutnant Herbert Meyer's *U-804*
had been around. Meyer had done an excellent job of shoot-

ing and evading the Americans. However, he was not so good at counting. Upon his return to base he put in a claim for two destroyers sunk.

The *Fiske* finally twisted apart, and her bow section sank at 1242. Her stern portion remained afloat for several hours until the *Howard* sank it with gunfire.[40] After the recovery of survivors, the task group pulled away to the west. The *Farquhar* was detached on 3 August to proceed to Argentia with her load of survivors. The next day the *George W. Ingram* and the *Schmitt* joined TG 22.6 to bring the carrier's screen back up to strength. Operations were then begun against a supposed nearby U-boat, but nothing was found. With the *Bogue*'s group coming out to relieve TG 22.6, the group set course for Norfolk.

The *Wake Island* docked on 15 August. The loss of the *Fiske* threw a damper on the task group's homecoming. There was even more of a letdown when the ASW Unit issued its analysis of the cruise. The Unit was quite blunt in its assessment, saying:

"This cruise was the most disappointing yet reviewed by this Unit. Two positive and one probable contacts were made with the enemy. No certain damage was inflicted on him and the TG lost one ship. [The ASW Unit was unaware that *U-543* had been sunk.] Some failures may be charged to fortune or exceptional circumstances, but failures to heed sound advice, failures of equipment at crucial times, inaccurate estimates of individual situations, improper employment of forces at hand, lack of readiness for battle in known proximity to the enemy, and inefficiency in individual units, even though apparently minor in themselves, when occurring with the frequency which they did in this Task Group, cannot but contribute to the overall failure of the Task Group to accomplish its mission."[41]

These were strong words, but in a way they pointed up just how far the escort carrier groups had come since the *Bogue*'s first faltering steps in early 1943. All the units—carriers, destroyer escorts, aircraft squadrons—were much better trained and disciplined than those of the year before. It was just the *Wake Island* group's misfortune to be a bit less efficient and disciplined than their peers. The *Wake Island* would not make any more antisubmarine missions in the Atlantic. She was employed in a pilot-training role until October; then she headed for the Pacific.

While the *Wake Island* was operating around the Azores, the *Card* was looking for action near Nova Scotia. The latter ship, which had spent the last few months on ferry trips to Casablanca and on carrier qualification (CarQual) exercises, followed the *Wake Island* out of Hampton Roads on 25 June. She was now commanded by Captain Rufus C. Young.

Young also commanded TG 22.10, which consisted of the *Card* with VC-12 boarded and Commander G. A. Parkison's CortDiv 48 (the *Thomas, Bronstein, Breeman, Baker,* and *Bostwick*). After puting to sea, the task group exercised near Bermuda, then turned north toward Argentia. On 2 July one of the *Card*'s planes sighted a yellowish oil slick. Escorts sent to investigate got a weak sound contact, but this was soon lost and not regained.

The task group remained in the area for the next few days. Bad weather prevented the VC-12 planes from operating, but the DEs kept looking for the probable submarine. Early on the evening of the 5th their quarry was finally "treed" about 100 miles south of Sable Island. It was the big minelayer *U-233* bound for Halifax to lay her eggs. This was the first voyage for this snorkel-less U-boat. The *Baker* (whose codename was "Setter") was the first to sniff out the U-boat. At 1908 she radioed excitedly, "Scent dead ahead 1,500 yards! Going to attack with full powder charges!"[42]

The *Baker* rushed the contact to drop a full pattern. Below the surface, the unsuspecting crew of *U-233* were doing some torpedo servicing and torpedo tube repairs in the aft compartment. The first the Germans knew that a hunter-killer group was in the vicinity was when they heard a loud whining sound, then screw noises. Almost immediately afterward numerous depth charges exploded around the boat. *U-233* was severely shaken, with lights knocked out and loose gear flying all over.

U-233 began to sink out of control rapidly. Water poured into her aft compartment, and she became very stern-heavy. A torpedo that was on the loading rails was jarred loose and slid into its tube, disemboweling an unfortunate sailor standing in its way. This torpedo may have damaged the tube cap also, thus letting more water in. The U-boat continued to sink at an alarming angle. More depth charges exploded near the submarine but caused little damage. Kapitanleutnant Hans Steen ordered the tanks blown, and *U-233* began to rise slowly.

In the meantime, Commander Parkinson was rushing to the scene in the *Thomas*. At 1931 the huge bulk of *U-233* broached in a welter of foam. The *Baker*'s gunners opened fire immediately, scoring hits all over the wallowing U-boat. The boat's chief engineer had been the first to get topside, and he promptly had his head blown off.[43] Lieutenant Commander N. C. Hoffman ordered his torpedomen to fire two torpedoes at the submarine. The *Baker*'s torpedoes ran hot and true, but the distance was too close, and they failed to arm. They did not explode, but the sight of them bubbling toward their vessel must have hastened a few submariners' departure from their boat.

The Germans had been intent on abandoning ship, not fighting back, when *U-233* surfaced, but the *Baker*'s crew believed their adversaries were shooting at them. To stop this the *Baker* roared past the sub laying a shallow depth charge pattern around the minelayer. The ocean heaved, and tons of water inundated the U-boat.

"Is the bastard shooting back at you?" asked Parkinson.

"Wait. Submarine is on fire. The submarine has stopped firing," the *Baker* replied.

"That is a swell show you are putting on!" Parkinson continued.

Lieutenant Commander D. M. Kellogg's *Thomas* was getting in the act now, peppering the sub with her own gunfire. Kellogg called Hoffman: "You go and pick up a prisoner. I am going to sink the bastard for sure."[44]

Kellogg lined his ship up and drove her into *U-233*. There was a shudder, a screech of metal against metal, as the *Thomas*'s bow ripped into the submarine just aft of her conning tower. Men on board the submarine were knocked into the water by the impact. *U-233*'s bow rose into the air as water rushed into her cracked hull; then she was gone. The screams of men thrashing about in the water echoed through the air.

The two destroyer escorts picked up thirty survivors, including *U-233*'s badly wounded captain. All of the survivors were transferred to the *Card* that evening. Steen's wounds were so severe that he died the following morning. He was buried at sea with full military honors. On 7 July TG 22.10 docked in Boston to put the prisoners ashore, and three days later the group departed for the Caribbean.[45]

German submarines had been operating in the Caribbe-

an infrequently for some time, but beginning in March
several had arrived to make nuisances of themselves. Admiral
Ingersoll decided that the Caribbean Sea Frontier forces
needed reinforcements. The *Card* and the *Guadalcanal* groups
were sent south to see if they could find anything. Both
groups ran across *U-539*, but that boat was lucky, evading all
attacks. The *Card* was lucky, too. While air attacks were
being conducted against *U-539*, the carrier's low pressure
turbine burned out. For several hours the *Card* lay dead in
the water, unable to recover her aircraft. The planes were
sent to Puerto Rico, and after repairs were finally made, the
Card limped into San Juan.

Following full-fledged repairs, the *Card* and her consorts
left San Juan looking for a U-boat leaving the Caribbean.
VC-12 planes had a radar contact on a submarine on 31 July
and dropped Fidos after the boat dove. These attacks were
unsuccessful, though, and a search by two escorts also came
up empty. There was another attack on a sub on 6 August,
but again the U-boat escaped. The carrier then headed north
to help the *Bogue* look for submarines, but nothing else was
discovered, and TG 22.10 anchored in Hampton Roads on 24
August.[46]

Abe Vosseller's *Bogue* group was back out on patrol after
a three-week stay in Norfolk. Vosseller's TG 22.3 included the
CortDiv 51 DEs *Haverfield, Willis, Swenning, Janssen,* and
Wilhoite. The *Bogue*'s new squadron was Lieutenant Commander Joseph T. Yavorsky's VC-42. Among the twelve Avengers and nine Wildcats of VC-42 were four new TBM-1Ds.

These four planes, with searchlights and improved radars, but minus rockets and launching rails, would enable the
aviators to make more accurate night attacks. The assignment
of these aircraft was the result of a message from King to
Ingersoll on 9 July directing Ingersoll to assign four of the
searchlight planes to each of the next three task groups to
sail. This message also ordered searchlight training to be
expedited. This cruise would see the first use of a searchlight
plane in an attack from an American CVE.[47]

On board the *Bogue* to observe her tactics were a naval
captain and an army colonel. Also on board, oddly, were five
fighter director officers. Vosseller was not impressed, saying
later, "The training these officers had received may be and
probably is excellent from the standpoint of air-to-air work.

However, not one of them had the slightest conception of the operations in which this ship is currently engaged and it has been necessary to train them practically from the ground up. . . . It is submitted that there should be a course in at least one of the Navy's fighter director schools which fits officers in this classification for duty in the Combat Information Center aboard ships engaged in ASW operations as well as strict fighter direction work."[48]

Vosseller was eager to begin flight operations, which did begin on 25 July. It was his intent to do a lot of night flying, so he decided to let the torpedo pilots fly the Avengers at night and some of the more experienced fighter pilots fly the TBMs during the day. There was one problem with this plan—none of the fighter pilots was qualified in an Avenger. The answer was to qualify them at sea.

However, on the morning of the 26th Lieutenant (jg) John Sulton, Jr. "disproved Captain Vosseller's theory definitely and irrevocably."[49]

Sulton was making his first TBM landing. His approach was normal, but just as he passed over the fantail, his plane settled slightly, and the Avenger's tailhook struck the ramp. The hook was weakened, but not broken, by the impact. Sulton caught the Number 7 wire, and it appeared that his plane was hooked. The barrier operators lowered the first two barriers.

But the arresting hook pulled out, and Sulton scooted down the deck over the first two barriers and through the third one. Lieutenant John B. Watson had just landed and was folding the wings on his Avenger when bits of metal flew through the air past him. Sulton's right wing had clipped the tail and folded left wing of Watson's Avenger. Watson tried to dig a hole in the floor of his cockpit.

Sulton's plane careened on, smashing into two TBMs parked side by side on the starboard bow. Three men working on the outboard plane took an unwanted bath as they and the Avenger went over the side. Bruised and soaking, they were picked up immediately by the *Haverfield*. The inboard Avenger was pushed off the flight deck onto the forecastle. Sulton's plane finally came to rest on its nose at the edge of the deck, and Sulton hopped out of his battered plane uninjured.

It had not been a good start for VC-42 and the *Bogue*.

Four Avengers had been wrecked, two of them "Dogs" —searchlight planes. This one accident had halved the *Bogue's* complement of these aircraft.[50]

The task group spent the next few days conducting antisubmarine exercises with the submarine *R-6*. A mock attack on Convoy UGS-49 was also made. Task Group 22.3 then headed for Bermuda, where replacement Avengers (but no searchlight aircraft) were picked up.

On 1 August the *Bogue* left Bermuda with orders to locate an enemy submarine near 46°00′N, 38°00′W. En route it was learned that the *Fiske* had been sunk and that the *Wake Island* was short of planes. Captain Tague was requesting that the *Bogue* expedite her arrival on station. Task Group 22.3 bent on the speed and relieved the *Wake Island's* group on the 5th.

For the next ten days a number of radar and sound contacts were made, but none could be developed into an attack. Weather played a large role in this lack of success; it was bad enough to prevent flying on five of the ten days. The planes were back out on the evening of 14 August. At 0300 the next morning Lieutenant (jg) Wayne A. Dixon reported a radar contact. Dixon's contact was *U-802*, heading for the Gulf of St. Lawrence. Nothing more was heard from Dixon, and he may have crashed while investigating his contact or had an attack of vertigo.[51]

Several other radar and sound contacts were made over the next few days, but once again the escorts and aircraft were unsuccessful in tracking down any U-boats. On the 16th the *Bogue* almost became a statistic herself when she unknowingly crossed the path of *U-802*. Before the U-boat could get into position, the flattop had zigged out of range.[52] Then, on the 19th, *U-802* turned up again, and VC-42 almost had a kill to log in its records.

The night of 19 August was moonless, with a few scattered clouds to break up the unrestricted visibility. Lieutenant Carl E. Lair, Jr. had been launched at 2117 the night before, but three hours of monotonous droning through the sky had produced nothing. At 0030 Lair's crew came fully alert when the radioman called out a blip on his radarscope. The target was 20 miles ahead.

Coached in by his radar operator, Lair closed with the target and descended from 2,000 feet to 150 feet. When the

Avenger was about three-quarters of a mile from the target, its searchlight was switched on. Dead ahead, pinned in the terrifyingly bright beam, was the thoroughly surprised *U-802*. One man could be seen on her bridge.

Lair attacked immediately. At 0040 he toggled out three Mk. XI British 250-pound torpex depth bombs from seventy-five feet. Plumes of water obscured the submarine as the bombs exploded; then she disappeared into the darkness. Lair circled back to find the U-boat gone. He dropped several sonobuoys but could not regain contact with the submarine, as *U-802* slipped away to make a remarkably unproductive patrol in the Gulf of St. Lawrence. Though the U-boat had escaped, Lair's attack (the first searchlight attack by a CVE plane) had proved that the TBM "Dogs" were excellent aircraft in the night search role.[53]

Further searches in the vicinity of Lair's attack found nothing. A warm front, with its associated bad weather, was approaching, and Captain Vosseller had an idea. He split his force, leaving three DEs to cover the U-boat's estimated course, while he took the *Bogue* and the other two escorts southwest to get in the clear behind the front as soon as possible. Because his force was now fragmented, Vosseller was assigned six Canadian frigates of Escort Group 16.

Vosseller later told what he had in mind, "It was believed that the submarine had been held down for some time, was probably damaged, would be anxious to surface and would be apt to do so since he would feel safe from aircraft in the bad weather prevailing in that area. Since our weather information was obviously better than his, an opportunity was presented to get ahead of him into clear weather and surprise him by having planes waiting for him when he broke out of the front."[54]

Vosseller's plan worked—but not on *U-802*. Instead, the *Bogue*'s planes came up with *U-1229*. Early on the 20th the *Bogue* passed into the clear and turned north to begin searching behind the front. Later in the morning the *Card*, operating nearby, asked if she could help. Vosseller requested that she cover the area where Lieutenant Lair had attacked *U-802*. The *Card*, of course, didn't find anything and soon returned to Norfolk.

It wasn't long before the VC-42 planes found something. *U-1229* had left Trondheim on 26 July for a special mission.

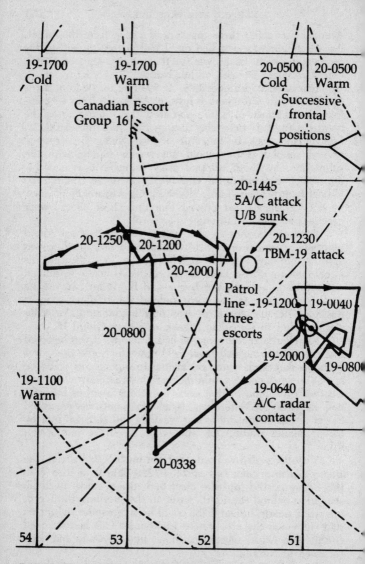

Bogue track during attacks on *U-1229*.

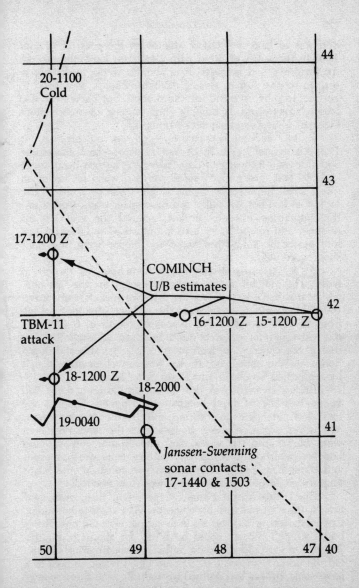

44

20-1100
Cold

43

17-1200 Z

COMINCH
U/B estimates

42

16-1200 Z   15-1200 Z

TBM-11
attack

18-1200 Z

18-2000

41

19-0040

Janssen-Swenning
sonar contacts
17-1440 & 1503

50   49   48   47 40

She was to land one Oskar Mantel on the coast of Maine. Though the sub was fitted with a snorkel, Korvettenkapitan Armin Zinke had not used it in about a week, preferring to remain on the surface during daylight. Zinke's crew tried to get him to submerge and use the snorkel, but Zinke (who was later characterized as ranking "high among the more inept German U-boat commanders") refused.[55]

Zinke's decision was fatal for both him and his boat. At 1227 Lieutenant (jg) A. X. Brokas ran across the U-boat some 300 miles south by east of Cape Race. Brokas was flying south at 1,500 feet, just under a solid overcast, when his radioman saw a small blip appear on his scope, distance 5 miles. The radioman had not yet called out his contact when Brokas saw the submarine himself. Brokas "poured the coal" to his Avenger and roared in for a rocket attack. The Germans saw him before he got within range and began firing, but their shots were wild.

At 1,200 yards Brokas began launching his rockets in pairs. They all hit short, however, except for the last one, which may have scored. As the last two rockets were fired, U-1229 began to swing left, and the rockets were approaching from an oblique angle. But in making the turn, U-1229 was left wide-open for a perfect depth bomb run. Despite the fact that it was contrary to doctrine to release rockets and depth bombs on the same pass, Brokas was so well positioned that he really had no choice but to drop the bombs.

Brokas zoomed over the U-boat at 100 feet, doing 230 knots. Two Mk. 54 depth bombs were dropped. The first one exploded very close to the port side by the conning tower. The other exploded about 40 feet from the bow. Five men were blown into the water, and one 20-mm gun was also knocked overboard. Numerous battery cells were cracked, and though no deadly chlorine gas was released, the boat's engines could not develop the power they needed.

The U-boat made a quick figure-eight turn, zigzagged briefly, then settled with little way on. As U-1229 went under, Brokas darted in to drop a sonobuoy pattern. On one of the buoys propeller beats could be heard for almost a minute. These stopped suddenly to be replaced by hammering sounds. On the ocean's surface U-1229's life blood began to pool in a large slick. Brokas had radioed his sighting, and three Avengers already in the air were vectored to the scene. Two more

TBMs and two FM-2s were also launched to relieve Brokas. Finally, Vosseller sent four of his escorts to help.[56]

The first reinforcements arrived about an hour after U-1229 had submerged. One Avenger was directed to orbit the area at 7,500 feet and provide the carrier a radar range and bearing to vector the other planes to the scene and to act as a radio relay. Soon all the planes had gathered at the scene. An oil slick could be seen extending about a mile in a U-shaped pattern.

Two planes began investigating the northwestern tip of the slick, while the remainder concentrated on its other end. The latter group finally found the sub. They soon noticed that oil was bubbling at the end of their slick, and at 1419 one of the pilots picked out the dim outline of the U-boat just under the surface. The hunt was over, and U-1229's ordeal would be relatively brief. The fliers were extremely eager to attack, perhaps too eager as their first attacks showed.

At 1425 U-1229 began to surface slowly. With little battery power, Zinke had tried to raise his snorkel under water and get air to start the diesels. This effort had been unsuccessful, and Zinke had to surface to get the snorkel to work. Before the conning tower was visible, Lieutenant (jg)s Bernard C. Sissler and Milton J. Sherbring made virtually simultaneous depth bomb runs. When they discovered they were approaching each other almost head-on, they each dropped their bombs about 200 feet short of the sub and pulled out sharply to avoid a collision. "In this case, too much eagerness instead of coordination, spoiled the attacks."[57]

Sissler still had rockets and returned to deliver a successful attack. Seven of his rockets punched into the sub just below the waterline. While the Avengers were attacking, the Wildcats were making virtually continuous strafing runs. Two minutes after Sissler's pass, U-1229 was fully surfaced, hardly moving. Men could be seen in her conning tower and on deck donning life jackets and launching rafts. Soon they began leaping into the water.

Lieutenant (jg) W. S. Porter arrived from the other end of the U-boat's oil slick to drop the last depth bombs. Unfortunately, one of his bombs hung up, and the other was a dud. Shortly after this drop an explosion was seen in U-1229's conning tower, and at 1440 she began to sink by the bow. Soon only her conning tower was visible; then her stern reared out of the water, and she slid sharply under the waves. A moment later a tremendous explosion blew her to bits, debris and water shooting 100 feet into the air.[58]

Forty-two survivors (one of whom died later) were pulled from the water by the DEs. Zinke was not among the survivors. One of those rescued was Oskar Mantel, self-styled "Propaganda expert" and spy. Found to be carrying $1,940.00 in twenty-dollar bills, he was promptly relieved of this burden. (Mantel had lived in Yorkville, New York prior to the war. After the war some of Mantel's Yorkville friends had the gall to instigate a lawsuit against Captain Vosseller to get the money back. They claimed it belonged to his mother in Germany.)[59]

On 22 August the *Bogue* received orders to proceed to Argentia where VC-42 would get two searchlight Avengers. The task group docked on the 24th and transferred the prisoners to naval intelligence personnel the next day. It turned out the TBM "Dogs" were not there—just standard Avengers—but the *Bogue* had some very distinguished visitors instead.

Admiral Ingersoll and his staff came on board to present awards to the VC-42 fliers involved in the sinking of *U-1229*. Speaking to the *Bogue's* crew, Ingersoll said, "It is not often that I am so fortunate as to be able to make awards for successful action against the enemy so promptly and under such auspicious circumstances. Here on this ship you have the dramatic evidence [the POWs] of your success."[60]

After informing those present that he had recommended the *Bogue* and her associated units (including VC-42) for the Presidential Unit Citation for their successes since 1943, Admiral Ingersoll awarded Distinguished Flying Crosses, Air Medals, and Letters of Commendation to a number of VC-42 officers and men. "As the Admiral fastened the medals to the pilots' khaki blouses, several recipients noticed his fingers bled from the pin pricks, but he took no notice of this and appeared to enjoy making the presentations."[61]

Following several days of relaxation (including a nonstop party by VC-42), TG 22.3 departed Argentia on the afternoon of 28 August. This portion of the cruise would be the most frustrating for the officers and men of the task group. Numerous sound and radar contacts were made, but none of these could be developed. One contact that was thought to be a

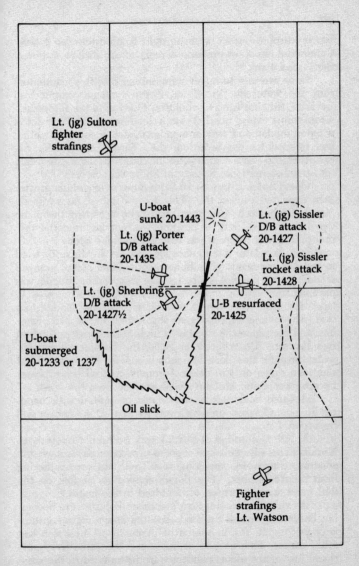

Final attacks on *U-1229* by VC-42 aircraft, 20 August 1944.

snorkel turned out to be an upright floating telephone pole. Other contacts were probably wrecks in the shallow waters of the Grand Bank.[62]

In an attempt to inject some humor into this maddening state of affairs, the VC-42 intelligence officer compiled an "awards" list. For the award of the "Survival of the Blippiest," seven blips were needed for a leather medal, five for a wooden medal, and two for a paper medal. A snorkel sighting was needed for the award of the "Three Schnorts for the Schnorchiest—and a guarantee of induction at a later date into the International Society of Short Schnorchers."[63]

One TBM was lost on 16 September when winds greater than expected caused the plane to run out of gas while on patrol. Fortunately, the Bogue had been vectoring the plane when it ditched, and its position was not far from the task group. The entire crew was rescued an hour later.

Two days later Lieutenant (jg) Robert T. McGusty tried to match Lieutenant (jg) Sulton's record of four planes pranged at one time. He fell short by one plane. The Bogue was pitching and yawing violently when McGusty attempted to land. He mistakenly took a waveoff as a cut and landed in a skid. The Avenger's right gear sheared off in the hard landing, and the plane then bounced high in the air over the first two barriers. Its tailhook engaged the Number 3 barrier, which brought the plane to a stop in midair. McGusty's TBM slammed down on two other Avengers, and all three planes became washouts. McGusty walked away from the crash.

McGusty and Sulton were later presented with handmade "Iron Crosses" on which was written "Der Fuehrer will be proud."[64]

On 19 September TG 22.3 was ordered to return to Norfolk. This was welcome news to everyone, particularly the aviators, who were becoming very tired and were suffering from "acute blipitis." The Bogue arrived at Norfolk on the 24th, and another cruise was entered in the books.[65]

As evidenced by the Bogue's cruise, U-boat were becoming harder and harder to find. But the escort carrier groups kept putting to sea in search of them. The CVEs also had other duties, such as pilot training and the usual ferry missions. Two more escort carriers were introduced in the summer for ferry runs. The Shamrock Bay was a new carrier commissioned in March of that year. Despite the lack of enthusiasm for the Kaiser carriers, she was sent to the East Coast in July to ferry planes to Casablanca, and left New York on 26 July with a load of P-47s. On her return passage she brought back another load of AAF aircraft plus a captured Do 217. She spent two and one-half weeks in New York, and then it was back to Casablanca with another load of aircraft. She returned to the United States on 23 October. Her stay in the Atlantic was short, for she soon left for the Pacific. These two ferry missions were the extent of her operations in the Atlantic.[66]

The *Prince William*, a *Bogue*-class vessel, had been operating in the Pacific since 1943. In May 1944 she was transferred to the Atlantic to operate as a CarQual carrier. Except for one ferry mission to Casablanca in August and September, she spent the rest of the war in the Atlantic in a training capacity.

The *Core* had followed the *Bogue* out of Hampton Roads by about two weeks, leaving on 8 August. Her cruise, like those of so many of the other groups now, would be disappointing. Doenitz was sending fewer U-boats to the western Atlantic, and most of those he did send were equipped with a snorkel. The CVE groups were expending a lot of effort, but finding very little.

After a stay in Bermuda for antisubmarine exercises, the *Core*'s TG 22.4 headed northeast to look for a weather picket near 46°30′N, 31°30′W. She had no luck at all, for there really wasn't much around. However, two U-boats (*U-1221* and *U-1223*), helped by new radar detection gear, were able to slip by the *Core*'s group and made a small nuisance of themselves off the North American coast.[67]

The *Core*'s cruise was devoid of much action, mainly because there were few U-boats about. The escorts and aircraft of VC-13 tried their best, tracking down several HF/DF fixes and attacking some supposed radar and sound contacts, but these were spurious. Weather on 27 August, though, caused a near disaster for VC-13. The weather had been poor for several days, but cleared enough on the morning of the 27th for four Avengers and five fighters to be launched to investigate a "Huff-Duff" bearing. Then fog settled in, and the *Core* was in the middle of it. With their gas running low, all nine planes were directed to ditch beside three of the task group's escorts, which, fortunately, were

operating away from the carrier and were in the clear. Lucki-
ly, too, all the crews were recovered uninjured.[68] The *Core's*
aircraft strength had been halved by this one incident.

The flattop put in to Argentia on 10 September to pick
up replacement aircraft and to fuel. She returned to sea on
the 17th. This portion of the cruise was no more successful
than the first part, and TG 22.4 anchored in Hampton Roads
on 8 October with little to show for the mission except for a
lot of miles covered.

The sinking of *U-1229* had been the only U-boat sinking
by a CVE group in August. There would be only one in
September, too; that down near the Cape Verdes Islands.

10

BITTER TO THE END

There had been no escort carrier in the Fourth Fleet area since the *Solomons* left Recife in early July, as Tenth Fleet could see "no profitable employment for a CVE" there.[1] With a few subs again putting in an appearance, the *Tripoli* was sent south to see if she could find them. The carrier, now commanded by Captain Thayer T. Tucker, had spent the previous couple of months in carrier qualification training off Quonset Point, Rhode Island. Now her crew were ready to see some action.

The *Tripoli*'s squadron was still VC-6, and for her voyage down to Recife the flattop was screened by the *O'Toole* and the *Edgar G. Chase*. The group left Norfolk on 1 August. For the fliers there was little excitement as not much flying was accomplished. Their main excitement came with the crossing of the equator. "The initiation of the pollywogs was tough. There were bones broken and heads shaved; however, no one was killed."[2]

For the *O'Toole*, though, the passage south almost resulted in the sinking of a U-boat. On 11 August the destroyer escort caught a submarine in her sonar web and raced in for the attack. Several hedgehog projectiles and depth charges disturbed the water with their explosions, and soon a large quantity of oil and debris could be seen coating its surface. The *O'Toole*'s crew were sure they had got the U-boat. But, as happened many times before, the submarine was tough, and she escaped.[3]

The *Tripoli* docked at Recife on 13 August and set back

out on the 23rd. Tucker's group was now organized as TG 41.7, with the *Straub, Gustafson, Alger,* and *Marts* providing the screen. Although several contacts were made during this mission, nothing was found. The VC-6 fliers put in a lot of night flying using three TBM-1D searchlight aircraft almost exclusively. The cruise was very disappointing, and TG 41.7 returned to Recife on 11 September.[4]

Thirty-six hours later the task group returned to sea. "Huff-Duff" had picked up the scent of a U-boat off Sierra Leone. As TG 41.7 headed northeast, Tenth Fleet provided the group with some new information. On the 18th the Tenth Fleet HF/DF operators decided that the submarine they were tracking was about to rendezvous with another U-boat west of the Cape Verdes. As usual, Tenth Fleet knew what it was talking about. *U-1062,* homeward-bound from Penang with a cargo of petroleum products, was to fuel *U-219,* heading for Japan.[5]

As the *Tripoli* plowed northeast, another CVE group was coming out to meet her. This group was built around the *Mission Bay,* now under the command of Captain John R. Ruhsenberger. After the flattop's mission to India earlier in the year, she had made one more ferry voyage to Casablanca in June. On her return from that mission she suffered an unfortunate collision with a dredge that put her in the yards for a couple of months.[6]

Once again in top shape, she was back on the prowl. Ruhsenberger's TG 22.1 (the *D. E. Howard, Farquhar, J. R. Y. Blakely, Hill,* and *Fessenden,* with VC-36 as the air group) left Norfolk on 8 September for the South Atlantic. The task group was to look for a south-bound U-boat before heading to Dakar for fuel. The submarine didn't show up, and TG 22.1 docked at Dakar on 20 September.

The next day the *Mission Bay* left port to work on the submarine (*U-219*) reported to be heading for the Far East. A couple of tentative contacts were made, but nothing else. A few days later TG 22.1 was ordered to join the *Tripoli* and break up the rendezvous of *U-219* and *U-1062* in the vicinity of 11°30′N, 34°40′W. Tenth Fleet estimated that the two boats would be meeting on 28 September.

On the 28th both task groups began receiving indications that the U-boats were nearby. A radar contact was made by the *Mission Bay* early that morning only 18,000 yards from

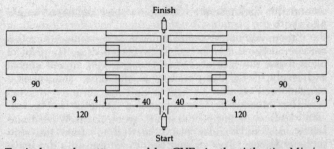

Typical search pattern used by CVEs in the Atlantic. *Mission Bay* two VT/two VF day beam search, August–October 1944.

the carrier, but there appears to have been no attempt to track this contact down. It was only later in the day that any attack was made on this contact. A Fido drop brought the welcome sound of an explosion and "deafening rushing sounds" over sonobuoys, but no sub was sunk (if one had even been present).[7]

Shortly after this attack *Mission Bay* group reported to TG 41.7 for duty. (Captain Tucker would command this joint operation.) Within minutes of this rendezvous the action began.

The sun had gone down about 1900, and there was almost complete darkness except for the fitful light of the moon through some clouds. Lieutenant William R. Gillespie had been launched before sunset to search ahead of the *Tripoli*. At 1940 Gillespie radioed the carrier (code-named "Tiger"), "Tiger, do you have any Committee away from group?"

"Wait," came the reply. "Negative, Committee all in formation."

Then, just a short time later, Gillespie excitedly radioed, "I've got him! I've got him! He's shooting at me! I'm going in to make a run!"[8]

It was Gillespie's last transmission. The submarine, probably *U-219*, shot his plane down with the loss of all hands. Lieutenant (jg) Joseph W. Steere (on his own search pattern) was just a few miles away when he saw the flash of gunfire from the sub and possibly some rocket fire from Gillespie's plane. He peeled off and headed in that direction, now shrouded in darkness after Gillespie's plane had been swatted into the sea.

Steere was having difficulty locating the submarine when antiaircraft fire suddenly flashed by his left wing. He jinked a bit and saw the boat almost underneath him. Steere circled and launched his eight rockets at the boat. Their flashes blinded him, so that he had to pull out abruptly to avoid crashing. Meanwhile, Lieutenant (jg) Douglas R. Hagood, who had been flying over the task group in his Wildcat and acting as a radio relay plane, arrived to strafe the still-surfaced U-boat. This strafing beat down the sub's defensive fire and enabled Steere to return and lay a depth bomb near the boat's starboard quarter. The U-boat dove, and Steere let loose his Fido to follow her.

The Mk. 24 missed, and Steere laid a sonobuoy pattern. Submarine noises were quite evident over the buoys; but even with ships and planes from both task groups scouring the area over the next few days, the U-boat escaped.[9]

The two groups were operating about 120 miles apart, heading north, on the 30th when the *Mission Bay* group got a hot contact. The VC-36 planes had been picking up continual contacts on radar and sonobuoys throughout the morning and into the afternoon. A number of Fidos were dropped, with indications of explosions. But the submarine (or submarines) kept operating.

Three DEs from the *Mission Bay*'s screen were sent to investigate the aviators' last attack near 11°37′N, 34°43′W. (This point was within 15 miles of Tenth Fleet's estimated position of the U-219/U-1062 rendezvous.) At 1617 the *Fessenden* obtained a sonar contact at 1,000 yards. She closed to 600 yards before this contact was classified as a submarine. Lieutenant Commander W. A. Dobby took his ship back out to 1,600 yards to ready his hedgehog, then charged the contact.

The hedgehogs were fired at 1630. Just fourteen seconds later four detonations were heard 320 feet below the surface. Two minutes later the *Fessenden* dropped a seventeen-charge depth charge pattern for good measure. These were unnecessary, as the hedgehogs had already done their work on U-1062. Her cargo from Penang had almost made it to Germany.[10]

U-219 was still in the vicinity. A VC-6 Avenger almost caught her napping on the surface on 3 October, but luck was not with the Americans this time. Lieutenant Charles A. Shortle, Jr. surprised *U-219* at night, but released his depth bombs prematurely. If they had been dropped normally, the U-boat would undoubtedly have been destroyed. After the U-boat dove, a sonobuoy pattern was laid (and later expanded by other planes) that showed the submarine was still nearby. After several hours of tracking, a Fido was dropped by one of the planes, and an explosion resulted, followed by hammering, clanking, and gurgling sounds. The VC-6 fliers were sure they had bagged the U-boat, but *U-219* escaped to reach Penang.[11]

Both carriers remained in the South Atlantic a while longer. Recife was the base for the *Tripoli*, and the *Mission Bay* used Bahia and Capetown as her bases, as both ships searched vainly for the rare U-boats reported to be in transit through the area. On 8 November both task groups joined forces to repel mock attacks by Fourth Fleet air and surface units. The exercise was well executed and all units received some very valuable training. After a short stay in Recife, both task groups left for Norfolk, arriving on 25 November. The *Tripoli* and the *Mission Bay* were the last CVEs to operate in the South Atlantic.[12]

The sinking of *U-1062* was to be the last made by the CVE groups until April of 1945. In fact, it would be the last sinking that U.S. forces would score in the Atlantic until January. Doenitz had pulled most of his boats back near the Continent, and only an average of 31 boats would be operating daily in the Atlantic in November 1944. This number would rise to 50 in April 1945, but this drop from a high of 108 boats in May 1943 showed that Doenitz had virtually conceded the run of the Atlantic to the Allies.[13]

The other "jeeps" operating in the Atlantic were just as frustrated by the lack of submarines as had been the *Tripoli* and the *Mission Bay*. The *Bogue* reported, "A contact now is a precious thing, only a few will occur in any cruise and they must be developed and held onto with every ounce of skill and endurance it is possible to muster."[14]

With a diminishing number of submarines to hunt, Admiral King thought it was time to change the emphasis of escort carrier operations. "Until there is a marked renewal of U-boat activity in Atlantic areas of U.S. responsibility," he wrote Admiral Ingersoll on 23 October, "it is considered that the present is an appropriate time to reduce (or suspend unless the U-boat estimate shows attractive targets) offensive sweeps of CVE support groups in the interest of concentrating more time on the training and material readiness of such groups for further intensive operations."[15]

Thus, a number of CVEs spent much of their time in the winter of 1944–45 in training roles or on ferry missions. After one offensive mission that saw fog so thick that the *Guadalcanal*'s planes had to be talked in by the landing signal officer listening to the sounds of the aircraft engines, the "Can Do" became a training center. She spent the rest of the war in this capacity.[16]

The *Bogue* had also been operating as a training career at Bermuda in January. She was replaced in that role by the *Croatan* and then joined the *Card* in a ferry run to Liverpool in mid-February. Upon their return to Norfolk together on 12 March, the *Card* entered the Norfolk yards for general overhaul, then spent until 25 May as a CarQual carrier off Quonset Point. The *Bogue* also operated off Quonset Point until April, when she began working against the U-boats one last time.[17]

The *Croatan*, in the meantime, was now commanded by Captain Kenneth Craig. On 24 January 1945 he took his carrier, screened by three DEs, to a meeting with another group of ships heading east. On board one of these ships, the cruiser *Quincy*, was President Roosevelt, heading for his last major conference at Yalta. The *Croatan* provided air cover for the president's coterie until she was relieved by aircraft from the Azores and Morocco. On Roosevelt's return the *Mission Bay* performed the same service between 23 and 27 February. Like the *Bogue*, though, the *Croatan*'s and the *Mission Bay*'s fighting days were not over just yet.

Of those escort carriers operating on offensive sweeps during the winter of 1944–45, the *Core*'s cruise in January and February came the closest to doing some damage to the U-boats. The *Core* had left Norfolk on 24 January to operate against a pair of U-boats in the mid-Atlantic. On the morning of 1 February a TBM pilot, running down a radar contact, caught sight of a U-boat, her decks awash. His attack, however, failed to damage the boat, and she escaped despite the efforts of several escorts to locate her.

More sonar contacts were made by the DEs over the

following days, but rough seas hampered the hunters, and no submarines were found. The *Core*'s aviators almost scored on diving submarines on 11 and 13 February, but the U-boats were too elusive. Several Tenth Fleet "Huff-Duff" fixes were run down, but these proved to be fruitless, and the *Core* group put into Argentia empty-handed on the 27th.

Against the *Core* group's lack of success with the U-boats, her squadron, VC-58, suffered actual losses. The tempestuous Atlantic created severe hazards for the fliers. A number of broken or lost airplanes and two fatalities were the result. There were a couple of unusual accidents during this mission. In one, the catapult holdback ring broke while an FM-2 was being run up on the catapult. The pilot tried to brake his plane, but forgot to cut his throttle. Seeing his plane skidding forward, the pilot tried to fly the Wildcat off. This didn't work, and the fighter dribbled off the bow. The pilot suffered only a good dunking.

The other accident involved an Avenger that had sustained some damage in a landing the day before. The plane was loaded on a crash dolly and tied down, wings spread, with some thirty 21-thread manila lines and two wire straps. These weren't enough to hold the plane. In mountainous seas with winds across the deck of 115 knots, the lines snapped, and the Avenger literally flew off the carrier to crash into the sea.[18]

While many of the "jeeps" had been involved in training and ferry missions, their air squadrons had not been sitting around doing nothing. In early 1945 reports had reached U.S. intelligence agencies that Hitler was planning a final blitz on the eastern seaboard using rockets launched from submarines. One of the earliest reports of this possibility had come from Oskar Mantel, the erstwhile spy who rode the wrong submarine (*U-1229*) on his mission.[19] This story had been strengthened when the snorkeler *U-1230* evaded all U.S. patrols to land two spies on the Maine coast on 29 November. The two hapless spies were soon caught, but their tale of a fleet of submarines carrying more German agents and armed with rockets caused the Americans grave concern.

And when *U-1230* stayed around to sink a Canadian vessel and then evade Tenth Fleet's inquisitive HF/DF ears and a search by the *Bogue*, the Americans did not find the situation to their liking.[20]

On 8 January Admiral Ingram (who had succeeded Admiral Ingersoll as CinCLant on 15 November) announced to the press the possibility of an attack on the East Coast. This announcement created quite a stir, and the press wanted to know just what kind of defenses the East Coast had. Of course, this couldn't be revealed, but the Navy, the Army, and the Army Air Forces were readying a hot welcome for the U-boats and rockets if they did come.

The VC squadrons were part of this "hot welcome." Besides their normal training schedules, the squadrons had to send groups of aircraft to various airfields along the East Coast. At these fields the planes were held at four-hour alert to act as "anti-buzzbombers." Needless to say, the rockets didn't come, and the four-hour alerts rapidly became a drag, but it was not long before the squadrons were back on their carriers.

When the squadrons reboarded their carriers, they were operating with a new mix of aircraft. After many months of recommendations and pleadings from carrier and squadron commanders, it was finally decided in January to increase the number of Avengers and reduce the number of Wildcats assigned to the squadrons. The number of Avengers was increased to sixteen and the number of Wildcats reduced to three.[21]

Doenitz *had* been planning a blitz on the East Coast, but when he put the operation in motion in late March 1945, Nazi Germany was bleeding to death, with less than two months of life left. The six Type IXC and IXC40 boats he was able to send (as Group *Seewolf*) on this operation hardly constituted a threat. Also, though equipped with snorkels, the U-boats did not have rockets or any other futuristic weapons.

Doenitz had sent his U-boats out only in the hope of creating as much havoc as possible. In a message to these boats on 3 April he exhorted, "For almost 1½ years the enemy has experienced no surface attacks on convoys and is prepared for only underwater U-boat operations . . . Attack ruthlessly and with determination."[22]

But once again, unfortunately for the Germans, through their penetration of Enigma, Tenth Fleet knew of Group *Seewolf*. With Tenth Fleet furnishing him the intelligence, Admiral Ingram planned an unwelcome reception (named

Operation Teardrop) for *Seewolf*. Two Barrier Forces were to be set up, each with two CVEs as the core of the barrier. The First Barrier Force was built around the *Mission Bay* and the *Croatan*.

For the CVE sailors accustomed to working with just three to five escorts, the Barrier Force was big-time stuff. Besides the two carriers, twenty destroyer escorts would be part of the operation. The First Barrier Force was made up of two sections (Northern and Southern) and four task groups. The Northern Force was composed of TGs 22.1 and 22.14. Captain John R. Ruhsenberger was the commander of the entire Barrier Force, as well as the Northern Force.

Captain Ruhsenberger's TG 22.1 consisted of the *Mission Bay* and Commander Evan W. Yancey's CortDiv 9 (the *D. L. Howard*, *Farquhar*, *J. R. Y. Blakely*, *Hill*, *Fessenden*, and *H. C. Jones*). Rounding out the Northern Force was an all–Coast Guard unit, TG 22.14. Commander Reginald H. French, USCG, as ComCortDiv 46, headed this task group. His ships, the *Pride*, *Menges*, *Mosley*, and *Lowe*, were well trained and had sunk *U-866* on 18 March.

Task Groups 22.5 and 22.13 constituted the Southern Force. Task Group 22.5 was built around Captain Craig's *Croatan*. Commander Giambattista's CortDiv 13 (the *Frost*, *Huse*, *Inch*, *Snowden*, *Stanton*, and *Swasey*) formed their usual screen around the carrier, with which they had operated for over a year. Adding his ships to the Barrier was Commander Morgan H. Harris. The *Carter*, *N. A. Scott*, *Muir*, and *Sutton* operated under the dual designation of TG 22.13 and CortDiv 79. Harris was also OTC of the picket line that would form ahead of the carriers.

The *Croatan* left Hampton Road on 25 March 1945, followed two days later by the *Mission Bay*. Initially the two carriers were to search for a west-bound submarine south of Newfoundland. This search was unsuccessful, being hampered by very bad weather and some operational problems. The *Mission Bay*'s catapult was out of service for several days. No sooner had this been remedied than it was discovered that ten of the sixteen VC-95 Avengers (all TBM-3Es with the new ASH radar) had gyro horizon failures that would make them unavailable for any instrument flying other than an emergency.[23] This problem would limit the squadron's activities considerably.

The *Croatan* had her own problems. Gale-force winds,

low clouds, frequent rains, and very rough seas plagued her. On 5 April a big wave hit the carrier, throwing men, food, and furniture from one side of the mess hall to the other. Then another wave struck, flinging everyone and everything back. Over 100 men were hurt, but the *Croatan*'s mission was not delayed by this mishap.[24]

Both carriers' squadrons (VC-55 and VC-95) had their problems operating in these conditions, and operations had to be suspended from time to time; but the squadrons were generally able to fly most of their search missions. Because of the increase in the number of Avengers carried and the consequent reduction in the number of Wildcats, several fighter pilots had to be retrained to fly the big torpedo planes. This didn't seem to be much of a problem as compared with Captain Vosseller's experience on the *Bogue*. The *Croatan* reported, "The pilots who had formerly flown only fighter type planes in the squadron could not be distinguished from the old VTB pilots in their capabilities except that the fighter pilots probably 'wrapped up' the TBMs a bit more in the final turn into the groove."[25]

The two flattops rendezvoused at mid-morning of 8 April. At daybreak the next morning the first barrier was erected along 30°00'W between 49°30'N and 47°30'N. There was a break in the northern sector until the 10th, however, because TG 22.14 was not able to be in position until that morning. The destroyer escorts (including four detached from the CVE screens) formed a north–south line at ten-mile intervals along the 30th meridian. The carriers, with four DEs each, were stationed 40 miles behind this screen. The *Mission Bay* and *Croatan* planes were to search eastward to the Barrier and 40 miles west of the carrier's positions. They were also to cover the areas north and south of the Barrier to prevent any end runs.[26]

It was not long after the Barrier had been established that possible contacts began popping up. On the afternoon of the 9th a VC-55 pilot tracking down a radar contact thought he saw a wake and some blue smoke. This contact disappeared, but the *Swasey*, which had been vectored to the scene, obtained a good sound contact on a target. A depth charge attack brought several explosions, but no debris rose to the surface, and the contact was lost.[27]

There were no other contacts until 15 April, when the

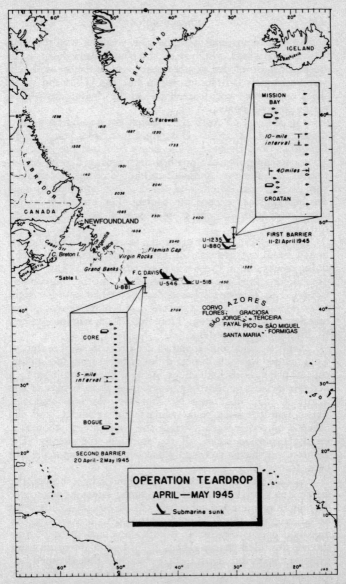

Operation Teardrop, April–May 1945. (From Morison, Vol. X)

action heated up considerably. The weather was still bad, with strong winds, rough seas, and cloud layers down to the deck. Because of the weather and because the snorkel subs were extremely hard for aircraft to find, the VC-55 and VC-95 fliers would play a very small role in the coming destruction of the *Seewolf* boats.

At 2135 on 15 April the *Stanton* got a radar target at a distance of 3,500 yards. This target was 5,000 yards off the *Croatan*'s bow. Because of the heavy seas that the force had been encountering, all ships had been moving slowly. Nevertheless, Lieutenant Commander John C. Kiley ordered his ship to increase speed, and the *Stanton* pounded through the heaving seas toward the contact. Fog hung low on the water, and visibility was quite restricted as the DE closed the distance.

At 1,000 yards Kiley ordered a searchlight turned on. Its pencil beam cut through the fog to dimly illuminate a dark hulk. It was one of the *Seewolf*'s boats, *U-1235*! The U-boat dove before the DE could fire her guns, but the sub couldn't escape. The *Stanton*'s sonar operators latched onto her right away. Meanwhile, as the *Croatan* beat a hasty retreat, Commander Giambattista sent Lieutenant Commander Andrew E. Ritchie's *Frost* to help.

With a solid sound contact on the U-boat, Lieutenant Commander Kiley had opened the distance from the submarine to prepare his hedgehogs. At 2147 the *Stanton* let fly a hedgehog pattern. Shortly a heavy underwater explosion was heard. *U-1235* had been hit—but she was not dead yet. Three minutes later sonar contact was regained, and the *Stanton* moved in again. Before she could attack, though, a terrific explosion shook all the ships in the vicinity. The *Stanton* was shaken so roughly that her crew thought she had been torpedoed.

U-1235 was still not done for, inching slowly through the water. The *Frost* and the *Stanton* joined forces to work over the painfully wounded submarine. More hedgehog hits were noted, but this tough U-boat continued to live. A smell of diesel oil permeated the air as both ships maneuvered across the fog-shrouded waters. Then, at 2314 a violent underwater explosion occurred. Both destroyer escorts thought they had been torpedoed. The *Croatan*, 12 miles away, was shaken by this explosion.

The sound of the explosion rolled through the water and faded away into silence. Commander Giambattista, riding in the *Frost,* radioed Captain Ruhsenberger, ". . . that is the end of sub! The explosion jarred us completely off the deck!"[28]

It was the end of *U-1235.* Her grave was located at 47°56'N, 30°25'W. Now only five of the original six *Seewolfs* were left, and one of these had only a couple of hours to live.

To make sure they had actually sunk the submarine, the destroyer escorts slowly combed the area for any signs of debris or oil scum. As the seas were still very high, any signs of the demise of *U-1235* were quickly swept away. But the probing eyes of the *Frost's* radar picked up something more interesting than debris. It was *U-880,* unwisely heading directly at the task group.

The *Frost* fired starshells, but the fog was so thick that they hardly illuminated the scene. The sub's skipper must have been aware of the presence of the destroyer escorts, but apparently believing the dense fog would cloak his boat in invisibility, he remained on the surface.

When the *Frost* was only 600 yards from *U-880,* her lookouts finally caught sight of the sub's ghostly shape gliding through the fog. Lieutenant Commander Ritchie opened fire with all the guns that would bear, and they were on target. Several 3-inch shells punched damaging holes in the U-boat's hull. Ritchie attempted to ram the submarine, but the heavy seas tossed the DE around so much that it was impossible to set a ramming course. *U-880* dove, and, for the time being, all contact with her was lost.

The *Frost* and the *Stanton* continued probing for their prey and were joined by the *Huse* and the *Swasey.* At 0122 the *Frost* obtained a good sound contact at a range of 300 yards. Ritchie opened the range and fired some hedgehogs. (It should be noted that the hedgehog crews on all the DEs were operating under very adverse conditions. Heavy seas continually washed over their forecastles and drenched the crews with cold water. Nevertheless, the crews were always ready when needed.) The *Frost's* hedgehogs missed, but Ritchie still had a good contact on the U-boat, and he took his ship out to coach in the other vessels.

Lieutenant Commander Kiley's *Stanton* was next up. As Ritchie coached him in, Kiley eased his ship toward the target. At 0203 the *Stanton* fired a volley of hedgehogs into the darkness. There were several minutes of silence, then four sharp cracks. The *Stanton* had scored. Silence again— but four minutes later a tremendous explosion that knocked sailors off their feet and could be felt miles away welled up from the deep. The *Frost* sailors thought their ship had been torpedoed.

It was *U-880*'s death rattle. The hunters regained sonar contact, and several more hedgehog salvos were fired, but they were not needed. The ships were just firing at the husk of a U-boat. At 0226 all four DEs lost contact with the dead vessel.[29]

The deaths of both U-boats had been extremely violent. Why this should have been so as compared with other submarines sunk is unknown, but the spectacular nature of their sinkings seemed to indicate that these boats did have some "secret weapons" on board. In fact, they did not, but the Americans redoubled their efforts to find the remaining U-boats.[30]

On the 16th Admiral Ingram ordered the First Barrier Force to begin moving west–southwest to keep in touch with the remaining U-boats. Captain Ruhsenberger decided to retire the Barrier at a rate of 100 miles a day, this rate conforming to the estimated speed of advance of the snorkelers. The Barrier was finally stopped on the 19th, with its center at 44°30′N, 38°00′W.

The weather remained quite bad, but the VC-55 and VC-95 pilots still flew frustrating (but dangerous) patrols in attempts to locate the elusive U-boats. Inevitably, the weather contributed to landing crashes aboard the twisting and tossing carriers. The *Croatan*'s major incident occurred on 18 April.

An Avenger pilot, a Lieutenant Mansell, just didn't have anything going for him on the night of the 18th. It was a black night; rain was coming down in sheets; the *Croatan* was pitching badly; and, to top it off, his plane developed an oil leak as Mansell was approaching to land. Mansell tried to land several times, but couldn't see the deck because his windscreen was coated with oil and rain.

Finally, Mansell asked the LSO for a cut by radio. On his last approach Mansell had his head completely out of the cockpit trying to see the LSO and the deck. As he neared the ramp, Mansell's goggles blew off and oil almost blinded him.

In pain and hardly able to see anything, he took his own cut. Just then the *Croatan* caught a wave and her stern shot up sharply. The *Avenger's* landing gear struck the ramp just below the flight deck level. Both struts sheared off, and the big plane bounced up the deck. It finally came to a stop, completely broken in half at the turret. Fortunately, there was no fire, and all the crew scrambled out of the wreckage safely.[31]

The *Seewolf* boats were still nearby, as was evidenced by the report from an Azores-based Liberator that had sighted and tracked a submarine for two hours early on the 18th. However, this report (which put the position of the sub less than 50 miles west of TG 22.1) did not reach the Barrier Force until that afternoon. By that time it was of little value. Nevertheless, the *Mosley* was detached to search for the U-boat. Her efforts were unsuccessful as the skipper of the sub (probably *U-805*) was exceedingly cautious.[32]

With the arrival of the Second Barrier Force imminent and the probability that the U-boats that were left were in range of that force, the dissolution of the First Barrier Force was scheduled for 22 April. Before that happened, though, another *Seewolf* was found.

Late in the evening of 21 April the *Mosley* gained a radar contact on a target that soon disappeared. Sonar contact was made a short time later. The *Mosley* crept in to deliver an attack that resulted in four explosions. Several more explosions were heard later over sonobuoys. Though the six DEs of TG 22.1's portion of the Barrier were put on the contact, and aircraft were also involved in the search, the contact was not regained. The submarine (which was probably *U-805* again) escaped.

Not so lucky was the *Seewolf U-518*. Late on the evening of 21 April the *Croatan* and her supporting vessels were preparing to break off from the Barrier and head for Argentia. Earlier in the day the *Croatan* had made one final air and surface sweep east of the Barrier. Nothing had been found because the U-boats were already west of the Barrier. In fact, one of the boats was right in the path of the *Croatan's* group.

Around 2200, in light fog illuminated by pale moonlight, the *Croatan* set course for Argentia. Fifty minutes later the *Carter,* flagship of Commander Harris's TG 22.13, made a sonar contact that was quickly evaluated as a submarine. Out of position, the *Carter* coached her sister ship, the *Neal A. Scott,* in. The *Scott* then obtained her own sound contact and fired a salvo of hedgehogs. A few seconds later two muted explosions rumbled up from below. *U-518* had been hurt.

The *Carter* took over. Lieutenant Commander F. J. T. Baker still had a good sound contact on the now-motionless submarine, and he conned his ship in for the kill. At 2309 the *Carter* fired a full hedgehog pattern. Sixteen seconds later three hits could be heard. Then, a tremendous underwater explosion occurred that shook the *Carter* so violently that her engineering officer (fearing possible damage) ordered her auxiliary boiler, evaporator, and all steam lines secured. This detonation was followed eleven minutes later by another heavy explosion that could be felt and heard three miles away. A third *Seewolf* had been eliminated.[33]

The day after the *Croatan* left for Argentia, the *Mission Bay* also departed the area for that port. It was on this day, 23 April, that the *Mission Bay* suffered her most grievous loss of the operation. During landing operations an Avenger landed hard, missed the wires, and bounced over the barriers. It then slammed into another TBM parked on the port side of the flight deck. Both planes went over the side. The crew of the landing aircraft were plucked from the chilly waters safely, but a pilot and a seaman who were working on the parked plane were killed, and another seaman was seriously injured. It was not a good conclusion to the operations of the First Barrier Force.[34]

As the First Barrier Force retired to Argentia, the Second Barrier Force was moving into position. The latter force was built around the *Bogue* and the *Core*. Captain George F. Dufek (skipper of the *Bogue*) was commander of the Second Barrier Force. The *Bogue*'s TG 22.3 formed the southern portion of the Barrier. Commander Theodore S. Lank's CortDiv 51 (the *Haverfield, Cockrill, Swenning, Willis, Janssen,* and *Wilhoite*) provided the screen for the carrier. Also under Captain Dufek's immediate command was TG 22.8. The destroyer escorts of this unit were the *Otter, Hubbard, Varian,* and *Hayter,* all commanded by Commander Jack F. Bowling, Jr.

The northern force, TG 22.4, consisted of Captain R. S. Purvis's *Core* and her screen of the *Moore, Sloat, Tomich, J. Richard Ward, Otterstetter,* and *Keith.* The screen was commanded by Captain T. S. Dunstan. The remainder of the DEs (the *Pillsbury, Pope, Flaherty, Chatelain, Neunzer,* and *Frederick C. Davis*) were organized as TU 22.7.1 and commanded by Commander Frederick S. Hall. Hall also acted as commander of the Barrier line.

The *Core* and her escorts came up from Guantanamo Bay, Cuba, via Bermuda, while the *Bogue* group sortied from Narragansett Bay, Rhode Island. All units of the Second Barrier Force rendezvoused on 20 April. The Barrier was set up immediately. Dufek's line was different from Ruhsenberger's. Each carrier retained a screen of four destroyer escorts, but instead of remaining some miles behind the barrier, the carriers were stationed about 25 miles to the north and south of the Barrier. The rest of the DEs formed a long patrol line with an interval of 5 miles between each ship. This formation resulted in an impressive 120-mile-long line. The CVE squadrons flew searches 80 miles east and west of the Barrier and overlapping in the center of the line.

Initially the Barrier had been set up along the 45th meridian, with the center at 43°00'N. This was changed to the 41st meridian, and the Barrier Force swept eastward to this meridian, arriving in position on the 21st. Despite the weather, which was still very poor, both carriers kept their planes in the air most of the time. The VC-19 and VC-12 fliers would have better luck than their comrades in the First Barrier Force in spotting U-boats, but virtually all of the action would still devolve on the surface craft.

On the 23rd several contacts were reported by the fliers. None of these contacts amounted to anything, though a *Core* pilot dropped a depth bomb on what appeared to be a snorkel wake. He then dropped some sonobuoys that recorded "submarine sounds" and a further explosion. However, when two escorts reached the scene, all they found was a dead whale.

There was a submarine nearby, though. On the 23rd Doenitz, unaware that half of his *Seewolf* boats were gone, dissolved the group and ordered them to proceed independently to the East Coast. *U-546* had received the order, and Kapitanleutnant Paul Just was preparing to head west when he became aware of the Barrier Force and its carriers. The idea of picking off one of the "jeeps" appealed to Just, who hung around hoping to put a torpedo in the right spot. He would have a success, but it would cost him his boat.

The skipper of the *Bogue*'s VC-19, Lieutenant Commander William W. South, was the first to find *U-546*. South was scouting 74 miles northeast of his carrier when he saw *U-546* surfacing at 1307. The sighting was the first real contact by any pilot since Operation Teardrop began. South attacked immediately, dropping his depth bombs just after the U-boat submerged. *U-546* escaped, however, but a massive surface search was begun in an attempt to catch her.

The sighting of *U-546* placed the submarine near the center of the Barrier line, and Commander Hall took a large group of DEs to hunt for the U-boat. This hunt was unsuc-

U.S.S. *Bogue* **(CVE 9)**

cessful though the ships and aircraft raked the area with a fine-toothed comb. The hunt was continued throughout the night. The next morning, at 0829, the *Frederick C. Davis* gained a solid sound contact on a target at 2,000 yards.

The target dropped aft of the DE and was lost in the racket of the ship's "Foxer." Lieutenant (jg) John F. McWhorter, the officer of the deck, immediately ordered hard right rudder. Simultaneously the *Davis*'s skipper, Lieutenant James R. Crosby, was summoned to the bridge, and battle stations was sounded. The "Fighting Freddy's" crew were quickly at their stations. Commander Hall was notified that the *Davis* was investigating a hot contact. At about 0834 the sound contact was regained, and a few minutes later the destroyer escort reversed course.

By 0840 the range had closed to 650 yards. Just then the *Frederick C. Davis* was struck on her port side abreast of the forward engine room by a torpedo. An enormous explosion whipped the ship back and forth. The devastation and carnage on the *Davis* was terrible. Within seconds the engine rooms and several compartments were flooded. Everyone in the wardroom was killed when the force of the explosion blew its deck up to the level of the portholes. The whipping of the ship snapped her mast, and lethal wire shrouds carved the air. One of these wire cut Lieutenant Crosby in half. Lieutenant (jg) McWhorter was flung into a gun tub and killed. Many on the flying bridge were thrown overboard.

Surviving officers attempted to organize damage control parties, but it was too late. The *Frederick C. Davis* had been disemboweled and was breaking apart. Ensign Philip K. Lundeberg ordered abandon ship. About 100 men were able to get off the foundering vessel. The survivors were not in much better shape in the water than they would have been on board their ship. The water was cold, and the sea was running heavy. Some men were injured or had no life jackets. As the ship went down, two depth charges that couldn't be set on safe exploded, causing further injuries.

After the *Davis* was hit, Commander Hall sent the *Flaherty* to rescue survivors and the *Hayter* and the *Neunzer* to find *U-546*. The *Flaherty* eased through the clots of survivors (her captain rightly apprehensive about stopping while an obviously aggressive U-boat was nearby), dropping rafts and empty depth charge cases as she passed by. As the *Flaherty* was going about her grim task, her sonar operations caught the scent of the U-boat. The DE broke off her rescue efforts, and the *Hayter* took over the task of pulling the men from the water. With the help of *Core* aircraft spotting several men away from the main group, the DE finally took aboard all that were left of the *Frederick C. Davis*'s crew. The number of those rescued was depressingly small. Only 66 men survived out of a crew of 192.[35]

The other destroyer escorts were not about to let the sinking of the *Frederick C. Davis* go unavenged. Commander Hall positioned his ships in a cordon around the U-boat's last known position. The *Flaherty* was the first to deliver an attack. Assisted by Hall's flagship, the *Pillsbury*, the *Flaherty* beat the water with hedgehog and depth charge attacks. *U-546* had gone deep, and the *Flaherty* missed, but time was beginning to work against the Germans.

The hours passed. The DEs queued up to take turns with *U-546*. Scores of depth charges were dropped, falling silently through the water to finally explode near the submarine. The U-boat was being battered, but had not yet been fatally damaged. The continuous pounding was beginning to tell on the submariners, though. Shortly before 1800 the hunters noted that the U-boat had come up to around 200 feet. Commander Hall decided to switch from depth charges to hedgehogs.

At 1810 the *Flaherty* delivered a hedgehog attack. It was *U-546*'s undoing. A hedgehog connected with the U-boat. A large hole was punched in her pressure hull, and batteries were broken. Kapitanleutnant Just decided to come up fighting. At 1838 *U-546* broached. As he surfaced, Just fired a torpedo at his nearest adversary, the *Flaherty*. The "fish" missed. This tactic offended the DE's captain who radioed, "That stinker fired a torpedo at me!"[36] In retaliation, he fired two torpedoes at the U-boat, but they were wide of the mark also.

Surrounded by a pack of destroyer escorts—all firing everything they had at the helpless sub—*U-546* was being ripped to pieces. Just ordered his ship abandoned, and the Germans jumped into the cold Atlantic waters. At 1845 the submarine's bow came out of the water almost vertically, then disappeared. The DEs closed in to save thirty-three of *U-546*'s crew, including Just. They proved to be a die-hard band of Nazis. It was only after a period in the marine brig at Argentia that they began talking to their interrogators. The information obtained from the prisoners showed that Doenitz had not planned any secret weapons offensive against the East Coast, and the Americans could relax a bit.[37]

There were still two boats of the *Seewolf* Group missing, *U-805* and *U-858*. Admiral Ingram ordered the Second Barrier Force to retire in hopes of catching this pair, and Captain Dufek took his force at a leisurely pace to the southwest. Even though several tenuous contacts were made, no submarines were actually in the vicinity. On 2 May the Second Barrier Force was split up. The *Core* and her coterie of

escorts covered an area east of 50°30'W, while the *Bogue*
searched to the west. In addition, the *Croatan* and *Mission
Bay* groups were ordered out of Argentia to set up another
barrier centered around 45°00'N, 42°30'W.[38]

These new barriers did not encounter anything and were
soon dissolved. However, the *Mission Bay*'s TG 22.1 later
came across a target. *U-881* had been sent on 8 April to beef
up the *Seewolf* boats. *U-881* and the *Mission Bay* group met
southwest of the Grand Banks on 6 May. The encounter was
terribly brief. At 0413 on the morning of the 6th the *Farquhar*
got a sonar contact at a range of 1,300 yards. The ship raced
in to drop a thirteen-charge pattern. The sea boiled as seven
explosions, followed by two more, resounded underwater.
The *Farquhar* and other escorts probed for several more
hours looking for signs of the submarine, but there were
none. The DE's first attack had been the end of the U-boat.
The sinking of *U-881* was the last hurrah for the escort carrier
groups in the Atlantic. The war in Europe ended the next
day.[39]

Hitler had committed suicide on 30 April, and Doenitz
had been named the new Fuehrer. Though Nazi Germany
was in her final death throes, Doenitz signaled his U-boats on
2 May, "In order to save hundreds of thousands of Germans
from annihilation and slavery, carry on with your old rigor."[40]
However, faced with the inevitable, on 4 May Doenitz ordered all German warships still at sea to stop hostilities and
return home. *U-881* apparently never received this order.
Then, on 7 May in Rheims, France, Germany surrendered
unconditionally. The next day, however, when Russia ratified
the surrender agreement, is officially recognized as VE day.

There were few spectacular demonstrations by the American sailors who had been fighting the Battle of the Atlantic,
no flares or guns firing wildly about—just a sense of relief
that the killing was finally over. And the killing had been
going on for a long time, from the first day of the war to VE
Day. For the sailors there was still a lot of work to do. The
Allies had ordered the U-boats still at sea to surface and
report their positions to the nearest Allied radio station.
When instructed, they were to head for port and fly a black
flag. The *Bogue, Core, Croatan,* and *Mission Bay* and their
escorts were directed to erect a barrier between 38°00' and
39°N', 60°00'W to accept the surrender of U-boats, and to

guard against any possible surprise attacks by unrepentant U-boat skippers.[41]

Several U-boats surrendered to units of the barrier, including *U-805* and *U-858* (late of Group *Seewolf*), *U-1228*, and *U-234*.[42] Then the war in the Atlantic was well and truly over for the CVEs and their escorts.

What had been the cost to the CVE hunter-killer groups, and what had been their impact on the Battle of the Atlantic? First, figures on the losses suffered by the U-boat arm vary from source to source, but a fairly accurate figure is 785 boats lost out of 1,162 built, and 28,000 to 32,000 submariners killed.[43] Of these 785 U-boats, the American escort carrier groups sank fifty-three and captured one. This comes out to only 7 percent of the total sinkings. But when compared to the total sinkings by U.S. forces, this percentage rises greatly. Some 177 U-boats were destroyed by the Americans solely, and the CVE groups' share of this is almost 31 percent.[44] Breaking these triumphs down further, the aircraft squadrons had been responsible for thirty of the sinkings, the escorts claimed another nineteen, and four sinkings and the capture of *U-505* had been shared.

It is obvious that the British–Canadian forces were responsible by far for the majority of the U-boat losses. Yet the American contribution, really taking effect only in 1943, cannot be denigrated. It is also quite obvious that the American escort carrier groups were better than their counterparts in the Royal Navy. Possibly this is so because the American CVE group commanders were aviation-trained. They were well aware of the advantages and limitations of the carriers and aircraft they had to use. More important, though, was the fact that they were able to operate relatively unencumbered by higher commands' restrictions. Conversely, the British CVE captains were, for the most part, surface sailors unfamiliar with aviation and were usually operating under the Admiralty's tight control. The CVE groups were a very important factor in the war in the Atlantic. Samuel Eliot Morison even states that the "escort carrier groups were probably the greatest single contribution of the United States Navy to victory over enemy submarines."[45]

Since World War II a rather sterile controversy has erupted over whether it was a waste of time and effort to send

the CVE hunter-killer groups to seek out the U-boats instead
of operating them in close support of the convoys. The British
view of this matter appears to be that the protection of the
convoys was the primary concern and the sinking of U-boats
was only a secondary consideration.[46] This line of thinking
seems to ignore the fact that a submarine not sunk will sooner
or later return to sink more ships. Also, the penetration of
even a well-defended convoy by a determined U-boat skipper
was not an impossible task.

By not sinking submarines, too, the Allies could run the
risk of allowing the German Navy to increased the number of
U-boats to dangerous (for the Allies) limits. It is one of the
ironies of World War II that though it is now conceded that
Germany lost the Battle of the Atlantic in May of 1943,
U-boat construction actually increased through 1944 (196
built in 1941, 244 in 1942, 270 in 1943, 387 in 1944, and 155
in 1945).[47] It should be noted, however, that while a number
of the U-boats built in 1944 and 1945 were the vastly improved and potentially very dangerous Type XXI and XXIII
boats, few of these became operational. It also should be
noted that many of the submarines that were operational in
the latter stages of the war were fitted with a snorkel and
were becoming harder to detect.

The key to the resolution of the controversy over hunter-
killer groups versus close convoy escort is Enigma. Royal
Navy Captain S. W. Roskill, in his book *The Navy at War,*
states that only those forces involved in convoy support were
really effective, and that it was only because of "accurate
intelligence" (in other words, Enigma) that the U.S. Navy's
hunter-killer groups were able to accomplish anything. He
also says that without Enigma information, the escort carrier
groups would have been wasting their time as the British did
in 1940 with their hunting groups.[48]

Roskill's comments, however, unwittingly underscore the
fact that the information gained from Enigma really forced
the Allies to use, if at all possible, this information for
offensive purposes. Without the knowledge gained from Enigma it would, indeed, have been much better for the Allied
antisubmarine forces to operate in close support of the convoys, for the U-boats would congregate about the convoys
and could be found more easily. However, this is a defensive

system and subjected the ships in a convoy to needless attack by a determined and aggressive enemy.

But with the knowledge of enemy positions and tactics that the breaking of Enigma conferred upon the Allies, it was preferable for the ASW forces (including the escort carrier groups) to seek out and destroy the U-boats before they got anywhere near the convoys or any other targets. There was one other factor that made it preferable to use offensive tactics—antisubmarine vessel construction. With increased numbers of destroyers, destroyer escorts, escort carriers, and so forth, available in 1943 and 1944, these vessels were wasted if not used. Only a certain number of these ships could be used efficiently on convoy escort. What could be done with the rest? Use them to man hunter-killer groups on offensive missions! And this is what the U.S. Navy did.

Enigma information, when available (since it was not always readable or current), enabled the Allies to route convoys around known U-boat positions. It also allowed (along with the increased numbers of ships available) the U.S. escort carrier groups to operate against the U-boat refueling points with deadly effect. Of the approximately 490 U-boats sunk by the Allies from January 1943 to the end of the war, the U.S. Navy's forces sank about 63 with the direct aid of Enigma, plus another 30 with the indirect aid of Enigma.[49] What results the British had using the same source is unknown.

However, it was not just in sinking U-boats that Enigma made a contribution. Many enemy submarines were attacked and damaged or forced to remain hidden underwater by the seemingly constant presence of Allied escort carriers, land-based aircraft, and surface vessels. The U-boats were harassed and hounded from the Arctic to the Cape of Good Hope by Allied antisubmarine forces. The German submariners were allowed no respite, no place to relax during their operations without feeling the gnawing fear of discovery by an enemy aircraft or surface vessel.[50]

As the Battle of the Atlantic dragged on, the U-boat arm became "less bold when pressing an attack which was sure to reveal their presence."[51] For the U-boats their operations, "once so boldly offensive, [came to take] on increasingly the character of makeshift and evasion, the search for counter measures and counter tactics."[52]

HUNTER-KILLER

Thus it was not just in sinking submarines that the escort carrier groups contributed to the winning of the Battle of the Atlantic, but their offensive operations also helped to diminish the aggressiveness of the U-boat skippers and, so, to keep the U-boats away from the vital convoys. The Op-20-G history, referring to the U-boat radio traffic read through Enigma intercepts, sees the German submariners despairing of the "inability of the U-boat to cope with surprise attack from the air" and of the "increasing intimidation of U-boat men as they began to appreciate the visibility and vulnerability of their weapon."[53]

The escort carriers, their aircraft, and their supporting ships did not win the Battle of the Atlantic. But neither can it be said that land-based aircraft, close support groups, or even the convoy system won it. "Superior leadership and tactics, quick initial action, and well-coordinated attack and defense played as much of a part in the defeat of the U-boats as did concentration of forces at the decisive points and weapon superiority."[54]

With these items, however, should be listed probably the most important factor in the winning (and losing) of the Battle of the Atlantic—Enigma. The Allies may still have won the battle without it, but they would have paid a far greater price for the victory.

APPENDIXES

I

ESCORT CARRIER
TECHNICAL DATA

Long Island Class

No. in class	5 (4 transferred to Royal Navy)
Hull numbers:	CVE-1
Displacement:	7,886 tons, standard; 14,055 tons, full load
Dimensions:	465′ (wl) 492′ (oa) × 69′6″ × 25′6″ (102′ extreme beam), flight deck 436′ after retrofit
Machinery:	1-shaft diesel engines, 8,500 SHP, speed 16 knots, fuel 1,429 tons
Armament:	1 5″/51, 2 3″/50, 20 20-mm (1945), 1 catapult, 21 aircraft
Complement:	970
Builder:	Sun S.B. as Maritime Commission C-3 type

Charger

No. in class:	1
Hull numbers:	CVE-30
Displacement:	11,800 tons; 15,126 tons
Dimensions:	465′(wl) 492′(oa) × 69′6″ × 25′2″ (111′2″ extreme beam), flight deck 436′
Machinery:	1-shaft diesel engines, 8,500 SHP, speed 17 knots, fuel 1,295 tons
Armament:	1 5″/51, 2 3″/50, 10 20-mm, 1 catapult, 21 aircraft
Complement:	856
Builder	Sun S.B. as Maritime Commission C-3 type

Bogue Class

No. in class:	44 (including 33 transferred to Royal Navy)
Hull members:	CVE-9, 11/13, 16, 18, 20, 21, 23, 25, 31

Displacement: 8,390 tons; 13,890 tons
Dimensions: 465′(wl) 495′8″(oa) × 69′6″ × 23′3″ (111′6″ extreme beam), flight deck 442′3″
Machinery: 1-shaft geared turbine, 8,500 SHP, speed 18 knots, fuel 3,420 tons
Armament: 2 5″/38, 20 40-mm (twin), 27 20-mm (1945), 1 or 2 catapults, 28 aircraft
Complement: 890 (generally exceeded up to 1,200)
Builder: Todd, Tacoma

Sangamon Class

No. in class: 4
Hull numbers: CVE-26/29
Displacement: 10,500 tons; 23,875 tons
Dimensions: 525′(wl) 553′6″(oa) × 75′ × 30′7″ (114′3″ extreme beam), flight deck 503′
Machinery: 2-shaft geared turbine, 13,500 SHP, speed 18 knots, fuel 4,780 tons (This ex-oiler class retained a large oil capacity that could be used over the listed figure.)
Armament: 2 5″/38, 8 40-mm (quad), 14 40-mm (twin), 21 20-mm, 1 catapult to 1944, then 2, 30 aircraft
Complement: 1,080
Builders: Federal (Kearny) and Sun S.B.

Casablanca Class

No. in class: 50
Hull numbers: CVE-55/104
Displacement: 8,200 tons; 10,900 tons
Dimensions: 490′(wl) 512′3″(oa) × 65′2″ × 20′9″ (108′1″ extreme beam), flight deck 477′
Machinery: 2-shaft reciprocating, 9,000 SHP, speed 19 knots, fuel 2,279 tons
Armament: 1 5″/38, 16 40-mm (twin), 20 20-mm (1945), 1 catapult, 28 aircraft
Complement: 860
Builder: Kaiser, Vancouver

Commencement Bay Class

No. in class: 19
Hull numbers: CVE-105/123
Displacement: 11,373 tons; 24,275 tons (postwar figures)
Dimensions: 525′(wl) 557′1″(oa) × 75′ × 32′2″ (105′2″ extreme beam), flight deck 502′
Machinery: 2-shaft geared turbines, 16,000 SHP, speed 19 knots, fuel 3,134 (Like the Sangamon-class ships, these vessels had additional oil storage capacity.)

Armament: 2 5″/38, 12 40-mm (quad), 24 40-mm (twin), 20 20-mm
               (1945), 2 catapults, 34 aircraft
Complement: 1,066
Builder: Todd-Pacific

Note: Data on escort carriers vary with the source. This listing is
compiled primarily from *Escort Carriers and Aviation Support Ships of
the U. S. Navy, U. S. Warships of World War II*, Volume XV of *History of
United States Naval Operations in World War II*, and *Escort Carriers
and Their Air Unit Markings During W. W. II in the Pacific*.

II

SUBMARINE SINKINGS
BY ESCORT CARRIER
GROUPS

Date	Submarine	Carrier	Sinking Credited to Unit	Enigma intelligence used
1942				
11 November	Sidi-Ferruch	Suwannee	VGS-27	No
1943				
22 May	U-569	Bogue	VC-9	Yes
5 June	U-217	Bogue	VC-9	Yes
12 June	U-118	Bogue	VC-9	Yes
13 July	U-487	Core	VC-13	Yes
14 July	U-160	Santee	VC-29	Yes
15 July	U-509	Santee	VC-29	Yes
16 July	U-67	Core	VC-13	Yes
23 July	U-613	Bogue	George E. Badger	Yes
23 July	U-527	Bogue	VC-9	Yes
30 July	U-43	Santee	VC-29	Yes
7 August	U-117	Card	VC-1	Yes
9 August	U-664	Card	VC-1	Yes
11 August	U-525	Card	VC-1	Yes
24 August	U-185	Core	VC-13	Yes
24 August	U-84	Core	VC-13	Yes
27 August	U-847	Card	VC-1	Yes
4 October	U-460	Card	VC-9	Yes

Date	Submarine	Sinking Credited to Carrier	Unit	Enigma intelligence used
4 October	U-422	Card	VC-9	Yes
13 October	U-402	Card	VC-9	Yes
20 October	U-378	Core	VC-13	Yes
28 October	U-220	Block Island	VC-1	Yes
31 October	U-584	Card	VC-9	Yes
1 November	U-405	Card	Borie	Yes
29 November	U-86	Bogue	VC-19	Yes
13 December	U-172	Bogue	VC-19, Badger, DuPont, Clemson, and Ingram	Yes
20 December	U-850	Bogue	VC-19	Yes
24 December	U-645	Card	Schenck	Yes
1944				
16 January	U-544	Guadalcanal	VC-13	Yes
1 March	U-709	Block Island	Thomas, Bostwick, and Bronstein	Yes
1 March	U-603	Block Island	Bronstein	Yes
13 March	U-575	Bogue	VC-95, Haverfield, and HMCS Prince Rupert	Yes
17 March	U-801	Block Island	VC-6, Corry, and Bronstein	Yes
19 March	U-1059	Block Island	VC-6	Yes
7 April	U-856	Croatan	Huse and Champlin (TU 27.6.1)	Yes
9 April	U-515	Guadalcanal	VC-58, Pillsbury, Pope, Flaherty, and Chatelain	Yes
10 April	U-68	Guadalcanal	VC-58	Yes
26 April	U-488	Croatan	Frost, Huse, Barber, and Snowden	Yes
6 May	U-66	Block Island	Buckley	Yes
13 May	RO-501 (U-1224)	Bogue	F M. Robinson	Yes
29 May	U-549	Block Island	Eugene E. Elmore and Ahrens	Yes
4 June	U-505	Guadalcanal		Yes
11 June	U-490	Croatan	Frost, Snowden, and Inch	Yes
15 June	U-860	Solomons	VC-9	Yes
24 June	I-52	Bogue	VC-69	Yes

Date	Submarine	Sinking Credited to		Enigma intelligence used
		Carrier	Unit	
2 July	U-543	Wake Island	VC-58	Yes
3 July	U-154	Croatan	Frost and Inch	Yes
5 July	U-233	Card	Thomas and Baker	Yes
20 August	U-1229	Bogue	VC-42	Yes
30 September	U-1062	Mission Bay	Fessenden	Yes
1945				
15 April	U-1235	Croatan	Frost and Stanton	Yes
16 April	U-880	Croatan	Frost and Stanton	Yes
21 April	U-518	Croatan	Carter and Neal A. Scott	Yes
24 April	U-546	Core	Flaherty, Pillsbury, Neunzer, and Hayter	Yes
6 May	U-881	Mission Bay	Farquhar	Yes

Sinkings by squadrons:
VC-9: 9; VC-13: 6; VC-1: 5; VC-29: 3; VC-58: 3 (1 shared); VC-19: 3 (1 shared); VC-6: 2 (1 shared); VC-42: 1; VC-69: 1; VGS-27: 1; VC-95: 1 (shared).

Sinkings by carriers:
Bogue: 12; *Card:* 11; *Croatan:* 7; *Block Island:* 7; *Core:* 6; *Guadalcanal:* 4, including *U-505; Santee:* 3; *Mission Bay:* 2; *Solomons:* 1; *Wake Island:* 1.

III

THE ANGLO-AMERICAN
CVE CONTROVERSY

It perhaps appeared to the Axis powers that the Allied war machine (particularly at the higher command levels) worked efficiently toward a single purpose. If only the enemy could have known what really went on behind the scenes. Each country—the United States, England, France, Canada, and so on—had its own war aims, its own ideas on how to win the war, its own ingrained prejudices. However, for the most part during World War II the Allies meshed like the parts of a smooth-running engine. Still, the Allies occasionally didn't see eye-to-eye on a subject, and a cog slipped in the engine, setting off a horrendous clamor. But with some tinkering here and there, the engine would soon be running smoothly again.

For a time during the Battle of the Atlantic a cog slipped when the British and American navies clashed verbally over the merits of the U.S.–built escort carriers and of their "proper" use in the Atlantic. Fortunately for the prosecution of the war against the U-boats, this relatively minor set-to was short-lived, and the two navies were soon operating together smoothly.

When the British received their first escort carriers from American shipyards, they were not impressed with their new acquisitions. The new vessels were thought to be quite unstable and lacking in many safety areas. This view was reinforced when the *Avenger* sank quickly after taking one torpedo on 15 November 1942, and the *Dasher* was destroyed by a gasoline explosion while anchored in the Clyde on 27 March 1943. The Admiralty decided to make extensive modifications to the CVEs they received.

Instead of following the U.S. Navy's practice of filling empty fuel tanks with salt water for ballast, the British decided that between 1,200 and 2,000 tons of extra ballast had to be added for stability. Then, the carriers had to have their fuel systems completely redone. More fighter direction equipment had to be fitted, as the British intended the ships for full fighter operations, not only antisubmarine work. Also, the British planned to lengthen the CVEs' flight decks. Needless to say, all these modifications took time, and it appeared to the Americans that the British CVEs were spending most of their time in the yards instead of on active operations.

This state of affairs was unacceptable to the Allied Antisubmarine Survey Board (a joint British–American board established on 8 March 1943 to study and survey all things involving antisubmarine warfare in the Atlantic). On 27 August 1943 the Survey Board, considering the delay in getting the British escort carriers operational, recommended that the next seven CVEs scheduled to be sent to the British instead be operated by the U.S. Navy. The Combined Chiefs of Staff agreed to this recommendation on 10 September 1943.

The recommendation of the Survey Board may have had some effect, for the British were eventually able to reduce the time their carriers spent in the yards. The British escort carriers later compiled an outstanding record in operations in Arctic waters.

In addition to the length of time it took the British to get their escort carriers into service, there was another bone of contention between the U.S. and British navies. This was over the best way to use the carriers and what type of officer was best suited to command the ships. In mid-October 1943 Captain Marshall R. Greer, the former skipper of the *Core*, was sent to England to discuss CVE operations with the British. His visit had little effect on changing British procedures, but his talks with numerous officers of all ranks were very valuable in establishing more lines of communication regarding CVE operations.

In his report of his visit, Captain Greer was very frank in his comments on British escort carrier operations:

"It is my belief," he reported, "that the carrier squadrons are being well trained but that due to inexperience the inability of the officers to efficiently operate the carriers is deplorable, even though the young captains in command are, and have been, exceptionally fine young gunnery and submarine officers; and I now can better understand why it is necessary to run the carriers from Headquarters ashore like a puppet show instead of giving them complete freedom of action which we are successfully employing. It is my opinion that we must continue to accept the unpleasant truth that we cannot expect much from British CVEs in the antisubmarine warfare [role] in the near future. This, to my mind, results directly from the fact that they have not had our good fortune of able leadership in Naval Aviation."

Greer's remarks were reinforced by Captain Kenneth Knowles in a memorandum for Admiral Low on 24 December 1943. In this memorandum Knowles stated:

My observation had been that there are two matters on

which there has been a marked divergence of opinion between Cominch and Admiralty, namely:

1. The most profitable disposition of CVEs and
2. Their method of employment (i.e., offensively or defensively).

There is slight probability of any reconciliation of the 1st primarily because it has its roots in the battle of operational control. If we accede to British demands it logically follows that they should operate our CVEs since such operations tie in with their convoys and the Biscay offensive.

While the British recently have professed their desire to go on the offensive against the U-boat, an objective analysis of their operations since the launching of this offensive fails to disclose any marked change from their tradition "divert-and-avoid" methods. On the contrary there appears to be a decided reluctance on the part of the British to go out of their way to engage the enemy offensively except in the Bay where no convoys are involved.*

In operations involving convoys the British continue to divert both the convoy and its supporting CVE, permitting the latter to attack only when the U-boats threaten the convoy.

Greer's and Knowles's remarks may overstate the case, but they do indicate how many American naval officers viewed their British counterparts. Nevertheless, an accommodation was secured between the two Allies concerning the use of their escort carriers and their spheres of operations.

Though the Americans remained skeptical and wary of the British regarding escort carrier operations and the operational control of such units (evidenced by this excerpt from a CominCh message to the Admiralty, "We stand ready to operate our CVEs in any profitable area but do not desire that they operate between your forces in such manner that confusion as to control would inevitably result."; and alongside this underlined sentence a somewhat smug marginal note—"I expect them to rise to this."), the two navies were able to work together efficiently and, most of the time, with remarkable good will toward each other.

To the Germans' misfortune, the work of the two navies proved to be an unbeatable combination.[1]

---

*Underlined in the original.

NOTES

Chapter 1

1. Edward P. Von der Porten, *The German Navy in World War II* (hereafter cited as Von der Porten), p. 32; David Mason, *U-Boat: The Secret Menace* (hereafter cited as Mason), p. 29; Harald Busch, *U-Boats at War*, p. 1.

2. Henry M. Dater, "Development of the Escort Carrier" (hereafter cited as Dater), p. 79.

3. Stefan Terzibaschitsch, *Escort Carriers and Aviation Support Ships of the U. S. Navy* (hereafter cited as Terzibaschitsch), pp. 22–23; Scot MacDonald, "Emergence of the Escort Carriers" (hereafter cited as MacDonald), p. 15.

4. Terzibaschitsch, pp. 22–23.

5. *ONI Weekly*, "Evolution of the Escort Carrier" (hereafter cited as *ONI Weekly*), p. 1310.

6. MacDonald, p. 16; Dater, p. 80.

7. *ONI Weekly*, pp. 1310–11; Terzibaschitsch, pp. 24, 31–33.

8. Norman Polmar, *Aircraft Carriers* (hereafter cited as Polmar), pp. 127–29; Peter Kemp, *Decision at Sea: The Convoy Escorts* (hereafter cited as Kemp), pp. 32–33.

9. *ONI Weekly*, p. 1312; Terzibaschitsch, pp. 24–25, 34.

10. Polmar, pp. 292–93.

11. Mason, pp. 68–72; Vice Adm. Friedrich Ruge, *Der Seekrieg: The German Navy's Story*, p. 252.

12. *Allied Communications Intelligence and the Battle of the Atlantic* (hereafter cited as Communications Intelligence), Vol. I, p. 10.

13. Von der Porten, p. 185; H. A. Jacobsen and J. Rohwer, *Decisive Battles of World War II: The German View* (hereafter cited as Jacobsen), pp. 271–72.

14. *ONI Weekly*, pp. 1312–13; Terzibaschitsch, pp. 36, 200–1.

15. Terzibaschitsch, p. 36.

16. *ONI Weekly*, pp. 1313–14; Terzibaschitsch, pp. 61, 200–2.

17. *ONI Weekly*, p. 1314.

18. Ibid., pp. 1314–15; Terzibaschitsch, pp. 68, 200–2; Dater, pp. 82–83.

19. Rear Adm. Daniel V. Gallery, Reminiscences, p. 64.

20. *ONI Weekly*, pp. 1315–16; Terzibaschitsch, pp. 128, 200–2; MacDonald, p. 18.

21. Dater, p. 89.

Chapter 2

1. Samuel E. Morison, *History of United States Naval Operations in World War II*, Vol II, *Operations in North African Waters* (hereafter cited as Morison II), pp. 12–31.

2. *Santee* Action Report, no serial, 28 November 1942, Enclosure A, p. 1.

3. Admiral J. J. Clark, with Clark G. Reynolds, *Carrier Admiral*, pp. 96–99; *Suwannee* History, pp. 1–2; Capt. J. J. Clark Interview, p. 1.

4. *Santee* Action Report, Enclosure A, p. 1.

5. *Chenango* Action Report, Serial 035, 2 December 1942, p. 1.

6. CTG 34.2 Action Report, Serial 0032, 3 December 1942, Enclosure A, p. 1.

7. Ibid., p. 2.

8. *Santee* Action Report, Enclosure A, p. 2.

9. *Santee* Action Report, Serial 019, 21 November 1942, p. 38.

10. *Santee* Action Report, Enclosure A, p. 2.

11. VGF-29 History, p. 8.

12. *Santee* Action Report, Enclosure A, p. 3; *Santee* Action Report, Serial 019, pp. 28–29.

13. VGF-29 History, pp. 8–9.

14. *Santee* Action Report, Enclosure A, p. 3.

15. Atlantic Fleet ASW Unit Report, Serial 01068, 18 December 1942; Morison II, p. 110.

16. *Santee* Action Report, Enclosure A, p. 5.

17. Ibid., Enclosure A, pp. 4–5; VGF-29 History, pp. 9–10.

18. VGF-29 History, p. 9; *Santee* Action Report, Serial 019, p. 28.

19. *Suwannee* Awards for Meritorious Achievement, Serial 024, 17 November 1942; Clark Interview, p. 3; Morison II, p. 109.

20. VGS-26 Report No. 1, 8 November 1942.

21. *Sangamon* Action Report, Serial 0224, 26 November 1942, pp. 5–6; VGS-26 Reports No. 1 and 2, 8 November 1942; *Sangamon* Action Report, Serial 054, 20 November 1942, p. 1.

22. Atlantic Fleet ASW Unit Report, Serial 01064, 17 December 1942.

23. *Santee* Action Report, pp. 6–7; VGF-29 History, p. 11; Morison II, p. 152.

24. Atlantic Fleet ASW Unit Report, Serial 01038, 8 December 1942; Morison II, p. 168.

25. *Sangamon* Awards of Distinguished Flying Cross, Serial 049, 20 November 1942 (note that dates of action are incorrect); Morison II, p. 128; CTG 34.2 Action Report, Serial 0032, Enclosure A, p. 3.

26. CTF 34 Preliminary Report on TORCH, Serial 00241, 28 November 1942, p. 10.

27. "Wartime History of *Chenango*," p. 2; *Chenango* Action Report, Serial 035, pp. 1–2; CTF 34 Preliminary Report, pp. 12–14.

28. CTG 34.8 Action Report, Serial 0224, 26 November 1942, p. 12; VGS-26 Reports No. 3 and 4, 10 November 1942.

29. VGF-29 History, p. 12.

30. Atlantic Fleet ASW Unit Report, Serial 01067, 18 December 1942; *Santee* Action Report, Enclosure A, p. 7.

31. *Santee* Action Report, Enclosure A, p. 9.

32. Morison II, p. 155.

33. VGF-29 History, p. 12; *Santee* Action Report, Enclosure A, p. 9; Morison II, p. 152.

34. *Chenango* Action Report, Serial 035, pp. 2–3; *Chenango* History, p. 2; *Sangamon* History, Serial 075, 3 October 1945, p. 2.

35. Morison II, p. 90.

36. Commander, Amphibious Force Atlantic Fleet, TORCH Operations Comments, Serial 00299, 22 December 1942, First Endorsement, p. 2.

37. Aircraft Operations During TORCH, Commander in Chief, Atlantic Fleet, Serial 0874, 30 March 1943, p. 7; ComAmphForLant Comments, pp. 21–22; CTG 34.2 Action Report, Serial 0032, Enclosure B, p. 1.

38. ComAmphForLant Comments, p. 21.

Chapter 3

1. Patrick Beesly, *Very Special Intelligence* (hereafter cited as Beesly), pp. 62–65; 72–74; Kemp, pp. 23, 56; Ronald Lewin, *Ultra Goes to War,* pp. 207–12; Terry Hughes and John Costello, *The Battle of the Atlantic* (hereafter cited as Hughes), p. 72; F. H. Hinsley et al., *British Intelligence in the Second World War: Its Influence on Strategy and Operations,* Vol. II (hereafter cited as Hinsley), p. 553.

2. Samuel Eliot Morison, Vol. X, *The Atlantic Battle Won* (hereafter cited as Morison X), pp. 16–20.

3. Ibid., p. 25.

4. Tenth Fleet Memos, 21 June and 1 July 1943, and CominCh Memo, 23 June 1943, all in Tenth Fleet Message Files—CVE Groups; Ladislas Farago, *The Tenth Fleet* (hereafter cited as Farago), p. 169.

5. Morison X, p. 24.

6. Beesly, p. 114.

7. Samuel Eliot Morison, Vol. I, *The Battle of the Atlantic* (hereafter cited as Morison I), p. 410.

8. Dr. Philip K. Lundeberg, *American Anti-Submarine Operations*

in the Atlantic, May 1943–May 1945 (hereafter cited as Lundeberg), p. 64.

9. Ibid., p. 68.

10. "History of USS *Bogue*," p. 1; Terzibaschitsch, p. 40; Theodore Roscoe, *United States Destroyer Operations in World War II* (hereafter cited as Roscoe), p. 287.

11. *Bogue* Narrative, 25 December 1944, p. 2; Terzibaschitsch, pp. 200–2.

12. *Bogue* History, p. 1; *Bogue* Narrative, pp. 2–3.

13. Hinsley, p. 750; Beesly, p. 183; Kemp, pp. 98–100; Hughes, pp. 262–63; Jurgen Rohwer, *The Critical Convoy Battles of March 1943* (hereafter cited as Rohwer), pp. 61, 241–42.

14. VC-9 ASW Report No. 1, 10 March 1943, and Second Endorsement to report.

15. Hughes, pp. 163–65; Rohwer, pp. 61–62; Capt. John M. Waters, Jr., *Bloody Winter* (hereafter cited as Waters), pp. 205–7.

16. VC-9 ASW Report No. 2, 11 March 1943; *Bogue* Chronology, 25 December 1944, p. 4.

17. *Bogue* Action Report, Serial 017, 14 March 1943, pp. 1–2.

18. B.d.U. War Diary, 26 March 1943; Communications Intelligence, Vol. II, p. 48.

19. B.d.U. War Diary, 16 April 1943.

20. *Bogue* Action Report, Serial 022, 2 May 1943, pp. 1–4.

21. Ralph Hiestand correspondence.

22. Morison X, pp. 65–76; Kemp, pp. 119–20.

23. Morison X, p. 77.

24. *Bogue* Action Report, Serial 022, Enclosure C, p. 1.

25. Ibid., Enclosure B.

26. Morison X, p. 80.

27. VC-9 ASW Report No. 4, 21 May 1943, and analysis; ASW Bulletin, June 1943, p. 19; Morison X, p. 80; Farago, p. 193; John Bishop, "The U-Boat Meets its Master" (hereafter cited as Bishop), 18 September 1943, p. 78.

28. Bishop, 18 September 1943, p. 80.

29. VC-9 ASW Report No. 5, 22 May 1943, and analysis; ASW Bulletin, June 1943, p. 19; Bishop, 18 September 1943, p. 80.

30. Bishop, 25 September 1943, p. 16; Hiestand correspondence.

31. VC-9 ASW Report No. 6, 22 May 1943, and analysis; ASW Bulletin, June 1943, p. 19.

32. VC-9 ASW Report No. 7, 22 May 1943, and analysis; ASW Bulletin, June 1943, p. 19; Morison X, p. 81.

33. VC-9 ASW Reports No. 8 and 9, 22 May 1943, and analysis; ASW Bulletin, June 1943, p. 19; Morison X, p. 81; B.d.U. War Diary, 22 May 1943; Bishop, 25 September 1943, pp. 41–42, 44.

34. Jacobsen, p. 306.

35. B.d.U. War Diary, 23 May 1943.

36. Communications Intelligence, Vol. I, p. 19.

37. Mason, p. 80.

38. B.d.U. War Diary, 5 March 1943.

39. Ibid., 3 May 1943; Adm. Karl Doenitz, *Memoirs: Ten Years and Twenty Days* (hereafter cited as Doenitz), p. 341.

40. Communications Intelligence, Vol. I, p. 24.

41. Ibid., pp. 24–27.

42. Kemp, p. 90.

43. Rohwer, pp. 198–200.

44. B.d.U. War Diary, 8 May 1943.

45. Ibid., 5 March 1943; Beesly, pp. 168–69; Hinsley, pp. 554–55; Rohwer, p. 241.

46. Doenitz, p. 143.

47. Beesly, p. 55.

48. Communications Intelligence, Vol. I, pp. 84–85; Beesly, p. 55.

49. B.d.U. War Diary, 24 May 1943.

50. Communications Intelligence, Vol. II, p. 78.

51. Both messages in B.d.U. War Diary, 24 May 1943.

52. Communications Intelligence, Vol. I, p. 34.

53. Morison X, p. 110.

54. Communications Intelligence, Vol. II, p. 105; Farago, p. 195.

55. Communications Intelligence, Vol. II, pp. 103–4, Vol. III, pp. 31–32; B.d.U. War Diary, 29 May 1943, 1 June 1943; Morison X, pp. 108, 111; *Bogue* Action Report, Serial 002, 11 June 1943, pp. 1–2. (Doenitz was unaware of UGS-9.)

56. *Bogue* Action Report, Serial 002, p. 2; Communications Intelligence, Vol. II, p. 105.

57. VC-9 ASW Report No. 11, 4 June 1943, and analysis; ASW Bulletin, July 1943, p. 18.

58. VC-9 ASW Reports No. 12, 13, and 14, 4 June 1943, and analysis; ASW Bulletin, July 1943, p. 18; Lundeberg, pp. 72–73; B.d.U. War Diary, 4 June 1943.

59. VC-9 ASW Report No. 15, 5 June 1943, and analysis; ASW Bulletin, July 1943, p. 18; Lundeberg, pp. 72–73; Alfred Price, *Aircraft Versus Submarine*, pp. 144–45.

60. B.d.U. War Diary, 4 June 1943 and 5 June 1943.

61. Ibid., 16 June 1943.

62. VC-9 ASW Report No. 16, 8 June 1943, and analysis.

63. Communications Intelligence, Vol IV, p. 43.

64. VC-9 ASW Reports No. 17 and 18, 8 June 1943, and analysis; ASW Bulletin, July 1943, pp. 18–19; Lundeberg, pp. 74–76; *Bogue* Action Report, Serial 002, p. 4; B.d.U. War Diary, 8 June 1943.

65. Communications Intelligence, Vol. IV, p. 44.

66. Ibid.; see also B.d.U. War Diary, 22 May 1943, for aircraft and aircraft defenses.

67. Waters, p. 237.

68. Communications Intelligence, Vol. II, pp. 135–37; B.d.U. War Diary, 11 June 1943.

69. B.d.U. War Diary, 12 and 13 June 1943.

70. VC-9 ASW Reports No. 19, 20, 21, and 22, 12 June 1943, and analysis; ASW Bulletin, July 1943, p. 19.

71. ASW Bulletin, July 1943, p. 19.

72. B.d.U. War Diary, 13 June 1943.

73. Communications Intelligence, Vol. II, pp. 139–42; B.d.U. War Diary, 5 June 1943.

74. This was a recurring theme in the analyses of VC-9 attacks.

75. Morison X, p. 114.

Chapter 4

1. *Santee* War Diary, Serial 076, 27 July 1945.

2. Ibid.

3. Morison I, p. 384.

4. *Eberle* Action Report, Serial 046, 14 March 1943; Capt. Walter Karig et al., "Battle Report," *The Atlantic War* (hereafter cited as Karig), pp. 440, 460–61; Hinsley, p. 544; Morison I, pp. 384–85.

5. VC-29 ASW Report No. 1, 16 March 1943.

6. VC-29 ASW Report No. 2, 16 March 1943.

7. VC-29 ASW Report No. 3, 16 March 1943.

8. *Santee* Action Report, Serial 038, 23 March 1943, Second Endorsement.

9. Capt. A. J. Isbell Interview, p. 1.

10. Morison X, p. 117.

11. Ibid., p. 110.

12. Ibid., p. 115; B.d.U. War Diary, 13 June 1943; CTG 21.11 Action Report, Serial 00020, 6 August 1943.

13. CTG 21.11 (*Santee*) Action Report, Serial 00020, p. 4; Morison X, p. 116.

14. CTG 21.11 Action Report, Serial 00020, pp. 2–3; Morison X, p. 116.

15. CTG 21.11 Action Report, Serial 00020, pp. 3–5.

16. Morison X, pp. 116, 130–31; B.d.U. War Diary, 29 and 30 June, 11 July 1943.

17. Lundeberg, p. 64.

18. Morison X, p. 117; "VC-13 Unit History," p. 5.

19. CTG 21.11 Action Report, Serial 00020, p. 6.

20. VC-13 ASW Report No. 1, 13 July 1943; ASW Bulletin, August 1943, p. 24.

21. VC-13 ASW Report No. 1; ASW Bulletin, August 1943, pp. 24–25; Morison X, pp. 117–18; Farago, p. 200.

22. Communications Intelligence, Vol. II, p. 376.

23. Ibid., Vol. II, p. 144, Vol. I, p. 30.

24. Allison W. Saville, "German Submarines in the Far East," pp.

80–85; B.d.U. War Diary, 30 June 1943; Communications Intelligence, Vol. II, pp. 375–78; Hinsley, p. 549; Beesly, pp. 195–96.

25. VC-13 ASW Report No. 2, 14 July 1943; ASW Bulletin, August 1943, pp. 25–26.

26. CTG 21.11 Action Report, Serial 00020, p. 7.

27. CTG 21.11 Action Report, Serial 084, 6 August 1943; VC-29 ASW Report No. 5, 14 July 1943; Morison X, p. 118; Farago, p. 201.

28. B.d.U. War Diary, 18 and 21 July 1943.

29. CTG 21.11 Action Report, Serial 084; VC-29 ASW Reports No. 6, 7, and 8, 14 July 1943; B.d.U. War Diary, 15 July 1943.

30. CTG 21.11 Action Report, Serial 084; VC-29 ASW Report No. 9, 15 July 1943; Morison X, p. 118.

31. CTG 21.11 Action Report, Serial 00020, p. 9.

32. Ibid.; VC-29 ASW Report No. 10, 15 July 1943; B.d.U. War Diary, 15 July 1943.

33. VC-13 ASW Report No. 3, 16 July 1943; ASW Bulletin, August 1943, pp. 26, 42; Morison X, p. 118; B.d.U. War Diary, 30 July 1943; Farago, p. 201; Karig, p. 438.

34. Morison X, pp. 118–19; B.d.U. War Diary, 21 July 1943.

35. "VC-13 Unit History," p. 6.

36. W. C. Heinz, "Hunting U-Boats on a Baby Flat-top" (hereafter cited as Heinz), 10 January 1944, p. 9.

37. VC-13 Unit History, pp. 6–7; Heinz, 10 January 1944, pp. 1, 9.

38. CTG 21.11 Action Report, Serial 00020, p. 10.

39. CTG 21.13 (Bogue) Action Report, Serial 006, 2 August 1943, p. 2.

40. ASW Bulletin, September 1943, p. 17.

41. Ibid.; Roscoe, p. 288; CTG 21.13 Action Report, Serial 006, p. 2; Morison X, pp. 119–21.

42. Summaries of Interrogations of Survivors of Enemy Submarines (hereafter cited as Interrogations), No. G/19, p. 17.

43. ASW Bulletin, September 1943, p. 32; Interrogations No. G/19; B.d.U. War Diary, 24 July and 29 July 1943; Morison X, p. 121.

44. VC-29 ASW Report No. 11, 24 July 1943; Morison X, p. 119; B.d.U. War Diary, 24 July 1943; CTG 21.11 Action Report, Serial 00020, p. 10.

45. CTG 21.13 Action Report, Serial 006, p. 3.

46. VC-29 ASW Reports No. 12A and 12B, 30 July 1943; CTG 21.11 Action Report, Serial 00020, pp. 11–12; Morison X, p. 119.

47. B.d.U. War Diary, 4 August 1943.

48. Ibid., 5 August 1943.

49. Ibid., 6 August 1943.

50. Ibid., 31 July 1943.

51. Ibid., 14 and 23 August 1943.

52. Ibid., 6 August 1943.

53. CTG 21.14 (Card) Action Report, Serial 0020, 10 September 1943, p. 1; Isbell Interview, p. 1.

54. VC-1 ASW Report No. 1-43, 4 August 1943.

55. B.d.U. War Diary, 3 August 1944.

56. Communications Intelligence, Vol. II, p. 154.

57. Isbell Interview, p. 2.

58. VC-1 ASW Report No. 1-43.

59. VC-1 ASW Reports No. 2-43 and 2B-43, 7 August 1943.

60. B.d.U. War Diary, 9 and 11 August 1943.

61. Ibid., 13 and 14 August 1943.

62. VC-1 ASW Report No. 3-43, 8 August 1943, Enclosure B.

63. VC-1 ASW Report No. 3-43; Isbell Interview, p. 2; Morison X, p. 123.

64. B.d.U. War Diary, 9 August 1943.

65. Interrogations No. G/27, p. 64.

66. CTG 21.14 Action Report, Serial 0020, p. 4.

67. VC-1 ASW Reports No. 5A-5E, 9 August 1943; ASW Bulletin, October 1943, pp. 22–23; Interrogations G/27; Morison X, p. 124.

68. VC-1 ASW Report No. 6-43, 11 August 1943; Morison X, p. 124.

69. CTG 21.14 Action Report, Serial 0020, p. 5.

70. Ibid., p. 6.

71. Morison X, pp. 220–22.

72. Interrogations No. G/26, p. 8.

73. VC-13 ASW Report No. 5, 24 August 1943; ASW Bulletin, September 1943, pp. 18–19; Interrogations No. G/26; Morison, p. 127.

74. Morison X, p. 127.

75. CTG 21.11 Action Report, Serial 0027, 12 October 1943, Enclosure E, pp. 1–2.

76. Ibid., Enclosure K, pp. 2–3.

77. VC-25 ASW Report No. 1, 21 August 1943; VC-6 History, pp. 3–4; Morison X, p. 125.

78. VC-6 Hstory, p. 4.

79. VC-6 ASW Report No. 2, 9 September 1943; Lundeberg, p. 519.

80. VC-6 History, p. 5.

81. Morison X, p. 126.

82. VC-1 ASW Report No. 7-43, 27 August 1943; Morison X, p. 128.

83. Communications Intelligence, Vol. II, pp. 156–57.

84. VC-1 ASW Report No. 8-43, 27 August 1943.

85. Ibid.; Morison X, p. 128; B.d.U. War Diary, 29 and 31 August 1943.

86. Communications Intelligence, Vol. II, p. 114.

87. Wolfgang Frank, *The Sea Wolves*, pp. 240–41; B.d.U. War Diary, 23 August 1943.

Chapter 5

1. Morison X, pp. 135–46.

2. J. P. Mallmann Showell,·*The German Navy in World War Two*, p. 50.

3. CTG 21.12 (*Bogue*) Action Report, Serial 097, 28 September 1943, p. 2.

4. CTG 21.12 Action Report, Serial 0102, 20 October 1943, pp. 1–2.

5. Farago, pp. 230–31; Morison X, p. 159.

6. CTG 21.14 Action Report, Serial 0043, 9 November 1943, p. 1.

7. VC-9 ASW Report No. 23, 4 October 1943.

8. Morison X, p. 160.

9. VC-9 ASW Report No. 23.

10. Ibid.; CTG 21.14 Action Report, Serial 0043, Annex A, pp. 4–5; Lundeberg, pp. 525–29; Morison X, pp. 159–60; B.d.U. War Diary, 5 October 1943.

11. B.d.U. War Diary, 7 October 1943.

12. VC-9 ASW Report No. 24, 4 October 1943; CTG 21.14 Action Report, Serial 0043, Annex A, p. 5; Morison X, p. 160.

13. CTG 21.14 Action Report, Serial 0043, p. 7; Morison X, p. 160.

14. Hiestand correspondence.

15. VC-9 ASW Report No. 25, 12 October 1943.

16. VC-9 ASW Report No. 26, 12 October 1943; Lundeberg, pp. 531–33; Morison X, p. 160.

17. VC-9 ASW Report No. 27, 13 October 1943; Lundeberg, pp. 534–35; Morison X, p. 160.

18. VC-9 ASW Report No. 28, 13 October 1943.

19. Ibid.; Morison X, p. 161.

20. VC-9 ASW Report No. 29, 13 October 1943; Waters, pp. 268–69; Morison X, p. 161.

21. VC-9 ASW Report No. 30, 13 October 1943; CTG 21.14 Action Report, Serial 0043, Annex A, pp. 11–12.

22. Heinz, 27 December 1943, p. 7.

23. Morison X, p. 161; "VC-13 Unit History," Part II, p. 8.

24. Morison X, p. 162; "VC-13 Unit History," Part II, p. 8.

25. "VC-13 Unit History," Part II, p. 8.

26. Lundeberg, pp. 541–42.

27. Howard Adams correspondence.

28. Wayne Lee correspondence.

29. CTG 21.16 (*Block Island*) Action Report, no serial, 25 November 1943.

30. VC-1 ASW Report No. 9-43, 28 October 1943; Lundeberg, p. 547; Morison X, p. 162.

31. VC-9 ASW Report No. 31, 30 October 1943; Morison X, p. 162.

32. VC-9 ASW Report No. 32, 31 October 1943; Lundeberg, pp. 549–51; Morison X, p. 162.

33. Roscoe, p. 290.

34. *Borie* ASW Report, 8 November 1943, Enclosure A; Morison X, p. 163; Lt. Comdr. Charles H. Hutchins Interview, pp. 1–2.

35. Morison X, p. 163.

36. John Hersey, "U.S.S. *Borie*'s Last Battle" (hereafter cited as Hersey), p. 106.

37. Ibid., p. 112.

38. Hutchins Interview, p. 7.

39. Hersey, p. 112.

40. Ibid., p. 114.

41. *Borie* ASW Report, Enclosure B; Hutchins Interview; Hersey, Morison X, pp. 163–67.

42. History of VF-29, pp. 17–18; *Santee* War Diary, Serial 076, 27 July 1945.

43. CTG 21.13 (*Bogue*) Action Report, Serial 0021, 5 December 1943, Enclosure H.

44. Lundeberg, pp. 577–79.

45. Ibid., pp. 579–80.

46. Ibid., p. 581.

47. CTG 21.13 Action Report, Serial 0040, 29 December 1943, including Analysis of Antisubmarine Action; VC-19 ASW Report No. 6, 13 December 1943; Morison X, pp. 169–70; ASW Bulletin, February 1944, pp. 28–32; Roscoe, pp. 291–92.

48. Interrogations No. G/29, p. 43.

49. Lundeberg, p. 585.

50. VC-19 ASW Report No. 7, 20 December 1943.

51. CTG 21.14 Action Report, Serial 003, 2 January 1944, p. 11.

52. Lundeberg, p. 584; Morison X, p. 172.

53. CTG 21.14 Action Report, Serial 003, p. 14.

54. B.d.U. War Diary, 23 December 1943; Lundeberg, p. 591.

55. CTG 21.14 Action Report, Serial 003, p. 16.

56. Morison X, p. 174.

57. CTG 21.14 Action Report, Serial 003, p. 17.

58. Ibid.

59. Lundeberg, pp. 591–99; Morison X, pp. 173–76; Roscoe, p. 293; History, USS *Card*, pp. 5–6.

60. CTG 21.14 Action Report, Serial 003, p. 17; Morison X, p. 176; B.d.U. War Diary, 23 and 24 December 1943.

61. Morison X, p. 176.

62. Communications Intelligence, Vol. III, p. 15.

63. Ibid., Vol. I, pp. 66–67.

Chapter 6

1. VC-6 ACA Report No. 1, 22 December 1943.

2. VC-6 ASW Reports No. 3 and 4, 2 January 1944.

3. CTG 21.16 Action Report, Serial 007, 13 February 1944, pp. 1–2; VC-58 History, Serial 87, pp. 2–3; Capt. S. W. Roskill, *The War at Sea, 1939–1945*, Vol. III, Part I, p. 74.

4. CTG 21.16 Action Report, Serial 007, p. 2.

5. Ibid., Annex A, pp. 1–6; Communications Intelligence, Vol. II, p. 182.

6. "TBF Pilots Describe Fireworks...," *All Hands*, July 1944, p. 18.

7. ASW Bulletin, March 1944, p. 27; VC-58 History, p. 3; *All Hands*, July 1944, p. 18; CTG 21.16 Action Report, Serial 007, p. 4.

8. B.d.U. War Diary, 15 January 1944.

9. Lundeberg, p. 617.

10 CTG 21.11 Action Reports, Serial 00020, 6 August 1943, p. 15, and Serial 0027, 12 October 1943, Enclosure H.

11. Commander in Chief, U.S. Atlantic Fleet, p. 679.

12. CTG 21.11 (*Mission Bay*) Action Report, Serial 009, 14 February 1944; *Mission Bay* History, 13 September 1943 to 19 November 1945, p. 1.

13. Gallery, Reminiscences, pp. 70–71.

14. Paul Silverstone, *U. S. Warships of World War II*, p. 167.

15. CTG 21.12 (*Guadalcanal*) Action Report, Serial 007, 26 April 1944, Annex A, p. 2.

16. "VC-13 Unit History," p. 9.

17. William Bowne correspondence; Rear Adm. Daniel V. Gallery, *Clear the Decks!*, pp. 119–20.

18. Bowne correspondence.

19. "VC-13 Unit History," p. 9.

20. ASW Bulletin, March 1944, pp. 32–33; "VC-13 Unit History," p. 10; B.d.U. War Diary, 12 and 17 January 1944.

21. Rear Adm. D. V. Gallery, ". . . Nor Dark of Night," p. 87; see also Gallery's *Twenty Million Tons Under the Sea*, pp. 252–56. The *Guadalcanal*'s experience was just a foretaste of what would happen six months later in the Battle of the Philippine Sea.

22. ". . . Nor Dark of Night," p. 88.

23. Gallery, Reminiscences, p. 75.

24. *Clear the Decks!*, pp. 164–65.

25. "VC-13 Unit History," p. 11.

26. Ibid.

27. CTG 21.14 Action Report, Serial 016, 9 March 1944, p. 2, Annex H, pp. 1–4.

28. Ibid., Summary of Crashes, p. 1; VC-55 Historical Report, Serial 193, 20 June 1945, p. 4.

29. Gordon Swanborough and Peter M. Bowers, *United States Navy Aircraft Since 1911*, pp. 207–9.

30. VC-6 History, p. 9.

31. Roscoe, p. 299; Morison X, p. 279; Karig, p. 447.

32. Interrogations No. G/33, p. 20.

33. Ibid., p. 21.

34. VC-6 History, pp. 10–11; ASW Bulletin, May 1944, p. 27.

35. CTG 21.16 Action Report, Serial 0010, 31 March 1944, p. 3.

36. B.d.U. War Diary, 2 April 1944.

37. CTG 21.16 Action Report, Serial 0010, Annex B, p. 7c.

38. Interrogations No. G/33, pp. 22–23.

39. Ibid., p. 23; CTG 21.16 Action Report, Serial 0010; ASW Bulletin, May 1944, pp. 27–28, 43; VC-6 History, pp. 10–15.

40. Roscoe, p. 302.

41. B.d.U. War Diary, 2 April 1944.

42. Interrogations No. G/37, p. 32.

43. VC-6 History, p. 16.

44. Ibid., p. 17. Whether Dowty stalled out or his plane was damaged by gunfire and crashed is unknown.

45. VC-6 History, pp. 16–17; Interrogations No. G/37; "U-Boat Hunters," *All Hands*, July 1945, p. 19.

46. VC-6 History, pp. 17–20.

47. Morison X, pp. 280–81.

48. VC-6 History, p. 20.

49. Hiestand correspondence.

50. Ibid.

51. *Bogue* Action Report, Serial 006, 14 February 1944; *Bogue* Chronology.

52. CTG 21.11 (*Bogue*) Action Report, Serial 0018, 19 April 1944, pp. 1–3; *Bogue* History, Appendix E; Interrogations No. G/32; Roscoe, pp. 300–1; B.d.U. War Diary, 17 March 1944.

53. VC-95 History, Serial 040, 1 January 1945, pp. 3–5.

54. "*Wake Island* History"; History of *Mission Bay*, p. 2.

55. CTG 21.12 Action Report, Serial 007, 26 April 1944, Annex B, p. 13.

56. Rear Adm. D. V. Gallery, *Twenty Million Tons Under the Sea* (hereafter cited as Gallery), p. 258.

57. CTG 21.12 Action Report, Serial 007, Annex A, pp. 3–4.

58. ASW Bulletin, June 1944, p. 28.

59. Gallery, p. 261.

60. Ibid.

61. CTG 21.12 Action Report, Serial 007; ASW Bulletin, June 1944, pp. 28–29; Interrogations No. G/36, pp. 40–45; Morison X, p. 282; Roscoe, pp. 302–3; Gallery, pp. 259–61; ". . . Nor Dark of Night," p. 88.

62. Interrogations No. G/36, p. 18.

63. Gallery, p. 266.

64. Ibid., p. 267.

65. Ibid., p. 269; Farago, p. 357.

66. ASW Bulletin, June 1944, p. 29; Morison X, p. 283.

67. B.d.U. War Diary, 8 and 10 April 1944.

68. ASW Bulletin, June 1944, pp. 29–30; Gallery, pp. 270–72; Morison X, p. 283; VC-58 History, p. 4; Interrogations No. G/36, pp. 58–60.

69. CTG 21.12 Action Report, Serial 007, Annex A, pp. 4–5.

70. Ibid., p. 1.

71. "VC-13 Unit History," p. 13.

72. CTG 21.14 (*Tripoli*) Action Report, Serial 003, 29 April 1944; Morison X, p. 283.

73. B.d.U. War Diary, 20 April 1944.

74. CTG 21.15 (*Croatan*) Action Report, Serial 0001, p. 6; LantFlt ASW Unit Study, Serial 0020, 22 May 1944, p. 11.

75. VC-42 History, Chapter 6, p. 5.

76. CTG 21.15 Action Report, Serial 0001, p. 6; LantFlt ASW Study, Serial 0020, p. 11.

77. ASW Bulletin, May 1944, p. 28.

78. LantFlt ASW Study, Serial 0020, pp. 3–4; VC-24 History, Chapter 6, pp. 6–9; CinCLant History, pp. 680–81; Interrogations G/35; ASW Bulletin, May 1944, pp. 28–31; Roscoe, p. 302.

79. B.d.U. War Diary, 22 April 1944.

80. LantFlt ASW Study, Serial 0020, p. 11.

81. B.d.U. War Diary, 26 and 28 April 1944.

82. LantFlt ASW Study, Serial 0020, pp. 5–7; VC-42 History, Chapter 6, pp. 11–13; Morison X, pp. 283–84; Roscoe, p. 304.

83. VC-42 History, Chapter 6, p. 13.

84. LantFlt ASW Study, Serial 0020, pp. 8–13; CTG 21.15 Action Report, Serial 0001, pp. 5–7.

85. B.d.U. War Diary, 28 April 1944.

86. CTG 21.16 (*Core*) Action Report, Serial 0021, 30 May 1944; VC-36 History, 30 May 1945, pp. 34–40.

Chapter 7

1. Morison I, p. 412; Morison X, p. 367. In October 1944 no ships were lost in the Atlantic to U-boat attacks.

2. CTG 21.11 (*Block Island*) Action Report, Serial 0025, 27 June 1944, Annex B, p. 1.

3. B.d.U. War Diary, 26 and 30 April 1944, 1 May 1944.

4. VC-55 Narrative of Events, 1–2 May 1944.

5. B.d.U. War Diary, 5 May 1944; Interrogations No. G/38, p. 22.

6. Morison X, p. 286.

7. Ibid.

8. CTG 21.11 Report on *U-66* Prisoners, Serial 0018, 18 May 1944, p. 13.

9. Ibid., p. 4; ASW Bulletin deletes "with their hands up."

10. ASW Bulletin, June 1944, p. 25.

11. Ibid.

12. Ibid., pp. 25–26.

13. Report on *U-66* Prisoners, p. 5; B.d.U. War Diary, 31 March 1944.

14. Report on *U-66* Prisoners, pp. 1–16; ASW Bulletin, June 1944, pp. 24–26; Morison X, pp. 285–88; Roscoe, pp. 306–7; CTG 21.11 Action Report, Serial 0025, Annex B, pp. 1–3.

15. CTG 21.11 Action Report, Serial 0025, Annex B, p. 3; Morison X, p. 288.

16. Lee correspondence.

17. Ibid.

18. CTG 21.11 Action Report, Serial 0025, Annex B, p. 9.

19. Ibid., p. 10; Lee correspondence.

20. Lee correspondence.

21. Ibid.

22. CTG 21.11 Action Report, Serial 0025, Annex B, pp. 11–12.

23. Ibid., pp. 4–13; ASW Bulletin, July 1944, pp. 27–29; Morison X, pp. 289–90; Roscoe, pp. 307–8; Lee correspondence.

24. Lee correspondence.

25. Morison X, p. 291.

26. VC-8 History, Serial 04, 5 March 1945, Narrative, pp. 9–10.

27. Farago, p. 266.

28. CTG 22.3 (*Guadalcanal*) Action Report, Serial 0021, 19 June 1944, p. 2.

29. Ibid.

30. VC-8 History, Addendum 1, 25 June 1945, Serial 012, Chronology, p. 2.

31. Roscoe, p. 310.

32. CTG 22.3 Action Report, Serial 0021, 19 June 1944, p. 4.

33. Ibid., p. 5.

34. Capt. Daniel V. Gallery Interview, 26 May 1945, p. 11.

35. Communications Intelligence, Vol. I, p. 27.

36. B.d.U. War Diary, 6 July 1944.

37. CTG 22.3 Action Report, Serial 0021, 19 June 1944, p. 8.

38. This entire section on the capture of *U-505* is based primarily on CTG 22.3 Action Report, Serial 0021, 19 June 1944, including all enclosures (particularly Enclosure D, Communications Log). The *Guadalcanal* file also includes a pair of letters from Dudley S. Knox to Rear Admiral Gallery written in January–February 1953, commenting on possible misconceptions in Gallery's book, *Clear the Decks*, which had been published a short time before. See also Gallery, pp. 275–311; Morison X, pp. 290–93; Farago, pp. 265–71; Roscoe, pp. 309–10; Karig, pp. 142–44.

Chapter 8

1. *Tulagi* History; *Kasaan Bay* Ship's History.

2. *Kasaan Bay* "A Brief History of an Active Small Carrier," p. 1.

3. *Tulagi* Action Report, Serial 002, no date, p. 1, Appendix D, p. 5; *Kasaan Bay* War Diary, Serial 0104, 10 July 1944; ". . . an Active Small Carrier," p. 1.

4. *Kasaan Bay* Action Report, Serial 0121, 11 September 1944, Enclosure E.

5. *Kasaan Bay* War Diary, Serial 0113, 12 August 1944, p. 23.

6. Samuel Eliot Morison, Vol. XI *The Invasion of France and Germany* (hereafter cited as Morison XI), pp. 279–80.

7. *Kasaan Bay* Action Report, Serial 0121, p. 3.

8. Ibid.; Morison XI, p. 242.

9. *Tulagi* Action Report, Serial 002, p. 1; *Kasaan Bay* Action Report, Serial 0121; Polmar, p. 306.

10. *Tulagi* Action Report, Serial 002, Appendix B, Appendix E, p. 7;

CTG 88.2 Action Report, Serial 0070, 6 September 1944, Enclosure B, p. 6; Barrett Tillman, *Hellcat* (hereafter cited as Tillman), p. 101.

11. *Kasaan Bay* Action Report, Serial 0121; CTG 88.2 Action Report, Serial 0010, Enclosure B, p. 6.

12. CTG 88.2 Action Report, Serial 0010, Enclosure A, p. 2.

13. *Kasaan Bay* Action Report, Serial 0121, Record of Flight Operations, pp. 7–9; Tillman, p. 101.

14. VOF-1 ACA Report No. 25; Tillman, pp. 101–2; Lt. (jg) John G. Norris, "Hellcats Over France," p. 144.

15. *Kasaan Bay* Action Report, Serial 0121, Record of Flight Operations, pp. 12–14.

16. Ibid., p. 13.

17. CTG 88.2 Action Report, Serial 0010, Enclosure B, p. 6.

18. Ibid., Enclosure A, p. 44

19. *Kasaan Bay* Action Report, Serial 0121, Record of Flight Operations, pp. 15–18.

20. VOF-1 ACA Report No. 28; Tillman, p. 103.

21. VOF-1 ACA Report No. 31.

22. Karig, p. 534.

23. VOF-1 ACA Report No. 33.

24. VOF-1 ACA Report No. 34.

25. Ibid.

26. *Tulagi* Action Report, Serial 002, Appendix E, p. 11; *Kasaan Bay* Action Report, Serial 0121; "Hellcats Over France," p. 150.

27. CTG 88.2 Action Report, Serial 0010, Enclosure B, p. 6.

28. Karig, p. 534.

29. Tillman, p. 104; Karig, pp. 534, 536.

30. *Kasaan Bay* Ship's History, Documentation, p. 3.

31. ". . . an Active Small Carrier," p. 3.

32. Report of Rear Admiral, Escort Carriers, Royal Navy, Serial 0675/14, 11 September 1944, p. 2.

33. Ibid.

Chapter 9

1. B.d.U. War Diary, 15 June 1944.

2. VC-6 History, p. 20.

3. Memo, Ingersoll to King, 13 May 1944 (in CVE Groups).

4. Lee and Hiestand correspondence.

5. *Bogue* Narrative, 25 December 1944, p. 11.

6. CTG 22.2 (*Bogue*) Action Report, Serial 0022, 3 July 1944, p. 3; Roscoe, p. 308.

7. CTG 22.2 Action Report, Serial 0022, Enclosure Y.

8. Ibid., p. 4.

9. Ibid.

10. Ibid., p. 5; *Bogue* Chronology.

11. B.d.U. War Diary, 31 July 1944; Martin Brice, *Axis Blockade*

Runners of World War II, pp. 146–47.

    12. CTG 22.2 Report of ASW Action, Serial 0023, 3 July 1944, p. 4.

    13. VC-69 ASW Report No. 1, 24 June 1944.

    14. VC-69 ASW Report No. 2, 24 June 1944.

    15. CTG 22.2 Action Report, Serial 0022, pp. 11–12.

    16. Ibid., pp. 7, 12.

    17. Ibid., p. 7.

    18. Ibid., pp. 7–8.

    19. B.d.U. War Diary, 7 August 1944.

    20. Interrogations No. G/42, p. 18; Morison X, p. 320.

    21. ComCortDiv 13 Action Report, no serial, p. 5, Endorsement of 25 June 1944 to *Frost* Action Report, Serial 07, 12 June 1944.

    22. Morison X, p. 321.

    23. Ibid., pp. 320–21; Roscoe, pp. 310–12; CTG 22.5 (*Croatan*) Action Report, Serial 0006, 22 July 1944, pp. 1–3.

    24. CTG 22.5 Action Report, Serial 0006, p. 3.

    25. Ibid., pp. 3–4; VC-95 History, Serial 040, 1 January 1945, p. 9; Morison X, p. 321; VC-95 ASW Report No. 2-44, 18 June 1944.

    26. B.d.U. War Diary, 8 July 1944.

    27. VC-95 History, p. 10.

    28. CTG 22.5 Action Report, Serial 0006, pp. 5, 7–8.

    29. Ibid.; VC-95 History, pp. 8–11.

    30. CTG 41.6 (*Solomons*) Action Report, Serial 003, 30 April 1944; Morison X, p. 295.

    31. CTG 41.6 Action Report, Serial 0016, 23 June 1944, Enclosure A, p. 2.

    32. VC-9 ASW Report No. 33, 15 June 1944.

    33. *Straub* Action Report, Serial 029, 22 June 1944.

    34. CTG 41.6 Action Report, Serial 0016, Enclosure A, p. 2; VC-9 History, p. 10; Terzibaschitsch, p. 83; B.d.U. War Diary, 1 August 1944.

    35. ASW Unit Report, Serial 0038, 6 September 1944, p. 1.

    36. Ibid., p. 2.

    37. Ibid., pp. 2–3.

    38. Ibid., pp. 3–4; CTG 22.6 (*Wake Island*) Action Report, Serial 00144, 15 August 1944, Annex B, p. 25; Morison X, p. 299.

    39. ASW Unit Report, Serial 0038, pp. 4–5.

    40. Ibid., p. 7–9; CTG 22.6 Action Report, Serial 00144, Annex B, pp. 79–81; Roscoe, p. 313; Morison X, p. 322.

    41. ASW Unit Report, Serial 0038, p. 10.

    42. CTG 21.10 (*Card*) Action Report, Serial 066, 23 August 1944, TBS Log, p. 2.

    43. Lundeberg, p. 910.

    44. CTG 21.10 Action Report, Serial 066, TBS Log, p. 4.

    45. VC-12 History; 13 January 1945, pp. 8–9; *Card* History, p. 7; Roscoe, p. 312; Morison X, p. 319; Interrogations No. G/45; B.d.U. War Diary, 11 August 1944.

    46. *Card* History, pp. 7–8; VC-12 History, pp. 9–10; Morison X, p. 298.

47. CominCh message, Serial 102040, 9 July 1944 (in CVE Groups).

48. CTG 22.3 (*Bogue*) Action Report, Serial 0035, 24 September 1944, p. 8.

49. VC-42 History, Chapter 7, p. 4.

50. Ibid., pp. 4–5.

51. Morison X, pp. 325–26; VC-42 History, Chapter 7, p. 9.

52. B.d.U. War Diary, 12 November 1944.

53. VC-42 ASW Report No. 5, 19 August 1944; CTG 22.3 Action Report, Serial 0035, p. 3; VC-42 History, Chapter 7, pp. 10–11.

54. CTG 22.3 Action Report, Serial 0035, p. 4.

55. Interrogations No. G/46, pp. 21–22.

56. VC-42 ASW Report No. 6, 20 August 1944; ASW Bulletin, September 1944, pp. 17–18.

57. VC-42 ASW Report No. 7, 20 August 1944.

58. Ibid.; ASW Bulletin, September 1944, pp. 18–19, 21.

59. VC-42 History, Chapter 4, pp. 13–15; Interrogationss No. G/46; B.d.U. War Diary, 2 December 1944; Morison X, p. 327.

60. VC-42 History, Chapter 4, p. 18.

61. Ibid., p. 19.

62. Morison X, pp. 328–29.

63. VC-42 History, Chapter 4, p. 24.

64. Ibid., pp. 26–27.

65. CTG 22.3 Action Report, Serial 0035, p. 9; VC–42 History, Chapter 4, p. 27.

66. *Shamrock Bay* Action Reports, Serial 048, 4 September 1944, and Serial 052, 27 October 1944.

67. Morison X, p. 329.

68. CTG 22.4 (*Core*) Action Report, Serial 0033, Enclosure A, p. 3; VC-13 History, p. 15.

Chapter 10

1. Tenth Fleet Memo, 27 July 1944 (in CVE Antisubmarine Operations).

2. VC-6 History, p. 21.

3. James L. Mooney, *Dictionary of American Naval Fighting Ships*, Vol. VII, p. 284.

4. CTG 41.7 (*Tripoli*) Action Report, Serial 083, 11 September 1944.

5. Morison X, pp. 295–96.

6. *Mission Bay* History.

7. CTG 22.1 (*Mission Bay*) Action Report, Serial 0026, 25 November 1944, Enclosure C, p. 2.

8. VC-6 History, p. 22; CTG 41.7 Action Report, Serial 090, 12 October 1944, p. 2.

9. VC-6 History, pp. 22–24; CTG 41.7 Action Report, Serial 090, pp. 2–3.

10. ASW Bulletin, January 1945, p. 30; CTG 22.1 Action Report, Serial 0026, Enclosure C, p. 4.

11. VC-6 History, pp. 24–28; CTG 41.7 Action Report, Serial 090,

pp. 4–5; B.d.U. War Diary, 2 and 4 December 1944; Morison X, p. 296.

12. CTG 41.7 Action Report, Serial 0109, 12 November 1944; CTG 22.1 Action Report, Serial 0026, pp. 5–8.

13. Morison X, p. 366.

14. *Bogue* Narrative, 25 December 1944, pp. 12–13.

15. CominCh message, Serial 003093, 23 October 1944 (in CVE Antisubmarine Operations).

16. CTG 22.7 (*Guadalcanal*) Action Report, Serial 0052, 6 November 1944, Enclosure A, p. 2.

17. *Bogue* Chronology; *Card* History.

18. CTG 22.4 Action Report, Serial 005, 28 February 1945.

19. Farago, p. 7; Communications Intelligence, Vol. II, p. 228.

20. Farago, pp. 8–11; Morison X, pp. 330–31.

21. VC-95 History, Serial 061, 1 April 1945, p. 1; VC-12 History, 7 June 1945, p. 2; VC-58 History, Serial 087, p. 5.

22. Communications Intelligence, Vol. II, p. 228.

23. CTG 22.1 Action Report, Serial 0044, 27 April 1945, p. 1.

24. Morison X, p. 346.

25. CTG 22.5 (*Croatan*) Action Report, Serial 005, 14 May 1945, Report on Air Operations.

26. Ibid., p. 2; Morison X, p. 346.

27. CTG 22.5 Action Report, Serial 005, p. 2.

28. Ibid., p. 3.

29. Ibid., pp. 2–3; Morison X, pp. 346–48; Roscoe, p. 508.

30. CTG 22.5 Action Report, Serial 005, p. 3; Roscoe, pp. 508–9; Morison X, pp. 348–49.

31. CTG 22.5 Action Report, Serial 005, Enclosure C, p. 3.

32. Morison X, p. 349; CTG 22.1 Action Report, Serial 0044, p. 3.

33. CTG 22.5 Action Report, Serial 005, p. 4; Roscoe, p. 510; Morison X, pp. 349–50.

34. CTG 22.1 Action Report, Serial 0044, p. 4, Enclosure A, p. 48; VC-95 History, Serial 089, 28 June 1945, Narrative, pp. 2–3.

35. Morison X, pp. 351–53; Roscoe, pp. 510–11; CTG 22.1 Action Report, Serial 0044, p. 3; VC-12 History, p. 4.

36. Morison X, p. 355.

37. Ibid., pp. 353–55; Roscoe, pp. 511–13; VC-12 History, p. 4.

38. CTG 22.5 Action Report, Serial 005, p. 4; CTG 22.4 Action Report, Serial 0020, Enclosure A, p. 3; Morison X, p. 355.

39. Roscoe, pp. 513–14; Morison X, p. 355.

40. Communications Intelligence, Vol. II, p. 235.

41. VC-95 History, Serial 089, p. 4; VC-12 History, p. 5; CTG 22.5 Action Report, Serial 005, p. 5.

42. CTG 22.5 Action Report, Serial 005, p. 5; Morison X, p. 360.

43. Thomas Parish, *Simon & Schuster Encyclopedia of World War II*, p. 228; John Keegan, *Rand McNally Encyclopedia of World War II*, p. 242; Hughes, p. 303; Barrie Pitt, *The Battle of the Atlantic*, pp. 86, 179.

44. Roscoe, p. 516.

45. Morison X, pp. 362–63.

46. Tweed Wallis Ross, Jr., *The Best Way to Destroy a Ship* (hereafter cited as Ross), p. 129.

47. Morison X, p. 60.

48. Capt. S. W. Roskill, *The Navy at War, 1939–1945*, pp. 404–5.

49. Communications Intelligence, Vol. I, p. 30.

50. Ross, p. 129.

51. Communications Intelligence, Vol. I, p. 55.

52. Ibid., Vol. II, pp. 101–2.

53. Ibid., Vol. I, p. 53.

54. C. M. Sternhell and A. M. Thorndike, *Antisubmarine Warfare in World War II*, p. 37.

Appendix III

1. Report of Capt. M. R. Greer, 15 November 1943 (in CVE ASW Ops); Memo from Capt. K. A. Knowles, 24 December 1943 (in CVE ASW Ops); CominCh dispatch 052215, 5 January 1944 (in CVE Groups); Morison X, pp. 16, 39, 307; Roskill, *The War at Sea, 1939–1945*, Vol. III, Part I, pp. 34–36.

BIBLIOGRAPHY

Documentary Sources: American

Note: Carrier reports can be found in naval records in the Operational Archives at the Washington Navy Yard under the carrier's name or task group designation because CVE captains, generally, also commanded the task groups.

Block Island
    Action Reports—various serials.
    "USS *Block Island*, CVE-21 and CVE-106," no date.

Bogue
    Action Reports—various serials.
    War Diaries—various serials.
    "History of USS *Bogue* (CVE-9)," with narrative and chronology, 25 December 1944.
    USS *Bogue* Unit History for December 1944–February 1945, no serial.
    USS *Bogue* Unit History for March–August 1945, no serial.

Card
    Action Reports—various serials.
    "History of USS *Card*," no date.

Chenango
    Action Report, Serial 035, 2 December 1942.
    "Wartime History of *Chenango*," no date.

Core
    Action Reports—various serials.

Croatan
    Action Reports—various serials.
    War Diaries—various serials.

Guadalcanal
    Action Reports—various serials.
    Letters of Dudley S. Knox in *Guadalcanal* files.

Kasaan Bay
    Action Report, Serial 0121, 4 September 1944.
    War Diary, Serial 0113, 12 August 1944; Serial 002, 14 September 1944.
    "A Brief History of an Active Small Carrier," no date.
    "Ship's History: Authorization to 1 July 1945," no date.

Mission Bay
    Action Reports—various serials.
    War Diaries—various serials.
    "History of *Mission Bay*, 13 September 1943 to 19 December 1945," no date.

Sangamon
    Action Reports—various serials.
    Awards of Distinguished Flying Cross—various serials.
    "History of USS *Sangamon*," Serial 075, 3 October 1945.
    "History of USS *Sangamon*," no date.

Santee
    Action Reports—various serials.
    War Diary, Serial 076, 27 July 1945.

Shamrock Bay
    Action Reports, Serial 084, 4 September 1944; Serial 052, 27 October 1944.

Solomons
    Action Reports—various serials.

Suwannee
    Action Reports, Serial 029, 28 November 1942.
    Awards for Meritorious Achievement, Serial 024, 17 November 1942.
    "*Suwannee* War History," Serial 488, 5 November 1945.
    "History of USS *Suwannee*," no date.

Tripoli
    Action Reports—various serials.

Tulagi
    Action Report, Serial 022, no date.
    War Diaries—various serials.
    "History of *Tulagi*," no date.

Wake Island
    Action Report, Serial 00144, 15 August 1944.

Atlantic Fleet ASW Unit Operations Study, Serial 0038, 6 September 1944.

"*Wake Island* History," no date.

VC-1

ASW Reports—various numbers.

VOF-1

ACA Reports—various numbers.

VC-6

ASW Reports—various numbers.

ACA Report No. 1, 22 December 1943.

Historical Report, no serial, 3 July 1945.

VC-8

ASW Reports—various numbers.

History (in four parts)—various serials and dates.

VC-9

ASW Reports—various numbers.

"History of VC-9, August 1942–July 1945," no serial, 23 July 1945.

VC-12

"History of VC-12" (in two parts), no serials, 13 January 1945 and 7 June 1945.

VC-13

ASW Reports—various numbers.

War Diaries—various serials.

"VC-13 Unit History," no date.

VC-19

ASW Reports—various numbers.

VC-19 History, no date.

VC-25

ASW Report No. 1, 21 August 1943.

VGS-26

Reports No. 1 and 2, 8 November 1942; 3 and 4, 10 November 1942.

VGS-27

ASW Report No. 1, 11 November 1942.

VC-29

ASW Reports—various numbers.

VGF-29

ACA Reports—various numbers.

"VF-29 (VGF-29) History and Chronology," no date.

VGS-29

ACA Reports—various numbers.

ASW Reports—various numbers.

VC-36

"History of Composite Squadron 36," 30 May 1945.

VC-42

ASW Reports—various numbers.

"History of Composite Squadron 42, 15 April 1943–24 September 1944," no date.

"Supplement No. 1, 24 September 1944–10 December 1944," no date.

VC-55

   Narrative of Events, 1 and 2 May, 4 May 1944.

   VC-55 Historical Report, Serial 193, 20 June 1945.

VC-58

   History of VC-58, Serial 87, 5 June 1945.

VC-69

   ASW Reports—various numbers.

   Report of Operations, 4 May–3 July 1944, no serial, 3 July 1944.

   "History," Serial 126, 31 May 1945.

VF-74

   ACA Reports—various numbers.

VC-95

   ASW Reports—various numbers.

   VC-95 History, Serial 040, 1 January 1945; Serial 061, 1 April 1945; Serial 089, 28 June 1945.

   War Diary, Serial 039, 31 May 1944.

Office of Naval Intelligence

   Summaries of Interrogations of Survivors of Enemy Submarines.

United States Fleet Antisubmarine Bulletins, June 1943–June 1945.

Atlantic Fleet ASW Unit

   Reports—various serials.

Atlantic Fleet

   Report of Aircraft Operations during TORCH, Serial 0874, 30 March 1943.

Commander, Amphibious Force, U.S. Atlantic Fleet

   Report, Serial 00299, 22 December 1942, and First Endorsement, 1 March 1943.

Tenth Fleet

   Message Files—in Box 33/ASM under 1: CVE Antisubmarine Operations and 2: CVE Groups.

   Allied Communications Intelligence and the Battle of the Atlantic. (Four volumes.)

Task Force 34

   Occupation of French North Africa: Outline History.

   Preliminary Report on TORCH, serial 00241, 28 November 1942.

Task Group 21.11

   Report on *U-66* Prisoners, Serial 0018, 18 May 1944.

Task Group 34.2

   Action Report, Serial F-0032, 3 December 1942.

Task Group 34.8

   Action Report, Serial 0224, 26 November 1942.

Task Group 88.2

   Action Report, Serial 0010, 6 September 1944.

   Rear Admiral, Escort Carriers, Report of Proceedings Operation DRAGOON, E.C. No., 0675/14, 11 September 1944.

Commander Escort Division 4
  Action Report, Serial 001, 8 June 1944.

Savannah
  Action Report, no serial, 10 March 1943.

Borie
  ASW Reports of 31 October 1943 and 1 November 1943, no serial, 8 November 1943.

Eberle
  Action Report, Serial 046, 14 March 1943.

Frost
  Action Report, Serial 07, 12 June 1944, with ComCortDiv 13 endorsement of 25 June 1944.

Jenks
  Action Report, Serial 0001, 9 June 1944.

Straub
  Action Report, Serial 029, 2 June 1944.

Lundeberg, Dr. Philip K. *American Anti-Submarine Operations in the Atlantic, May 1943–May 1945.*

Sternhell, C. M., and A. M. Thorndike,. *Antisubmarine Warfare in World War II.* Operational Evaluation Group Report No. 51, Washington, 1946.

U.S. Naval Administration in World War II
  "Commander in Chief, U.S. Atlantic Fleet." Washington, D.C., 1946.
  "Air Force Atlantic Fleet History." Norfolk, 1946.

U.S. Naval Administration in World War II, DCNO (Air)
  "Air Task Organization in the Atlantic Ocean Area." Washington, 1945.

Interviews and Oral Histories:
  Capt. J. J. Clark, 27 November 1942.
  Lt. Comdr. Charles H. Hutchins, 15 November 1943.
  Capt. Arnold J. Isbell, 24 December 1943.
  Capt. Daniel V. Gallery, 26 May 1945.
  Rear Adm. Daniel V. Gallery, Reminiscences.

Documentary Sources: German

  B.d.U. War Diary, 1942–1945.

Correspondence with Author

  Wayne J. Lee, Jack Reidy, Howard Adams: *Block Island;* Ralph Hiestand: *Bogue;* Charlie Thompson, Patrick T. O'Dowd: *Core;* William L. Bowne, Mylo C. Keck: *Guadalcanal;* William H. Barnett:

Mission Bay; Thomas A. Matthews: *Tripoli;* and Stanley E. Sykes, A. B. Speed, James Dresser.

Books

Beesly, Patrick. *Very Special Intelligence.* New York: Ballantine Books, 1981.

Brice, Martin, *Axis Blockade Runners of World War II.* Annapolis: Naval Institute Press, 1981.

Brown, David. *Carrier Operations in World War II: The Royal Navy.* Annapolis: Naval Institute Press, 1974.

Buchanan, Lt. A.R., USNR, editor. *The Navy's Air War: A Mission Completed.* New York: Harper, 1946.

Buell, Thomas B. *Master of Sea Power.* Boston: Little, Brown, 1980.

Burchard, John E., editor. *Rockets, Guns and Targets.* Boston: Atlantic—Little, Brown, 1948.

Busch, Harald. *U-Boats at War.* New York: Ballantine Books, 1955.

Clark, Adm. J. J., USN (Ret.), with Clark G. Reynolds. *Carrier Admiral.* New York: McKay, 1967.

Craven, Wesley Fank, and James Lea Cate, editors. *The Army Air Forces in World War II,* Vol. 2, *Europe: Torch to Pointblank.* Chicago: University of Chicago Press, 1949.

Doenitz, Adm. Karl. *Memoirs: Ten Years and Twenty Days.* Cleveland: World, 1959.

Farago, Ladislas. *The Tenth Fleet.* New York: Ivan Obolensky, 1962.

Frank, Wolfgang. *The Sea Wolves.* New York: Rinehart, 1955.

Gallery, Rear Adm. Daniel V., USN (Ret.). *Twenty Million Tons Under the Sea.* Chicago: Henry Regnery, 1956.

—— *Clear the Decks!* New York: Warner Books, 1967.

U. S. S. *Guadalcanal Memory Logg.* Privately printed, no date.

Hinsley, F. H., et. al. *British Intelligence in the Second World War: Its Influence on Strategy and Operations,* Vol. II. New York: Cambridge University Press, 1981.

Hughes, Terry, and John Costello. *The Battle of the Atlantic.* New York: Dial Press/James Wade, 1977.

Jacobsen, H. A., and J. Rohwer, editors. *Decisive Battles of World War II: The German View.* London: Andre Deutsch, 1965.

Karig, Capt. Walter, USNR, et al. *Battle Report,* Vol II, *The Atlantic War.* New York: Rinehart, 1946.

Keegan, John, editor. *The Rand McNally Encyclopedia of World War II.* Chicago: Rand McNally, 1977.

Kemp, Peter. *Decision at Sea: The Convoy Escorts.* New York: Elsevier-Dutton, 1978.

King, Fleet Adm. Ernest J., and Walter Muir Whitehill. *Fleet Admiral King: A Naval Record.* New York: Norton, 1952.

Lewin, Ronald. *Ultra Goes to War.* New York: McGraw-Hill, 1978.

Love, Robert William, Jr., editor. *Changing Interpretations and New Sources in Naval History.* "Ultra and the Battle of the Atlantic: The German View," Jürgen Rohwer. New York: Garland, 1980.

Mason, David. *U-Boat: The Secret Menace.* New York: Ballantine Books, 1968.

Middlebrook, Martin. *Convoy.* New York: Morrow, 1977.

Mooney, James L., editor. *Dictionary of American Naval Fighting Ships,* Vol. VII. Washington, D.C.: Naval Historical Center, 1981.

Morison, Samuel Eliot. *History of United States Naval Operations in World War II.* Vol. I, *The Battle of the Atlantic.* Vol. II, *Operations in North African Waters.* Vol. X, *The Atlantic Battle Won.* Vol. XI, *The Invasion of France and Germany.* Vol. XV, *Supplement and General Index.* Boston: Atlantic—Little, Brown, 1957–1962.

Naval History Division. *United States Naval Chronology, World War II.* Washington, D.C.: Government Printing Office, 1955.

Parish, Thomas, editor. *The Simon & Schuster Encyclopedia of World War II.* New York: Simon & Schuster, 1978.

Pitt, Barrie. *The Battle of the Atlantic.* Alexandria: Time-Life Books, 1977.

Polmar, Norman. *Aircraft Carriers.* Garden City: Doubleday, 1969.

Potter, E. B., and Fleet Adm. Chester W. Nimitz, USN, editors. *The Great Sea War.* New York: Bramhall House, 1960.

Price, Alfred. *Aircraft Versus Submarine.* Annapolis: Naval Institute Press, 1973.

Rohwer, Jurgen. *The Critical Convoy Battles of March 1943.* Annapolis: Naval Institute Press, 1977.

Roscoe, Theodore. *United States Destroyer Operations in World War II.* Annapolis: United States Naval Institute, 1953.

Roskill, Capt. S. W., DSC, RN. *The War at Sea 1939–1945,* Vols. II and III. London: Her Majesty's Stationery Office, 1956, 1960.

——— *The Navy at War, 1939–1945.* London: Collins, 1960.

Ross, Tweed Wallis, Jr., *The Best Way to Destroy a Ship: The Evidence of European Naval Operations in World War II.* Manhattan: MA/AH Publishing, 1980.

Ruge, Vice Adm. Friedrich. *Der Seekrieg: The German Navy's Story, 1939–1945.* Annapolis: United States Naval Institute, 1957.

An Oil Can with Wings: The Story of the Sangamon. Baton Rouge: Army and Navy Publishing, no date.

Showell, J. P. Mallmann. *U-boats Under the Swastika.* New York: Arco, 1974.

——— *The German Navy in World War Two.* Annapolis: Naval Institute Press, 1979.

Silverstone, Paul H. *U. S. Warships of World War II.* London: Ian Allan, 1965.

U. S. S. Suwannee War Log. Baton Rouge: Army and Navy Publishing, 1946.

Swanborough, Gordon, and Peter M. Bowers. *United States Navy Aircraft Since 1911*. New York: Funk and Wagnalls, 1968.

Taylor, J. C. *German Warships of World War II*. London: Ian Allan, 1966.

Terzibaschitsch, Stefan. *Escort Carriers and Aviation Support Ships of the U. S. Navy*. Annapolis: United States Naval Institute, 1981.

Tillman, Barrett. *The Dauntless Dive Bomber of World War Two*. Annapolis: Naval Institute Press, 1976.

—— *Hellcat: The F6F in World War II*. Annapolis: Naval Institute Press, 1979.

—— *Avenger at War*. New York: Scribner's 1980.

Von der Porten, Edward P. *The German Navy in World War II*. New York: Galahad, 1969.

Waters, Capt. John M., Jr., USCG. *Bloody Winter*. Princeton: Van Nostrand, 1967.

Articles

"Anti-Sub." *All Hands*, May 1946.

Bishop, John. "The U-Boat Meets its Master." *Saturday Evening Post*, 18 and 25 September 1943.

Dater, Henry M. "Development of the Escort Carrier." *Military Affairs*, Summer 1948.

"Evolution of the Escort Carrier." *ONI Weekly*, 18 April 1945.

Gallery, Capt. D. V., USN. "We Captured a German Sub." *Saturday Evening Post*, 4 August 1945.

Gallery, Rear Adm. Daniel V. ". . . Nor Dark of Night." United States Naval Institute *Proceedings*, April 1969.

Grosvenor, Melville Bell. "Cruise on an Escort Carrier." *National Geographic*, November 1943.

Heinz, W. C. "Hunting U-Boats on a Baby Flat-top." (A series of 24 articles.) New York *Sun*, 20 December 1943–18 January 1944.

Hersey, John. "U.S.S. *Borie*'s Last Battle." *Life*, 13 December 1943.

MacDonald, Scot. "Emergence of the Escort Carriers." *Naval Aviation News*, December 1962.

"The Navy's Babies." *Time*, 4 September 1944.

Norris, Lt. (jg) John G. "Hellcats Over France." *Flying*, January 1945.

Saville, Allison W. "German Submarines in the Far East." United States Naval Institute *Proceedings*, August 1961.

"TBF Pilots Describe Fireworks in First Rocket Attack on U-boat." *All Hands*, July 1944.

"U-boat Hunters." *All Hands*, July 1945.

"The Welcome Escorts." *Time*, 26 July 1943.

Wise, James E., Jr. "Victory of the Woolworth Brigade." *Sea Classics*, September 1975.

INDEX

THIS VIOLENT CENTURY

*Bantam War Books Tell the Story of Military Conflicts
Throughout the World*

1918

April 21   Baron Manfred von Richthofen's career comes
to an end. *A History of the Luftwaffe* by John Killen.

1919

Jan. 1   More than a thousand Soviet troops attack
American soldiers entrenched around the village of
Nijni Gora in northern Russia. *The Ignorant Armies*
(April 1990).

1927

Oct. 18   HMS *L 4*, a British submarine under the
command of Lt. Frederick J. C. Halahan, R.N.,
rescues the crew and passengers of the SS *Irene* from
Chinese river pirates. *Submarine Warriors* by Edwyn
Gray (July 1990).

1932

Dec. 26   Chesty Puller drives off sandinista "bandits" who are attacking his train just outside El Sauce, Nicaragua. *Marine! The Life of Chesty Puller* by Burke Davis (February 1991).

1937

April 10   German bombers attack the Spanish town of Guernica. It is the town's market day and 1,600 civilians die. *Full Circle* by Air Vice Marshal J. E. Johnson.

Aug. 17   Having missed their fighter escort, eleven out of twelve Japanese carrier-based attack bombers are shot down over Hangchow by defending Chinese fighter planes. *The Ragged, Rugged Warriors* by Martin Caidin.

1939

Sept. 14   The author, a young British aviator, is called to active duty. It is going to be a very long war. *Tale of a Guinea Pig* by Geoffrey Page.

1940

April 7   HMS *Sealion* in the middle of the German invasion fleet on its way to Norway watches the ships sail past. Rules of engagement prevent an attack. *Submarine Commander* by Ben Bryant.

May 10   The Phony War is over. German troops invade Belgium and Holland. *Churchill and His Generals* by Barrie Pitt.

Sept. 15   The critical day in the Battle of Britain. The

Luftwaffe is beaten back from her daylight skies and Stanford Tuck, one of Britain's greatest air aces, shoots down a German Me 100. *Fly for Your Life* by Larry Forrester.

Nov. 11 British Swordfish torpedo bombers attack the Italian fleet anchored in the harbor of Taranto. *To War in a String Bag* by Charles Lamb.

1941

March 15 A hunter killer group commanded by Captain Donald MacIntyre sinks a U-99 and captures its captain, submarine ace Otto Kretschmer. *U-Boat Killer* by Donald MacIntyre.

April 16 Egyptian liner *Zamzam* sunk in South Atlantic by German surface raiders. *The German Raider Atlantis*, by Rogge and Frank.

May 24 "I turned around to look for *Hood* and stared and stared and stared. It was clear to the horizon and *Hood* was no longer there. She'd had a crew of nearly fifteen hundred. Three of them survived." *Heart of Oak* by Tristan Jones.

May 27 German battleship *Bismarck* sunk. HMS *Hood* is avenged. *Pursuit* by Ludovic Kennedy.

July 4 The 10th Gurkhas with the 2nd Bn. of the 4th in reserve attack Vichy French and Syrian troops defending Deir-es-Zor, Syria. *The Road Past Mandalay* by John Masters.

ug. 9 Douglas Bader loses a leg as his fighter plane is shot down over France. Fortunately it was one of his two artificial ones. *Reach for the Sky* by Paul Brickhill.

t. 31 U.S. destroyer *Rubin James* sunk by German ubmarine. *Tin Cans* by Theodore Roscoe.

. 22 Major Robert Crisp fights his "Honey" tank ainst Rommel's panzers at Sidi-Rezegh in the North

African desert. *Brazen Chariots* by Donald Crisp.

Dec. 7 Japanese carrier-based aircraft attack the U.S. fleet at Pearl Harbor. *Day of Infamy* by Walter Lord.

Dec. 24 The gallant defenders of Wake Island are overwhelmed by a Japanese amphibious landing force. *The Story of Wake Island* by Brig. Gen. James P. S. Devereux.

Dec. 27 British and Norwegian commandos attack the German garrison at Vaagso, Norway. *The Vaagso Raid* by Joseph H. Devins, Jr.

1942

Jan. 27 Lt. Commander Joe Grenfiel, commanding USS *Gudgeon*, sinks the Japanese submarine *I-173* near Midway Island. *Combat Patrol* by Clay Bair, Jr.

Feb. 8 From the embattled fortress of Corregidor the submarine USS *Trout* loads two tons of gold bars and 18 tons of silver pesos for transport to Pearl Harbor. *Pig Boats* by Theodore Roscoe.

Feb. 11 Three German capital ships are making a run from the French port of Brest up the English Channel toward a safe haven in Germany. *Breakout!* by John Deane Potter.

March 6 Operation Nordpol commences with the capture of a British radio operator in Holland by Abwehr personnel. The problem now is to turn the agent so that he sends false messages to England. *London Calling North Pole* by H. J. Giskes.

May 8 British commandos blast their way into St. Nazaire harbor so as to destroy the Normandy dock. *The Greatest Raid of All* by C. E. Lucas Phillips.

June 1 Captain Frederic John Walker, R.N., in *Starling*, with *Wild Goose* and *Kite* in support as a hunter killer group stalk Captain Poser's *U-202*. This German submarine is hidden 800 feet below them in the depths of the Atlantic. *Escort Commander* by T. Robertson.

June 4 Nazi General Reinhard Heydrich dies of wounds received on May 27 when his car was bombed by Czech OSS agents. His side had neglected to develop penicillin. *Seven Men at Daybreak* by Alan Burgess.

June 16 Sub. Lt. C. L. Page captured and then executed by the Japanese. He'd stayed behind as a coastwatcher to radio intelligence reports on Japanese troop and naval movements from the Tabar Islands to Australia. *The Coast Watchers* by Eric A. Feldt.

June 21 Rommel captures the British North African fortress of Tobruk. *With Rommel in the Desert* by H. W. Schmidt.

June 27 Russian submarine *K-21* fires a spread of four torpedoes at the German battleship *Tirpitz*. *Russian Submarines in Arctic Waters* by I. Kolyshkin.

July 27 Special Air Service jeeps destroy Rommel's precious Ju 52 transport planes at Sidi Haneish airfield in North Africa. *Stirling's Desert Raiders* by Virginia Cowles.

Aug. 7 U.S. marines land on Guadalcanal. *The Battle for Guadalcanal* by Samuel B. Griffith II (November 1990).

Aug. 8 Wounded and nearly blind, Japanese ace Saburo Sakai nurses a shattered Zero fighter over five hundred miles of ocean after attacking the Americans on Guadalcanal. *Samurai* by Sakai and Roger Pineau.

Aug. 9 British bombers lay mines in the Channel to block the *Prince Eugen* from the Atlantic. *Enemy Coast Ahead* by Guy Gibson.

Aug. 15 The American tanker *Ohio* finally docks at

the besieged island of Malta in the Mediterranean. *Red Duster, White Ensign* by Ian Cameron.

Sept. 13 Over the North African desert, German ace Hans-Joachim, "The Star of Africa," with 158 victories, dies as he fails to successfully exit his burning Me 109. *Horrido!* by Raymond R. Toliver and Trevor J. Constable.

Sept. 17 Admiral Donetz secretly orders his U-boat commanders not to attempt to assist or reach the survivors of their attacks. *The Laconia Affair* by Leonce Peillard.

Oct. 4 British motor torpedo boats in battle action against German convoys off the Dutch coast. *Night Action* by Peter Dickens.

Dec. 11 British commandos who had paddled their fold-a-boats through sixty miles of German-occupied territory mine and sink several large German merchant ships tied up in the French harbor of Bordeaux. *Cockleshell Heroes* by Lucas-Phillips.

1943

Jan. 31 General Von Paulus surrenders the German 6th Army at Stalingrad. *Enemy at the Gates* by Walter Craig.

Feb. 7 Commander Howard W. Gilmore, wounded on the bridge of the USS *Growler*, gives the order, "Take her down." He does but his ship survives. *Sink 'Em All* by Charles A. Lockwood.

Feb. 26 British agent Yeo-Thomas, "The White Rabbit," parachutes behind German lines into occupied France. *The White Rabbit* by Bruce Marshall.

Feb. 28 Norwegian commandos sabotage the heavy-water plant at Vemork, Norway. *Assault in Norway* by Thomas Gallagher.

March 30 Upon landing in Norway, his unit is destroyed

by the Germans and this Norwegian commando, Jan Baalsrud, embarks on an incredible journey of survival. *We Die Alone* by Horwith.

May 12 The German Afrika Korps in Tunisia surrenders. One unit, the 164th Light Afrika Division, fights on until the following day. *The Foxes of the Desert* by Paul Carell.

May 16 Lt. Machorton returns to Imphal from the jungles of Burma. Wounded, he had been left to die. *The Hundred Days of Lt. Machorton* by Machorton and Henry Maule.

May 17 Guy Gibson and Squadron 617 destroy the Moehne and Eder dams. *The Dam Busters* by Paul Brickhill.

May 30 Although American troops have secured the island of Attu in the Aleutians, individual Japanese defenders still lurk in the surrounding hills. *The Thousand Miles War* by Brian Garfield (October 1990).

July 8 Rudel's cannon-firing Stuka takes part in the biggest tank battle of World War II, Kursk, Russia. *Stuka Pilot* by Hans Ulrich Rudel (November 1990).

July 11 Allied troops invade Sicily. *One More Hill* by Franklyn A. Johnson.

July 11 General George Patton is very much there too. *War As I Knew It* by George S. Patton.

July 27 The German city of Hamburg is consumed by a firestorm. *The Night Hamburg Died* by Martin Caidin (December 1990).

Aug. 17 British bombers attack the German doomsday missile development base at Peenemünde. *V-2* by Walter Dornberger.

Sept. 9 Fresh from his triumphs in North Africa, Popski along with his jeeps is landed in Teranto harbor by the USS *Boise* so that his private army can commence its invasion of Italy. *Popski's Private Army* by Lt. Col. Peniakoff.

Sept. 12 Colonel Skorzeny rescues Mussolini. *Commando Extraordinary* by Charles Foley.

Sept. 14 Russ Carter parachutes into Paestum, which is just south of the Salerno beachhead. *Those Devils in Baggy Pants* by Russ Carter.

Oct. 11 Running on the surface in La Pérouse Strait, one of America's greatest submarines fails to survive an attack by Japanese aircraft. *Wahoo: The Patrols of America's Most Famous World War II Submarine* by Rear Admiral Richard H. O'Kane (Ret.).

Oct. 14 The Schweinfurt Ball Bearing works were the target. Sixty B-17s failed to return from it. *Black Thursday* by Martin Caidin.

Oct. 29 Three British POWs escape from Stalag-Luft III. *The Wooden Horse* by Eric Williams.

Nov. 2 American destroyers in battle action against the navy of Imperial Japan at the Battle of Empress Augusta Bay. *Admiral Arleigh (31 Knot) Burke* by Ken Jones and Hubert Kelley.

Nov. 5 Donald R. Burgett wins his paratrooper wings. *As Eagles Screamed* by Donald R. Burgett.

Nov. 13 The Japanese battleship *Hiei* goes to the bottom, sunk by marine and navy airmen. *The Cactus Air Force* by Thomas G. Miller, Jr.

Nov. 20 American marines land on the Japanese island of Tarawa. *Tawara* by Robert Sherrod.

Dec. 2 Bari, Italy. German bombers sink twenty Allied merchant ships, and a deadly, secret cargo is released. *Disaster at Bari* by Glen Infield.

1944

Jan. 3 "Pappy," after chalking up 25 victories gets shot down over Rabaul. *Baa, Baa, Black Sheep* by Gregory "Pappy" Boyington.

Feb. 1 American and Filipino guerrillas launch an offensive against the Japanese. *American Guerrilla in the Philippines* by Ira Wolfert.

Feb. 22 Heinz Knoke shoots down a B-17 Flying Fortress over his home town of Hameln, Germany. *I Flew for the Führer* by Heinz Knoke.

March 5 Brig. Tom Churchill takes command on the island of Vis in the Adriatic Sea. *Commando Force 133* by Bill Strutton.

March 18 Chindit units battle hand to hand with the Japanese invaders of Burma. *Fighting Mad* by "Mad" Mike Calvert.

March 20 USS *Angler* surfaces off Panay Island in the Japanese-occupied Philippines to rescue 58 refugees. *Guerrilla Submarines* by Ed Dissette.

April 13 Over Hamburg, Germany, an FW 190 becomes the author's 25th aerial victory. *Thunderbolt* by Robert S. Johnson, with Martin Caidin (September 1990).

June 6 In the first minutes of this day the green light goes on in a C-47 flying over the Cherbourg peninsula. *As Eagles Screamed* by Donald R. Burgett. *D-Day* by David Howarth.

June 9 Normandy beachhead. Keith Douglas KIA near Tilly-sur-Seulles. *Alamein to Zem Zem* by Keith Douglas.

June 22 An American pilot uses a 1,000-pound bomb to cure a long-standing rat problem in his old barracks now occupied by the Japanese. *Into the Teeth of the Tiger* by Donald S. Lopez.

June 24 Marine General "Howlin' Mad" Smith relieves Major General Ralph Smith from command of the 27th Infantry Division on the island of Saipan. *Coral* *and Brass* by General Holland "Howling Mad" Smith.

June 25 German ace Robert Spreckels shoots down British ace J.R.D. Braham in air combat over Denmark. *Night Fighter* by J.R.D. Braham.

June 26 The French port of Cherbourg falls to Allied invasion forces. *Invasion: They're Coming!* by Paul Carell.

June 29 An SS squadron in Russia on the Mogilev-Minsk road is shooting German officers found to be moving toward the rear without proper written orders. *The Black March* by Peter Neumann.

July 18 The city of St. Lô is finally secured. *The Clay Pigeons of St. Lô* by Grover S. Johns, Jr.

Aug. 15 Operation "Anvil," the allied landing in the South of France. "The best invasion I ever attended." *Up Front* by Bill Mauldin.

Sept. 15 A young marine goes ashore on Peleliu Island which was one of the most bitterly contested of the Pacific island landings. *Helmet for My Pillow* by Robert Leckie.

Sept. 17 Disguised as a slave laborer, British Sgt. Charles Coward, a prisoner of war in Germany, has just spent the night in hell, locked inside the Auschwitz concentration camp. He now knows the secret of the camp and has vowed to tell it to the world. *The Password Is Courage* by John Castle.

Oct. 3 A young infantry captain enters Germany. It is 11:15 A.M. and the war in Europe is a long way from being over. *Company Commander* by Charles Mac-Donald (August 1990).

Oct. 25 Lt. Seki successfully crashes his plane into the USS *St. Lô* (CVE-63) and sends this escort carrier to the bottom. *The Divine Wind* by Roger Pineau.

Having attacked a Japanese convoy with unbelievable

ferocity, *Tang* fires a final misfunctioning torpedo which turns back and sinks this famous submarine. *Clear the Bridge* by Richard O'Kane (November 1990).

Nov. 26   If you have ever wondered where some of our best writers are. Flying a P-51 on an escort mission over Hanover, Germany, Bert Stiles is KIA. *Serenade to the Big Bird.*

1945

Jan. 4   The 761st Tank Bn. attacks the town of Tillet. It is just to the west of Bastogne. *Hit Hard* by David J. Williams (May 1990).

Feb. 3   Convoy JW-64 sails north from England on its way to Russia. *A Bloody War, 1939-45* by Hal Lawrence.

Feb. 23   U.S. marines raise the American flag on the peak of Mt. Suribachi. *Iwo Jima* by Richard Newcomb.

Feb. 28   Company K attacks the town of Hardt just to the west of Düsseldorf, Germany. *The Men of Company "K"* by Leinbaugh and Campbell (November 1990).

March 15   Bob Clark, Clostermann's No. 4, flying a Hawker Tempest, shoots down an Me 262 piloted by Walter Nowotney, one of the Luftwaffe's greatest aces. *The Big Show* by Pierre Clostermann (November 1990).

April 1   The Japanese island of Okinawa is invaded. *Okinawa: Typhoon of Steel* by Belote and Belote.

April 16   A German steamship with 7,000 evacuees aboard is sunk outside of Hela, Prussia, by a Russian submarine. There are 170 survivors. *Defeat in the East* by J. Thorwald.

April 26   Adolph Galand leads a flight of Me 262 jet fighters in one of the last air battles of the European war. *The First and the Last* by Adolph Galand.

April 29 General Patton climbs down from one of his tanks to liberate the American POW camp of Mooseburg in Germany. *Prisoner of War* by Kenneth W. Simmons.

April 30 British "Crocodile" flame-throwing tanks take up positions outside the German town of Oldenburg. *Flame Thrower* by Andrew Wilson.

May 3 American armor overruns Jagvelband 44 at Salzburg-Maxglan,. Germany, and the war is over for this squadron of futuristic German fighters. *Rocket Fighter* by Mano Ziegler.

May 8 German ace Erich Hartman chalks up his 352nd and final aerial victory. *Horrido!* by Raymond F. Toliver and Trevor J. Constable.

On a leave train bound for the South of France, the author learns that the war in Europe, at long last, is officially over. *To Hell and Back* by Audie Murphy.

June 2 The USS *Tinosa* recovers the crew of a ditched B-29 just south of the Japanese island of Kyushu. *Sink 'Em All* by Charles A. Lockwood.

June 21 The Japanese commander on Okinawa, General Ushijima, commits suicide. *Marine at War* by Russell Davis.

The U.S. high command declares Okinawa to be secured. *With the Old Breed* by Eugene B. Sledge (April 1991).

June 22 With her last two torpedoes, and just before heading home, USS *Crevalle* sinks a Japanese destroyer. *Hellcats of the Sea* by Lockwood and Adamson.

July 25 U.S. carrier aircraft raids Japan's Kure naval base, destroying or damaging most of what was left of the Imperial fleet. *Combat Command* by Frederick C. Sherman.

July 30 Japanese submarine *I-58* sinks the USS *Indianapolis*. *Abandon Ship!* by Richard E. Newcomb.

Aug. 17 A German U-boat commander surrenders to the Argentinian navy only to be accused of having brought Hitler to Antarctica. *U-Boat 977* by Heinz Schaeffer.

Sept. 2 General Wainwright, recently released from a Japanese POW camp, is present on the deck of the USS *Missouri* as the Japanese formally surrender. *General Wainwright's Story* by General Jonathan M. Wainwright. Edited by Robert Considine.

Sept. 11 After three and a half years of imprisonment, Australian soldiers and American sailors liberate the Kuching prison camp in North Borneo. *Three Came Home* by Agnes Newton Keith.

1950

June 25 The North Korean army moves south and the world is once more at war. *This Kind of War* by T. R. Fehrenbach (March 1991).

Dec. 10 Their breakthrough is now completed, and the marines who fought their way down from the Chosin Reservoir are finally in the clear. *The March to Glory* by Robert Leckie (June 1990).

1951

April 22 In the Battle of Solma-Ri, waves of Chinese infantry engulf the British Gloucester regiment. The survivors fight their way out to the south. *Now Thrives the Armourers* by Robert O. Holles.

1955

Jan. 4   On the Foum-Toub-Arris road four men are ambushed and burnt to death in their jeep by Algerian rebel forces. *The War in Algeria* by Pierre Leulliette.

1956

Oct. 10   Dedean Kimathi, the most wanted Mau Mau terrorist, is taken by four Kikuyu tribal policemen. *Manhunt in Kenya* by Sir Philip Goodhart and Ian Henderson.

1958

April 5   A 28-year-old police constable accepts the surrender of Hor Lung, the last of the top level Chinese Communist leaders at large in Malaya. *The War of the Running Dogs* by Noel Barber.

1963

June 11   A Buddhist monk burns himself to death on a street corner in Saigon. *The New Face of War* by Malcolm Browne.

1964

Nov. 24   Belgian Paras and the Lima One Flying Column of mercenaries save the lives of a thousand hostages in the Congo. *Save the Hostages* by David Reed.

1965

May 15   *SR-71*, the legendary recon U.S. aircraft, sets an 80,000-foot Mach 3.12 record. Twenty-five years later the *New York Times*, on February 24, 1990, reports that the air force will retire it. *Air War Vietnam* by Frank Harvey.

June 17 Navy Phantoms shoot down the first MiGs to be destroyed over Vietnam. *The Story of Air Fighting* by J. E. Johnson.

Dec. 18 Air cavalrymen are going into a hot landing zone at Ben Khe, Vietnam. *Year of the Horse—Vietnam* by Col. Kenneth D. Mertel.

1966

Jan. 17 A B-52 collides with its KC-135 tanker and a hydrogen bomb is lost. *One of Our H-Bombs Is Missing!* by Flora Lewis.

Oct. 13 A navy flyer's wife receives a telegram listing her husband as MIA. His plane was seen to explode over enemy-occupied territory. No parachute was observed and no radio distress calls were received. *Touring Nam* by Greenburg and Norton.

1967

Sept. 15 The Brown Water Navy's Force 117 goes into battle along the Rach Ba Rai against the 263rd Vietcong Main Force Bn. *Seven Firefights in Vietnam* by John A. Cash, John Albright, and Allan W. Sandstrum.

1968

Jan. 29 The Tet offensive starts and a marine doctor has no clue as to what the next two days will bring. *12, 20 & 5, a Doctor's Year in Vietnam* by John A. Parrish, M.D.

Feb. 25 Khe Sanh. A marine patrol is ambushed. One third of it returns to the perimeter. *Welcome to Vietnam, Macho Man* by Ernest Spencer.

July 3 A long year starts for an American soldier who has just landed in Vietnam. *One Soldier* by John Shook.

Nov. 15 Near Binh Tri village a scout dog finds a Vietcong mine. Casualties: dead 1 dog, 1 PRU, 12 others wounded. *The Advisor* by John L. Cook.

1970

Oct. 10 There is a patrol just outside the village of Truong Lam, and the word is "Incoming!" *Platoon Leader* by James R. McDonough.

1972

April 1 An EB-66 meets a SAM 2 just south of the DMZ and the co-pilot punches out at 30,000 feet *Bat-21* by William C. Anderson (January 1991).